Application of Machine Learning and Optimization Methods in Engineering Mathematics

Application of Machine Learning and Optimization Methods in Engineering Mathematics

Guest Editors

Miljan Kovačević
Borko Đ. Bulajić

MDPI

Basel • Beijing • Wuhan • Barcelona • Belgrade • Novi Sad • Cluj • Manchester

Guest Editors
Miljan Kovačević
Faculty of Technical Sciences
University of Pristina
Kosovska Mitrovica
Serbia

Borko Đ. Bulajić
Department of Civil
Engineering and Geodesy
University of Novi Sad
Novi Sad
Serbia

Editorial Office
MDPI AG
Grosspeteranlage 5
4052 Basel, Switzerland

This is a reprint of the Special Issue, published open access by the journal *Axioms* (ISSN 2075-1680), freely accessible at: https://www.mdpi.com/journal/axioms/special_issues/YE4N4PIJQ4.

For citation purposes, cite each article independently as indicated on the article page online and as indicated below:

Lastname, A.A.; Lastname, B.B. Article Title. *Journal Name* **Year**, *Volume Number*, Page Range.

ISBN 978-3-7258-4745-7 (Hbk)
ISBN 978-3-7258-4746-4 (PDF)
https://doi.org/10.3390/books978-3-7258-4746-4

Contents

About the Editors

Miljan Kovačević

Miljan Kovačević is an Associate Professor at the Faculty of Technical Sciences, University of Pristina, Serbia. His research focuses on addressing the complex challenges of mathematical modeling in civil engineering, particularly the difficulties in accurately representing real-world construction processes and structural behaviors under uncertainty. Specializing in the application of artificial intelligence and optimization methods, he targets key areas such as project management, machine learning for structural analysis, and the prediction of construction productivity. Miljan Kovačević has led and contributed to numerous multidisciplinary projects that combine theoretical mathematical models with practical engineering problems, improving model reliability and computational efficiency. His work contributes to overcoming inherent uncertainties and nonlinearities in engineering systems, supporting more sustainable, optimized, and data-driven design and management solutions. He has published extensively in international journals and serves as a reviewer and editor for various scientific publications, advocating for the integration of innovative AI and optimization techniques to tackle complex modeling problems in engineering.

Borko Đ. Bulajić

Borko Đ. Bulajić is a Full Professor at the Faculty of Technical Sciences at the University of Novi Sad, Serbia, following five years of working as an Assistant Professor in the same institution. Over the past 10 years, he has delivered lectures on a variety of topics, including Natural Hazards, the Role and Importance of Prevention in Risk Reduction, Risk Analysis Methods, Civil Engineering Design Fundamentals, and Earthquake Impacts on Civil Engineering Structures. He has overseen the completion of numerous B.Sc. and MSc. theses, as well as two Ph.D. dissertations. He has produced more than 100 scientific publications (including a book) on diverse themes linked to earthquake engineering and seismic hazard and risk assessment. As a member of an international team of experts from the USA, Serbia, Croatia, Bosnia and Hercegovina, North Macedonia, and India, he has participated in a number of seismic microzonation studies in these six countries. All this work has demonstrated that both shallow geology features and deep geological site surroundings are crucial for establishing accurate seismic hazard assessments. In addition to working in academia, Borko Bulajić has more than 20 years of experience as a civil engineer. In addition to his role overseeing the construction or maintenance of numerous bridges, culverts, and retaining walls, as a Team Leader and Chief Resident (Supervision) Engineer on a number of road and bridge construction and/or rehabilitation projects, he has also overseen the stabilization of major landslide zones. Between 2020 and 2022 he provided civil engineering consultancy services for the Nordic market. Since 2014, Borko Bulajić has also been employed in the field of civil engineering as a Court Expert.

Preface

The present Reprint is the result of a focused effort to collect high-quality contributions at the intersection of applied mathematics, engineering, and computer science. Our goal was to provide a platform for research that bridges the gap between theory and practice through innovative uses of machine learning, optimization, and mathematical modeling. We hope that this publication will serve as a useful reference for researchers and professionals seeking effective computational tools in engineering applications.

Miljan Kovačević and Borko Đ. Bulajić
Guest Editors

axioms

Article

Identification of the Yield Rate by a Hybrid Fuzzy Control PID-Based Four-Stage Model: A Case Study of Optical Filter Industry

You-Shyang Chen [1], Ying-Hsun Hung [2,*], Mike Yau-Jung Lee [3], Chien-Jung Lai [4], Jieh-Ren Chang [5,*] and Chih-Yao Chien [5]

1 College of Management, National Chin-Yi University of Technology, Taichung 411030, Taiwan
2 Department of Finance, Chaoyang University of Technology, Taichung 413310, Taiwan
3 Department of Business Administration, China University of Technology, Taipei City 116, Taiwan
4 Department of Distribution Management, National Chin-Yi University of Technology, Taichung 411030, Taiwan
5 Department of Electronic Engineering, National Ilan University, Yilan City 26047, Taiwan
* Correspondence: t2010102@cyut.edu.tw (Y.-H.H.); jrchang@niu.edu.tw (J.-R.C.)

Abstract: With the vigorous development of emerging technology and the advent of the Internet generation, high-speed Internet and fast transmission 5G wireless networks contribute to interpersonal communication. Now, the Internet has become popular and widely available, and human life is inseparable from various experiences on the Internet. Many base stations and data centers have been established to convert and switch from electrical transmission to optical transmission; thus, it is entering the new era of optical fiber networks and optical communication technologies. For optical communication, the manufacturing of components for the purpose of high-speed networks is a key process, and the requirement for the stability of its production conditions is very strict. In particular, product yields are always low due to the restriction of high-precision specifications associated with the limitations of too many factors. Given these reasons, this study proposes a hybrid fuzzy control-based model for industry data applications to organize advanced techniques of box-and-whisker plot method, association rule, and decision trees to find out the determinants that affect the yield rate of products and then use the fuzzy control Proportional-Integral-Derivative (PID) method to manage the determinants. Since it is unrealistic to test the real machine online operation at the manufacturing stage, the simulation software supersedes this for improved results, and a mathematical neural network is used to verify the given data to confirm whether its result is similar to that of the simulation. The study suggests that excessive temperature differentials between substrate and cavity can lead to low yields. It suggests using fuzzy control technology for temperature management, which could increase yield, reduce labor costs, and accelerate the transition to high-speed networks by mass-producing high-precision optical filters.

Keywords: optical filter; big data mining; fuzzy PID control; neural network; yield rate

MSC: 03E75; 62P30

1. Introduction

In this section, we describe optical filters and related industrial application research and important problems encountered in the manufacturing process, then explain the purpose of relevant research, and finally introduce the paper structure of this study.

1.1. Research Background with Research Importance

With the development of emerging optical communication network technology, there is an existing need for loading more data and traffic, and it is necessary to make signal transmission faster and more real-time; thus, optical filters have become one of the most important optical communication components. Figure 1 shows the related products for the optical filter industry, which are usually stacked by the physical phenomenon of evaporation. Evaporation is a kind of physical process; it refers to heating the evaporated medicinal materials to a certain sufficient vapor pressure in a vacuum state, so that the medicinal materials are coated with evaporate naturally. Condensation into a thin film layer by layer on the substrate has many advantages, such as simplicity and convenience, fast film formation speed, high efficiency, large coating area, and low cost.

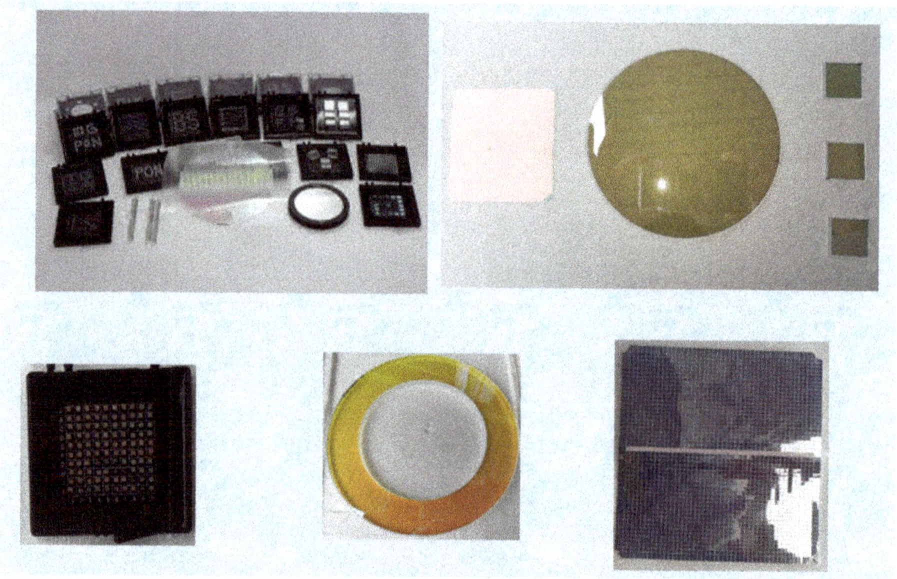

Figure 1. Related products in the optical filter industry.

Specifically, the evaporated atomic energy is relatively low, the ionization rate is not high, the binding to the substrate is poor, and the distribution is not good. For narrow-band filters, since the film is thicker and the number of coating layers is more than 200, the evaporated waveform must consider the central wavelength, head width, bottom width, and ripple stability [1], which results in that good products are usually not enough. Therefore, some conditions of the equipment itself must be stable, including temperature control, cooling water system, stable vacuum control, electron gun, ion source, and other related peripherals. It is also an important benefit to have stable water, gas, and electricity around the equipment. These benefits include the process of ice water, such as cooling water temperature, cooling water pressure, cooling water flow rate, and environmental temperature and humidity control, etc., which affect the yield rate of this product.

For the optical filter products, the fronthaul part is the user end for industry applications, such as mobile phones, computers, and driverless cars. The midhaul part is passive components used in the telecommunications room, including fixed networks, area networks, and passive components of optical communication called Edge/Dense wavelength division multiplexing (DWDM)/beamsplitter (BS). The backhaul part is used for the cloud database that passive components of optical communication for optical filters are called Coarse Wavelength Division Multiplexing (CWDM)/Lan-Wavelength Division Multiplexing (LWDM)/Optical Block [2]; thus, optical filters are one of the most important modern network communication components.

With the above statements, the related emerging importance of manufacturing optical filters has piqued a variety of interest in this study for the key topics of the manufacturing process. Thus, these core issues are highlighted as the main research focus, and it becomes the key research object emphasized in this study.

1.2. Research Motivation

With the advent of the high-speed network era, human beings rely heavily on the convenience of the network for different purposes, and the demand for optical components in the market is increasing continually. Smartphones and home computers of various 3C products have connected to the Internet with the function of extensive applications, and these applications related to daily life can no longer be separated from human beings. In 2021, due to more than 200 million people worldwide confirmed with the severe coronavirus disease 2019 (COVID-19) and the death toll reaching more than 4.5 million, many countries will use remote video teaching to avoid human-to-human contact infection; thus, the Internet generation has brought great benefits and convenience to human beings. In order to make the network high-speed and stable, it is an important key point to have a high-speed base station, and thus it is a requirement to have good optical filters for this key point. In addition, with the 5G generation, the demand for optical filters, which are one of the key components used in 5G base stations, is increasing gradually in the application market; more base stations need to be set up around the world to improve the transmission signal. Importantly, optical filters have become so popular that demand exceeds supply now; thus, it is important to improve the yield rate of production to increase the output of optical filter productivity.

The research motivation of this study is to use some effective models or methods, like the main concept of fuzzy set and artificial neural networks (ANN) to better process optical filters for benchmarking their yields for the 5G optical communication industry. Specifically, the processing flow of manufacturing optical filters is very time-consuming; improving the yield rates can directly reduce costs of both manpower and materials and indirectly increase production quantity. Furthermore, the techniques of data mining are developing sustainably. Many factories use data mining techniques to solve problems faced on the production line. For aquaculture production, Gladju et al. [3] used the framework of data mining techniques and machine learning methods to provide a solution for smart decision-making for solving the complex problems of aquaculture and fisheries. In the study of Guo et al. [4], they offered some sub-modules with different MIS (manufacturing management system) functions, such as material management, order management, and assembly line logistics scheduling, or system management, based on data mining techniques in artificial intelligence (AI) for energy-saving resources. In research by Du et al. [5], they optimized a high-dimensional design space for the supercritical CO_2 recompression cycle (abbreviated as sCO_2-RC) by using deep learning and data mining techniques of machine learning to measure decisional variables for optimizing systems. Moreover, Coşkun et al. [6] used both integrating lameness scores and some image parameters by using a data mining technique to process thermal images with the ImageJ program in order to measure the early detection of lameness in Brown Swiss cattle. Clancy et al. [7] provided a method to decide a methodology to enable data-driven quality management in order to reduce the waste from manufacturing processes using data mining techniques. A study by Tu et al. [8] explored the principles and characteristics of acupuncture for treating major depressive disorder (MDD) by analyzing its clinical trials using data mining techniques. Chien and Chuang [9] made a detection framework for batch processing systems of semiconductor manufacturing by a big data mining analysis, and in the study of Lyu et al. [10], they used a data analysis membrane filter by a data-driven approach to identify possible manufacturing processes and production parameters that lead to defects in produced products.

From these documents in the literature review above, we understand that data mining techniques used for industrial data analysis bring convenience and important benefits to all walks of life and industry applications, particularly for improving the yield rate of the manufacturing industry. Thus, for the data mining learning techniques, it should be an effective trigger-based challenge used to underline the research importance of this study to trigger with the more data-driven models in advance to identify potential industry applications for lowering manufacturing process costs from highlights on optical filter industries.

1.3. Research Gap and Research Question

According to the problems faced in the production of optical filters [11], the manufacturing process is limited by the need for longer time, machine working conditions, quality of raw materials, and stable peripheral equipment, such as electricity, temperature and pressure of cooling water, air pressure, the status of the central air conditioning system, humidity control, water quality, etc. Production needs also include the design of the coating program and the operating skill of the operator. If one of these requirements is not met, it will affect the output yield rate. Interestingly, past research has studied evaporation machines for measuring the electricity, water, and gas of a factory and found that it is better for the manufacturing process when the water temperature is set at 19–21 degrees, the cooling water pressure is set at 2.6–3.0 kg, the cooling water conductivity is set at 151–200 um/cm, and the air pressure is set at 4.1–4.5 kg. However, these are only the experimental results of the manufacturing process for the requirements of the factory service, and there is still a lack of controllable data from important features related to other equipment. Notably, this study proposes the use of an effective method to add some useful conditions to the manufacturing process and collects more real data to be further explored to benefit some manufacturing operations from further analysis. In particular, the controllable conditions of the evaporation equipment are the key to success in correctly identifying the yield rate of output, and the product of the optical filter is a high-precision part processed; each link in the manufacturing process is very important. Given the above reasons, this study emphasizes how to improve the yield rate of optical filters for evaporation manufacturing to outline these emerging areas of industry application-oriented research. It is a major objective for this study that we are dedicated to finding out the related conditions and resources, including production time, product type, production equipment, substrate size, substrate temperature, cavity temperature, the temperature difference between the substrate and the cavity, the cooling water temperature, the cooling water pressure, status of yield, distribution of yield, analysis of failure causes, and the adjustment references of the light spots of the two medicinal materials, etc., when the manufacturing process is handled. We propose an effective mathematical model with some components and corresponding work: (1) To further identify more than thousands of collected raw data points and analyze them with a valuable data mining technique such as the distribution status of box-and-whisker plots (abbreviated as boxplots) and the analysis of association rules, (2) to find out the related problems faced and the correlation or associativity between good products and bad products by using a decision tree model, and (3) to then use effective control methods, such as intelligent control, fuzzy control, and neural networks (NN), to solve and improve the critical problems. Thus, we have three important steps to take to implement the proposed model. (1) The study first uses the control system of evaporation manufacturing and establishes a mathematical factory model. (2) Then, mathematical software and circuit software are used to imitate the factory structure to simulate the evaporation process of an optical filter. (3) During the simulation process, we process the data changes of some collected features, collect further relevant information from the manufacturing process, and use the ANN to confirm the effectiveness of the research, correct the factors that cause adverse effects of products, and gradually increase the yield rate.

This study is motivated by exploring the potential challenges of the optical filter's manufacturing process and thereby studying an interesting and important issue for both academics and industry practitioners meaningfully.

1.4. Research Purpose

This study collects thousands of real data points produced by the process of evaporation in order to measure the proposed hybrid model; accordingly, this study has the following major research purposes to identify and overcome the issue of yields:

(1) Propose an efficacious hybrid model to properly identify the yield rate with the main objective of reducing the output of defective products, which can not only directly save production time and reduce labor and material cost losses but also indirectly increase the number of outputs in the operating process of manufacturing optical filters.
(2) Use package software for big data mining techniques to analyze the given real data to find out the regularities related to the yield.
(3) Use the empirical method of research experiments to create the association rules to discover the problem of poor production.
(4) Find the suitable control methods of fuzzy control, intelligent control, and the NN model to further identify the manufacturing problem of optical filters.
(5) The main purpose of this study is to improve the yield rate of optical filters quickly and effectively.

1.5. Research Structure

The structure of this study has five sections, described as follows: Section 1 mainly discusses the background and relevant problems of addressing the production line to reduce the occurrence of defective products, as well as highlighting the purposes of the study. The second section is to describe the literature review and theoretical background of this study. Section 3 describes the main research methods and techniques used for this study, mainly box-and-whisker analysis, association rule analysis, decision tree analysis of a data mining technique of machine learning, fuzzy control method, and NN model. Section 4 is to analyze the empirical results and effectiveness of the research through experimental examples. The final section concludes the study results from a variety of empirical analyses with a discussion of differences and prospects for future research from experiencing this empirical work. The research flowchart for the study is shown in Figure 2.

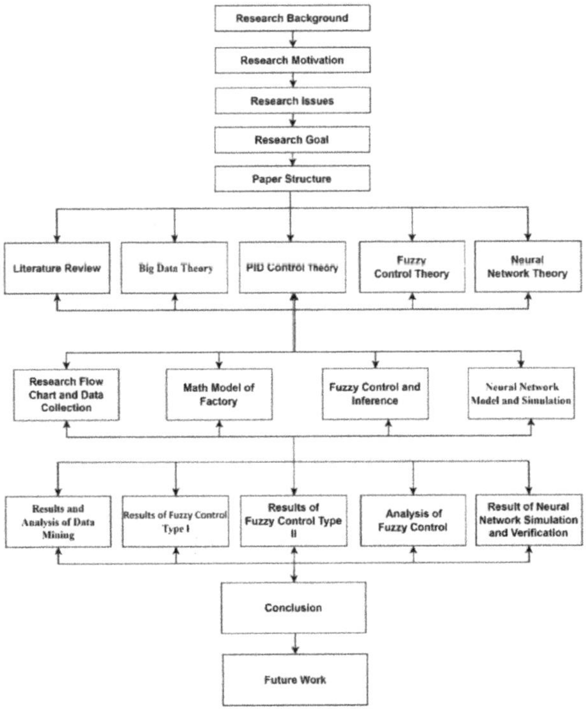

Figure 2. Research architecture of this study.

2. Related Work

This section is to make a literature review of relevant industrial applications and theoretical backgrounds of this study, including industrial background and applications of optical communication thin film filters, related data mining techniques and applications, Proportional–Integral–Derivative (PID) control theory and applications, fuzzy control theory and applications, and NN theory and applications.

2.1. Industrial Background and Applications of Optical Communication Thin Film Filters

Optical communication thin film filter is a type of thin film filter, and its manufacturing process is to use the principle of thin film evaporation, to use the method of physical gas deposition, and to use the principle of dielectric material to apply two kinds of medicinal materials SiO_2 and Ta_2O_5, which are exchanged layer by layer using the high voltage and low current of the electron gun. This generates high-voltage arcs, shooting on the medicinal materials [12–15], melting under vacuum to generate airflow heat convection, and so attaching the medicinal materials to the steam. The size of the substrate has three specifications: 95 mm, 150 mm, and 228 mm in diameter, and the number of evaporated layers of the finished product can be 200–300 layers. By controlling the thickness of the coating film and the sequence of the arrangement, the wavelengths required by customers can pass through, and different wavelengths are filtered out when the light passes through the filters of different products. Therefore, it is possible to achieve the effect that a single optical signal source is divided into multiple project channels. Due to the continuous increase in the number of channels requested, the evaporated layers need more than a hundred layers, and thus the manufacturing of optical filters is very difficult for achieving sufficient yields to lower operating losses. Practically, optical filters are often used for the well-functioning dense wavelength division multiplexer (DWDM) with over 8 channels. Due to the different uses, specifications, channels, or wavelengths, many derived items are created for the categories of optical filters. As for the application fields, it covers a wide range of domains, such as optical communications, optics, medicine, lasers, and space science. The following descriptions of different components for optical filters are their relevant basic applications:

(1) The DWDM system is a very efficient optical transmission method that can accommodate more than four channels under the conditions of the original optical fiber equipment. Thus, its most important application is focused on the use of a backbone network. Due to the fact that DWDM is mainly used in the backbone network, the transmission capacity has increased by more than four times. As for the lack, this system uses several different wavelengths to share a single optical fiber, resulting in a technical difficulty for manufacturing.

(2) Coarse wavelength division multiplexer (CWDM) is also a direct way for the purpose of optical transmission; it uses the thin-film filter technique for optical fiber transmission modules, so it only accommodates two channels, and their wavelength spacing can be compared. Its new-generation design is directly applied to the optical transceiver module at the end of use, and its usage will far exceed the speed of the LAN. CWDM is mainly used in post-transmission cloud databases and LAN use-site transceiver modules. It has the benefits of low technical difficulty, small data transmission volume, and low manufacturing cost, but it has two features: only two channels and wavelength spacing as large as 20 nm.

(3) Gain flattening filters (GFFs) are mainly used to compensate and make the signal more stable. Raman fiber amplifier (RFA) provides a wide gain bandwidth of up to 100 nm. Erbium-doped fiber amplifier (EDFA) on broadband can extend the transmission distance. Currently, they can be applied in the system for combinations of three networks.

(4) Band separators filters (BSFs) are optical carrier signals of different wavelengths on various signals. At the sending end, they will be integrated by a multiplexer and

coupled to the same optical fiber to make the transmission. The optical signals of various wavelengths are separated by a demultiplexer at the receiving end.

(5) Broad band pass filter (BBPF) and narrow band pass filter (NBPF): they can be used for CWDM and CWDM to improve the quality and bandwidth of the system.

(6) Anti-reflection coating (ARC) is an optical thin-film filter. Usually, the coating on the reverse side is called the AR side, and the coating on the front side is called the coating side of the product. Its applications can be extended to digital cameras, projectors, cameras, medical instruments, camera lenses for mobile phones, telescope lenses for viewing astronomy, and special eyeglass lenses, as well as optical films necessary for various optical components.

(7) The edge filter is a multiplexing wave splitter (WDM) for each band; it can be regarded as the function of a switch in application. Thus, it can pass certain wavelengths or prevent certain wavelengths from passing. This is a variety of optical filters required for fiber-to-the-user (FTTx), optical transceiver modules, and passive optical networks (PON), and it is also very commonly used in the industry.

Interestingly, we can connect several computers in a factory or company's office or at home via ultra-broadband wireless, and this is called a local area network [16,17]. We can also connect the computers in the whole city, and this network is called the backbone network; however, these backbone networks must be approved by the country before they can be directly connected to the Internet abroad. Subsequently, it is only possible to use the Internet through these backbone networks. Thus, it implies that optical filters are very important to the era of the Internet, simultaneously, it is needed to understand how to process and highlight the optical filters.

Figure 3 shows the flow chart of the main processing for the production of optical filters. From Figure 3, it is indicated that when the materials first enter the manufacturing factory, the substrates are cleaned by ultrasonic waves and coated with an anti-reflection coating (i.e., AR coating), and then the substrate is ground and degraded. Thick processing for the coater is coating the surface. Then, the coated substrate is cut into optical filters, and the optical filters are taken out for measurement; if the specifications meet the standards, they can be accordingly packaged and shipped.

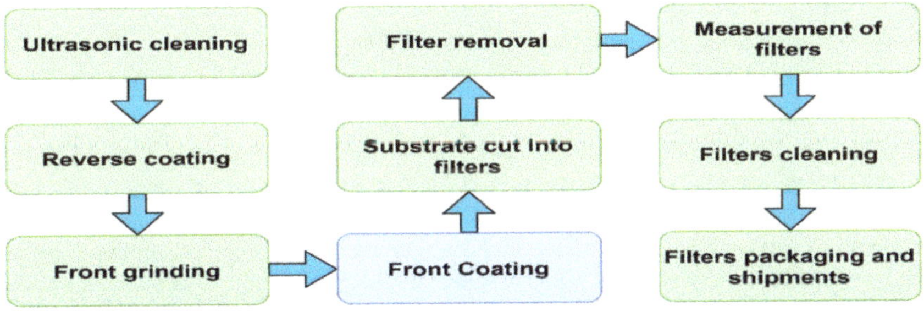

Figure 3. The flowchart of processing optical filters.

2.2. Related Data Mining Techniques and Application

Data mining is an effective process that involves the functions of data collection, data warehousing, and computer processing to analyze a given large raw dataset from real-life problems faced in order to identify potential relationships, uncover trends or patterns, and extract valuable information and knowledge. Figure 4 presents the flowchart of the data mining method. From Figure 4, we can see that the data mining process for a real-time processing framework can be divided into three main stages: the ordering of data, data processing, and data presentation [18]. Furthermore, as to the many functions of data mining techniques, three brilliantly technical methods, including box-and-whisker analysis, association rule analysis, and decision tree classifier, have become the frameworks of professionally emerging models or technologies for challenges and alternatives in industry applications, and thus they are selected and emphasized in this study. The three stages are described in detail as follows, and the three techniques are introduced in the following three subsections, respectively.

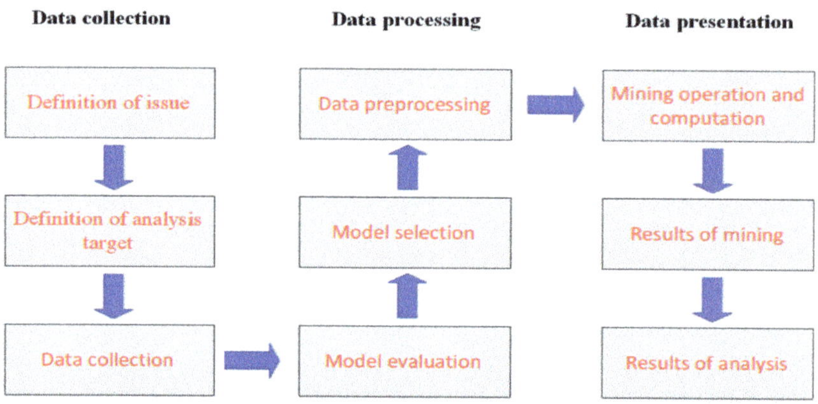

Figure 4. The flowchart of processing data mining functions.

(1) Data collection: For industry application, first clarify the problem to be solved, analyze the definition and structure of the problem, know how to set the data analysis goals, and further collect relevant data from industries for facilitating the setting conditions of experiments to achieve the pre-established objectives like yields of production outputs.
(2) Data processing: After collecting and organizing a large amount of industrial data, we accordingly employ appropriate tools and suitable models to further analyze the defined problem and dig out useful information about decisional features like association rule algorithms from the given huge amount of data.
(3) Data presentation: Based on the information obtained from the results of data analysis, find out the insights of empirical results, and then apply visualization presentation or communication analysis to further formulate appropriate action plans to assist decision-making in industry for purposes of improvement.

2.2.1. Box-and-Whisker Analysis

The result of box-and-whisker analysis is a box plot as a visual tool and a very simple and easy-to-understand statistical method, which has a statistical graph showing the distribution of data with a combination of the maximum, minimum, median, first quartile, and third quartile. In particular, the difference between the first quartile and the third quartile is called the interquartile range (IQR), which is commonly used to assess the variability of statistical dispersion. Thus, when drawing a box-and-whisker plot, it is necessary to first determine the fence; the fence is the first quartile $-1.5 \times$ IQR and the third quartile $+1.5 \times$ IQR. Importantly, this kind of box plot can be learned and interpreted easily and clearly from the outcome of statistical charts; with the helpful benefit that box-and-whisker plots have a wide application field, such as the analysis of lung data in medicine [19] and the data analysis in stores [20].

By highlighting industry applications, this study thus selects it to judge and visualize the distribution features of the given data and benefit the outcome by resulting in a measurable improvement.

2.2.2. Association Rule Analysis

Association rule analysis refers to searching and analyzing events or records that occurred concurrently through some given real data, and the analyzed results can reveal some associated rules for a real-life problem. For example, in a practical purchase record of supermarket customers, it is found that if customer A bought beer, then this customer also bought diapers simultaneously; thus, the beer and diapers form a relevant link, which is called an association rule [21]. Even if a customer buys diapers, there is still a high chance that he or she will also buy beer at the same time; however, it can practically help supermarket decision-makers further formulate a set of cross-selling strategies in order to accelerate the promotion of related products by using the association rule constructed. That is, the operator can change the way that the store is displayed to make it easier for customers to purchase the related products and further increase the probability of sales. In addition, fuzzy association rules (FARs) are a variant of association rules, and they can be used for a variety of industry applications, such as using FARs to find out the power energy loss analysis to achieve the effect of energy savings [22] and using association rules to judge the cause of transformer faults and improve production efficiency for making the power transformer fault diagnosis [23]. In mining, the process of association rules includes two main phases, its key functions are described as follows:

(1) In the first phase, all high-frequency project groups must be found from the original data collected to set the interval number of equal-frequency discretization in the default discretization, which can be slowly adjusted to a suitable demand value or can be selected to set equal-width discretization, and then complete the setting of individual attributes. The high frequency means that the frequency of a certain item group must reach a certain level relative to all records. The frequency at which an item group appears is called the support degree. To further define frequency, if we take two projects, A and B, we can obtain the support degree of the project group containing A and B. If the support degree is greater than or equal to the set minimum support threshold value, then A and B are called a high-frequency project group. A K-itemset that satisfies the minimum support is called a high-frequency K-item group, which is generally expressed as a large K or a frequent K. The algorithm generates a larger K + 1 from the large K item group, and the search will not stop until no high-frequency item groups can be found and generated.

(2) Accordingly, the second phase is to generate association rules. First, set the appropriate parameters of high-frequency item groups, such as equal-frequency discretization and interval number, which are based on the previous step for high-frequency K-item groups used to generate rules. If the reliability calculated by a rule satisfies the minimum reliability, this rule is just an association rule.

More importantly, due to the complexity of the production process of optical filters, it is a nonlinear system, so this study uses the characteristics of association rules to formulate its relevant regulations in order to obtain good classification results.

2.2.3. Decision Tree Classifier

In machine learning fields, a decision tree is a good predictive model in a variety of applications; it is a mapping feature between object attributes and object values. Each node in the tree represents an object, and each branch path represents a certain attribute value. The node of each leaf corresponds to the value of the object represented by the path experienced from the node at the root of the tree to the leaf node. A decision tree can generate and learn a decision-making tree-based structure from given data. In particular, for its application, it has many benefits in industrial domains, such as analysis of distribution line fault causes [24], real-time migration of fault trees to decision trees for fault detection at the International Space Station (ISS) [25], misconfiguration detection usage analysis for addressing large-scale cloud data centers [26], etc.

For the illustrious classifier, it has some key algorithms with various advantages, such as classification and regression trees (CART), C4.5, and C5.0.

(1) CART: The Gini coefficient (abbreviated as Gini in this study) [27] is a statistical measure of inequality on a scale between 0 and 1, indicating that the higher the value, the higher the inequality; thus, it can be used as the criterion for determining the branch variables. Each branch node is separated from the data, and a dichotomous tree structure of decision is established to find out the critical branch variables. Given the features of the binary branching CART algorithm, it can deal with classification problems by benefiting categorical variables and continuous variables. First, given a node t, the branch variable is divided into two elements by the Gini, assuming that the branch level of the attribute is s, t_{left} and t_{right} are the left and right child nodes of the node t, respectively, and the purity before and after the branch is compared with their difference, $\Delta Gini(s,t)$ is an increment under the (s,t) of the Gini, which is formatted as in Equation (1):

$$\Delta Gini(s,t) = Gini(t) - \left[Gini\left(t_{left}\right) + Gini\left(t_{right}\right)\right] \quad (1)$$

(2) C4.5: In C4.5, the ratio of information gain [28] is used as the criterion for determining the branch variables with a multi-branch. In practice, the C4.5 algorithm is most commonly used to handle categorical data, but in the case of continuous data, it first needs to be converted into a category variable. Compared with these features of prediction accuracy, complexity degree, tree pruning, and training time for other classifiers or algorithms, the C4.5 decision tree algorithm provides better advantages in classification accuracy and data interpretation ability.

(3) C5.0: Its core algorithm for C5.0 [29] is a modified version based on C4.5. C5.0 adopts the concept of pessimistically estimating the classification error rate and directly uses the results of training data to estimate the classification error rate. The confidence level (CL) is a measure of the mean of a certain variable and is formatted as Equation (2); where p represents the probability of misclassification of the leaf node, N is the number of data points in the node t, x represents the number of data that may be misclassified in the node, and E represents the maximum number of data in the node that is misclassified.

$$CL = \sum_{x=0}^{E} C_x^N p^x (1-p)^{N-x} \quad (2)$$

Due to the strong industrial applicability of the decision tree classifier, specific advantages make the utilization rate in learning industrial applications much higher than other algorithms. Therefore, this study applies this classifier to identify practical classification problems with good research results in the real world, such as the problem of filter production processes.

2.3. PID Control Theory and Its Application

For a PID controller, P is proportional, I is integral, and D is differential. Its attributes can be adjusted by adjusting the three benefits of K_P, K_i, and K_d [30], which is common in automatic controls. One of the control methods, such as multi-mecanum-wheeled mobile robot [31], wind power generation system [32], heat exchanger [33], vehicle active suspension based on road [34], water and fertilizer control system [35]. PID control is used for automatic control to improve stability. It is mainly divided into three key functions, described as follows:

(1) The P controller is a very simple control method. The output of its controller is proportional to the input error signal, and the control amount of proportional control is proportional to the error. When the error is large, the control amount will be relatively large, and the response will rise quickly. Although proportional control can quickly reduce the error, the biggest problem is that when the control amount is less than a certain value, the goal cannot be achieved, and it will cause a steady-state error. This error will not be eliminated by proportional control over time, so

it will be presented in the paragraph below. Its proportional control is formatted as Equation (3).

$$u(t) = K_{pe}(t) \tag{3}$$

(2) The I controller is the output of the controller and is proportional to the integral of the input error signal. How can the steady-state error be eliminated? It will continue to accumulate the value of the error, so that the control amount will increase. As time increases, the integral term will become larger. If the error is small, the integral term will also increase with time, but if the value is large, the value will keep rising. Finally, under the action of this mechanism, the steady-state error is successfully eliminated, and the output of the controller is increased to further reduce the steady-state error until it is equal to zero and the target value can be reached. Therefore, the proportional + integral (i.e., PI) controller makes the system have no steady-state error after entering the steady state. The integral control is cumulative error and directly added to the control quantity for the integral error function, and its formation is defined as Equation (4).

$$u(t) = Kp\left(e(t) + \frac{1}{T_1}\int_0^t e(t)dt\right) \tag{4}$$

(3) The D controller, also an output controller, is directly proportional to the differential of the input error signal; that is the rate of change of the error. Differential is the function of dealing with interference sources. If the machine equipment is affected by external forces and changes rapidly, the error will also increase rapidly. At this time, the differential control can show its unique ability. The differential controller calculates the rate of change of the errors. When the rate of change fluctuates rapidly, the amount of differential controller will increase with the increase in the rate of change of the errors, so that more force will be quickly returned to the target position, making it more stable. When the target is close, the error decreases rapidly, so the derivative of the error is negative. The item function for the differential controller will reduce the control amount, making the speed smaller to prevent exceeding the target value. In summary, the integral controller provides a certain inertia, but the differential controller provides a certain damping; this is the understanding of a simple and intuitive PID controller. The proportional + differential (i.e., PD) controller can suppress the control effect of the errors in advance to be equal to zero or even a negative value, thereby avoiding serious overshoots of the controlled quantity. The PD controller can improve the dynamic characteristics of the system during the adjustment process. The differential control, to calculate the rate of change of the current errors and add it to the control quantity, is defined as Equation (5).

$$u(t) = Kp\left(e(t) + \frac{1}{T_T}\int_0^t e(t)dt + T_D\frac{de(t)}{dt}\right) \tag{5}$$

Figure 5 shows the output signal of the closed-loop control system for the PID thermostat. The output signal is fed back to the reference input signal through the sensor to adjust the proportional, integral, and differential values for the total value. After processing, it is inputted and returns to the setting after the input point to compare the error and correct the P, I, and D again until the temperature of the output value is close to the error value. The algorithm is formatted as Equation (6) below, and the steps are as follows: (1) The input signal is the heating current and the actual temperature; (2) the output has the three internal parameters, including P, I, and D, and can be adjusted up, but it is not adjusted down for the three regulation methods.

$$Kpe + Ki\int edt + Kd\frac{de}{dt} \tag{6}$$

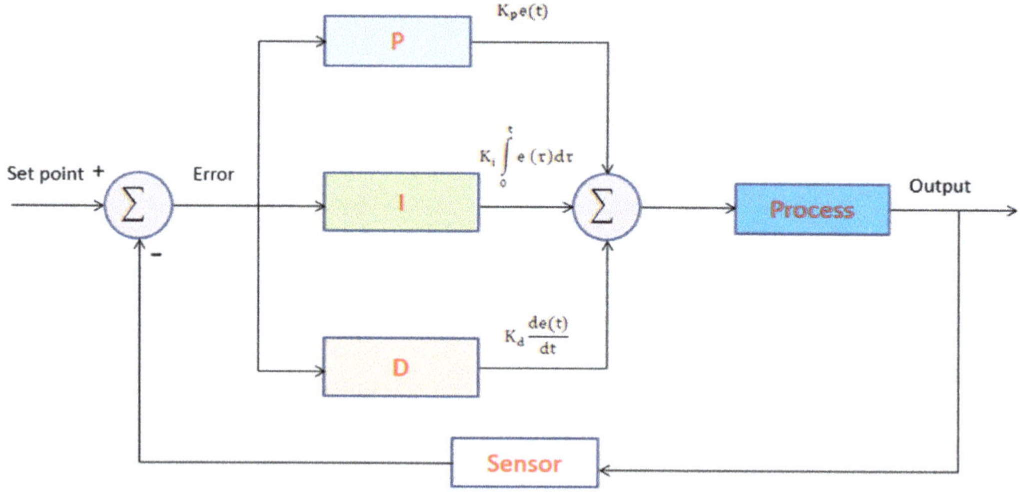

Figure 5. A diagram of PID temperature controller architecture.

2.4. Fuzzy Control Theory and Its Application

A fuzzy control system mainly has three data inputs, and after fuzzification, the adjustment of empirical rules is established by fuzzy rules, and after defuzzification, the results for output data come out. The basic structure of the fuzzy system has four functions, as follows:

(1) Fuzzifier: Its function as a fuzzifier is to convert external input data into semantic fuzzy information that can be communicated in the fuzzy system. That is, convert the given "data" to useful "information". The measurement value of the interface is used to carry out the quantification work, so that this value is transformed into the range of language variables and other pairs [36].
(2) Fuzzy-rules base: The fuzzy-rules base is composed of a collection in the form of IF-THEN statements that store the human operator's practical knowledge of the process. The rule base will be more flexible to calculate accurate prediction values. If the rules of the fuzzy-rules base are set well, the calculated results will be more accurate. This kind of fuzzy rule is used to describe the relationship between the input and output of the system; multiple inputs can be set according to the requirements, and a system with multiple outputs can be set according to the requirements.
(3) Fuzzy inference engine: This engine is the core of the fuzzy system, which can simulate human thinking and decision-making to determine the value. By means of approximate inference or fuzzy inference, it can be used to solve real-life problems.
(4) Defuzzifier: Defuzzification is the opposite activity of the function of the fuzzification process. Defuzzification must convert the inferred fuzzy output into a real and clear value to communicate with many external interfaces and facilities; that is to be able to find an unambiguous value suitable for representing fuzzy sets. (Note: the defuzzification in this study uses the approach of the center of gravity.

2.5. NN Theory and Its Application

The architecture diagram of basic backpropagation NN (BPNN) [37,38] is a good algorithm that simulates the nerves of organisms; it is composed of an input layer, a hidden layer, and an output layer. A connection in each layer represents a weight; when the weight reaches the threshold through the activation function output, the neuron is activated, and the data is passed to the next layer. The linear activation function can effectively deal with the problem of gradient disappearance. This form is the prototype of BPNN, and the meanings of each layer are described as follows: (1) Input layer X: It is an input set. (2) Output layer Y: It is an output set. (3) Hidden layer: It has a processing function F and the number of neurons; its constructional algorithm will determine the number of hidden layers, and it is dependent on the complexity of the problem faced, increasing from one layer to several layers. (4) Activation function: An input value is directly transmitted from the input layer to the hidden layer, and after the weight is accumulated, an output value can be converted through the activation function, and then it is passed back to the output layer.

In the learning process of the backpropagation (BP) algorithm, the data is composed of forward propagation and negative propagation, respectively, and the input can be obtained from the output through the weighting function (F). In the reverse transfer NN, the input value of the current calculation neuron is the output value of the previous neuron, and the output layer y_j^n of the NN can be calculated by Equation (7). In the Equation (8), net_j^n is expressed as the weight accumulation of the output value in the $n-1$ layer of the network, and w_{ji}^n represents the jth neuron of the ith neuron in the $n-1$ layer in the n-layer. In this study, the backward transfer neural architecture belongs to the supervised learning method, and the target value b is used as the purpose of learning so as to reduce the error between network input and target output.

$$y_j^n = f\left(\sum_i w_{ji} y_i^{n-1}\right) = f\left(net_j^n\right) \tag{7}$$

$$net_j^n = \sum_i w_{ji}^n y_i^{n-1} + b_j^n \tag{8}$$

In addition, after calculating the function of error (E), its purpose is to reduce the gap between the actual output and the target output, so that the network can correct the output network through E, and the process of making the minimizing E becomes the function of network. The learning process for the network is to process the minimizing the function of error E, and E can be represented by the following Equation (9). Among them, E can be regarded as the correction of the error function, d_k is the target output value of the neuron at position k, and y_k is the actual output value of the neuron network at position k. In the process of minimizing E, the network will adjust the size of the weight value each time the training data is input.

$$E = \left(\frac{1}{2}\right) \sum_K (d_k - y_k)^2 \tag{9}$$

In Equation (10), Δw_{ji} is the adjusted weight, and the degree of adjusted change is proportional to the weight connection value. η is the learning rate, usually set between 0.8 and 1.2.

$$\Delta w_{ji} = -\eta \frac{-\partial E}{\partial w_{ji}} \tag{10}$$

In reviewing many studies, such as optimizing fuzzy neural network (FNN) for tuning the use of orthogonal simulated annealing (OSA) algorithm for PID controller [39], a learning rule for simultaneous perturbation of recurrent neural network (RNN) and its implementation using a field-programmable gate array (FPGA) [40], using the NN structure for a dynamic system cycle to adaptive global sliding-mode control based on a double hidden layer RNN (DHLRNN) [41], all were found to achieve good results. Through continuous iterations of the NN, a robust approach for a supervised learning NN can be trained. Therefore, this study selects a NN model and applies it to effectively monitor the production process of optical filters.

From the literature reviews mentioned above, it is clear that focusing on the optical filter production process with a wide variety of useful benefits associated with practical industry applications is an interesting issue, particularly concerning the generation of high-speed 5G wireless networks.

3. Materials and Methods

This section primarily introduces the research methods used and the proposed mathematical model. The main aim is to describe the methods, including box-and-whisker diagram analysis, association rule analysis, and decision tree analysis, and the advantages of big data mining. After discovering the practical problem, we first use the fuzzy control method to adjust and find out the optimal parameters, then use the simulation software to simulate the result, and then use the NN to verify the effectiveness. The structure of the proposed hybrid model is described in Section 3 in detail, and it has four subsections, including Section 3.1 research process structure and data collection, Section 3.2 mathematical model and factory model establishment, Section 3.3 fuzzy control method and inference, and Section 3.4 NN simulation and verification.

3.1. Research Structure for the Proposed Model

Regarding the proposed hybrid model, there are seven core steps addressed, including data collection and preprocessing, data mining technique, manufacturing model establishment, fuzzy control technology, effect comparison of simulation, effect verification of NN, and drawing conclusions. In detail, the first step of the proposed hybrid model is the data stage, including data collection and data preprocessing. Next, use data mining techniques to find out the important factors that affect the yield rate. The third step is to build a suitable model for the factory manufacturing process and use this mathematical model to apply radiant heat in a vacuum to imitate the structure of a physical factory. The following step accordingly uses the fuzzy control technique in order to control the found factors. With the comparison benefits, this study uses two types of fuzzy control methods and compares their experimental effects to see which structure is more ideal and suitable. The two types are presented as follows: (1) Type I: Uses fuzzy control to control PID in order to automatically adjust the three key parameters of Kp, Ki, and Kd to generate current (u) and to handle the controlled object to produce heat. (2) Type II: Uses the three key parameters of Kp, Ki, and Kd generated by the PID control in the previous method (1), and concurrently add the ΔKp, ΔKi, and ΔKd generated by the fuzzy control of the PID to produce current u; the mathematical equation for current is $u = \text{Kp} + \Delta\text{Kp} + \text{Ki} + \Delta\text{Ki} + \text{Kd} + \Delta\text{Kd}$. The electric current is generated by the thermal energy generated by the controlled body. Accordingly, the fifth step is to make the effect comparisons after implementing software simulation for the fuzzy control method. In the sixth step, we use the NN model to verify whether the effect of fuzzy control has reached the expected improvement goal. Finally, we confirm the empirical results with a meaningful conclusion. Figure 6 displays the flow chart for the seven steps in this research architecture. Importantly, algorithms of the proposed hybrid model in four stages are implemented stage-by-stage to show its detailed procedure in the following four sections, mainly including data preprocessing, modeling a mathematical model of a factory, modeling a fuzzy control model, and simulation verification. Initially, in the first stage, there are four main procedures (data collection, data classification, data exploration and calculation, and data analysis) described in the following four subsections.

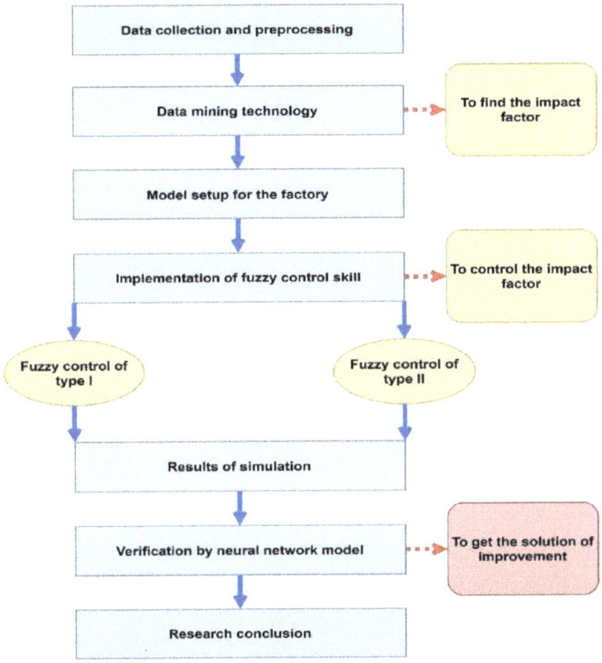

Figure 6. Research flow chart of this study.

3.1.1. Data Features and Data Collection from Factory with Its Equipment

This research is first aimed at the process of acquiring peripheral equipment for the coating machine from an optoelectronic company. The peripheral equipment process is presented in the following three key sub-processes: (1) After the ice water host is cooled, the ice water is stored in the water tower of this process, and then it is pumped into the filter by the ice water pump so that after the ice water is filtered, it can reenter the host for the cooling water cycle. (2) After cooling, the temperature is regulated by a plate heat exchanger, and then it is used for coating equipment, so that the cooling cycle continues repeatedly. (3) The main function of the cooling water tower is to prevent the host of ice water from overheating and causing a shutdown; in particular, the main function of the softening system of water is to control the water quality so as not to let the water quality deteriorate or let scale accumulate, causing the cooling water pipes to be blocked. Accordingly, the factory data is mainly focused on the three core features, including cooling water inlet pressure, cooling water return pressure, and cooling water temperature. However, in the processing system of a factory, the three features play an extremely important and interesting role. That is, if the pressure and temperature for the cooling water are insufficient, the components with heat sources in the equipment will be damaged due to overheating, and in severe cases, the equipment will be broken and the functions of evaporation will be stopped. Thus, the conditions for the three features must be given a high priority and be specifically considered. Moreover, the 12 attributes of the process equipment identified by professional experts include production month, job number, product type, equipment code, substrate size, yield rate, cause of failure, yield distribution, substrate temperature, cavity temperature, and the two spot positions of medicinal materials, SiO_2 and Ta_2O_5. The data collection of the 12 attributes is conducted, and the instances collected from the 12 attributes of product lines can be used for further statistics and analysis purposes from the perspective of industrial data. Especially in this era of data explosion, it is important to quickly organize the data into usable information. When data is sorted and analyzed, it can become an important information asset, and after the evolution process, it can become key knowledge in the factory. Thus, we can benefit from the four knowledge forming processes of data collection → useful information → critical knowledge → higher wisdom.

3.1.2. Data Preprocessing for Further Automatic Classification

It is necessary that the data of products collected, including 50G, 100G, 800G, and CWDM, from the factory be first preprocessed and classified for further speeding the automatic classification in order to advantage the effective analysis of big data mining; thus, the decisional attributes of products are classified into the three classes of good, normal, and bad. Figure 7 shows the flow chart for well-used data mining techniques in this study. From Figure 7, it is seen that after collecting the industrial data, there are three effective analysis techniques: box-and-whisker analysis, association rule, and decision tree, for data mining functions in order to figure out and confirm the problem faced and the decisional rules generated from the decision tree. Specifically, we can accordingly create association rules after extracting frequent item sets.

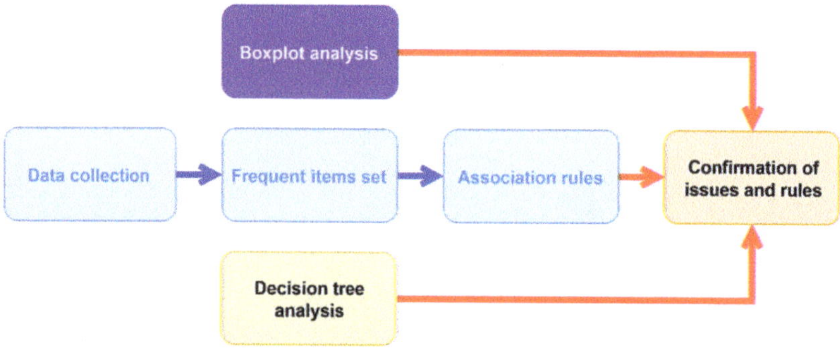

Figure 7. Flow chart of further data analysis for the hybrid proposed model.

3.2. Modeling a Mathematical Model

In order to make the simulation more realistic and practical based on the industrial data of the case study, this research will imitate a mathematical model similar to the on-site environment of a factory. For the detailed process, we first refer to the related literature for radiation heat transfer in a vacuum state, and we apply the equation of radiation heat transfer to establish a mathematical model of simulation for an evaporation factory. There are a lot of parameters used in the peripheral equipment of the factory; especially, five key elements, such as temperature, vacuum degree, electron gun, ion source, and cooling water, are identified as core factors for evaporation equipment. Among them, temperature is the most important factor, so we used temperature as the main consideration to establish a mathematical model of simulation and set up a set of effective fuzzy control methods to improve the yield rate of the factory production process. The mathematical model of simulation can be used as a future reference to increase the processes in factories. Next, five subsections are addressed for the proposed model with a variety of experiments, as follows:

3.2.1. Establish a Mathematical Model with Temperature Changes

When the testing object is placed in the heated test chamber with temperature T_e (in a vacuum state at this time), its temperature T will gradually rise due to the absorption of radiant heat from the wall of the test chamber. According to the principle of energy conservation, the change of T in the heating process can be expressed and formatted as Equations (11) and (12) [42,43] as a differential equation:

$$MCdT = \varepsilon A\sigma\left(T_e^4 - T^4\right)dt \tag{11}$$

or

$$qR = MC\frac{dT}{dt} = \varepsilon A\sigma\left(T_e^4 - T^4\right) \tag{12}$$

where qR is the radiative heat transfer rate, and the rate of change of the temperature T of the test substrate with time t. The Y_R' is expressed and defined in an Equation (13) as follows:

$$Y_R' = \frac{dT}{dt} = \frac{\varepsilon A\sigma}{MC}\left(T_e^4 - T^4\right) \tag{13}$$

In the above equation, q is energy, and R is radiant heat. The reflected part is qR, σ is a proportional constant, also known as Stephen—Boltzmann constant, the true value is 5.67×10^{-8} W/m^{2}K^4, A is the thermal radiation on the surface area of the body, and T is the temperature of the heat radiator (in K), also known as "Boltzmann's law of thermal radiation".

To derive the above equations related to the experiments, the following parameters are used: (1) the mass of the testing object M = unit (in g), (2) the specific heat of the testing object C = degrees in unit (J/kg), (3) the surface area for the testing object A = unit cm^2, (4) the emissivity ε of the surface for the testing object, (5) the temperature T_e (K) of the heating test chamber, (6) the temperature T(K) of the testing object, and (7) the time t.

3.2.2. Building a Fuzzy Control Method

The substrate processing in the evaporation chamber is in a vacuum environment, which has two sets of heaters. One is the substrate heater; it is easy to control the temperature, and thus the temperature is relatively stable because the heater area is relatively small. The other is the cavity heater; it is relatively difficult to control the temperature stably because of its large area and the interference of two sets of high-temperature interference sources. Thus, this study uses the method of fuzzy control in order to effectively control the cavity heater, minimize the influence of interference sources, and adjust the temperature difference to be close to the substrate temperature so that the yield rate of production output can be effectively improved. Given the above reasons, there are three experiments addressing the substrate, chamber, and cavity wall for inducing dynamic equation derivation in the following descriptions of three subsections.

3.2.3. Dynamic Equation Derivation for Substrate Experiments

This study further analyzes the heat conduction system of vacuum coating. According to the theory of heat conduction, there are three types: conduction heat, convection heat, and radiation heat. In a vacuum environment, radiation heat transfer is the main method used. Therefore, this study focuses on the dynamic equation of thermal radiation and thermal conduction.

Furthermore, the effects of the cavity wall, the exchange of the two electron guns, and the radiation temperature of the cavity are considered based on the dynamic equation of the substrate temperature, as shown in Equations (14) and (15); where u is the substrate heating controller, with the mass M_1, specific heat C_1 of the substrate, surface area A_1 of the substrate, surface emissivity ε of the substrate, temperature T_1 of the substrate, and temperature T_2 of the cavity.

$$e = T_2 - T_1 \tag{14}$$

$$\frac{dT_1}{dt} = \frac{\varepsilon A_1\sigma}{M_1C_1}\left(T_W^4 - T_1^4\right) + \frac{\varepsilon A_1\sigma}{M_1C_1}\left(Te_1^4 - T_1^4\right) + \frac{\varepsilon A_1\sigma}{M_1C_1}\left(Te_2^4 - T_1^4\right) + \frac{\varepsilon A_1\sigma}{M_1C_1}\left(T_2^4 - T_1^4\right) + u \tag{15}$$

3.2.4. Dynamic Equation Derivation for Chamber Experiments

Similar to the previous method, all the influences on some key substance materials, including the cavity wall, the two electron guns for the heater, and the radiation temperature of the substrate, are concurrently considered by the chamber dynamic equation, which is shown in Equation (16); where u_1 is the infrared (or IR) lamp heating controller, the mass of the cavity M_2, specific heat C_2 of the cavity, surface area A_2 of the cavity, surface emissivity ε of the cavity, temperature T_2 of the cavity, and temperature T_1 of the substrate.

The dynamic equation for chamber temperature change is then formatted as follows:

$$\frac{dT_2}{dt} = \frac{\varepsilon A_2 \sigma}{M_2 C_2}\left(T_W^4 - T_2^4\right) + \frac{\varepsilon A_2 \sigma}{M_2 C_2}\left(Te_1^4 - T_2^4\right) + \frac{\varepsilon A_2 \sigma}{M_2 C_2}\left(Te_2^4 - T_2^4\right) + \frac{\varepsilon A_2 \sigma}{M_2 C_2}\left(T_1^4 - T_2^4\right) + u_1 \quad (16)$$

3.2.5. Dynamic Equation Derivation for Cavity Wall Experiments

Similarly, the temperature influence of the cavity and room temperature are also considered in the dynamic equation of the cavity wall, which is shown in Equation (17):

$$\frac{dT_W}{dt} = \frac{\varepsilon A_3 \sigma}{M_3 C_3}\left(T_2^4 - T_W^4\right) - \frac{\varepsilon A_4 \sigma}{M_4 C_4}\left(T_W - T_P\right) \quad (17)$$

where M_3 is the mass of the cavity wall, the specific heat C_3 of the cavity wall, the surface area A_3 of the cavity wall, the surface emissivity ε of the cavity wall, the temperature T_2 of the cavity body, the temperature T_W of the cavity wall, and the normal temperature T_P of the indoor environment.

3.3. Research Method and Inference of Fuzzy Control PID

PID controllers are popular and advantageous in general factories. Importantly, a PID controller is needed when the water pressure or temperature need to be controlled at a fixed constant value. However, there are two serious flaws in the PID controller for controlling some conditions about temperature, as follows: (1) Internal interference determinants. The traditional PID controller is always used in the manufacturing factory, and its disadvantage is that the parametric conditions of the controller have not been corrected due to no use for too long. The parametric conditions may have some serious problems, such as the varying condition of the heating body, the aging of the temperature sensor, the declining of the power of the heater, and the varying space for the heating body. These problems lead to the parametric conditions being inaccurate, resulting in ineffective communication for the controller, and more seriously, damage and decrease the yield rate of the factory. Thus, these PID parameters must be adjusted appropriately and in a timely manner in order to control the temperature or other features accurately. (2) External interference sources: In addition, some external cases exist in the problem of an interference source, such as the different power outputs of two electron guns used to alternately interfere, or the heat interfering ion source, etc., which also results in inaccurate temperature control. Interestingly, using the fuzzy control method to continuously correct the parametric conditions of a PID controller is a novel industrial application that can solve these traditional problems. Based on this trigger, this study motivates the use of two types of different fuzzy control PIDs for the above issues faced by the optical filter industry and provides the rationale for proposing the hybrid model. Figure 8 first shows the processing environment for proposing Type I of fuzzy control PID. It is noted that the universal value's intervals for the input and output variables of the fuzzy controller are obtained from industry experts' recommendations for the two types (Type I for Simulation 1 and Type II for Simulation 2) used in this study.

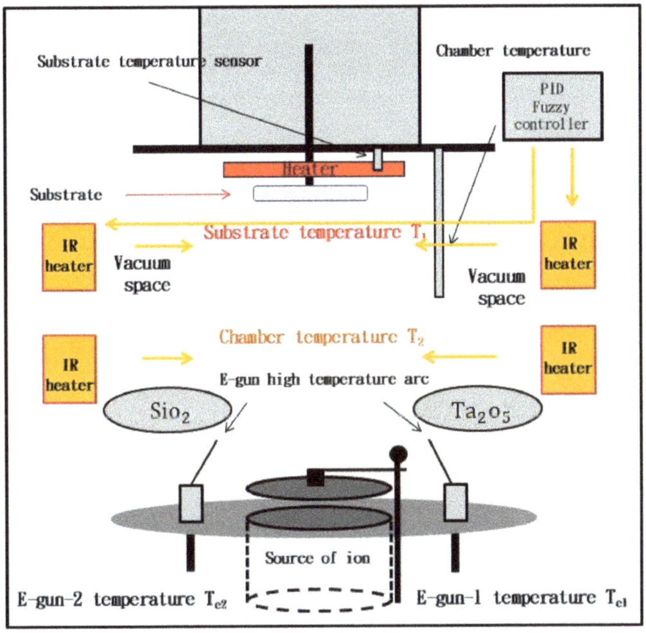

Figure 8. The processing environment diagram for Type I of the fuzzy control PID.

3.3.1. Type I of Fuzzy Control PID with Its Research Simulation 1

In the Type I fuzzy control PID, it has a main processing flow in that it first adopts a fuzzy controller and receives the signal source of input *e*. After implementing the fuzzification with fuzzy rules and using fuzzy inference to make defuzzification, three kinds of output, Kp, Ki, and Kd [44], are produced, respectively. Figure 9 shows an architecture diagram of the fuzzy control PID [45]; it can be set for the input temperature starting at 25 degrees, and the maximum temperature is set at 175 degrees. Then, the fuzzy rules of fuzzy control are based on creating the three parameters Kp, Ki, and Kd and generating current *u* to the heater and heat the coating cavity; however, because of the high temperature of the two sets of electron guns, the output has the error of comparison on the cavity temperature feedback and is continuously adjusted to the set value of 175 degrees for finally reaching the effect of steady-state average temperature. Figure 10 shows the output and input diagram of the fuzzy control, which is the *e* (error value) of the set temperature for each input. After executing the fuzzy rules of fuzzy control, three adjusted parameters of Kp, Ki, and Kd are outputted and transmitted to *u* (current), and then continuously adjust the *e* value to the approximate value.

To further help understand the process of the Type I fuzzy control PID, there are four core directions addressed as follows: (1) Figure 11 presents the membership function for the input *e* of fuzzy control. From Figure 11, it is shown that the *e* value set for an input temperature and then its related membership functions have the following four situations: range of the NL (negative & large) is (−20~−5.5), range of the NS (negative & small) is (−6.5~−1.5), range of the ZE (zero) is (−2.5~2.5), range of the PS (positive & small) is (1.5~6.5), and range of the PL (positive & large) is (5.5~20.0). (2) Next, it is also shown that the input Kp value set for an output Kp is highlighted, and its related membership functions also have the following four situations: range of the NL is (−20.0~−5.0), range of the NS is (−7.0~−1.0), range of the ZE is (−2.0~2.0), range of the PS is (1.0~7.0), and range of the PL is (5.0~20.0). (3) In addition, for the input Ki of fuzzy control, there is a set output Ki highlighted, and its related membership functions also have the following four cases: range of the NL is (−15.0~−5.0), range of the NS is (−7.0~−1.0), range of the Z is

(−2.0~2.0), range of the PS is (1.0~7.0), and range of the PL is (5.0~15.0). (4) Finally, the set input Kd of fuzzy control on an output Kd is highlighted, and its related membership functions are the same as the output Ki in the following four cases: range of the NL is also (−15.0~−5.0), range of the NS is also (−7.0~−1.0), range of the ZE is also (−2.0~2.0), range of the PS is also (1.0~7.0), and range of the PL is also (5.0~15.0).

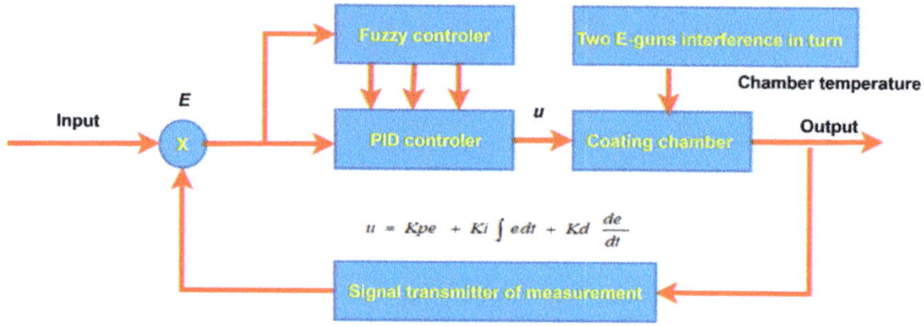

Figure 9. The architecture diagram of the fuzzy control PID.

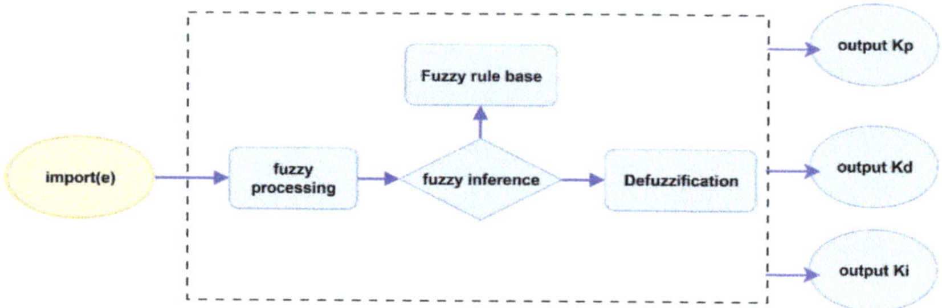

Figure 10. The diagram of input and output values for the fuzzy control.

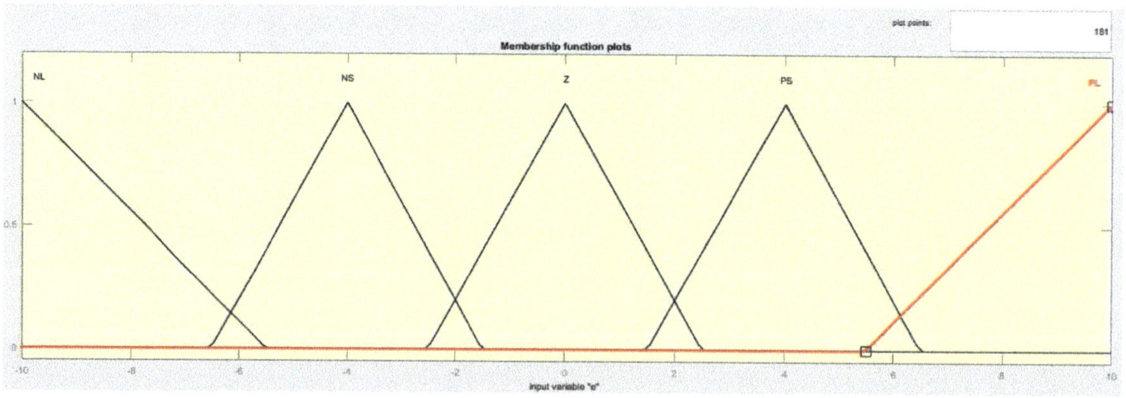

Figure 11. Input *e* of membership function diagram for the fuzzy control.

3.3.2. Fuzzy Rules-Based System for PID

The rule base for processing the fuzzy control PID is addressed in a single input error value *e*. After implementing the fuzzy rules, a single output is generated: the three adjusted values of Kp, Ki, and Kd. First, the fuzzy rules base uses the input *e* value; that is, the e is entered into the rule base in order to adjust the PID parameters by matching the temperature set, and the current u generated accordingly flows into the cavity and then heats it. Next, the output value of temperature is compared with the value preset, and the temperature is constantly corrected and adjusted to make an approximate result of the temperature between the value preset and the output value achieved. Among them, the output value for the three parameters, Kp, Ki, and Kd, has been classified into meaningful semantic values of fuzzy; thus, there are three semantic situations productively determined by Simulink simulation results in this study. (1) The input e value has been identified as five kinds of semantic values of input, PL, ZE, NL, NS, and PS, for the Kp, which are used to generate the output Kp value by identifying the changing quantity for the five semantic values of output, NL, ZE, PL, NS, and PS. (2) The e value for the Ki value also has five variations of semantic values of input, ZE, NS, PL, NL, and PS, used to generate the changing quantity for the Ki value with five semantic values of output, ZE, PS, NL, PL, and NS. (3) The e value for the Kd value also has five variations of input, which are ZE, NS, PL, NL, and PS, used to generate the changing quantity for the Kd value with five semantic values of output, ZE, PS, NL, PL, and NS. Figure 12 shows the practical decision rules of the fuzzy-rules base; from Figure 12, we know that there are 15 rules in the fuzzy-rules base under the fuzzy control PID. In processing the implementation, when the set temperature e value is input, it first goes throughout the 15 fuzzy rules bases to adjust the values of the three output parameters Kp, Ki, and Kd, controls the output current u to feedback, and compares with e until it approaches the approximate value.

Fuzzy Control PID Rule Base							
1	IF	e(error amount)	PL	Then	output value	NL	Kp
2	IF	e(error amount)	ZE	Then	output value	ZE	Kp
3	IF	e(error amount)	NL	Then	output value	PL	Kp
4	IF	e(error amount)	PS	Then	output value	NS	Kp
5	IF	e(error amount)	NS	Then	output value	PS	Kp
6	IF	e(error amount)	ZE	Then	output value	ZE	Ki
7	IF	e(error amount)	NS	Then	output value	PS	Ki
8	IF	e(error amount)	PL	Then	output value	NL	Ki
9	IF	e(error amount)	NL	Then	output value	PL	Ki
10	IF	e(error amount)	PS	Then	output value	NS	Ki
11	IF	e(error amount)	ZE	Then	output value	ZE	Kd
12	IF	e(error amount)	NS	Then	output value	PS	Kd
13	IF	e(error amount)	PL	Then	output value	NL	Kd
14	IF	e(error amount)	NL	Then	output value	PL	Kd
15	IF	e(error amount)	PS	Then	output value	NS	Kd

Figure 12. Fuzzy decision rule base for the fuzzy control PID.

Next, we accordingly use Simulink simulation to design the four core control situations to implement the process of fuzzy control PID as follows:

(1) For Equation (15): Uses the substrate of the PID control to derive the circuit diagram according to Equation (15) for the substrate experiment. In particular, the PID control allows the substrate to reach a stable temperature in a short time.

(2) For Equation (16): Uses the chamber of PID control, and the circuit diagram is derived from Equation (16) for the chamber experiment; its temperature is set at 175 degrees plus 25 degrees at room temperature, two sets of interference sources of electron guns are added to switch alternately, and the cavity temperature is affected by the interference sources, making the temperature of PID control unsatisfactory. If we want to have a good control effect, constant adjustment of the current u of the output is needed to control the temperature by the PID.

(3) For fuzzy-rules base: Uses the fuzzy control, according to Section 3.3.1, the concepts of fuzzy control and the fuzzy rules base in Figure 12, to adjust the three parameter variations of output to control the influence of the two sets of interference sources by the PID so that the temperature can be controlled close to ideal.
(4) For Equation (17): Uses the circuit diagram derived from Equation (17) for the cavity wall experiment, and it will be affected by the evaporation coefficient at room temperature because the cavity wall is made of stainless steel which has the property of high thermal conductivity.

3.3.3. Type II of Fuzzy Control PID with Its Research Simulation 2

The second method of fuzzy control PID in this study is to mainly use the fuzzy controller to receive the input signal source of e (error) and d/dt (differentiator); after conducting the fuzzification and fuzzy-rules base and concurrently performing fuzzy inference to defuzzification, three kinds of output are obtained, including ΔKp, ΔKi, and ΔKd. Figure 13 shows the structure of the fuzzy PID algorithm [46,47], which is the result of fine-tuning ΔKp, ΔKi, and ΔKd for the fuzzy control after PID adjustment is applied. In implementing this Type II method, after tuning the PID controller, the variation of the temperature difference between the two sets of electron guns under high-temperature alternating interference has been greatly reduced. All the Kp, Ki, and Kd of PID plus the output ΔKp, ΔKi, and ΔKd of fuzzy control, respectively, are added to generate a current u transferring to the heater, which can provide feedback for error comparison of temperature between the heating cavity and the coating cavity after tuning continuous adjustment to measuring up the preset value of 175 degrees in order to achieve the effect of steady-state average temperature. Figure 14 presents the results for the input and output of the fuzzy control with the fine-tuning ΔKp, ΔKi, and ΔKd. From Figure 14, the input values of e and d/dt for the set temperature are determined, and the three outputs of ΔKp, ΔKi, and ΔKd are identified after tuning the fuzzy rules; afterwards, the three adjusted parameters are transmitted to u (current), and repeatedly, in this way, the e value is continuously adjusted to an approximate value. Similar to the previous method of Type I, there are five main directions for the e and d/dt addressed in the following explanations. (1) Figure 15 shows a membership function of fuzzy control for the input e of the set temperature. Based on the membership function of Figure 15, there are the following four situations: for the NL, its range is (−1.0~−0.5), its range is (−0.7~−0.1) for the NS, its range is (−0.2~0.2) for the ZE, its range is (0.1~0.7) for the PS, and its range is (0.5~1.0) for the PL. (2) Moreover, add the membership function of input d/dt and set the d/dt of the temperature for each input. Based on the membership function, there are also the following four situations: the range of the NL is (−1.0~−0.5), the range of the NS is (−0.7~−0.1), the range of the ZE is (−0.2~0.2), the range of the PS is (0.1~0.7), and the range of the PL is (0.5~1.0). (3) For the input ΔKp membership function and the setting ΔKp for each output, there are the following four situations: its range of the NL is (−2.0~−0.5), its range of the NS is (−0.7~−0.1), its range of the ZE is (−0.2~0.2), its range of the PS is (0.1~0.7), and its range of the PL is (0.5~2.0). (4) For the input ΔKi membership function and the setting ΔKi for each output, there are the following four situations: the range of the NL is (−1.5~−0.5), the range of the NS is (−0.7~−0.1), the range of the ZE is (−0.2~0.2), the range of the PS is (0.1~0.7), and the range of the PL is (0.5~1.5). (5) Finally, for the input ΔKd membership function and the setting ΔKd for each output, there are also the following four situations: the range of the NL is (−1.5~−0.5), the range of the NS is (−0.6~−0.01), the range of the ZE is (−0.05~0.05), the range of the PS is (0.01~0.6), and the range of the PL is (0.5~1.5).

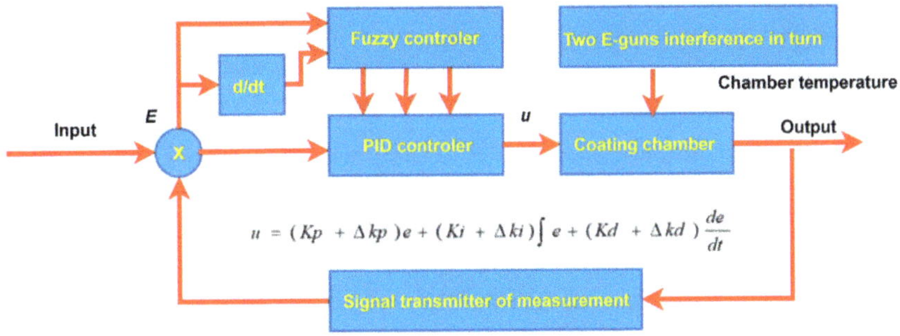

Figure 13. Processing flow of fine-tuning ΔKp, ΔKi, and ΔKd by fuzzy control after tuning PID adjustment.

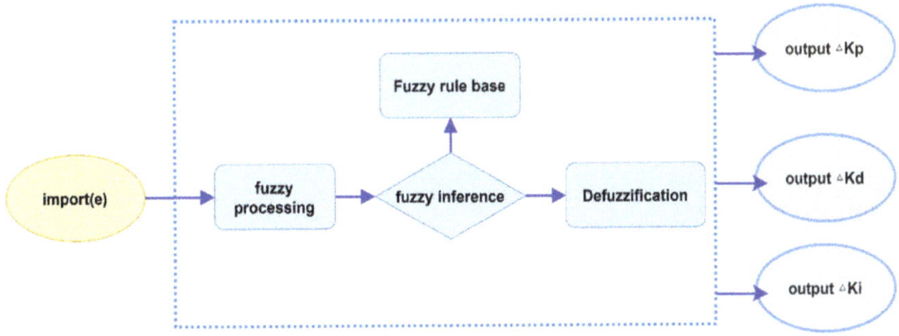

Figure 14. Results of the fine-tuning ΔKp, ΔKi, and ΔKd by the fuzzy control PID.

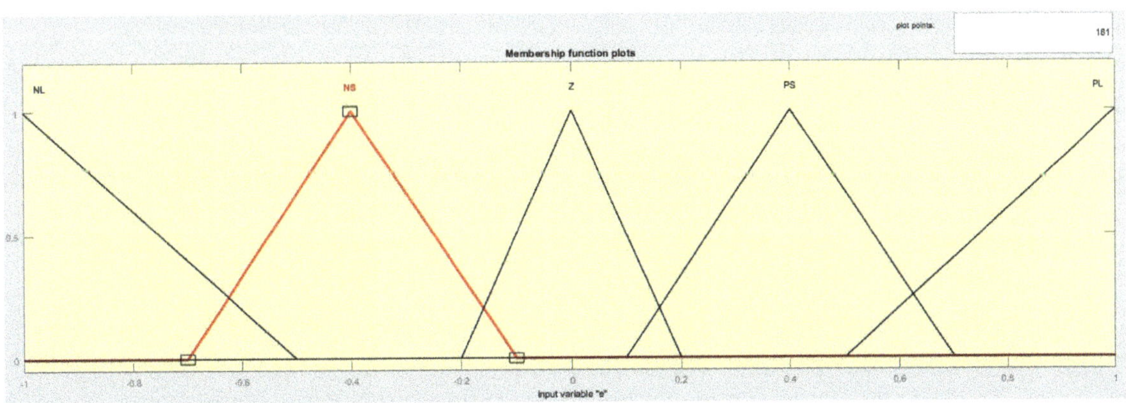

Figure 15. Membership function of input *e* using the fuzzy control.

3.3.4. PID + Kp, Ki, and Kd of Fuzzy-Rules Base

The rules used in this study in processing the fuzzy PID control have multiple input values, such as *e* value and d/dt (d/dt is an operational expression; d is not a differential but refers to a very small amount of change; d/dt differentiates with respect to t). After tuning the fuzzy rules, the single output is created and addressed in the adjustment values of three parameters, ΔKp, ΔKi, and ΔKd. After implementing the PID to control the temperature, add the ΔKp, ΔKi, and ΔKd of the fuzzy control PID, and then through the fuzzy-rules base, the input *e* value and d/dt enter the outputs, ΔKp, ΔKi, and ΔKd plus PID, of the fuzzy control for the set temperature; the generated current *u* is passed to the cavity for heating, and then the generated temperature is compared with the preset value. Accordingly, the temperature is continuously adjusted to produce a similar result for the difference between the set value and the output value obtained. Among them, the three output values, ΔKp, ΔKi, and ΔKd, have their fuzzy semantic values, respectively. The input of *e* value and d/dt for the ΔKp value has five kinds of semantic values, including PL, ZE, NL, PS, and NS, and it is used to generate the output value of the ΔKp with five fuzzy semantic values: NL, ZE, PL, ZE, and ZE. Likewise, the input *e* value and d/dt for the ΔKi value also have 5 kinds of fuzzy semantic values, ZE, NS, PL, NL, and PS, used to generate the output ΔKi for five semantic values of all zeros, i.e., ZE, ZE, ZE, ZE, and ZE. Similarly, the input *e* value and d/dt for the ΔKd value have five fuzzy semantic values, ZE, NS, PL, NL, and PS, used to generate the output value of ΔKd with five fuzzy semantic values, ZE, ZE, PS, NS, and ZE. Figure 16 shows the fuzzy rule base for the fuzzy control PID + ΔKp, ΔKi, and ΔKd. From Figure 16, there are 15 fuzzy decision rules defined. In implementing the process of Type II, it first goes through the 15 fuzzy rules after setting the temperature of input *e* and d/dt and then adjusts the output values of the three parameters, ΔKp, ΔKi, and ΔKd, to control the output current in the way of feedback until it reaches an approximate value in continuous adjustment for *e*. Afterwards, according to the fuzzy control and the fuzzy rules, we constantly adjust the output variations of parameters by the PID to effectively control the influence of the two sets of interference sources so that the temperature can be controlled close to the idealized effect.

Fuzzy Control PID + ΔKp , ΔKi , ΔKd Rule Base							
1	IF	(e)and(d/dt)	PL	Then	output value	NL	ΔKp
2	IF	(e)and(d/dt)	ZE	Then	output value	ZE	ΔKp
3	IF	(e)and(d/dt)	NL	Then	output value	PL	ΔKp
4	IF	(e)and(d/dt)	PS	Then	output value	NS	ΔKp
5	IF	(e)and(d/dt)	NS	Then	output value	PS	ΔKp
6	IF	(e)and(d/dt)	ZE	Then	output value	ZE	ΔKi
7	IF	(e)and(d/dt)	NS	Then	output value	PS	ΔKi
8	IF	(e)and(d/dt)	PL	Then	output value	NL	ΔKi
9	IF	(e)and(d/dt)	NL	Then	output value	PL	ΔKi
10	IF	(e)and(d/dt)	PS	Then	output value	NS	ΔKi
11	IF	(e)and(d/dt)	ZE	Then	output value	ZE	ΔKd
12	IF	(e)and(d/dt)	NS	Then	output value	PS	ΔKd
13	IF	(e)and(d/dt)	PL	Then	output value	NL	ΔKd
14	IF	(e)and(d/dt)	NL	Then	output value	PL	ΔKd
15	IF	(e)and(d/dt)	PS	Then	output value	NS	ΔKd

Figure 16. Decision rules of fuzzy-rules based of the fuzzy control PID + ΔKp, ΔKi, and ΔKd.

3.4. Simulation Verification of an Intelligent NNs Model

Figure 17 shows a structural diagram for processing a NN model. As shown in Figure 17, after collecting the industry data, the data are divided into two types: training and testing sets. The data contain the parameter values set and controlled by the peripheral control equipment and the evaporation machine equipment of the factory, respectively. We use the original conditions to establish a learning NN model through the training data. Then, we introduce the testing data into the learning process, set the neurons in the hidden layer of the NN, and choose Tanh(·) as the output activation function [48]; the Tanh function is also called the hyperbolic tangent function, which is proposed to solve the mean value problem on the basis of the Sigmoid function [49]. The range of values for the function is [−1, 1], and the corresponding average value of the output is 0. Tanh function will have a good effect when the characteristics are significantly different. The solver is set to use the stochastic gradient descent (SGD) method [50]; its advantage is that for large data sets, and the training speed is fast. A batch is randomly selected from the training set samples to calculate the gradient once, and the model parameters are updated once. The maximum number of iterations is selected to be 50 times. The testing results, testing scores, and predicted results can be obtained in a short period of time. It is one of the most useful and fast neural algorithms, designed to predict this kind of big data structure.

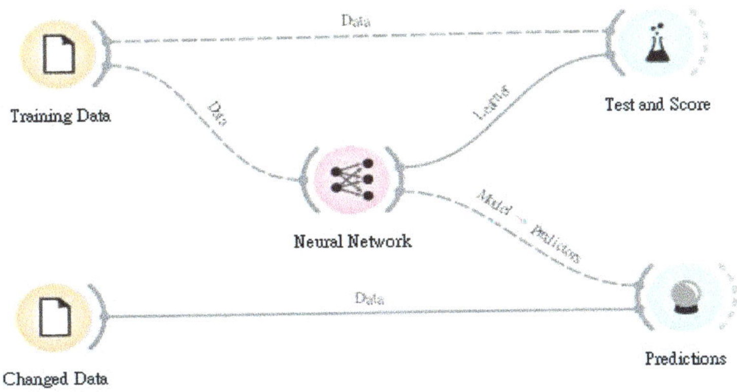

Figure 17. Architecture of a NN model.

Applied to the practical cases of this study, the NN has two sets of input values, the training data and the testing data; after implementing the neural algorithm, two sets of corresponding output values for the testing score and prediction result can be obtained, respectively. Thus, the data obtained by the PID tester are used as the input layer to input $X = \{r_1, r_2, \ldots, r_N\}$. The sampling time will be every Δt seconds, the impedance value of the *ith* measurement is $r(i\Delta t) = r_i$, the impedance value from the 1st to the *Nth* will be used as the input layers 1~N neurons, calculate the network weight value through Equation (6), and then guide the input weight value to the output layer through Equation (5). A set of input X and output Y data will be obtained. Not every training instance achieves the ideal network weight value immediately; thus, it is necessary to continuously correct the weight of each connection, and the weight value is connected to the neurons of the hidden layer and the output layer. Therefore, this study corrects the weight value in the way of supervised learning, supplemented by the form of BPNN, to correct the weight of the error function E in the form of Equation (7). Afterwards, we calculate in the hidden layer, and then calculate the calculated data with the Equation (8) and multiply the weight w_{ji}^n of the hidden layer and the output layer. Accordingly, the output layer summarizes the data, and the output layer compares the result with the target value (i.e., whether there exists a PID phenomenon). If the calculated output does not meet the expected target value, it will be returned to the input layer, and then recalculate the weight value of the connection weight value in Equation (7) with the hidden layer; repeat Equation (5) to calculate the output value of the hidden layer and the output layer until we get what we want: knowing whether there exists a PID phenomenon.

In addition, it is necessary to eliminate the data that may cause training errors in the input data and use other input data to supplement it. After finishing the supplement, re-enter the data into the input layer and calculate the output value for the input layer and hidden layer again. Finally, other validation data is fed into this modified and trained NN model [51]. Therefore, the construction of a NN model in this study is divided into three stages, namely training, verification, and testing, described separately. (1) Training: After the input data and structure size are determined in the training phase, the weights are adjusted; the training phase must provide enough data T_R for the learning phase of the NN model. (2) Verification: Provide part of the data T_V in the verification phase to verify whether the parameters and architecture of the training phase are appropriate, and select the most suitable model from them as the best architecture of the NN model used in the testing phase. (3) Testing: The testing phase mainly uses testing data T_T to test whether the trained and verified NN model can meet the practical industry data application.

4. Data Analysis and Demonstration Results

After implementing the real-life case study, this section mainly describes the research results and evidence of effectiveness in three parts. First, we collect the practical data and, accordingly, use the analytical techniques. Second, we find out the relevance of the cause of the defect rate and use the fuzzy control PID to formulate fuzzy rules and make a comprehensive analysis [52]. Third, we use the Simulink simulation package to simulate the effect of fuzzy control with its experimental results. Thus, we have five sections to address the above processing scheme with results, including analysis results of data mining techniques, analysis results of Simulation 1 using fuzzy control, analysis results of Simulation 2 using fuzzy control, summary analysis of fuzzy control research, and verification results of NNs, respectively.

4.1. Analysis Results of Data Mining Techniques

We need to first define and describe the yield rate of the case study. Figure 18 shows the distribution of products for the yield rate in this case. From Figure 18, it is clear that we have defined three classes of products to distinguish the yield rate: 60% or more is good, 30%–60% is normal, and 0%–30% is bad. Interestingly, the bad rate is unacceptable.

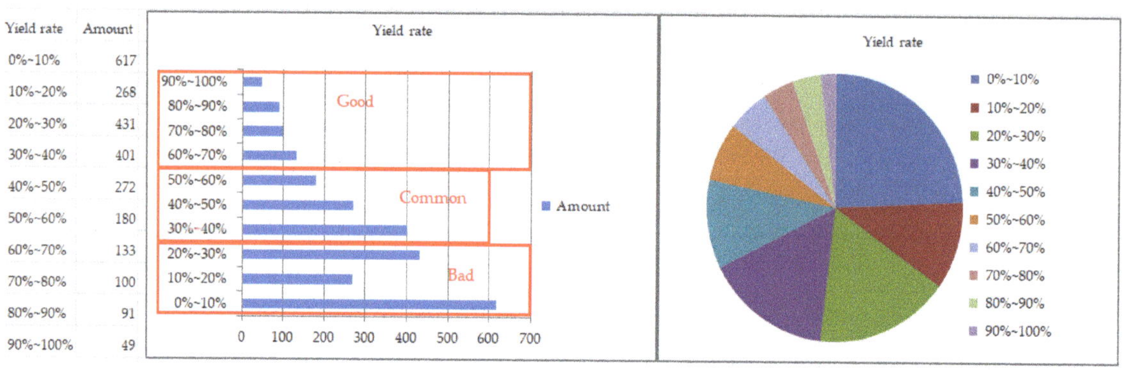

Figure 18. Distribution status of the yield rate for the case study.

Accordingly, based on actual features to analyze the industrial data from an optoelectronic company, Table 1 shows the partial data collected from factory affairs and equipment, and Table 2 shows the integrated partial data classified into three classes with sorting in decisional attribute (i.e., test result) for more convenient experimental operation and use. The three classes are good, normal, and bad. (Note the following abbreviations are defined for these terms: production month (P.M.), job number (J.N.), product code (P.C.), equipment code (E.C.), substrate size (S.S.), yield rate (Y.R.), cause of failure (C.F.), yield distribution (Y.D.), substrate temperature (S.T.), and cavity temperature (C.T.), cooling water temperature (C.W.T.), inlet water pressure (I.W.P.), return water pressure (R.W.P.), temperature difference between the cavity and the substrate (T.D.), good (G), normal (N), and bad (B)).

Table 1. Original partial data collected from an optoelectronic company.

P.M.	J.N.	P.C.	E.C.	S.S.	Y.R.	C.F.	Y.D.	S.T.	C.T.	C.W.T.	I.W.P.	R.W.P.	Ta_2O_5	SiO_2	Result
January	G2101001	100G	K011	95	1.16	1	3	195	184	20	4	0.6	−1	−1.5	B
January	G2101002	MBS	B002	150	20.1		2	195	185	20	2.4	0.6	0	0.5	B
January	G2101003	100G	C003	95	38.5		2	178	179	21	2.8	0.6	3	0.5	N
January	G2101004	800G	A001	150	36.6		2	175	180	20.5	3.3	0.8	0	−0.5	N
January	G2101005	MBB	D004	95	34.28		6	178	193	21	2.5	0.8	2	0	N
January	G2101006	100G	F006	95	35.47		6	201	185	20	2.8	0.6	2	1	N
January	G2101007	100G	J010	95	0	1	8	188	208	23.5	3.6	0.2	0	−0.5	B
January	G2101008	100G	I009	95	20.42	10	2	177	183	19	3.8	0.9	−2	1.5	B
January	G2101009	CWDM	E005	150	82.76		6	176	175	21	2.8	0.8	0	0	G
January	G2101010	800G	G007	150	38.20		6	215	180	20.5	2.8	0.9	−2	0	N
January	G2101011	MWB	H008	150	7.08	2	3	176	185	19.5	3.6	0.1	0	3.5	B
January	G2101012	100G	K011	95	15.99		3	184	184	20	4	0.6	−1	−4.5	B
January	G2101013	800G	A001	150	65.53		6	176	180	20.5	3.3	0.8	0	−0.5	G
January	G2101014	MBS	B002	150	90.21		6	195	185	20	2.4	0.6	1	−1	G
January	G2101015	100G	C003	95	31.53		2	180	178	21	2.8	0.6	3	0.5	N
January	G2101016	100G	F006	95	37.30		4	200	187	20.5	2.7	0.4	4	1.5	N
January	G2101017	MBB	D004	95	44.92		2	178	193	21	2.5	0.8	0	1	N
January	G2101018	100G	J010	95	18.81		3	188	211	23.5	3.6	0.2	0	−1.5	B
January	G2101019	CWDM	E005	150	53.99		6	176	178	21	2.8	0.8	0	−0.5	N
January	G2101020	100G	I009	95	39.01		2	178	178	18.5	3.8	1.0	0	0.5	N
January	G2101021	800G	G007	150	30.62		2	212	181	20	2.8	0.6	−2	0	N
January	G2101022	800G	A001	150	87.77		6	176	179	20	3.3	0.8	0	0	G
January	G2101023	MWB	H008	150	28.63		2	176	188	19.5	3.6	0.1	0	0.5	B
January	G2101024	100G	K011	95	14.51		4	185	185	20	4.0	0.6	0	−0.5	B
January	G2101025	100G	C003	95	33.16		2	181	179	21.5	2.8	0.5	2	0	N
January	G2101026	MBS	B002	150	90.21		6	196	185	21	2.4	0.6	0	1.5	G
January	G2101027	100G	J010	95	28.08		2	187	190	24.3	3.6	0.1	0	0.5	B
January	G2101028	MBB	D004	95	0	2	8	178	193	21	2.5	0.8	0	0	B
January	G2101029	CWDM	E005	150	6.28	8	1	180	170	21	2.8	0.6	0	0	B
January	G2101030	800G	G007	150	43.34		6	210	175	20	2.8	0.6	−3	0	N
January	G2101031	100G	I009	95	32.25		2	177	186	18.5	3.8	0.8	−1	0.5	N
January	G2101032	100G	F006	95	5.73	2	2	199	188	21	2.8	0.5	4	1.5	B
January	G2101033	800G	A001	150	60.49		6	175	176	20	3.2	0.8	0	0	G
January	G2101034	MBB	D004	95	0	2	8	178	193	21	2.5	0.8	0	0	B

Table 2. Partial data after performing classification process of decision attribute.

P.M.	J.N.	P.C.	E.C.	S.S.	Y.R.	C.F.	Y.D.	S.T.	C.T.	C.W.T.	I.W.P.	R.W.P.	Ta_2O_5	SiO_2	T.D.	Result
January	G2101003	100G	C003	95	38.5		2	178	179	21	2.8	0.6	3	0.5	1	N
January	G2101006	100G	F006	95	35.47		6	201	185	20	2.8	0.6	2	1	−10	N
January	G2101015	100G	C003	95	31.53		2	180	178	21	2.8	0.6	3	0.5	−2	N
January	G2101016	100G	F006	95	37.30		4	200	187	20.5	2.7	0.4	4	1.5	−13	N
January	G2101020	100G	I009	95	39.01		2	178	178	18.5	3.8	1.0	0	0.5	0	N
January	G2101025	100G	C003	95	33.16		2	181	179	21.5	2.8	0.5	2	0	−2	N
January	G2101031	100G	I009	95	32.25		2	177	186	18.5	3.8	0.8	−1	0.5	9	N
January	G2101037	100G	C003	95	40.91		2	180	178	21	2.8	0.6	4	0	−2	N
January	G2101042	100G	F006	95	32.92		3	202	195	21	2.8	0.6	3	1	−7	N
January	G2101054	100G	K011	95	40.97		3	186	192	19.5	3.8	0.7	−2	0.5	6	N
January	G2101064	100G	K011	95	38.34		3	188	189	19.5	4.0	0.6	0	0.5	1	N
January	G2101068	100G	C003	95	32.47		2	176	182	21	2.8	0.6	2	0.5	6	N
January	G2101072	100G	F006	95	44.21		3	185	188	20.5	0.8	0.6	4	0.5	3	N
January	G2101075	100G	K011	95	33.47		3	188	188	19.5	4.0	0.6	0	0.5	0	N
January	G2101083	100G	C003	95	53.61		4	170	175	21	2.8	0.6	2	0.5	5	N
January	G2101087	100G	K011	95	37.26		4	188	187	19.5	4.0	0.6	−3	0.5	−1	N
January	G2101088	100G	F006	95	45.15		4	199	189	20	2.8	0.6	2	0.5	−10	N
January	G2101093	100G	C003	95	51.06		6	172	178	21	2.8	0.6	0	0	6	N
January	G2101096	100G	K011	95	38.34		3	184	189	19.5	3.2	0.6	0	0	5	N
January	G2101099	100G	F006	95	33.19		4	192	195	20.5	2.8	0.6	3	1	3	N
January	G2101106	100G	K011	95	40.85		2	186	187	19.5	3.8	0.6	−2	0.5	1	N
January	G2101107	100G	F006	95	33.32		4	192	186	21	2.6	0.4	5	0.5	−6	N
January	G2101109	100G	J010	95	41.15		3	186	195	23.5	3.8	0.2	0	1.5	9	N
January	G2101113	100G	C003	95	35.47		2	169	175	21	2.8	0.6	3	−0.5	6	N
January	G2101117	100G	F006	95	55.38		4	198	187	21	2.7	0.4	2	0.5	−11	N
January	G2101128	100G	F006	95	39.64		4	192	182	20	2.8	0.6	2	0.5	−10	N
January	G2101133	100G	C003	95	46.50		2	170	176	21	2.8	0.4	2	−0.5	6	N
January	G2101139	100G	F006	95	39.64		2	189	182	20	2.8	0.6	4	0.5	−7	N
January	G2101143	100G	C003	95	33.23		2	170	176	21	2.8	0.4	2	−0.5	6	N
January	G2101148	100G	F006	95	51.91		4	185	182	20	2.8	0.6	4	0.5	−3	N
January	G2101150	100G	K011	95	49.58		6	185.5	186.5	19.5	3.9	0.6	−2	0.5	1	N
January	G2101160	100G	K011	95	33.21		2	186	194	19.5	3.9	0.6	0	0.5	8	N
January	G2101168	100G	D004	95	55.27		6	178	189	21.5	2.7	0.8	−3	0	11	N
January	G2101171	100G	K011	95	47.30		6	186	193	19.5	3.9	0.6	0	0.5	7	N

4.1.1. Analysis Results of Box-and-Whisker Plot

After performing the analysis of the box-and-whisker plot, Table 3 lists its summary for the analytical experiment. From Table 3, we can obtain characteristic results of seven items by the box-and-whisker plot, including substrate temperature, cavity temperature, cooling water temperature, inlet water pressure, Ta_2O_5 spot position, SiO_2 spot position, and the temperature difference between the cavity and the substrate. It is clear that no significant difference exists in the first six items; conversely, the temperature difference in the seventh item has a significant difference. Thus, the temperature difference between the cavity and the substrate is a key determinant that influences the yield rate. From the perspective of temperature difference, there are three fuzzy levels identified. (1) In particular, the correlation outcome between the yield rate and the temperature difference within 2 °C to 3 °C is very good; (2) the correlation is normal when the temperature difference is within 3 °C to 9 °C; and (3) it is not a good correlation if the temperature difference is above 4 °C to 13.5 °C. Therefore, based on the above experimental results, we have found an important fact: the larger the temperature difference, the lower the yield rate. Based on the above interesting fact, this research is aimed at controlling the temperature difference to being as small as possible. It is most likely that the yield rate of the products can be improved by improving the temperature difference. Furthermore, it is also clear that there are obvious differences in the distribution from the evidence of the box-and-whisker plot for the conditional temperature difference of the product equipment. Regarding the box-and-whisker plot in Table 3, there are three categories, good, ordinary, and bad, for the yield rate, which is also proved and determined by the cavity and the substrate. (1) In terms of temperature difference, the average temperature difference is about 2.37 degrees when the yield rate is good, and its distribution range is relatively low and concentrated. (2) The average temperature difference is about 6.12 degrees when the yield rate is normal, and its distribution range is relatively large. (3) When the inspection outcome is not good, the average temperature difference is about 9.25 degrees, and its distribution range is relatively larger and less concentrated when compared to the other two cases. Furthermore, from a distribution analysis of the box-and-whisker plot for the cooling water pressure, it is also clear that there are three categories, very good, ordinary, and bad, addressed and identified for the yield rate. (1) From the perspective of cooling water pressure, the yield rate is good when the average water pressure is about 3.46 kg, the water pressure range is from 3.3 kg to 3.8 kg, and it is implied to need stronger water pressure for "cooling" temperature. (2) The yield rate is normal when the average water pressure is 3.32 kg, the water pressure range is from 2.8 kg to 3.8 kg, and the water pressure tends to be at a "weak cooling" temperature. (3) The yield rate is bad when the average water pressure is about 3.2 kg, the water pressure range is from 2.8 kg to 3.6 kg, and the water pressure is also identified as a biased "weak cooling" temperature. Therefore, focusing on the above experimental results, there also exists a significant difference in the cooling water pressure, and when the cooling water pressure is stronger, the yield rate has a better outcome.

Table 3. Summary of box-and-whisker method after analytical experiments.

Item No.	Feature	Good	Normal	Bad	Good A.	Normal A.	Bad A.	S.D.
1	Substrate T.	180–188 °C	178–189.5 °C	175–190 °C	183.8 °C	185.3 °C	184.1 °C	No
2	Cavity T.	181–191 °C	181–192 °C	180–191 °C	185.5 °C	187.1 °C	186.4 °C	No
3	Cooling water T.	19–21 °C	19.5–21.5 °C	19.5–21.5 °C	20.33 °C	20.86 °C	21.16 °C	No
4	Cooling water inlet P.	3.3–3.8 kgs	2.8–3.8 kgs	2.8–3.6 kgs	3.45 kgs	3.32 kgs	3.22 kgs	No
5	Ta2o5 spot position	0~−1	0~−1	0~−1	−0.54	−0.14	−0.16	No
6	Sio2 spot position	0.5~−0.5	0.5~−0.5	0.5~−0.5	−0.18	0.06	0.15	No
7	T. D. between the cavity and the substrate	2~3 °C	3~9 °C	4~13.5 °C	2.3 °C	6.1 °C	9.25 °C	Yes

Note: A. refers to average, S. refers to significant, T. refers to temperature, P. refers to pressure, and D. refers to difference.

4.1.2. Analysis Results of Association Rule

After implementing the association rule, Table 4 shows its analytical results for the seven conditional attributes mentioned above. From Table 4, the results of seven featured attributes for the correlation with the one decisional attribute (i.e., the yield rate) can be observed. There are also seven features in the previous subsection, and the seventh item, the temperature difference between the cavity and the substrate, has a significant difference. There are four key points to address in the analytical results. (1) If the average temperature difference is within 2.3 degrees, the yield rate is very good; the yield rate is normal if the average temperature difference is within 6.1 degrees, and the yield rate will be bad if the average temperature difference is within 9.25 degrees. (2) The above results are the same as the results of the box-and-whisker method. Interestingly, we also have an important research finding: the greater the average temperature difference, the worse the yield rate. Thus, this study also needs to mainly control the average temperature difference close to the ideal value in order to improve the yield rate of products. (3) Afterwards, with the discretization of numerical items, we can obtain the 5 frequent items of high-density products when the number of intervals of equal-frequency discretization is set to 2, the number of itemsets is 2 when the minimum support is set at 3%, the support achieves 3.67% when the temperature difference between the cavity and the substrate is less than or equal to 6.75, and thus, the yield rate is very good. (4) Moreover, according to the analytical results of association rules, two decision rules are generated if the minimum support is set at 37.0% and the minimum reliability is set at 74.0%. This implied two important industry rule findings. Rule 1: The cooling water temperature is greater than 20.75 degrees if the inlet water pressure is less than 3.25 kg. Rule 2: The yield rate is bad when the temperature difference between the cavity and the substrate is greater than 6.75 degrees.

Table 4. Summary of feature correlation from performing the association rule method.

Item No.	Feature	Good	Normal	Bad	Good A.	Normal A.	Bad A.	S.D.
1	Substrate T.	175–186 °C	176–188 °C	175–188 °C	182.1 °C	183.5 °C	183.4 °C	No
2	Cavity T.	179–190 °C	180–190 °C	179–190 °C	185.3 °C	185.2 °C	184.6 °C	No
3	Cooling water T.	20–21 °C	19.5–21.5 °C	19.5–21.5 °C	20.6 °C	20.9 °C	20.9 °C	No
4	Cooling water inlet P.	2.4–3.1 kgs	2.8–3.6 kgs	2.8–3.6 kgs	2.84 kgs	3.15 kgs	3.16 kgs	No
5	Ta2o5 spot position	0~−1	0~−1	0~−1	−0.32	−0.27	−0.30	No
6	Sio2 spot position	0.5~−0.5	0.5~−0.5	0.5~−0.5	0.05	0.148	0.159	No
7	T. D. between the cavity and the substrate	2~3 °C	3~9 °C	4~13.5 °C	2.3 °C	6.1 °C	9.25 °C	Yes

Note: A. refers to average, S. refers to significant, T. refers to temperature, P. refers to pressure, and D. refers to difference.

4.1.3. Analysis Results of Decision Tree

Subsequently, Table 5 shows the analytical summary for the decision tree technique. From Table 5, similar to the results of the first two methods, a total of seven features are also defined, and the seventh item, the temperature difference between the cavity and the substrate, has a significant difference in the yield rate. We also have four directions for determining the analytical results. (1) The yield rate is very good if the temperature difference is within 2 degrees, but it accounts for only 3.7%; the yield rate is normal if the temperature difference is within 2 degrees to 8.59 degrees, and its ratio has 40.10%; the yield rate is bad if the temperature difference is above 8.5 degrees to 17 degrees, and its ratio has 56.20%; therefore, the larger the temperature difference, the worse the yield rate. From the analysis results of the decision tree, similar to the previous two methods, this research is still moving towards the goal of controlling the temperature difference to make it close to the ideal value to improve the yield rate. (2) There are three classes for bad, normal, and good yield rates, which are executed for decisional rules, respectively. The first is the results of the decision tree analysis of the bad yield rate. There are 1008 items; among them, 567 items have a temperature difference greater than 8.5 degrees to 17 degrees, and 56.2% of them indicate that if the temperature difference is too large, the yield rate is obviously bad. (3) The second is the result of the decision tree analysis with the normal yield rate. There are 404 items defined with a temperature difference between less than 2 degrees and 8.5 degrees; there are 40.1% of them. It can be identified that if the temperature difference is within this range, the yield rate is normal. (4) The last are the results of the decision tree analysis with a good yield rate. There are 37 items with a temperature difference of less than 2 degrees, accounting for a total of 3.7%. It can also be defined that the temperature difference falls within this range, and then the yield rate is very good. Productively, through the above analysis results from the decision tree technique, it is identified that we should be committed to adjusting and controlling the temperature difference between the substrate and the cavity. If it can be controlled within 2 degrees, it will greatly help produce better products in the production process.

Table 5. Summary of analysis results from the decision tree technique.

Item No.	Feature	Good	Normal	Bad	S.D.
1	Substrate T.	167–195.5 °C	167–195.5 °C	167–195.5 °C	No
2	Cavity T.	184.5–198 °C	184.5–198 °C	184.5–198 °C	No
3	Cooling water T.	18–22 °C	18–22 °C	18–22 °C	No
4	Cooling water inlet P.	2.1–3.4 kgs	2.1–3.4 kgs	2.1–3.4 kgs	No
5	Ta_2O_5 spot position	0~+2	0~+2	0~+2	No
6	SiO_2 spot position	0~−4.5	0~−4.5	0~−4.5	No
7	T. D. between the cavity and the substrate	≤ 2 °C	2~8.59 °C	8.5~17 °C	Yes
	Yield rate %	3.7%	40.10%	56.20%	-

Note: S. refers to significant, T. refers to temperature, P. refers to pressure, and D. refers to difference.

4.1.4. Analysis Results of Fuzzy Control

Regarding the fuzzy control analysis, Table 6 shows the parameters of the mathematical model for the case factory after performing fuzzy control. From Table 6, it means that these parameters are approximate practice data from the factory site, and they are brought into the simulation system constructed. In order to make the experimental results more simulated and realistic, the three most important factors include the substrate, cavity, and cavity wall. The parameters are set according to the setting values of the actual field.

Table 6. Parameter list of the mathematical model from the case factory.

Object	Mass	Specific Heat	Surface Area	Emissivity	Substrate T.	Cavity T.	Cavity Wall T.	Constant of P.	T. Setting	Normal T.
	M	C	A	ε	T_1	T_2	T_w	σ	T_s	T
	g	°C	cm²	aλ	°C	°C	°C	W/m²K⁴	°C	°C
Substrate	250	700	17,662	11.75	175	175	175	5.67×10^{-8}	175	25
Cavity	20,000	500	35,000	0.95	173–177	173–177	173–177	5.67×10^{-8}	175	25
Cavity wall	10,000	500	22,000	0.45	173–177	173–177	173–177	5.67×10^{-8}	175	25

Note: T. refers to temperature and P. refers to proportionality.

4.2. Analysis Results of the Fuzzy Control PID Simulation Method 1

Following the previous section on using data mining techniques, we accordingly perform the fuzzy control PID simulation method. First, we show the PID control of the cavity for the original job site. Next, it is known that there are two electron guns: one is an electron gun with a larger change and a higher power, and the other is an electron gun with a smaller change and a lower power. The two electron guns operate alternately; the highest temperature is about 190 degrees; when another electron gun with a lower power is replaced, the temperature drops to about 160 degrees, and their temperature difference is about 30 degrees. However, because the power of the two electron guns in some processes is different, the temperature difference may vary even more, and the difference may be between 20 and 30 degrees; it is a key to note that this difference may cause poor yield rates. Moreover, because the heater area of the substrate for the optical coating machine is relatively small, it is easier to control the temperature. While the cavity area is larger, the IR heaters surround the four sides of the cavity. In particular, there are two electron guns alternately melting the powder, and a large voltage and a low current are used for melting the powder at high temperatures; the temperature can reach up to 1000 degrees or more, and thus, it is very difficult to control the temperature because of the huge factors of temperature variation. Importantly, the temperature control of the cavity is mainly emphasized in this study, and the way of using the fuzzy control method is to majorly control the nonlinear temperature in the cavity so as to achieve the effect that the temperature difference between the substrate and the cavity can be closer. Given the above problem from the original job site, this study makes an adjustment and improvement with the electron gun after the fuzzy control; the improvement includes one electron gun with a higher power and the other with a lower power. In particular, after the fuzzy control of PID in this experimental method, the higher-power electron gun is set to about 176 degrees, and the lower-power electron gun is set to about 174 degrees. Their temperature difference has a significant low range of only about 2 degrees, and productively, this excellent result can significantly increase the yield rate for the products of the case study.

4.3. Analysis Results of the Fuzzy Control PID Simulation Method 2

For the comparison benefits, we make another simulation method of the fuzzy control PID. This study has analyzed results of fine-tuning ΔKp, ΔKi, and ΔKd by the fuzzy control after PID adjustment; the adjustment has the one with the higher power of the electron gun and the other with the lower power. Therefore, the two electron guns operate alternately; when the first electron gun operates, the temperature rises to about 178 degrees at the beginning, and after about 100 s after the fuzzy control adjustment, the temperature slowly drops to about 177 degrees. Consequently, after about 500 s, the temperature is set to fit the target value of 175 degrees, and then the steady-state situation is reached. However, when the second electron gun is turned on, the temperature drops to 172 degrees, and then it can reach 174 degrees because of the adjustment made by the fuzzy control PID. Finally, the minimum temperature difference is reduced to about 1 degree, and it is proven that this method can make the temperature difference less, smoother, and better, thereby benefiting the yield rate. Interestingly, this method 2 significantly improves the yield rate of the case study factory.

4.4. Research Summary for the Analysis Results of the Fuzzy Control

Subsequently, we make a comparable study for the above methods. In the original method for the case study factory, the following descriptions are for the current status of the manufacturing process site. When the high-power electron gun is turned on, the temperature is above 190 degrees, and it will be pulled back to 177 degrees after the PID control. However, when the high-power electron gun is turned off and the low-power electron gun is turned on, the temperature drops to 162 degrees, and we compensate the temperature to 173 degrees through the PID control. In order to solve the above problem of large temperature differences, we have the following two methods: (1) Experimental method 1 of the fuzzy control research: For the experimental result of the fuzzy control PID, when the electron gun interference source input is after fuzzy control, the temperature is quickly adjusted to 176 degrees, but when the second electron gun is turned on, the temperature first drops and then pulls back to 174 degrees, so the temperature difference is about 2 degrees. (2) Experimental method 2 of the fuzzy control research: For the result of fine-tuning ΔKp, ΔKi, and ΔKd using the fuzzy control after the PID control, when the first electron gun is turned on, the temperature is about 178 degrees; importantly, after tuning the fuzzy control adjustment for about 100 s, the temperature slowly drops to about 177 degrees. Accordingly, after about 500 s, the temperature reaches the target value of 175 degrees, and then it reaches a good steady-state status. However, when the second electron gun is turned on, the temperature drops to 172 degrees, and after tuning the fuzzy control adjustment again, it reaches 174 degrees, which has a temperature difference of one degree. It seems to have a good outcome for the yield rate.

4.5. Verification Results of the NN Model Simulation

Subsequently, Figure 19 shows a graph for the verification results of performing the NN model. From Figure 19, the X-axis is the temperature difference in degrees, and the

Y-axis is the yield rate in terms of percent. Moreover, Table 7 lists the detailed verification outcomes of the NN model. It can be determined that the total number of records is 700 after using the NN algorithms. From Table 7, the verification results show the following facts: The temperature differences are identified from 0, 1, 2, 3, 4, 5, 6, 7, 8, 9, 10, ... to 20 degrees, and concurrently, their yield rates are achieved, corresponding to 98.57%, 98.57%, 92.85%, 85.71%, 74.28%, 71.4%, 59.71%, 57.14%, 54.28%, 47.14%, 42.85%, 31.42%, 22.8%, ... to 0%, respectively. Interestingly, based on the above results, an important research finding is unearthed: it is the best choice for positively influencing the yield rate to effectively control the temperature difference between the temperatures of substrate and cavity within one degree, and it is a key industrial contribution for benefiting the case study factory to proactively identify its manufacturing processing with the benefit of better-quality products and productivity. Productively, the smaller the temperature difference, the better the yield rate. The new production process can significantly improve the stability and operation performance of the products compared to the original processing.

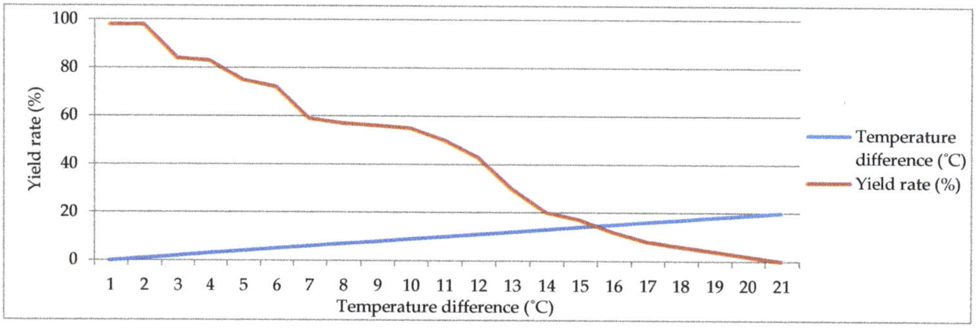

Figure 19. Verification results for line chart of NN model.

Table 7. Verification results for the NNs model.

Temperature difference (°C)	0	1	2	3	4	5	6
Yield rate (%)	98.57	98.57	92.85	85.71	74.28	71.40	59.71
Temperature difference (°C)	7	8	9	10	11	12	13
Yield rate (%)	58.57	57.14	54.28	47.14	42.85	31.42	22.80
Temperature difference (°C)	14	15	16	17	18	19	20
Yield rate (%)	15.71	8.57	5.71	5.71	4.28	1.42	0

The equipment cost and time cost of the physical manufacturing process are both very high, and the product defect rate is also high, which will affect the company's profitability and competitiveness. Before carrying out the physical manufacturing process, this study used fuzzy control technology to improve the temperature difference based on empirical data provided by professionals and used neural networks to verify the effect. Finally, a method to improve the yield rate was derived to ensure that manufacturing costs can be reduced and product quality can improve in the physical process in the future.

The results of this study show that before the problem is solved, when the difference between the substrate temperature and the cavity temperature is too large, the yield is not good. The results after improvement through two fuzzy control technologies, Types I and Types II, are as follows: (1) After improvement of Type I, after fuzzy control simulation and online correction PID, the average temperature difference can be controlled to about 2 degrees, but the shortcoming is that it cannot reach the target value of 175 degrees. (2) After improvement of Type II, after PID control, fuzzy control is added to fine-tune Kp, Ki, and Kd. After correction by fuzzy control online, the average temperature difference can be controlled by about 1 degree, and the correction speed is slow.

5. Conclusions and Future Research

This section has mainly made a conclusive summary with a subsequent direction for the issue of the yield rate in the optical filter industry, including three concerns about conclusions with research findings and contributions, a summary of important achievements, and the future prospects of this study.

5.1. Conclusions with Research Findings and Contributions

The research object of this study is focused on processing the optical filter of optical communication components, and the processing is an advanced optical precision process. Due to the rapid development of information technology, the transmission of the network is getting faster and faster, from early 2G communication to current 5G communication with continuing development, and the progress has moved towards the era of future 6G. Therefore, in the manufacturing process of products related to optical communication, to maintain their advantage of a high yield rate, the related processes become extremely important. Based on alleviating this concern, the relevant techniques used in this study have been improving in the optical filter industry for industrial value. Thus, this study makes good use of data mining techniques to deal with various classification problems and dig out some consequential research findings, and we chose an appropriate method for addressing a good industrial data analysis. Thus, this study has proposed a hybrid model with an important technical contribution from the perspective of industrial application. In the detailed processing for the proposed hybrid model, there are five key points highlighted. (1) This study uses the statistical analysis of yield rate distribution, association rules, and decision tree classifiers in order to find out the potential reasons for the defect rate of the products on the production process line and then to improve it. (2) In the use of data mining techniques, it has been found that the main reason for the defect rate is that the temperature difference between the substrate and the cavity during the product manufacturing process is too large, which causes reduced output. (3) In order to overcome the problem of excessive temperature difference, this study uses the tool of fuzzy control PID to dominate the varied changes of the three temperature parameters, Kp, Ki, and Kd, and then further change its output current u. (4) We further used Simulink simulation software to completely simulate the experimental results. By analyzing the results to explore the real cause of the problem, this problem is reduced and solved, and the yield rate is improved; thus, we have industrial applicability value based on the application's context. (5) Finally, it is expected that the yield rate can be further improved, and by rapidly driving the production speed of 5G for 100G optical filters, the manufacturing cost can be further reduced, and the technology of the future optical communication industry can be improved.

Furthermore, there are eight points that summarize this study and the implemented experiments:

(1) Motivation of the study: In response to the strong demand for optical filters after the market upgrade from 4G to 5G, a serious problem has emerged. However, because of the long manufacturing process, high manufacturing cost, low yield rate, and many influencing factors, the market faces short supply and cannot keep up with demand. Thus, the study is motivated by this interesting issue and provides an effective hybrid model to identify and improve the yield rate of optical filters for the communication industry and increase its production quantity while maximizing efficiency in order to meet market demand. Therefore, this study offers valuable industry experience in this important domain of the optical communication industry.

(2) Data mining analysis methods used: This study uses three data mining analysis techniques, including the box-and-whisker method, the association rule method, and the decision tree method. After analyzing the experimental results, it is found that temperature is the key determinant influencing the output of products, and the main results are as follows: (a) Among the 1008 cases where temperature differences between the cavity and the substrate occurred, 567 cases were between 8.5 °C and above 17 °C; that is, 56.2% of the yield rate of products was bad. (b) There are 404 cases

between 2 °C and 8.5 °C, and 40.1% of the yield rate is normal. (c) Only 37 cases have a temperature of less than 2 °C, and only 3.7% of the yield rate is good.

(3) Important research finding: From the analysis results of data mining techniques, there is an important research finding; that is, it is found that the correlation between the yield rate of the process and the interference source of temperature has a significant influence on affecting the output rate of products and easily causes a high defective rate in bad situations.

(4) Another research finding: From the empirical results, it is also found that when the temperature difference between the substrate and the cavity is too large, it is one of the main reasons for poor yield rate. This research finding can be further explored in subsequent research.

(5) Types I and II of two fuzzy control techniques: In order to better control the temperature variation, this study uses two types (I and II) of fuzzy control techniques, and the results obtained are as follows: (a) The result of the Type I method can make the temperature difference between the cavity and the substrate controlled within two degrees; (b) the result of the Type II method can first control the temperature difference within about six degrees at the beginning; however, after continuous fuzzy control correction, it can be controlled with one degree close to the approximate value and ideal value and achieve the best situation for the yield rate of the case study factory.

(6) One significant verification result: The verification result of the alternative research method is to consider and use the simulation function on the NN model with the following three research highlights: (a) it is verified that if the temperature difference is less than two degrees, the yield rate is good; (b) if the temperature difference is less than eight degrees, the yield rate is normal; and (c) if the temperature difference is greater than 10 degrees, the yield rate has a bad effect on the bottom line.

(7) Poor performance for identifying temperature difference: After the important analysis of industry data from benefiting the data mining techniques, this study finds that the yield rate has an obvious poor performance when the temperature difference between the substrate and the cavity is too large. It is defined that the larger the temperature difference, the poorer the performance.

(8) Valuable contribution for industry application: This study has important industrial application contributions; that is, the use of the fuzzy control PID technique [53] to better control temperature can significantly improve the yield rate and reduce manufacturing costs, direct labor costs, direct material consumption, etc. Concurrently, it can mass-produce high-precision optical filters, thereby quickly driving the technology era of 5G with high-speed network products such as the Internet of Things (IoT), unmanned autonomous driving, and AI. They have made it more stable and mature, thereby adding a small step to the applicable contribution for industry data of the Internet generation with a major development.

5.2. Summary of Important Achievements

The research object of this study is optical filters for 5G and optical coating; it is the main component of future optical communication, but it has some disadvantages in the manufacturing process, such as production difficulty, long time, high cost, and low yield rate. In order to solve these plights, this study has some important achievements and advantages: (a) This study employs big data mining technology to find out the potential cause of the yield rate problem and employs the fuzzy control technique to control the PID thermostat [47], further facilitating model simulation; (b) it continuously adjusts the interference from the interference source to improve the temperature difference with some strengths, such as the improved yield rate of processing optical filters. The filters can be produced quickly, manpower is reduced, time is shortened, and cost loss is reduced.

The reason for using fuzzy control technology to simulate and improve the temperature difference is because the manufacturing cost of the process is high and the manufacturing time is long, so it is challenging to conduct real experiments. Fuzzy PID controller is a control algorithm based on fuzzy logic, which combines the advantages of fuzzy control and PID control. Compared with traditional PID controllers, fuzzy PID controllers can better adapt to complex nonlinear systems and show better performance in terms of control effect and stability. The fuzzy PID controller uses the control parameter adjustment principle derived from the practice of empirical rules to define a fuzzy rule table; the fuzzy controller is used to instantly correct the parameters of the PID controller; on the basis of the traditional PID, the parameters KP, KI, and KD are each increased by one amount of change. Fuzzy PID has better performance than PID. In the future, we will move towards using the researched fuzzy controller to use a combination of software and hardware to bring it into the actual process to verify its effect.

5.3. Future Directions

Although this study uses big data mining technology to see the reasons for the defect rate of the production line and efficiently uses fuzzy control technology to improve the difference degrees of temperature, and the actual research output has conclusively achieved remarkable results, there is still room for improvement in several key areas: (1) In the future, actual experiments can be performed instead of using simulation methods, and then the two experimental results can be practically compared. (2) For the Simulink simulation, many parameter values can be further adjusted continuously, hoping to achieve the desired absolute goal. (3) It is also expected that the academic research results can be fully disclosed to companies in order to achieve the combination of both academic theory and industrial practice, which can greatly improve the production yield and make production more efficient. Thus, the technological development of this industry can be rapidly improved.

Author Contributions: Conceptualization, J.-R.C. and Y.-S.C.; Methodology, J.-R.C. and Y.-S.C.; Software, C.-Y.C.; Visualization, C.-Y.C., Y.-H.H. and M.Y.-J.L.; Writing—original draft, C.-Y.C.; Writing—review and editing, Y.-H.H., Y.-S.C., C.-J.L. and M.Y.-J.L. All authors have read and agreed to the published version of the manuscript.

Funding: This research was partially supported by the National Science and Technology Council of Taiwan for grant number 111-2221-E-167-036-MY2.

Institutional Review Board Statement: Not applicable.

Informed Consent Statement: Not applicable.

Data Availability Statement: No new data were created or analyzed in this study. Data sharing is not applicable to this article.

Conflicts of Interest: The authors declare no conflicts of interest.

References

1. Haddi, S.B.; Zugari, A.; Zakriti, A.; Achraou, S. 5G narrow-band band-pass filter using parallel coupled lines and L-shaped resonator. In Proceedings of the 2020 International Symposium on Advanced Electrical and Communication Technologies (ISAECT), Marrakech, Morocco, 25–27 November 2020; pp. 1–4. [CrossRef]
2. Dzogovic, B.; Van Do, T.; Santos, B.; Feng, B.; Jacot, N. Thunderbolt-3 backbone for augmented 5G network slicing in cloud-radio access networks. In Proceedings of the 2019 IEEE 2nd 5G World Forum (5GWF), Dresden, Germany, 30 September–2 October 2019; pp. 415–420. [CrossRef]
3. Gladju, J.; Kamalam, B.S.; Kanagaraj, A. Applications of data mining and machine learning framework in aquaculture and fisheries: A review. *Smart Agric. Technol.* **2022**, *2*, 100061. [CrossRef]
4. Guo, Y.; Zhang, W.; Qin, Q.; Chen, K.; Wei, Y. Intelligent manufacturing management system based on data mining in artificial intelligence energy-saving resources. *Soft Comput.* **2023**, *27*, 4061–4076. [CrossRef]
5. Du, Y.; Yang, C.; Zhao, B.; Hu, C.; Zhang, H.; Yu, Z.; Gao, J.; Zhao, W.; Wang, H. Optimal design of a supercritical carbon dioxide recompression cycle using deep neural network and data mining techniques. *Energy* **2023**, *271*, 127038. [CrossRef]
6. Coşkun, G.; Şahin, Ö.; Delialioğlu, R.A.; Altay, Y.; Aytekin, İ. Diagnosis of lameness via data mining algorithm by using thermal camera and image processing method in Brown Swiss cows. *Trop. Anim. Health Prod.* **2023**, *55*, 50. [CrossRef]
7. Clancy, R.; O'Sullivan, D.; Bruton, K. Data-driven quality improvement approach to reducing waste in manufacturing. *TQM J.* **2023**, *35*, 51–72. [CrossRef]

8. Tu, M.; Xiong, S.; Lv, S.; Wu, X.; Hu, H.; Hu, R.; Fang, J.; Shao, X. Acupuncture for major depressive disorder: A data mining-based literature study. *Neuropsychiatr. Dis. Treat.* **2023**, *19*, 1069–1084. [CrossRef] [PubMed]
9. Chien, C.F.; Chuang, S.C. A framework for root cause detection of sub-batch processing system for semiconductor manufacturing big data analytics. *IEEE Trans. Semicond. Manuf.* **2014**, *27*, 475–488. [CrossRef]
10. Lyu, J.; Liang, C.W.; Chen, P.S. A data-driven approach for identifying possible manufacturing processes and production parameters that cause product defects: A thin-film filter company case study. *IEEE Access* **2020**, *8*, 49395–49411. [CrossRef]
11. Pan, H.Y.; Chen, X.; Xia, X.L. A review on the evolvement of optical-frequency filtering in photonic devices in 2016–2021. *Renew. Sust. Energy Rev.* **2022**, *161*, 112361. [CrossRef]
12. Chen, C.; Wang, Y.; Feng, J.; Wang, Z.; Chen, Y.; Lu, Y.; Zhang, Y.; Li, D.; Cui, Y.; Shao, J. Effect of ionic oxygen concentration on properties of SiO_2 and Ta_2O_5 monolayers deposited by ion beam sputtering. *Opt. Mater.* **2023**, *136*, 113349. [CrossRef]
13. Sakharov, Y.V. Structure and properties of nanoporous oxide dielectrics modified by carbon. *Mater. Phys. Mech.* **2020**, *44*, 110–115.
14. Kol, S.; Oral, A.Y. Hf-Based High-κ Dielectrics: A Review. *Acta Phys. Pol.* **2019**, *136*, 873–881. [CrossRef]
15. Huang, Y.; Wang, B.; Wang, X.; Li, J.; Zou, H.; Liu, L.; Yu, W.; Huang, J.; Yang, X.; Huang, L. A proposal for eliminating the zeroth order with polarization independence by mixing SiO2/Ta2O5 metamaterials. *Optik* **2022**, *271*, 170198. [CrossRef]
16. Rischke, J.; Sossalla, P.; Itting, S.; Fitzek, F.H.; Reisslein, M. 5G campus networks: A first measurement study. *IEEE Access* **2021**, *9*, 121786–121803. [CrossRef]
17. Huchard, M.; Weiss, M.; Pizzinat, A.; Meyer, S.; Guignard, P.; Charbonnier, B. Ultra-broadband wireless home network based on 60-GHz WPAN cells interconnected via RoF. *J. Light. Technol.* **2008**, *26*, 2364–2372. [CrossRef]
18. Zheng, Z.; Wang, P.; Liu, J.; Sun, S. Real-time big data processing framework: Challenges and solutions. *Appl. Math. Inf. Sci.* **2015**, *9*, 3169–3190.
19. Thirumalai, C.; Vignesh, M.; Balaji, R. Data analysis using Box and Whisker plot for Lung Cancer. In Proceedings of the 2017 Innovations in Power and Advanced Computing Technologies (i-PACT), Vellore, India, 21–22 April 2017; pp. 1–6. [CrossRef]
20. Vignesh, V.; Pavithra, D.; Dinakaran, K.; Thirumalai, C. Data analysis using box and whisker plot for stationary shop analysis. In Proceedings of the 2017 International Conference on Trends in Electronics and Informatics (ICEI), Tirunelveli, India, 11–12 May 2017; pp. 1072–1076. [CrossRef]
21. Parvez, M.R.; Hu, W.; Chen, T. An association rule mining approach to predict alarm events in industrial alarm floods. *Control Eng. Pract.* **2023**, *138*, 105617. [CrossRef]
22. Li, J.Q.; Niu, C.L.; Gu, J.J.; Liu, J.Z. Energy loss analysis based on fuzzy association rule mining in power plant. In Proceedings of the 2008 International Symposium on Computational Intelligence and Design, Wuhan, China, 17–18 October 2008; pp. 186–189. [CrossRef]
23. Zhou, M.; Wang, T. Fault diagnosis of power transformer based on association rules gained by rough set. In Proceedings of the 2nd International Conference on Computer and Automation Engineering (ICCAE), Singapore, 26–28 February 2010; pp. 123–126. [CrossRef]
24. Li, Y.; Song, X.; Zhao, S.; Gao, F. A line-fault cause analysis method for distribution network based on decision-making tree and machine learning. In Proceedings of the 2020 5th Asia Conference on Power and Electrical Engineering (ACPEE), Chengdu, China, 4–7 June 2020; pp. 1–5. [CrossRef]
25. Lee, C.; Alena, R.L.; Robinson, P. Migrating fault trees to decision trees for real time fault detection on international space station. In Proceedings of the 2005 IEEE aerospace conference, Big Sky, MT, USA, 5–12 March 2005; pp. 1–6. [CrossRef]
26. Uchiumi, T.; Kikuchi, S.; Matsumoto, Y. Misconfiguration detection for cloud datacenters using decision tree analysis. In Proceedings of the 2012 14th Asia-Pacific Network Operations and Management Symposium (APNOMS), Seoul, Republic of Korea, 25–27 September 2012; pp. 1–4. [CrossRef]
27. Han, Y.; Xu, K.; Qin, J. Based on the CART decision tree model of prediction and classification of ancient glass-related properties. *Highl. Sci. Eng. Technol.* **2023**, *42*, 18–27. [CrossRef]
28. Sulistiyono, M.; Wirasakti, L.A.; Pristyanto, Y. The effect of adaptive synthetic and information gain on C4.5 and Naive Bayes in imbalance class dataset. *Int. J. Adv. Sci. Comp. Eng.* **2022**, *4*, 1–11. [CrossRef]
29. Ariska, F.; Sihombing, V.; Irmayani, I. Student graduation predictions using comparison of C5.0 algorithm with linear regression. *Sinkron Jurnal dan Penelitian Teknik Informatika* **2022**, *7*, 256–266. [CrossRef]
30. Ambroziak, A.; Chojecki, A. The PID controller optimisation module using Fuzzy Self-Tuning PSO for Air Handling Unit in continuous operation. *Eng. Appl. Artif. Intell.* **2023**, *117*, 105485. [CrossRef]
31. Cao, G.; Zhao, X.; Ye, C.; Yu, S.; Li, B.; Jiang, C. Fuzzy adaptive PID control method for multi-mecanum-wheeled mobile robot. *J. Mech. Sci. Technol.* **2022**, *36*, 2019–2029. [CrossRef]
32. Zhou, C.; Shen, Y. A PID Control Method Based on Internal Model Control to Suppress Vibration of the Transmission Chain of Wind Power Generation System. *Energies* **2022**, *15*, 5919. [CrossRef]
33. Al-Dhaifallah, M. Fuzzy fractional-order PID control for heat exchanger. *Alex. Eng. J.* **2023**, *63*, 11–16. [CrossRef]
34. Han, S.Y.; Dong, J.F.; Zhou, J.; Chen, Y.H. Adaptive fuzzy PID control strategy for vehicle active suspension based on road evaluation. *Electronics* **2022**, *11*, 921. [CrossRef]
35. Huang, M.; Tian, M.; Liu, Y.; Zhang, Y.; Zhou, J. Parameter optimization of PID controller for water and fertilizer control system based on partial attraction adaptive firefly algorithm. *Sci. Rep.* **2022**, *12*, 12182. [CrossRef] [PubMed]

36. Zhao, T.; Yu, Q.; Dian, S.; Guo, R.; Li, S. Non-singleton general type-2 fuzzy control for a two-wheeled self-balancing robot. *Int. J. Fuzzy Syst.* **2019**, *21*, 1724–1737. [CrossRef]
37. Su, M.; Liu, J.; Kim, M.K.; Wu, X. Predicting moisture condensation risk on the radiant cooling floor of an office using integration of a genetic algorithm-back-propagation neural network with sensitivity analysis. *Energy Built Environ.* **2024**, *5*, 110–129. [CrossRef]
38. Sun, B.; Xu, Z.D.; Zhou, H. A multiple back propagation neural network fusion algorithm for ceiling temperature prediction in tunnel fires. *Eng. Struct.* **2023**, *280*, 115601. [CrossRef]
39. Ho, S.J.; Shu, L.S.; Ho, S.Y. Optimizing fuzzy neural networks for tuning PID controllers using an orthogonal simulated annealing algorithm OSA. *IEEE Trans. Fuzzy Syst.* **2006**, *14*, 421–434. [CrossRef]
40. Maeda, Y.; Wakamura, M. Simultaneous perturbation learning rule for recurrent neural networks and its FPGA implementation. *IEEE Trans. Neural Netw.* **2005**, *16*, 1664–1672. [CrossRef]
41. Chu, Y.; Fei, J.; Hou, S. Adaptive global sliding-mode control for dynamic systems using double hidden layer recurrent neural network structure. *IEEE Trans. Neural Netw. Learn. Syst.* **2019**, *31*, 1297–1309. [CrossRef]
42. Yih, K.A. Radiation effect on natural convection over a vertical cylinder embedded in porous media. *Int. Commun. Heat Mass Transf.* **1999**, *26*, 259–267. [CrossRef]
43. Kumar, K.G.; Archana, M.; Gireesha, B.J.; Krishanamurthy, M.R.; Rudraswamy, N.G. Cross diffusion effect on MHD mixed convection flow of nonlinear radiative heat and mass transfer of Casson fluid over a vertical plate. *Results Phys.* **2018**, *8*, 694–701. [CrossRef]
44. Vasu, S. Fuzzy PID based adaptive control on industrial robot system. *Mater. Today Proc.* **2018**, *5*, 13055–13060.
45. Wang, Y.; Zou, H.; Tao, J.; Zhang, R. Predictive fuzzy PID control for temperature model of a heating furnace. In Proceedings of the 2017 36th Chinese Control Conference (CCC), Dalian, China, 26–28 July 2017; pp. 4523–4527. [CrossRef]
46. Xue, P.; Wang, H.; Hou, J.; Li, W. Based on the fuzzy PID brushless DC motor control system design. In Proceedings of the 2012 International Conference on Measurement, Information and Control, Harbin, China, 18–20 May 2012; pp. 703–706. [CrossRef]
47. Liu, Y.; Fan, K.; Ouyang, Q. Intelligent traction control method based on model predictive fuzzy PID control and online optimization for permanent magnetic maglev trains. *IEEE Access* **2021**, *9*, 29032–29046. [CrossRef]
48. Kovilpillai, J.J.A.; Jayanthy, S. A transfer learning approach for effective motor fault identification of industrial machines used in tile manufacturing. *Natl. Acad. Sci. Lett.* **2022**, *45*, 405–409. [CrossRef]
49. Issa, A.H.; Mahmood, S.A.; Humod, A.T.; Ameen, N.M. Robustness enhancement study of augmented positive identification controller by a sigmoid function. *IAES Int. J. Artif. Intell.* **2023**, *12*, 686–695. [CrossRef]
50. Zhu, W.; Chen, X.; Wu, W.B. Online covariance matrix estimation in stochastic gradient descent. *J. Am. Stat. Assoc.* **2023**, *118*, 393–404. [CrossRef]
51. Chen, J.; Liu, Z.; Yin, Z.; Liu, X.; Li, X.; Yin, L.; Zheng, W. Predict the effect of meteorological factors on haze using BP neural network. *Urban Clim.* **2023**, *51*, 101630. [CrossRef]
52. Wang, X.Y.; Liu, Z.W.; Jiang, Y.; Sun, L.H. A fuzzy-PID controller based on particle swarm algorithm. In Proceedings of the 2008 Fifth International Conference on Fuzzy Systems and Knowledge Discovery, Jinan, China, 18–20 October 2008; pp. 107–110. [CrossRef]
53. Zhao, X.; Zheng, W. Generalized fuzzy PID algorithm and its application. In Proceedings of the 2009 Sixth International Conference on Fuzzy Systems and Knowledge Discovery, Tianjin, China, 14–16 August 2009; pp. 284–286. [CrossRef]

axioms MDPI

Article

Enhanced Remora Optimization with Deep Learning Model for Intelligent PMSM Drives Temperature Prediction in Electric Vehicles

Abdul Latif [1], Ibrahim M. Mehedi [2,3,*], Mahendiran T. Vellingiri [2], Rahtul Jannat Meem [4] and Thangam Palaniswamy [2]

1 Department of Mathematics, King Abdulaziz University, Jeddah 21589, Saudi Arabia
2 Department of Electrical and Computer Engineering (ECE), King Abdulaziz University, Jeddah 21589, Saudi Arabia
3 Center of Excellence in Intelligent Engineering Systems (CEIES), King Abdulaziz University, Jeddah 21589, Saudi Arabia
4 Electrical and Electronic Engineering Department, North South University, Dhaka 1229, Bangladesh
* Correspondence: imehedi@kau.edu.sa

Abstract: One of the widespread electric motors for electric vehicles (EVs) is permanent magnet synchronous machine (PMSM) drives. It is because of the power density and high energy of the PMSM with moderate assembly cost. The widely adopted PMSM as the motor of choice for EVs, together with variety of applications urges stringent monitoring of temperature to ignore high temperatures. Temperature monitoring of the PMSM is highly complex to accomplish because of complex measurement device for internal components of the PMSM. Temperature values beyond a certain range might result in additional maintenance costs together with major operational problems in PMSM. The latest developments in artificial intelligence (AI) and deep learning (DL) methods pave a way for accurate temperature prediction in PMSM drivers. With this motivation, this article introduces an enhanced remora optimization algorithm with stacked bidirectional long short-term memory (EROA-SBiLSTM) approach for temperature prediction of the PMSM drives. The presented EROA-SBiLSTM technique mainly focuses on effectual temperature prediction using DL and hyperparameter tuning schemes. To accomplish this, the EROA-SBiLSTM technique applies Pearson correlation coefficient analysis for observing the correlation among various features, and the *p*-value is utilized for determining the relevant level. Next, the SBiLSTM model is used to predict the level of temperature that exists in the PMSM drivers. Finally, the EROA based hyperparameter tuning process is carried out to adjust the SBiLSTM parameters optimally. The experimental outcome of the EROA-SBiLSTM technique is tested using electric motor temperature dataset from the Kaggle dataset. The comprehensive study specifies the betterment of the EROA-SBiLSTM technique.

Keywords: PMSM drives; remora optimization algorithm; deep learning; electric vehicles; artificial intelligence

MSC: 52B55; 74P10; 68Q32

1. Introduction

In pure electric vehicles (EVs), the permanent magnet synchronous motor (PMSM) was commonly utilized because of its higher efficiency, high power density, and high torque [1]. The major difficulties of PMSM development are thermal safety peak and performance. The main sources for the increasing temperature are the iron and the copper losses of rotor magnetic steels, and this temperature would determine the period of the peak power of the motor. The heat loss of the PMSM is copper loss, mechanical loss, and iron loss [2]. The mechanical loss hinges on the rotor speed whereas iron loss hinges on the stator's voltage. Unlike mechanical loss and iron loss, copper loss affects the stator winding heating degree [3]. From one perspective, the heat of the stator winding is sent to the insulation. In contrast, compared with the core and winding, the insulation in the motor has the worst heat resistance of all motor materials. So, the study of the rotor temperature estimation enhances the motor peak performance and ensures motor thermal safety as well [4]. In the meantime, the coercive forces of magnetic steel were closely relevant to temperature, which declines with increasing temperature. The irreversible demagnetization will occur only in cases where the temperature of the rotor magnetic steel surpasses the limit values. Generally, under the working condition of the motor, irreversible demagnetization must be avoided [5]. Certainly, compared to actual torque capacity, the PMSM torque capacity was lower which prevent overheating failure of the motor lacking the high-accuracy rotor temperature estimation. In recent years, the integration of renewable energy sources, advanced control strategies, and intelligent management techniques has gained significant attention in the field of electric vehicle (EV) drives and power management systems (PMS). Achieving efficient operation and optimal control of these systems while ensuring reliable performance has become a critical challenge, considering the dynamic nature of power generation, consumption, and the integration of smart technologies. To address these challenges, researchers have explored various strategies that leverage game theory, advanced observer designs, stochastic frameworks, and optimization techniques. One notable recent work by Smith et al. presents a three-layer game theoretic-based strategy for optimal scheduling of microgrids [6]. By incorporating a dynamic demand response program designer, this approach harnesses the potential of smart buildings and electric vehicle fleets to enhance the overall efficiency of microgrids. The synergistic interaction between microgrid components is optimized, leading to improved energy utilization and cost savings.

In the realm of induction motor control, advancements have been made in observer designs for accurate estimation of flux and speed. Johnson et al. introduce an improved double-surface sliding mode observer for induction motors [7]. This observer enhances the accuracy of flux and speed estimation, contributing to more precise control strategies for electric drives. Moreover, the integration of energy storage systems into smart communities has driven the development of sophisticated frameworks. Recent research by Williams et al. proposes a tri-layer stochastic framework for managing electricity markets within smart communities [8]. Energy storage systems play a pivotal role in balancing energy demand and supply, thereby ensuring grid stability and promoting efficient energy trading within the community. In the context of coordination between transmission system operators (TSOs) and distribution system operators (DSOs), optimization frameworks have emerged to harness the flexibility offered by smart buildings and EV fleets. Davis et al. present an interval-based nested optimization framework for deriving flexibility from these distributed resources [9]. This approach facilitates effective coordination between TSOs and DSOs, enhancing grid reliability and optimizing resource allocation.

To guarantee safe operation, many scholars and experts have devised techniques to measure the PMSM temperature [10]. The conventional motor temperature prediction algorithm has used the finite element technique. That particular technique uses the finite element approach to simulate the transient temperature, establishes the temperature field, and forecasts the temperature of the motor [11]. This method cannot tackle vast amount of nonlinear historical data instead it only process and compute the current linear data. Contrarily, machine learning (ML) based technique could be preferred that potentially solve this issue, and the estimated effect can be prominently improved than the conventional techniques. Several scholars and experts have made much more research and using ML endeavoured many different to forecast motor temperature [12]. One method used to forecast the temperature of PMSM drives in EV that is integration of ML approaches and thermal methods. This technique builds a thermal method and by making use of ML, techniques adjust the model parameters based on real-time data from sensors of the vehicles. This can offer precise temperature forecasts while changing thermal characteristics and driving conditions of the PMSM drive [13]. To forecast the PMSM temperature of drive directly another technique called data-driven ML approach was used. This technique trains an ML method on historical dataset gathered from the vehicle's sensors, like motor current, battery temperature, and vehicle speed [14]. After the trained model is used to forecast the PMSM drive temperature in real-time, permitting for decreasing the risk of failure and proactive temperature management. No optimization algorithm can guarantee with absolute certainty that it will always converge to the global optimum, especially for non-convex and multimodal optimization landscapes.

In this paper, we propose an Enhanced Remora Optimization combined with a Deep Learning Model for intelligent PMSM drive temperature prediction in electric vehicles. Building upon the advancements made in the aforementioned recent works, our methodology aims to provide accurate temperature predictions for PMSM drives by leveraging the synergy between enhanced optimization techniques and deep learning models. We consider the dynamic nature of EV operation, the intricate interplay between various components, and the potential for optimized control. This article introduces an enhanced remora optimization algorithm with stacked bidirectional long short-term memory (EROA-SBiLSTM) method for temperature prediction of the PMSM drives. The EROA-SBiLSTM technique applies Pearson correlation coefficient analysis for observing the correlation among various features, and the *p*-value is utilized for determining the relevant level. Next, the SBiLSTM model is used to predict the level of temperature that exists in the PMSM drivers. Finally, the EROA based hyperparameter tuning process is carried out to adjust the SBiLSTM parameters optimally. The experimental outcome of the EROA-SBiLSTM technique is tested using electric motor temperature dataset from the Kaggle dataset.

2. Related Works

Pietrzak and Wolkiewicz [15] introduced an ML related demagnetization fault diagnosis approach for PMSM drives. In the PM fault feature extraction, time-frequency domain analysis relevant to short-time Fourier transform (STFT) is enforced. Further, two ML-related approaches were compared and verified in the automated fault detection of demagnetization fault. Such methods were MLP and KNN. In [16], the CNN structure of DL has been utilized for diagnosing a demagnetization fault that happened in PMSM under stationary speed circumstances. Faults in motors diminish the production capacity and rise maintenance costs. In the study, a novel CNN structure has been made for identifying demagnetization faults in PMSM.

In [17], devised a rotor temperature prediction technique related to the lumped parameter thermal network and dual H infinity filter. First, to determine power loss, rotor, the bearing, and stator which is lumped parameter thermal network of 3 nodes was formulated numerically. Hence, for time-step iterative solution, discretized state-space expressions were listed. Then, dual H infinity filters were utilized in rotor temperature prediction to solve model parameter uncertainty. Bingi et al. [18] emphases on developing a stator and torque temperature estimation method for PMSM utilizing NNs. This technique can forecast torque and 4 other temperature parameters at winding, permanent magnet surface, tooth, and stator's yoke. The temperatures and motor's torque were projected without deploying any additional sensors into it. The predicted method has the optimal performance with the best R^2 values and least mean square error through the training data including Bayesian regularization algorithm and Levenberg-Marquardt optimization.

Xu et al. [19] present a technique for motors that depends on the principle of stacked denoising AE (SDAE) integrated with SVM method. First, the input data have been damaged randomly by including noise and motor signals. Further, the network structure of SDAE was built as per the experimental outcomes; noise reduction coefficient, the optimal learning rates, and the other parameters were set. In [20], the shape optimization of PMSM for EV was carried out through an MLP, which was a kind of DL method. By referring to Renault's Twizy, the targeted specifications have been decided, which is small EV. To fulfil the constraints and multi-objective functions, the angle between rib thickness of the rotor and V-shaped permanent magnets were chosen as design variables.

In [21], an SVM is developed through sparse representation for performing sensor fault diagnosis of PMSM. To produce set of labelled trained sets, a PMSM drive system for automotive applications was utilized that the SVM utilizes for determining margins between faulty operating and normal conditions. The PMSM method contains disturbance as a constant road grade and input as torque reference profile, against both of which faults should be detectable. Fatemi Moghadam et al. [22] presented a new AI related technique for PMSM current and speed control with the use of DNN. The necessity for such controllers rises as traditional proportional integral (PI) controllers not perform well in such variations. Similarly, the application of such control techniques is enabled by the enhanced controller hardware. This study assesses the robustness and performance of the presented DNN related controllers if the load and motor parameters differ.

3. The Proposed Model

In this article, a new EROA-SBiLSTM model was developed for accurate temperature prediction of the PMSM drives. The presented EROA-SBiLSTM technique majorly concentrated on effectual temperature prediction using DL and hyperparameter tuning schemes. It encompasses several subprocesses namely correlation analysis, SBiLSTM based temperature prediction, and EROA based hyperparameter tuning. Our research presents an integrated approach that combines established techniques from different domains to achieve accurate temperature prediction for Permanent Magnet Synchronous Motor (PMSM) drives. While there exist various efficient approaches in both academic research and practical applications, the convergence of multiple methodologies in a singular framework as presented in our work offers distinct advantages that were not previously explored. This section aims to elucidate why this specific integration and its resultant contributions may not have been readily undertaken by other researchers, as well as highlight the challenges that have propelled our approach into a unique space. The complexity of combining diverse techniques often poses significant challenges. Our EROA-SBiLSTM algorithm synthesizes concepts from Deep Learning (DL), hyperparameter tuning, and statistical analysis. This intricate interplay demands an in-depth understanding of each domain, making the research process intricate. Researchers seeking to embark on this endeavor would need to possess expertise in multiple areas, which could potentially hinder the adoption of such an integrated approach.

The synergy achieved through the integration of techniques like Pearson correlation coefficient analysis, Sequential Bidirectional Long Short-Term Memory (SBiLSTM) networks, and Enhanced Remora Optimization Algorithm (EROA) introduces a novel level of complexity. This combined technique leverages the strengths of each method to address the limitations of individual approaches. The specific expertise required to seamlessly integrate and optimize these techniques might be a significant barrier for researchers who are predominantly specialized in one specific domain. While there are existing techniques that address certain aspects of temperature prediction for PMSM drives, a comprehensive framework that orchestrates these methods cohesively is often missing. Our research bridges this gap by providing a holistic solution that encapsulates the intricacies of temperature prediction through a well-defined framework. Researchers might face difficulties in conceptualizing and designing such comprehensive frameworks, which could have contributed to the delay in addressing this research problem.

Implementing and validating an integrated approach requires access to relevant datasets, computational resources, and expertise. The absence of appropriate data, the high computational demands of some techniques, and the lack of familiarity with cross-disciplinary methodologies could deter researchers from embarking on such a multifaceted endeavor.

Figure 1 represents the overall process of EROA-SBiLSTM technique.

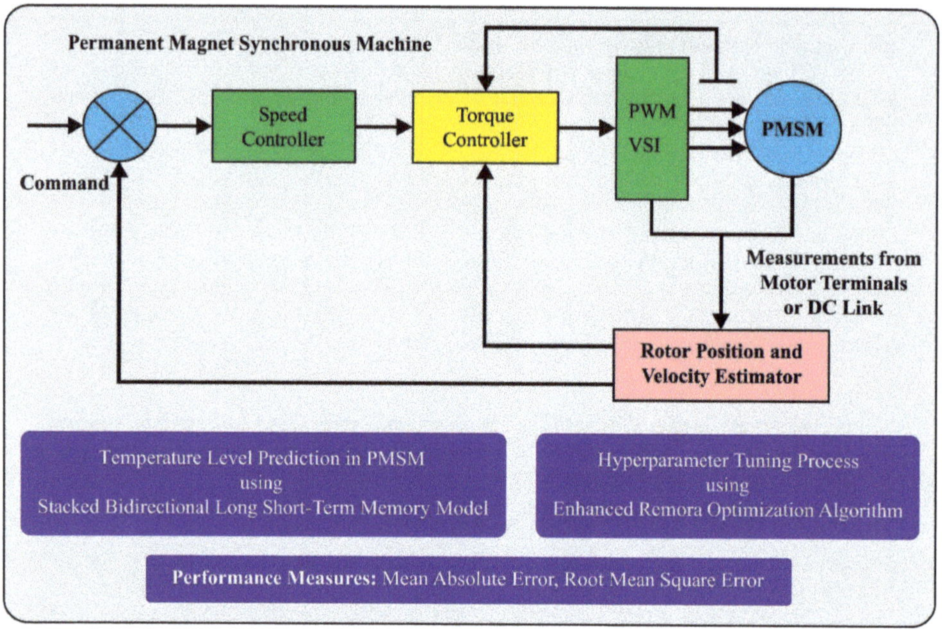

Figure 1. Overall process of EROA-SBiLSTM approach.

3.1. Modeling of PSPM

Changing input current based on the PMSM principle tends to produce of changing electric field that might lead to the formation of (B_s) rotating magnetic field. The intensity of rotating magnetic field relies on value of input voltage [23]. The permanent magnet of rotors produces (B_r) constant magnetic field once the three phase alternate voltage conducts the stator winding. Once powered on, the B_s generates electromagnetic torque that creates the rotor magnetic field for pursuing stator magnetic field, and it generates a three-phase alternating induction electromotive force (E_0) in stator winding by B_r. The single phase equivalent circuit of PMSM has been demonstrated in Figure 2.

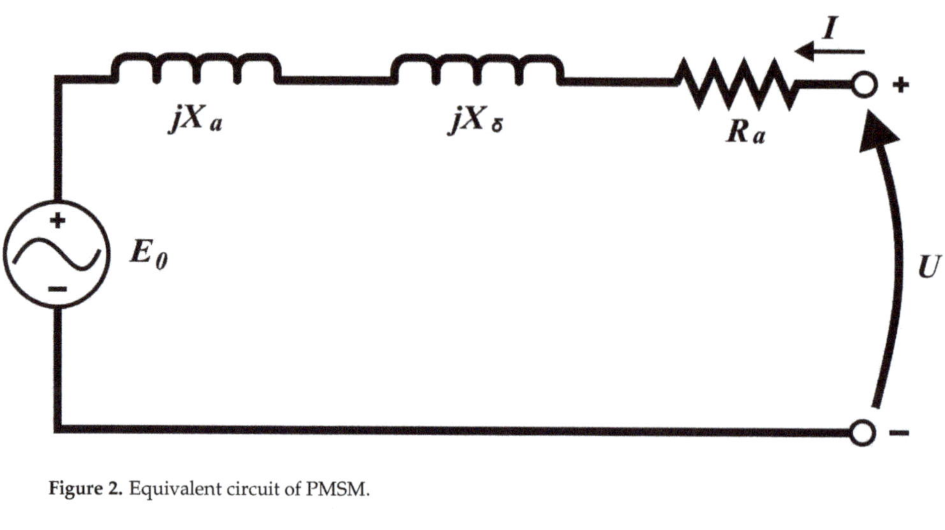

Figure 2. Equivalent circuit of PMSM.

From utilizing Kirchhoff's law produces the subsequent formula:

$$U = E_0 + I(R_a + jX_t) \tag{1}$$

$$X_t = X_a + X_\delta \tag{2}$$

Here, U indicates the input voltage, R_a signifies resistance of the stator winding; X_δ characterizes the armature reaction reactance; X_a denotes leakage reactance of the stator; X_t signifies the synchronous reactance; and I denote the input current. The amplitude of E_0 is proportional to the rotation speed of rotor magnetic field and the magnetic flux, as shown in Equation (3).

$$E_0 = K\phi\omega \tag{3}$$

In Equation (3), ω indicates the motor rotating speed, K signifies the motor constant, and β denotes the magnetic flux of the rotor magnetic field. As of the known rotating speed and constant magnetic flux, E_0 is defined. If the angle between B_s and B_r is evaluated, E_0 can be attained. Thus, Equation (4) is shown in the following:

$$U - E_0 = U' = I(R_a + jX_t) \tag{4}$$

3.2. Correlation Analysis

At the initial stage, the EROA-SBiLSTM technique applied the Pearson correlation coefficient analysis to monitor the correlation amongst various features, and the p-value is utilized for determining the relevant level and this can be expressed below:

$$r_{xy} = \frac{cov(x,y)}{\sigma_x\sigma_y} = \frac{E[(x-\mu_x)(y-\mu_y)]}{\sigma_x\sigma_y} \tag{5}$$

In Equation (5), σ_x and σ_y denotes the SD of x and y parameters, correspondingly. Furthermore, μ_x and μ_y indicates the average value of variables x and y and, $cov(x,\ y)$ denotes the covariance of the two variables, correspondingly. Generally, If the covariance of x and y is equal to 0, the variable x the variable y is independent. If the covariance of x and y is greater than 0, the variables x and y were correlated positively. Or else, parameters x and y are correlated negatively. The significance level p-value is calculated, and the relationship between data features is deliberated. To assess the relationship between the benchmark and the monitoring target data, the Pearson correlation value of every feature.

3.3. Temperature Prediction Using SBiLSTM Model

The SBiLSTM model is used in this work to predict the level of temperature that exists in the PMSM drivers. BiLSTM is used for obtaining the series data of the time-dependent input, along with the hidden relationships between the destination and the input features [24]. It is intended for recording long-term past knowledge and handling it by using memory cells. Noted that the door component doesn't provide data; rather, it is applied for restricting access to data. In reality, adding the gateway control model is a multilevel feature collection approach. LSTM provides a series of advantages while projecting and analyzing time series data. In RNN and LSTM, a chain structure is existing in the network module. In LSTM, the module consists of cells with 3 gates, while RNN module was composed of one neuron structure. The cell chooses features leveraging the forget, the input, and the output gates. The subsequent formula shows the computing technique for the three forms of gates:

$$input\ (t) = \sigma(W_i x(t) + V_i h(t-1) + b_i) \tag{6}$$

In Equation (6), W_i and y_i denotes the input gate's weights, $h(t-1)$ denotes the output of prior cell, $x(t)$ represents existing cell's input, and σ shows the sigmoid function:

$$forget\ (t) = \sigma\left(W_f x(t) + V_f h(t-1) + b_f\right) \tag{7}$$

These gates state that data in cell should be rejected, and W_f and y_f values in the calculation are forgotten gate weights. The update process was performed by using the following expression:

$$\widetilde{C}(t) = tanh\ (W_c x(t) + V_c h(t-1) + b_c) \tag{8}$$

$$C(t) = forget\ (t) * C(t-1) + inpuf(t) * \widetilde{C}(t) \tag{9}$$

Equation (8) represents the candidate unit for memory that generates current data. Furthermore, Equation (9) shows the process of renewing condition of the cells. Moreover, the lost data for gate was combined with the upgraded data for deriving the newest condition, where WV_c and y_c characterize the weight of the substitute and current conditions. The symbol $*$ represents the Hadamard product.

$$output\ (t) = \sigma(W_o x(t) + V_o h(t-1) + b_o) \tag{10}$$

$$h(t) = output(t) * tanh(C(t)) \tag{11}$$

Equations (10) and (11) analyze the output gate. Firstly, the sigmoid layer is exploited for obtaining the cell state to be output. Next, the upgraded cell state can be processed through *tanh* function, and the upgraded state was multiplied by output (t) for obtaining $h(t)$. y_o represents the output gate weight. To extract data features, a BLSTM network is created by these frameworks. In contrast with typical LSTM, BLSTM extracts more context data. To further generate accurate time-series prediction, the network uses backward and forward time series for gaining data about the existing timestamp in the previous and the future. In SBiLSTM model, further BLSTM layer is added to the stacked layer for complete representation and to establish a more abstract. Figure 3 illustrates the architecture of BLSTM. Consequently, output representation from the stacked layer is transmitted to FC and the regression layers for determining the temperature value. To mitigate disappearing gradient problem, the ReLU function was exploited as an activation function in resultant layer:

$$temperature = ReLU\left(W_o h_f + b_o\right) \tag{12}$$

In Equation (12), h_f suggests the output of FC layer. W_o and b_o denotes the weight matrix and bias in the last regression layer, correspondingly:

$$Loss = \frac{1}{T}\sum_{r=1}^{T}\left(\left|temperature_r - temperature_r'\right|\right)^2 \tag{13}$$

The presented method is trained by the BP through time. The forecasted output $temperature_r'$ is evaluated by the input dataset. The gradient of loss between the predicted output value $temperature_r'$ and the observed output value $temperature_r'$ concerning the parameter was defined in the backward pass as:

$$temperaturer_e' = ReLU\ ((dropout\ (\left(W_o h_f + b_o\right), P_m \tag{14}$$

Now, P_m denotes the masking probability of the dropout layer.

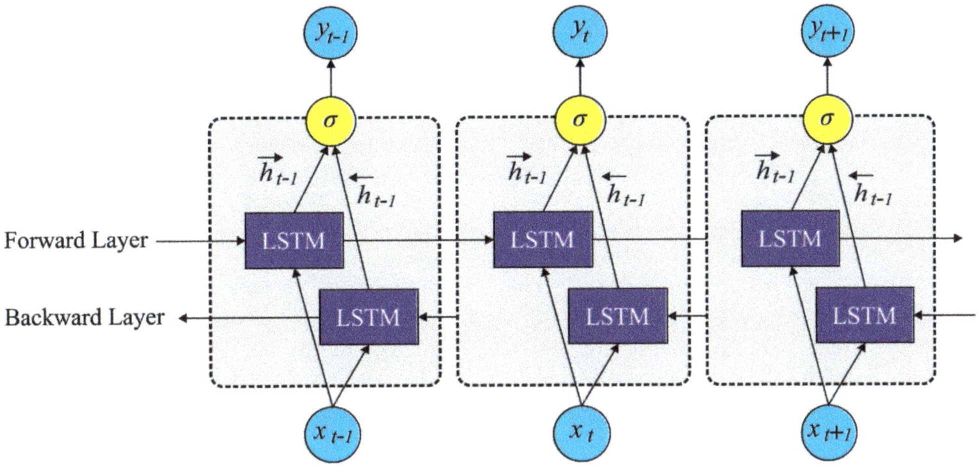

Figure 3. Structure of BLSTM.

3.4. Hyperparameter Tuning Using EROA

At the final stage, the EROA based hyperparameter tuning process is carried out to adjust the SBiLSTM parameters optimally. The original ROA has been enhanced by using the parasitic property of the remora [25]. Initialization was first implemented, and then individuals of the population arbitrarily begin their respective initial position within lower and upper bounds. Consequently, the fitness function of every individual can be evaluated, and the optimum location and fitness were upgraded. Using Equation (15), the individual attempt a new position:

$$R_{att} = R_i^t + \left(R_i^t - R_{pre}\right) \times rand_1, \tag{15}$$

In which R_{aii} refers to the attempted new location, R_i^t shows the i-th individuals at t-th iteration, R_{pre} shows the last historical location, and $rand_1$ denotes a uniformly distributed random integer within $[0, 1]$. The fitness $f(R_{att})$ of the attempted new location and the fitness $f\left(R_i^t\right)$ of existing individuals are compared and calculated:

$$R_i^{t+1} = R_i^t + (2V \times rand_2 - V) \times \left(R_i^t - C \times R_{best}\right) \tag{16}$$

$$V = 2 \times \left(1 - \frac{t}{max\_iter}\right) \tag{17}$$

where R_{best} denotes the global optimal position, R_i^{t+1} indicates the i-th individual at t-th iteration process, max_iter shows the maximal amount of iterations, $rand_2$ shows randomly generated value within $[0, 1]$, C indicates a fixed coefficient of 0.1, t represents the existing iteration amount, and V refers to the host feeding range. Or else, the host is changed and the SFO or WOA technique is used for updating the position:

$$R_i^{t+1} = \left|R_{best} - R_i^t\right| \times e^{\alpha} \times cos\,(2\pi\alpha) + R_i^t \tag{18}$$

$$\alpha = rand_3 \times \left(-\left(1 + \frac{t}{max\_iter}\right) - 1\right) + 1, \tag{19}$$

where $rand_3$ indicates a randomly generated value within $[0,1]$ and α denotes the random integer between [1, 1]. The equation for the SFO technique is shown below:

$$R_i^{t+1} = R_{best} - \left(rand_4 \times \frac{(R_{best} + R_m^t)}{2} - R_m^t \right), \tag{20}$$

In Equation (20), R_m^t indicates the random individual in the population and $rand_4$ represents the randomly generated value $[0,1]$. Lastly, the abovementioned stages are reiterated until the maximal amount of iterations is attained. In the original ROA, the SFO technique was related to individuals in population, and replacement host diversity was not higher. Thus, the study applied 3 better randomness approaches for replacing the original SFO technique as follows:

$$R_i^{t+1} = R_i^t + rand_5 \times \left(R_i^t - \frac{R_k^t + R_h^t}{2} \right) \tag{21}$$

$$R_i^{t+1} = R_{best} + R_d^t + rand_6 \times \left(R_e^t - R_f^t \right) \tag{22}$$

$$R_i^{t+1} = rand_7 \times R_i^t + rand_8 \times (R_{best} - R_i^t), \tag{23}$$

Now R_k^t, R_h^t, R_d^t, R_e^t, and R_f^t denotes the other random individuals at the iteration method and *rand*, rand, and $rand_8$ shows randomly generated values within $[0,1]$. In comparison to the original single strategy, the better randomness approach strengthened the connection with others in the population, rises the diversity of the replacement host and strengthens the connection with optimum individuals. In the presented EROA, original trial approach was substituted by the Poisson-like randomness approach.

The Algorithm 1 appears to be a hybrid optimization approach that combines elements of multiple optimization techniques. It initializes a population of agents and iteratively updates their locations to find an optimal solution. Here's a breakdown of the main components:

1. **Initialization:** The algorithm begins by initializing the pre-population data **R_pre** and defining parameters such as the maximum number of iterations **max_iter**, fitness function **f**, population bounds **[lb, ub]**, and the population of agents' initial locations **R_j**.
2. **Main Loop:** The algorithm enters a main loop where it performs optimization iterations until the maximum iteration count **max_iter** is reached.
3. **Boundary Handling:** Agents that go out of the defined bounds **[lb, ub]** are adjusted to stay within the bounds. This helps maintain feasible solutions.
4. **Fitness Evaluation:** The fitness function **f** is evaluated for all agents' locations. The **R_best** is updated to store the best-performing agent's location and fitness encountered so far.
5. **Agent Updates:** For each agent indexed by **i**, the algorithm attempts to improve its solution by following different strategies based on fitness comparisons and random factors.
    - If the attempted solution (**R_att**) has better fitness than the current solution ($\boldsymbol{R_i^t}$), the agent's location is updated using an "host feeding" strategy.
    - If the attempted solution doesn't improve fitness, the algorithm performs a series of location updates based on different policies (WOA and SFO) using equations defined in the algorithm.
6. **Population Management:** After updating the agents' locations, the current population is added to the **R_pre** data to keep track of previous solutions.
7. **Iteration Update:** The iteration count **t** is incremented.
8. **Termination:** The main loop continues until the maximum number of iterations is reached (**t < max_iter**).

The EROA is employed in this work to determine the hyperparameter added in the MABLSTM and is described by Equation (24).

$$MSE = \frac{1}{T}\sum_{j=1}^{L}\sum_{i=1}^{M}\left(y_j^i - d_j^i\right)^2 \tag{24}$$

where as M and L correspondingly characterize the resultant value of layer and data, y_j^i and d_j^i indicates the obtained and suitable magnitudes for j-th unit from the output layer of network in t time.

Algorithm 1: Pseudocode for these EROAs

Input: population location $R_j(1, 2, \ldots, n)$, the amount of iterations max_iter, fitness function f, and bound $[lb,\ ub]$.
Output: optimum location, optimum fitness, and fitness history.
Initialize the pre-population data R_{pre},
While $t < max\_iter$ perform
Adjust agent if out of bound $[lb, ub]$,
Evaluate $f(R_i^t)$ of all the agents;
Upgrade R_{best} and $f(R_{best}^t)$,
For all the agents indexed by i perform
Based on Equation (22) to make the experience attempt R_{att} with Poisson-like 7: distribution;
Evaluate $f(R_{att})$ and $f(R_i^t)$,
If $f(R_i^t) > f(R_{att})$ then
Implement host feeding using Equation (16);
Else
If random(i) = 1 then
Based on Equation (18) for updating the location using WOA policy;
If random (i) in $[2,4]$ then
Based on Equation (23) to upgrade the location with better randomness SFO policy;
End if
End if
Add present population to R_{pre},
End for
$t = t + 1$,
End while

4. Experimental Setup

In this section, we outline the experimental setup used to evaluate the proposed Enhanced Remora Optimization with Deep Learning Model for intelligent PMSM drive temperature prediction in electric vehicles. Specifically, we detail the hardware and software configuration of the computer used for simulations.

The simulations were conducted on a workstation with the following hardware specifications:

- **Processor:** Intel Core i7-9700K (8 cores, 16 threads)
- **RAM:** 32 GB DDR4
- **Graphics Card:** NVIDIA GeForce RTX 2080 Ti (11 GB GDDR6)
- **Storage:** 1 TB NVMe SSD

The simulations were performed using the following software and tools:

- **Operating System:** Windows 10 Professional
- **Programming Languages:** Python and matlab
- **Deep Learning Framework:** TensorFlow
- **Optimization Library:** SciP
- **Simulation Environment:** Simulink

- **Statistical Analysis:** NumPy pandas
- **Data Visualization:** Matplotlib, Seaborn

Simulation Parameters

The simulation parameters were set as follows:

- **Population Size**: 100
- **Number of Generations**: 500
- **Learning Rate for Deep Learning**: 0.001
- **Optimizer for Deep Learning**: Adam
- **Convergence Threshold**: 1e-6

Data Source

Real-world sensor data collected from electric vehicle PMSM drives was used for training and validation of the deep learning model. The data included parameters such as temperature, current, voltage, and speed.

5. Results and Discussion

In this section, the temperature prediction results of the EROA-SBiLSTM technique are examined under three cases: stator yoke temperature (SYT), Stator Tooth Temperature (STT) and Stator Winding Temperature (SWT). In Table 1 and Figure 4, the comparative predictive results of the EROA-SBiLSTM technique under SYT are provided [26]. The results imply that the EROA-SBiLSTM technique reaches closer predictive outcomes over other models. For instance, with 50 min and actual value of −0.0231, the EROA-SBiLSTM technique has predicted a temperature of −0.0411. Next, with 150 min and actual value of 0.0721, the EROA-SBiLSTM method has forecasted a temperature of 0.1031. Similarly, with 200 min and actual value of 0.2982, the EROA-SBiLSTM method has forecasted the temperature of 0.3042. Finally, with 300 min and actual value of 1.0120, the EROA-SBiLSTM technique has predicted a temperature of 1.0100.

Table 1. Predictive outcome of EROA-SBiLSTM approach with other systems under SYT.

		Temperature; Stator Yoke Temperature			
Time in Minutes	**Actual**	**EROA-SBiLSTM**	**PPO-RL**	**RNN**	**LSTM**
0	−1.4747	−1.4867	−1.4577	−1.3677	−1.5987
50	−0.0231	−0.0411	−0.0581	−0.0731	0.1419
100	1.1786	1.2106	1.1336	1.1326	1.1336
150	0.0721	0.1031	0.1551	0.0291	0.0221
200	0.2982	0.3042	0.1782	0.4122	0.2692
250	0.8217	0.8268	0.8927	0.7737	0.8277
300	1.0120	1.0100	0.8930	0.9360	1.0780

In Table 2 and Figure 5, the comparative predictive outcomes of the EROA-SBiLSTM method under STT are provided. The results imply that the EROA-SBiLSTM technique reaches closer predictive outcomes over other models. For instance, with 50 min and actual value of −0.1293, the EROA-SBiLSTM method has forecasted the temperature of −0.1213. Next, with 150 min and actual value of 0.1472, the EROA-SBiLSTM method has forecasted a temperature of 0.1782. Similarly, with 200 min and actual value of 0.1833, the EROA-SBiLSTM method has predicted a temperature of 0.1783. Finally, with 300 min and actual value of 0.7121, the EROA-SBiLSTM method has predicted a temperature of 0.7241.

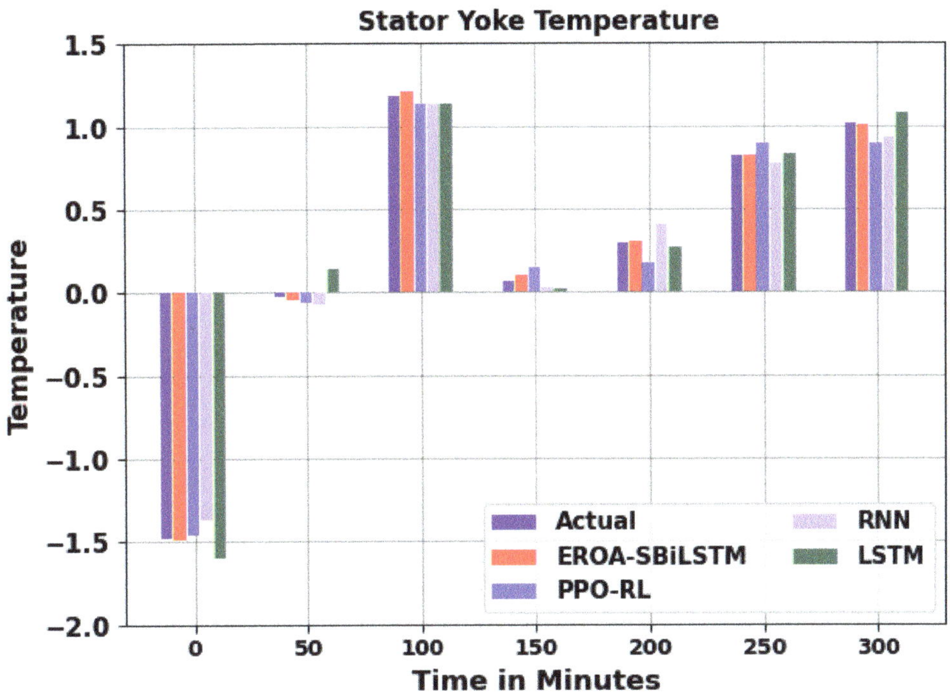

Figure 4. Predictive outcome of EROA-SBiLSTM approach under SYT.

Table 2. Predictive outcome of EROA-SBiLSTM method with other systems under STT.

	Temperature; Stator Tooth Temperature				
Time in Minutes	**Actual**	**EROA-SBiLSTM**	**PPO-RL**	**RNN**	**LSTM**
0	−1.4875	−1.4925	−1.5695	−1.5915	−1.4505
50	−0.1293	−0.1213	−0.0003	−0.0943	0.0597
100	0.8083	0.7953	0.8603	0.5643	0.5423
150	0.1472	0.1782	0.2422	0.0592	0.2622
200	0.1833	0.1783	0.2253	0.2343	0.2943
250	0.3636	0.3616	0.3516	0.4186	0.4056
300	0.7121	0.7241	0.5761	0.8151	0.4871

In Table 3 and Figure 6, the comparative predictive outcomes of the EROA-SBiLSTM technique under SWT are provided. The results imply that the EROA-SBiLSTM method reaches closer predictive outcomes than other models. For example, with 50 min and actual value of −0.2058, the EROA-SBiLSTM technique has predicted a temperature of −0.1278. Next, with 150 min and actual value of 0.0306, the EROA-SBiLSTM method has predicted a temperature of 0.0856. Similarly, with 200 min and actual value of −0.0369, the EROA-SBiLSTM method has forecasted a temperature of −0.0479. Lastly, with 300 min and actual value of 0.4922, the EROA-SBiLSTM method has forecasted the temperature of 0.4962.

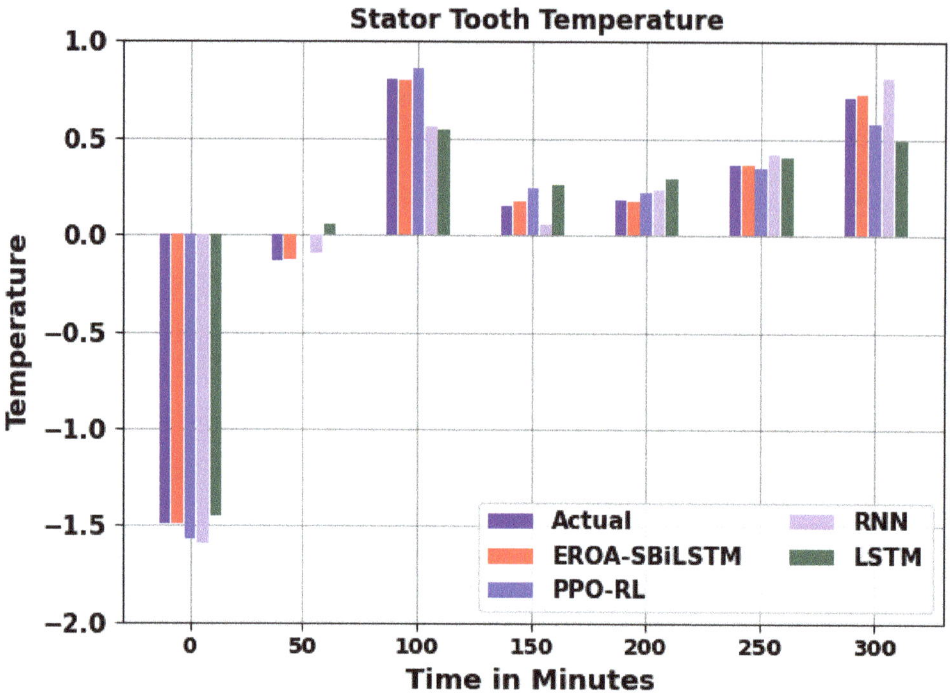

Figure 5. Predictive outcome of EROA-SBiLSTM approach under STT.

Table 3. Predictive outcome of EROA-SBiLSTM approach with other systems under SWT.

Temperature; Stator Winding Temperature					
Time in Minutes	**Actual**	**EROA-SBiLSTM**	**PPO-RL**	**RNN**	**LSTM**
0	−1.4779	−1.4519	−1.3989	−1.3849	−1.6119
50	−0.2058	−0.1278	−0.0858	−0.0538	−0.2908
100	0.4922	0.4802	0.6312	0.5822	0.2952
150	0.0306	0.0856	0.1216	−0.0564	0.1886
200	−0.0369	−0.0479	−0.0939	−0.1109	−0.1679
250	0.0531	0.0401	0.0911	−0.0069	0.0231
300	0.4922	0.4962	0.4122	0.3292	0.5732

In Table 4 and Figure 7, the EROA-SBiLSTM technique is compared with recent models in terms of RMSE. The results indicate that the PPO-RL model reaches worse outcomes with maximum RMSE values. Next, the LSTM and RNN models accomplish resulted in closer RMSE values. However, the EROA-SBiLSTM technique accomplishes enhanced performance with minimal RMSE values of 0.0596, 0.1025, and 0.0931 under SYT, STT, and SWT cases.

In Table 5, and Figure 8, the EROA-SBiLSTM method is compared with recent techniques in terms of MAE. The outcomes indicate that the PPO-RL method obtains worse outcomes with maximum MAE values. Next, the LSTM and RNN approaches accomplish resulted in closer MAE values. However, the EROA-SBiLSTM method achieves superior performance with minimal MAE values of 0.0623, 0.0509, and 0.0714 under SYT, STT, and SWT cases.

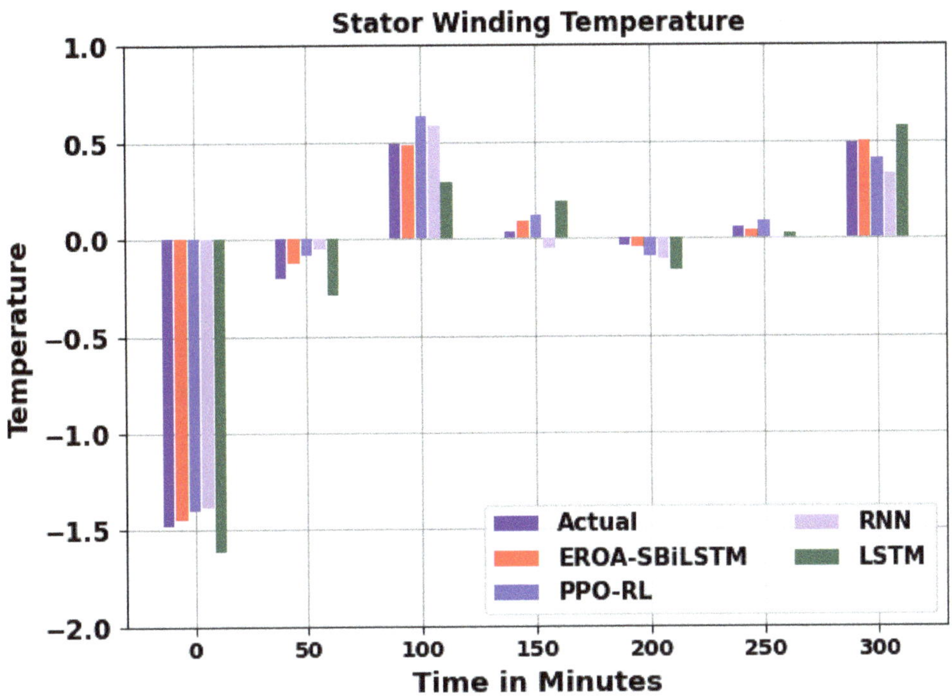

Figure 6. Predictive outcome of EROA-SBiLSTM approach under SWT.

Table 4. RMSE analysis of EROA-SBiLSTM approach with recent algorithms.

	RMSE		
Methods	**SYT**	**STT**	**SWT**
LSTM	0.1919	0.3742	0.3114
RNN	0.1627	0.2862	0.1329
PPO-RL	0.2190	0.1244	0.1938
EROA-SBiLSTM	0.0596	0.1025	0.0931

Table 5. MAE analysis of EROA-SBiLSTM method with recent algorithms.

	MAE		
Methods	**SYT**	**STT**	**SWT**
LSTM	0.1601	0.2682	0.2154
RNN	0.1627	0.2033	0.1038
PPO-RL	0.2165	0.1044	0.1708
EROA-SBiLSTM	0.0623	0.0509	0.0714

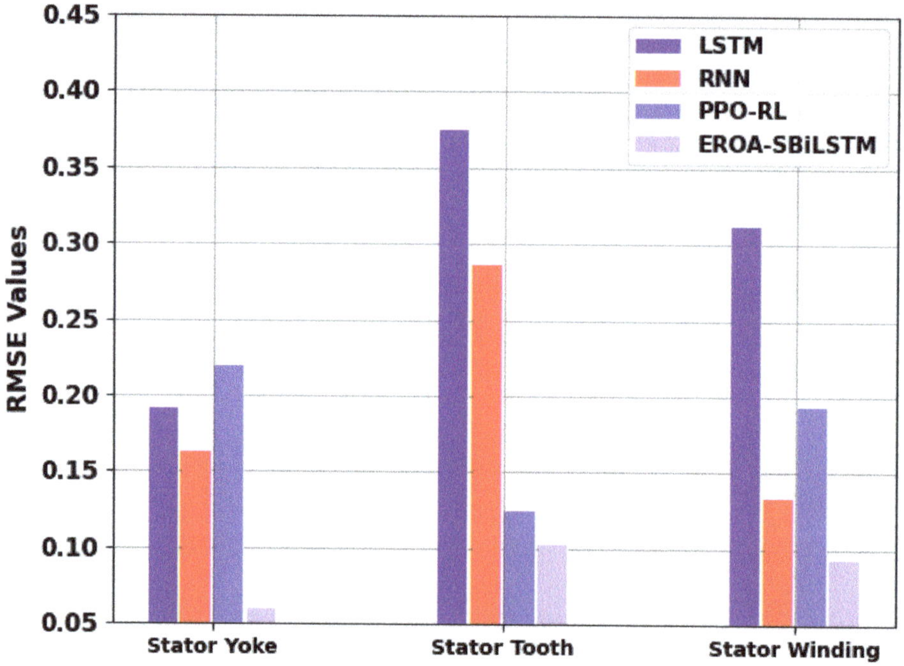

Figure 7. RMSE analysis of EROA-SBiLSTM method with recent algorithms.

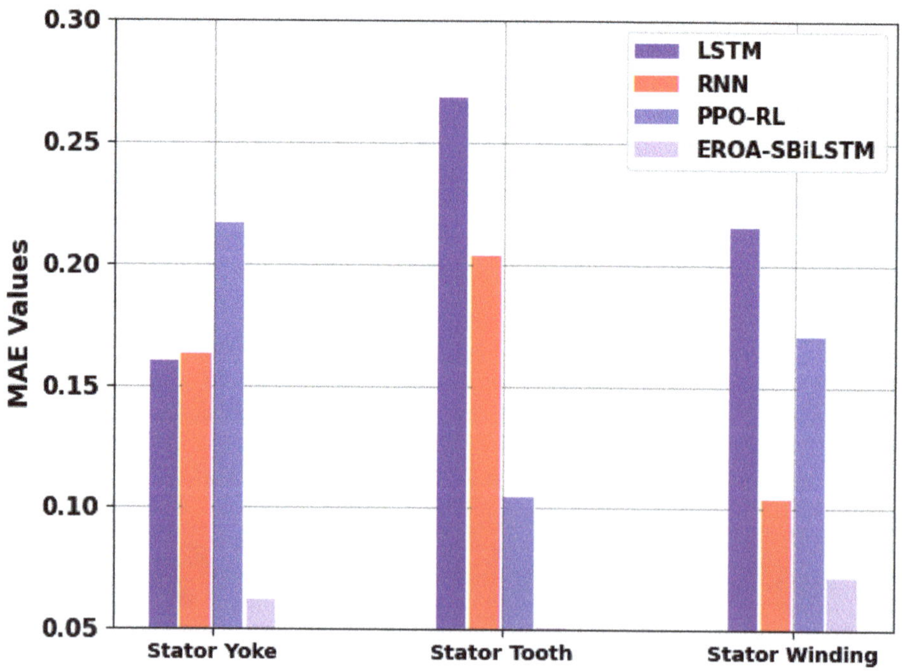

Figure 8. MAE analysis of EROA-SBiLSTM approach with recent algorithms.

In Table 6 and Figure 9, the EROA-SBiLSTM method is compared with recent models in terms of CT (Training). The results indicate that the PPO-RL technique attains worse outcomes with maximum CT values. Next, the LSTM and RNN approaches accomplish resulted in closer CT values. However, the EROA-SBiLSTM method accomplishes enhanced performance with minimal CT values of 152.16, 189.22, and 183.74 under SYT, STT, and SWT cases.

Table 6. CT (Training) analysis of EROA-SBiLSTM method with recent algorithms.

Computational Time (Training)			
Methods	**SYT**	**STT**	**SWT**
LSTM	269.19	249.80	234.04
RNN	723.50	781.71	707.88
PPO-RL	827.69	831.31	832.04
EROA-SBiLSTM	152.16	189.22	183.74

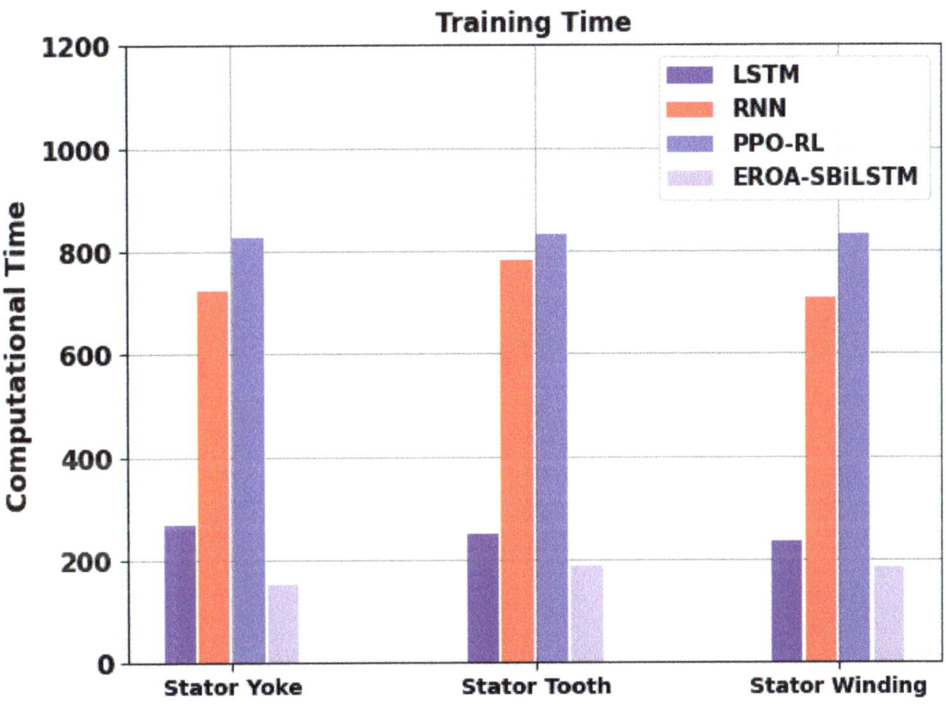

Figure 9. CT (Training) analysis of EROA-SBiLSTM approach with recent algorithms.

In Table 7 and Figure 10, the EROA-SBiLSTM technique is compared with recent models in terms of CT (Testing). The outcomes indicate that the PPO-RL method attains worse outcomes with maximum CT values. Next, the LSTM and RNN approaches accomplish resulted in closer CT values. However, the EROA-SBiLSTM method accomplishes enhanced performance with minimal CT values of 0.213, 0.175, and 0.180 under SYT, STT, and SWT cases.

Table 7. CT (Testing) analysis of EROA-SBiLSTM approach with recent algorithms.

Computational Time (Testing)			
Methods	**SYT**	**STT**	**SWT**
LSTM	0.326	0.314	0.350
RNN	0.400	0.340	0.246
PPO-RL	0.572	0.710	1.067
EROA-SBiLSTM	0.213	0.175	0.180

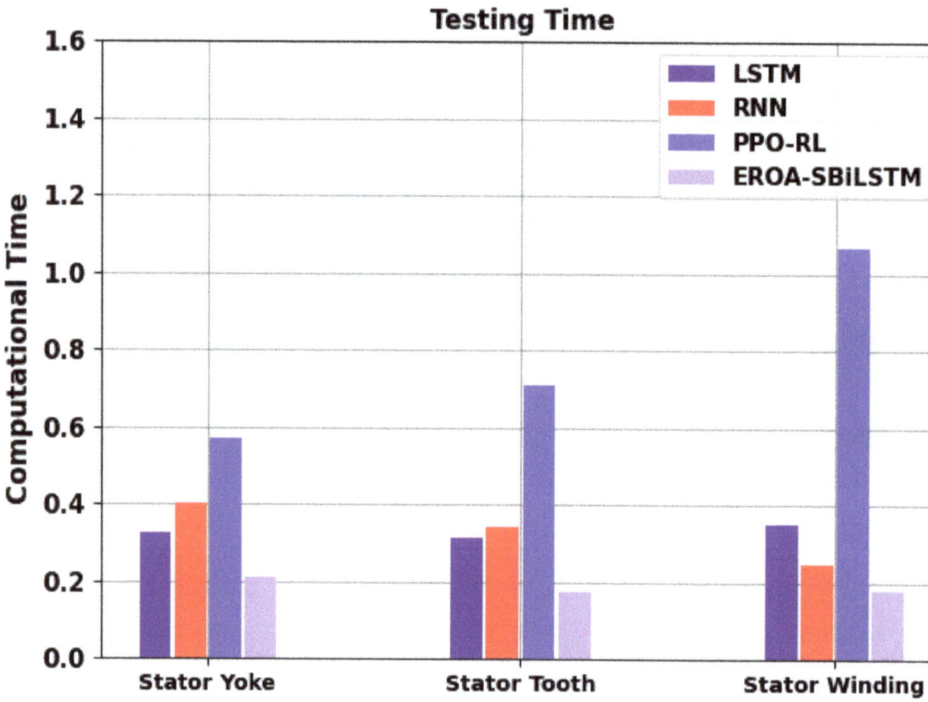

Figure 10. CT (Testing) analysis of EROA-SBiLSTM approach with recent algorithms.

These results highlighted that the EROA-SBiLSTM technique exhibits effective predictive ability over the other models.

6. Conclusions

In this article, we have introduced a novel EROA-SBiLSTM algorithm designed to enhance the accuracy of temperature predictions for Permanent Magnet Synchronous Motor (PMSM) drives. Our presented EROA-SBiLSTM technique focuses on achieving precise temperature predictions through the integration of Deep Learning (DL) and hyper-parameter tuning strategies. At its core, the EROA-SBiLSTM methodology incorporates a series of innovative steps. Initially, a comprehensive Pearson correlation coefficient analysis is applied to assess the relationships between various features. The utilization of p-values facilitates the identification of statistically significant correlations. This analytical phase serves as a crucial foundation for subsequent stages. The SBiLSTM model is then employed to forecast the temperature levels within PMSM drives. Leveraging the power of Sequential Bidirectional Long Short-Term Memory networks, our approach capitalizes on the sequence-based nature of the data to make accurate predictions. Furthermore, we introduce an EROA-based hyperparameter tuning process to dynamically optimize the parameters of the SBiLSTM model. This ensures that the model is configured optimally for the specific task of temperature prediction. To validate the efficacy of the proposed EROA-SBiLSTM technique, comprehensive experiments were conducted on a real-world electric motor temperature dataset sourced from Kaggle. The results of our study showcase the tangible improvements achieved by our EROA-SBiLSTM approach, underlining its potential for enhancing temperature prediction accuracy. Looking ahead, our future research endeavors will involve a more extensive evaluation of the EROA-SBiLSTM technique. Notably, the EROA-SBiLSTM method attained minimal RMSE and MAE values of 0.0596, 0.1025, and 0.0931 under SYT, STT, and SWT cases, demonstrating its precision and robustness across various scenarios. We plan to assess its performance on a larger and more diverse sample set, thereby providing deeper insights into its capabilities and uncovering its potential for broader applications within the realm of PMSMs. In conclusion, our EROA-SBiLSTM algorithm stands as a promising step forward in the pursuit of accurate temperature prediction for PMSM drives. By synergizing advanced DL techniques with meticulous hyperparameter tuning, we anticipate that our approach will contribute to further advancements in the field and open avenues for more sophisticated research and application.

Author Contributions: Conceptualization, A.L. and I.M.M.; methodology, M.T.V.; software, R.J.M.; validation, A.L., I.M.M. and T.P.; formal analysis, M.T.V.; investigation, A.L.; resources, M.T.V.; data curation, M.T.V.; writing—original draft preparation, M.T.V., T.P. and R.J.M.; writing—review and editing, A.L., I.M.M., M.T.V., R.J.M. and T.P.; visualization, I.M.M.; supervision, A.L.; project administration, A.L.; funding acquisition, I.M.M. All authors have read and agreed to the published version of the manuscript.

Funding: The Deanship of Scientific Research (DSR) at King Abdulaziz University (KAU), Jeddah, Saudi Arabia has funded this Project under grant no (G: 311-130-1443).

Data Availability Statement: Not applicable.

Acknowledgments: The Deanship of Scientific Research (DSR) at King Abdulaziz University (KAU), Jeddah, Saudi Arabia has funded this Project under grant no (G: 311-130-1443).

Conflicts of Interest: The authors declare no conflict of interest.

References

1. A, A.; AC, B.K. Optimal solution for PMSM rotor magnet demagnetization based on temperature estimation for EV application. In Proceedings of the 2021 International Conference on Communication, Control and Information Sciences (ICCISc), Idukki, India, 16–18 June 2021; pp. 1–6.
2. Chen, Z.; Zhao, H.; Zhang, Y.; Shen, S.; Shen, J.; Liu, Y. State of health estimation for lithium-ion batteries based on temperature prediction and gated recurrent unit neural network. *J. Power Sources* **2022**, *521*, 230892. [CrossRef]
3. Al-Gabalawy, M. Deep analysis of the influence of the different power system structures on the performance of the energy storage systems. *Int. J. Energy Res.* **2021**, *45*, 17805–17833. [CrossRef]
4. Ali, Z.M.; Aleem, S.H.E.A.; Omar, A.I.; Mahmoud, B.S. Economical environmental-technical operation of power networks with high penetration of renewable energy systems using multi-objective coronavirus herd immunity algorithm. *Mathematics* **2022**, *10*, 1201. [CrossRef]
5. Al-Gabalawy, M.; Hosny, N.S.; Dawson, J.A.; Omar, A.I. State of charge estimation of a Li-ion battery based on extended Kalman filtering and sensor bias. *Int. J. Energy Res.* **2021**, *45*, 6708–6726. [CrossRef]
6. Smith, A.B.; Johnson, C.D.; Davis, E.F. A three-layer game theoretic-based strategy for optimal scheduling of microgrids by leveraging a dynamic demand response program designer to unlock the potential of smart buildings and electric vehicle fleets. *Renew. Energy* **2022**, *175 Pt 2*, 1234–1248.
7. Johnson, C.D.; Williams, E.G.; Brown, F.H. Improved double-surface sliding mode observer for flux and speed estimation of induction motors. *IEEE Trans. Ind. Electron.* **2021**, *68*, 7890–7902.
8. Williams, E.G.; Davis, E.F.; Smith, A.B. A tri-layer stochastic framework to manage electricity market within a smart community in the presence of energy storage systems. *Energy Policy* **2023**, *150*, 112345.
9. Davis, E.F.; Johnson, C.D.; Williams, E.G. An interval-based nested optimization framework for deriving flexibility from smart buildings and electric vehicle fleets in the TSO-DSO coordination. *IEEE Trans. Power Syst.* **2020**, *35*, 3000–3012.

10. Foti, S.; Testa, A.; De Caro, S.; Scelba, G.; Scarcella, G. A general approach to sensorless estimation rotor and stator windings temperature in induction motor drives. *Electr. Eng.* **2022**, *104*, 203–215. [CrossRef]
11. Czerwinski, D.; Gęca, J.; Kolano, K. Machine learning for sensorless temperature estimation of a BLDC motor. *Sensors* **2021**, *21*, 4655. [CrossRef]
12. Dilshad, M.R.; Ashok, S.; Vijayan, V.; Pathiyil, P. An energy loss model based temperature estimation for Permanent Magnet Synchronous Motor (PMSM). In Proceedings of the 2016 2nd International Conference on Advances in Electrical, Electronics, Information, Communication and Bio-Informatics (AEEICB), Chennai, India, 27–28 February 2016; pp. 172–176.
13. Feng, G.; Lai, C.; Kar, N.C. Expectation-maximization particlefilter- and kalman-filter-based permanent magnet temperature estimation for PMSM condition monitoring using high-frequency signal injection. *IEEE Trans. Ind. Inform.* **2017**, *13*, 1261–1270. [CrossRef]
14. Feng, G.; Lai, C.; Kar, N.C. Speed harmonic based modeling and estimation of permanent magnet temperature for PMSM drive using Kalman filter. *IEEE Trans. Ind. Inform.* **2019**, *15*, 1372–1382. [CrossRef]
15. Pietrzak, P.; Wolkiewicz, M. Demagnetization Fault Diagnosis of Permanent Magnet Synchronous Motors Based on Stator Current Signal Processing and Machine Learning Algorithms. *Sensors* **2023**, *23*, 1757. [CrossRef] [PubMed]
16. Eker, M.; Gündogan, B. Demagnetization fault detection of permanent magnet synchronous motor with convolutional neural network. *Electr. Eng.* **2023**, *105*, 1695–1708. [CrossRef]
17. Ai, Q.; Wei, H.; Dou, H.; Zhao, W.; Zhang, Y. Robust Rotor Temperature Estimation of Permanent Magnet Motors for Electric Vehicles. *IEEE Trans. Veh. Technol.* **2023**, *72*, 8579–8591. [CrossRef]
18. Bingi, K.; Prusty, B.R.; Kumra, A.; Chawla, A. Torque and temperature prediction for permanent magnet synchronous motor using neural networks. In Proceedings of the 2020 3rd International Conference on Energy, Power and Environment: Towards Clean Energy Technologies, Shillong, India, 5–7 March 2021; pp. 1–6.
19. Xu, X.; Feng, J.; Zhan, L.; Li, Z.; Qian, F.; Yan, Y. Fault Diagnosis of Permanent Magnet Synchronous Motor Based on Stacked Denoising Autoencoder. *Entropy* **2021**, *23*, 339. [CrossRef] [PubMed]
20. You, Y.-M. Multi-Objective Optimal Design of Permanent Magnet Synchronous Motor for Electric Vehicle Based on Deep Learning. *Appl. Sci.* **2020**, *10*, 482. [CrossRef]
21. Zhao, C.; Li, Y.; Wessner, M.; Rathod, C.; Pisu, P. Support-Vector Machine Approach for Robust Fault Diagnosis of Electric Vehicle Permanent Magnet Synchronous Motor. In Proceedings of the Annual Conference of the PHM Society, Virtually, 9–13 November 2020; Volume 12, p. 10.
22. Fatemimoghadam, A.; Yan, Y.; Iyer, L.V.; Kar, N.C. Permanent Magnet Synchronous Motor Drive Using Deep-Neural-Network-Based Vector Control for Electric Vehicle Applications. In Proceedings of the 2022 International Conference on Electrical Machines (ICEM), Valencia, Spain, 5–8 September 2022; pp. 2358–2364.
23. Al-Gabalawy, M.; Elmetwaly, A.H.; Younis, R.A.; Omar, A.I. Temperature prediction for electric vehicles of permanent magnet synchronous motor using robust machine learning tools. *J. Ambient. Intell. Humaniz. Comput.* **2022**, 1–18. [CrossRef]
24. Tabrizchi, H.; Razmara, J.; Mosavi, A. Thermal prediction for energy management of clouds using a hybrid model based on CNN and stacking multi-layer bi-directional LSTM. *Energy Rep.* **2023**, *9*, 2253–2268. [CrossRef]
25. Yan, D.; Liu, Y.; Li, L.; Lin, X.; Guo, L. Remora Optimization Algorithm with Enhanced Randomness for Large-Scale Measurement Field Deployment Technology. *Entropy* **2023**, *25*, 450. [CrossRef]
26. Cen, Y.; Zhang, C.; Cen, G.; Zhang, Y.; Zhao, C. The Temperature Prediction of Permanent Magnet Synchronous Machines Based on Proximal Policy Optimization. *Information* **2020**, *11*, 495. [CrossRef]

axioms

MDPI

Article

Optimal Reinsurance–Investment Strategy Based on Stochastic Volatility and the Stochastic Interest Rate Model

Honghan Bei [1,2,3], Qian Wang [1], Yajie Wang [1], Wenyang Wang [1,2,*] and Roberto Murcio [4,5]

1 School of Maritime Economics and Management, Dalian Maritime University, Dalian 116026, China
2 Collaborative Innovation Centre for Transport Study, Dalian Maritime University, Dalian 116026, China
3 School of Management, Shanghai University, Shanghai 200444, China
4 Department of Geography, Birkbeck, London University, Malet Street, Bloomsbury, London WC1E 7HX, UK
5 Centre for Advanced Spatial Analysis, University College London, 90 Tottenham Court Road, London W1T 4TJ, UK
* Correspondence: wangwenyang@dlmu.edu.cn

Abstract: This paper studies insurance companies' optimal reinsurance–investment strategy under the stochastic interest rate and stochastic volatility model, taking the HARA utility function as the optimal criterion. It uses arithmetic Brownian motion as a diffusion approximation of the insurer's surplus process and the variance premium principle to calculate premiums. In this paper, we assume that insurance companies can invest in risk-free assets, risky assets, and zero-coupon bonds, where the Cox–Ingersoll–Ross model describes the dynamic change in stochastic interest rates and the Heston model describes the price process of risky assets. The analytic solution of the optimal reinsurance–investment strategy is deduced by employing related methods from the stochastic optimal control theory, the stochastic analysis theory, and the dynamic programming principle. Finally, the influence of model parameters on the optimal reinsurance–investment strategy is illustrated using numerical examples.

Keywords: Cox–Ingersoll–Ross model; Heston model; variance premium principle; HARA utility

1. Introduction

Insurance companies face significant risks in the financial market due to the high volume of insurance claims. Consequently, risk avoidance and management become paramount for these companies. Recently, reinsurance has emerged as an effective tool for risk management, garnering considerable attention in the insurance industry. When confronted with overwhelming claims, insurance companies transfer a portion of the risk to a reinsurer, relieving their burden. Simultaneously, they invest the premiums received to enhance their ability to make repayments, ensuring the smooth operation of their insurance business. This strategic approach significantly boosts their net profit while maintaining a delicate balance between profitability and risk. Therefore, the selection of an optimal reinsurance–investment strategy holds immense importance for insurance companies.

Several examples of the results of stochastic differential equations are applied to optimal control problems. Święch [1] proved the optimality inequalities of dynamic programming for viscosity sub- and super-solutions of the associated Bellman–Isaacs equations, where the value functions are the unique viscosity solutions of the Bellman–Isaacs equations and satisfy the principle of dynamic programming. Soner and Touzi [2] introduced a new dynamic programming principle for optimal stochastic control problems. They proved that the value function of the stochastic target problem is a discontinuous viscosity solution of the associated dynamic programming equation, proposing that financial mathematics should be the main application. Rami et al. [3] introduced the generalized (differential) Riccati equation, a new type of differential Riccati equation to both solve the algebraic equality/inequality constraints and matrix pseudoinverse, and to also prove that the solution to such an equation can identify all optimal controls. In recent years, some achievements have been made in applying the stochastic models: Zhu and Li [4] studied relevant questions by modeling interest rates in the market using the Vasicek model. They derived equilibrium reinsurance–investment strategies and value functions using a comprehensive dynamic programming approach. Ali and Khan [5] used an automatic procedure to solve the resultant algebraic equation after the discretization of the stochastic Lotka–Volterra operator and the proposed scheme was applied to the equivalent integral form of stochastic fractional differential equations under consideration. Their numerical simulations further demonstrate the effectiveness that the fractional Atangana–Baleanu operator approach produces.

Notably, the issue of investment and reinsurance of insurance companies has received much attention in recent decades. For example, Browne [6] considered a diffusion risk model and studied the optimal investment strategy to maximize the exponential utility function of terminal wealth and minimize the probability of bankruptcy. Yang and Zhang [7] studied the optimal investment strategy of an insurance company with a jump –diffusion risk process to minimize the ruin probability. Hipp and Plum [8] developed a compound Poisson risk model to determine the optimal investment strategy by minimizing the bankruptcy probability and the capital market index. For the reinsurance problem, Promisslow and Young [9] extended Browne's work by considering investing in risky assets and purchasing proportional reinsurance. They obtained the minimum bankruptcy probability and the optimal reinsurance–investment strategy. Bai and Zhang [10] studied the optimal ratio reinsurance and investment strategies in the classical and diffusion risk models because short-selling is prohibited. Ramadan et al. [11] came up with a new distribution method considering the appropriate transformation for half-logistic geometric (HLG) distribution and introduced an application in the insurance field to show its flexibility.

In addition, the logarithmic utility function, exponential utility function (CARA), and power utility function (CRRA) [12] commonly used in the field of actuarial insurance are exceptional cases of the hyperbolic absolute risk utility function (HARA). Therefore, the HARA utility function is more representative and has a more general mathematical structure and a more comprehensive range of applications. However, because the structure of the HARA utility function is more complex than the logarithmic utility, exponential utility, and power utility functions, there are few studies on the optimal reinsurance–investment strategy of insurance companies under the HARA utility function. Representative studies include the following: Jung and Kim [13] used the Legendre dual transformation method under the CEV model to solve the optimal investment problem under the HARA utility criterion and obtained a definitive solution. Chang and Chang [14] studied the consumption and investment problem under the HARA utility function when the interest rate was the same as the Vasicek stochastic interest rate model and obtained the explicit solution of the optimal strategy. Zhang and Zhao [15] studied the optimal reinsurance–investment problem related to sparse risk based on the HARA utility function, in which the CEV model drove the price of risky assets, and they obtained the closed-form expression of the optimal strategy. Zhang [16] studied the optimal asset–liability management problem under the framework of maximizing the expected utility, taking a variety of stochastic volatility models as a particular case and using the backward stochastic differential equation (BSDE) method to derive closed-form expressions for optimal investment strategy and optimal value function. Through the research literature, it was found that the HARA utility function was more widely used than the logarithmic utility function, exponential utility function, and power utility function. Regarding consumption investment and optimal asset–liability management, few studies in the literature have been applied towards studying the optimal portfolio strategies of insurance companies.

Although optimal reinsurance–investment strategies under the HARA utility criterion have been studied extensively, two aspects still require further exploration. First, most of the literature mentioned was studied with the precondition of constant or deterministic volatility, which differs from the facts observed in financial markets, such as volatility smiles and clustering. Therefore, in recent years, many studies have proposed various local volatility models and stochastic volatility models to serve as extensions of the deterministic volatility models, such as the CEV model [17], the Stein–Stein model [18], and the Heston model [19]. For example, Gu et al. [20] assumed that the insurance company's earnings process approximates the Brownian motion with drift and studied the optimal excess-of-loss reinsurance and investment strategy under the CEV model. Wang et al. [21] derived time-consistent reinsurance strategies before and after default using a game-theoretic framework that considers the strategy feedback time lag and the stock price following the CEV model. Huang et al. [22] studied the robust optimal investment and proportional reinsurance problems of general insurance companies, including insurers and reinsurers, under the Heston model. Zhu et al. [23] considered the relative performance problem. They derived the equilibrium investment reinsurance strategy's closed-form expression and corresponding value function based on the Heston model by applying the stochastic control theory. Zhang et al. [24] applied the Legendre transformation and stochastic control theory to obtain the optimal excess-of-loss reinsurance and investment strategy with dependent claims under the Heston model. Yan and Wong [25] first applied the open-loop LQ control framework to the reinsurance investment problem in general SV incomplete markets, deriving explicit solutions for the Hull–White SV model, the unleveraged Heston model, and the unleveraged 3/2 SV models, and gave uniqueness conditions for all of the above equilibrium controls that allow straightforward solutions.

Most of the above literature assumes that the interest rate was constant or deterministic, which ignores the application of some specific interest rate models in actual situations, such as the Vasicek model and the CIR model. Many scholars have studied the optimal reinsurance–investment problem with stochastic interest rates: Sheng [26] considered the reserve process with dynamic returns to study the reinsurance—investment problem of insurance companies under the Vasicek stochastic interest rate model; Zhang and Zheng [27] studied the optimal reinsurance—investment strategy of insurance companies under the Ho–Lee and Vasicek models, respectively, and explained the impact of two different stochastic interest rate models on the optimal decision-making of insurance companies. Yuan et al. [28] used the linear quadratic optimal control theory and the corresponding Hamilton–Jacobi–Bellman (HJB) equation to study the optimality of the interest rate subject to the Vasicek stochastic interest rate model in case the bond and stock processes are fully correlated. On investment and reinsurance issues, Guo and Zhuo [29] assumed that the extended CIR model described domestic and foreign nominal interest rates. They used dynamic programming principles to study the optimal reinsurance–investment strategy of insurance companies investing in domestic and foreign markets. Sun and Guo [30] studied insurance companies' optimal investment and reinsurance problems under the mean–variance criterion by applying reverse stochastic differential equations where the stock prices obey the Cox–Ingersoll–Ross (CIR) process.

In most of the literature reviewed on optimal reinsurance investments, only a random factor was considered. However, in real-world financial markets, it is better to consider the optimal reinsurance–investment strategy with random volatility and random interest rates. For example, Wang et al. [31] studied the time-consistent open-loop equilibrium reinsurance–investment strategy of insurance companies under Vasicek's stochastic interest rate model and Heston's stochastic volatility model. Guan et al. [32] introduced an inflation index and studied the robust optimal reinsurance and investment problem of fuzzy risk-averse insurance companies, where the stock prices are described using Heston's stochastic volatility model and the interest rates are described via Vasicek's model. Zhang et al. [33] introduced stochastic interest rates and stochastic volatility into optimal proportional reinsurance and investment strategies based on insurers' CRRA utility criterion and reinsurers' CARA utility criterion.

There are scattered results on the optimal reinsurance–investment strategy based on the HARA utility function in the stochastic financial market. To our knowledge, no research has yet been conducted on the optimal reinsurance–investment strategy under the HARA utility criterion, considering both the risk assets subject to the Heston model and the interest rates subject to the CIR model. The multiple stochastic factors and the variance premium principle are considered more practical and valuable for research. Here, we explore the optimal proportional reinsurance problem under a diffusion approximation claims model based on the stochastic factors, maximizing the HARA utility of the terminal wealth value.

We studied the optimal reinsurance–investment problem for insurers considering stochastic volatility and stochastic interest rates under the HARA utility function criterion. We use the arithmetic Brownian motion as a diffusion approximation to the insurer's surplus process. We assume that the financial market comprises risk-free assets, risky assets, and zero-coupon bonds. The insurance company can purchase proportional reinsurance and invest its surplus in a financial market of risk-free assets, risky assets, and zero-coupon bonds to maximize the expected ultimate return. The Heston model describes the price of this risky asset while the CIR model describes the risk-free rate. In addition, we assume that the proportion of reinsurance purchases must be non-negative and that there are no borrowing and short-selling constraints in the trading of financial assets. The HJB equation for the wealth process is established using dynamic programming principles. The nonlinear partial differential equation is solved using the Legendre transformations and pairwise theory. This ultimately leads to an optimal reinsurance–investment strategy for the insurance company and an analytical expression for the value function.

The rest of the paper is organized as follows: Section 2 establishes the model and gives the optimal reinsurance–investment problem of the insurance company in the stochastic financial market. Section 3 obtains the optimal reinsurance–investment strategy of the insurance company. In Section 4, several numerical examples are provided to illustrate our results. Finally, in Section 5, we present our conclusions.

2. The Model

In this section, we investigate the problem of optimal reinsurance–investment strategies with CIR rates under the Heston model from the perspective of insurance companies, using the HARA utility function as the criterion. The model in this section consists of equities S_1, zero-coupon bonds B, and risk-free assets S_0. Assuming that the price of risky assets follows the Heston stochastic volatility model and the stochastic interest rate meets the CIR interest rate model, and to maximize the HARA utility function of terminal wealth, the corresponding HJB equation was solved by applying the dynamic programming principle and employing both the Lejeune transformation and pairwise theory to solve the corresponding HJB equation, to obtain the analytical expressions for the optimal reinsurance–investment strategy and value function of the insurance company.

2.1. Surplus Process

Let $(\Omega, \mathcal{F}, \{\mathcal{F}_t\}_{0\leq t\leq T}, \mathbb{P})$ be a complete probability space, with $\mathcal{F}_t$ the total amount of information flow held by the insurance company up to time t. We assume that all stochastic processes are adapted processes in this probability space. The expression $\mathbb{F} = \{\mathcal{F}(t)|t \in [0,T]\}$ is the natural information flow generated using the $n+1$ dimensional Brownian motion $\left\{(W_0(t), W_1(t), \ldots, W_n(t))^T \middle| t \in [0,T]\right\}$, with $W(t)$ and $W_i(t)$ independent of each other, $i \in \{1,2\}$. In the classical risk model, the earnings process of insurance companies can be described using the following classical Cramér–Lundberg model:

$$C(t) = u + ct - S(t) = u + ct + \sum_{i=1}^{N_t} C_i. \tag{1}$$

where $u \geq 0.$ is the initial capital of the company, c is the premium rate, and the claim number process $\{N_t, t \geq 0\}$ is a time-homogeneous Poisson counting process with a density parameter of $\lambda \geq 0$, a positive random variable sequence with mutual independent and identically distributed random variables, and where $\{Y_i, i = 1,2,\ldots\}$ represents the amount of each claim and is also independent of the Poisson point process $\{N_t, t \geq 0\}$. For simplicity, let Y be a general random variable with the same distribution function as Y_i. The first and second moments of Y are $\mu_1 = EY$ and $\mu_2 = E[Y^2]$, respectively, and the generating function of the moment is recorded as $M_Y(\rho) = E(e^{\rho Y})$. Suppose there is a constant $0 < \zeta \leq +\infty$, and for $0 < \rho < \zeta$, we have $E(Ye^{\rho Y}) = M'_Y(\rho)$ and $E(Ye^{\rho Y}) = \infty$. According to Grandell [34], the claim process can be approximated using the diffusion of the Brownian motion with drift. That is, the diffusion claim model can be calculated using the following equation:

$$dC(t) = h_0 dt - \sigma_0 dW_0(t). \tag{2}$$

where $W_0(t)$ is a standard Brownian motion, h_0 is the claim rate; ${\sigma_0}^2$ is the volatility of the insurance company's claim process; $h_0 = \lambda\mu_1$, ${\sigma_0}^2 = \lambda\mu_2$; and μ_1 and μ_2 are the first and second moments of Y, respectively. Assuming that the premium is paid at the interest rate $c = (1+\theta_1)\mu_0$, μ_0 is the premium return rate, $\theta_1 > 0$ is the safe load of the insurance company, and $\theta_2 > 0$ is the safe load of the reinsurance company. When there is no reinsurance or investment, the surplus process of the insurance company is

$$\delta(q(t)) = \theta_2{\sigma_0}^2(1-q(t))^2 + (1-q(t))h_0, \tag{3}$$

and the earning process becomes

$$dR^q(t) = [c - \delta(q(t))]dt - h_0 q(t)dt + \sigma_0 q(t)dW_0(t). \tag{4}$$

2.2. Financial Market

To enrich the financial markets, we assume that they consist of risk-free assets, equities, and zero-coupon bonds.

For a risk-free asset, we set $S_0(t)$ as the price at the moment of t, $t \in [0, T]$ to satisfy the following differential equation

$$\begin{cases} dS_0(t) = r(t)S_0(t)dt, \ 0 \leq t \leq T, \\ S_0(0) = s_0 > 0. \end{cases} \tag{5}$$

The CIR model describes short-term interest rates:

$$dr(t) = (\varphi_r - \kappa_r r(t))dt + \sigma_r\sqrt{r(t)}dW_r(t), \tag{6}$$

where initial values are $r_0 \in R^+$, κ_r is the average regression velocity, $\frac{\varphi_r}{\kappa_r} \in R^+$ is the mean of the previous period, $\sigma_r \in R^+$ is the interest rate volatility and $2\varphi_r \geq \sigma_r^2$.

For a risky asset, we denote the price at the moment of t as $S_1(t)$, satisfying the Heston stochastic volatility model:

$$\begin{cases} dS_1(t) = & S_1(t)[(r(t) + \xi_s V(t) + \xi_v\mu_s\xi_r r(t))dt + \sqrt{V(t)}dW_s(t) \\ & +\xi_v\sigma_r\sqrt{r(t)}dW_r(t)], \\ dV(t) = & \kappa_v(\xi_1 - V(t))dt + \mu_v\sqrt{V(t)}dW_v(t), \end{cases} \tag{7}$$

where $S_1(0) = s_0 > 0$, $V(t) = s_0 > 0$, parameters $\xi_v, \kappa_v, \xi_r, \mu_v, \xi_s$, and ξ_1 are all positive numbers, and $2\kappa_v \geq \mu_v^2$.

For a zero-coupon bond, we assume that the expiration date is T and the price at t is noted as $B(t, T)$, which satisfies the following differential equation

$$\begin{cases} \frac{dB(t,T)}{B(t,T)} = (r(t) + \sigma_b(t)\xi_r\mu_s r(t))dt + \sigma_b(t)\sigma_r\sqrt{r(t)}dW_r(t), \\ B(T,T) = 1, \end{cases} \tag{8}$$

where

$$\sigma_b(t) = \frac{2(e^{m(T-t)} - 1)}{m - (\kappa_r - \sqrt{\sigma_r}\xi_r) + e^{m(T-t)}(m + \kappa_r - \sqrt{\sigma_r}\xi_r)}, \tag{9}$$

$$m = \sqrt{(\kappa_r - \sqrt{\sigma_r}\xi_r)^2 + 2\sqrt{\sigma_r}}. \tag{10}$$

2.3. Wealth Process

The insurance company purchases proportional reinsurance and invests in a financial market of equities, risk-free assets, and zero-coupon bonds. The reinsurance–investment strategy iis $\Pi(t) = \{q(t), \pi_s(t), \pi_b(t) : t \in [0, T]\}$; then, we set $X(t)$ as the wealth process of the insurer at the time of t. Assuming that the amount invested in risky assets is $\pi_s(t)$ and the amount invested in zero-coupon bonds is denoted as $\pi_b(t)$, then the amount invested in risk-free assets is $X(t) - \pi_s(t) - \pi_b(t)$. The wealth process $X(t)$ of the insurer under the strategy $\Pi(t)$ satisfies the following differential equation:

$$\begin{aligned} dX(t) = dR^q(t) + \pi_s(t)\tfrac{dS_1(t)}{S_1(t)} + \pi_b(t)\tfrac{dB(t,T)}{B(t,T)} \\ +(X(t) - \pi_s(t) - \pi_b(t))\tfrac{dS_0(t)}{S_0(t)}. \end{aligned} \tag{11}$$

Substituting the differential equations of (6), (7) and (8) into the wealth process (11) above gives the following equation:

$$\begin{aligned} X(t) = {} & [c - \theta_2\sigma_0^2 q^2(t) + 2\theta_2\sigma_0^2 q(t) - h_0 - \theta_2\sigma_0^2 \\ & + \pi_s(t)(\xi_s V(t) + \xi_v \mu_s \xi_r r(t)) + \pi_b(t)\sigma_b(t)\xi_r \mu_s r(t) \\ & + X(t) r(t)]dt + \sigma_0 q(t) dW_0(t) + \pi_s(t)\sqrt{V(t)} dW_s(t) \\ & + \left[\pi_s(t)\xi_v \sigma_r \sqrt{r(t)} + \pi_b(t)\sigma_b(t)\sigma_r\sqrt{r(t)}\right] dW_r(t), \end{aligned} \tag{12}$$

where the initial wealth $X(t) = x_0 > 0$.

Definition 1. *(Allowable strategy) The reinsurance–investment strategy $\Pi(t) = \{q(t), \pi_s(t), \pi_b(t)\}$ is defined as an allowable strategy if $t \in [0, T]$meets the following conditions:*

(i) $q(t)$, $\pi_s(t)$ and $\pi_b(t)$ are $\mathbb{F}$-measurable, $E\left[\int_0^T q^2(t)dt\right] < +\infty$, $E\left[\int_0^T {\pi_s}^2(t)dt\right] < +\infty$;

(ii) $E\left[\int_0^T \sigma_0^2 q^2(t)dt + \int_0^T \pi_s^2(t)V(t)dt + \int_0^T r(t)(\pi_s(t)\xi_v\sigma_r + \pi_b(t)\sigma_b(t)\sigma_r)^2 dt\right] < \infty$;

(iii) $\forall\Pi(t) = \{q(t), \pi_s(t), \pi_b(t) : t \in [0, T]\}$, the stochastic Equation (12) has a unique solution.

Let $\mathcal{L}$ be the space of all acceptable reinsurance–investment strategies. Assuming the optimal strategy $\Pi(t) = (q(t), \pi_s(t), \pi_b(t)) \in \mathcal{L}$, the insurer expects to find the optimal reinsurance–investment strategy $\Pi(t)$ that maximizes the expected utility of its terminal wealth, i.e.,

$$\max_{\Pi(t)\in\mathcal{L}} E[U(X(T))], \tag{13}$$

where $U(\cdot)$ is the utility function of the insurance company.

3. Optimization Problem and the Optimal Strategy

The optimization problem is considered in this section and the corresponding optimal strategy is derived. We examine the optimal reinsurance strategy of an insurer under the HARA utility function

$$U(x) = U(\gamma, m, n, x) = \frac{1-n}{mn}\left(\frac{m}{1-n}x + \gamma\right)^n, \tag{14}$$

where $m > 0, n < 1, \gamma \neq 0$.

At time t, we define the value functions for instantaneous volatility v, instantaneous interest rate r, and wealth x as

$$J^{\pi}(t,v,r,x) = E[U(X(T))|X(t) = x, V(t) = v, r(t) = r], \quad (15)$$

and then, the optimal value function can be expressed as

$$J(t,v,r,x) = \sup_{\Pi(t)\in\mathcal{L}} J^{\pi}(t,v,r,x), \quad (16)$$

where the boundary conditions meet

$$J(T,v,r,x) = U(x). \quad (17)$$

The arbitrary value function $J(t,v,r,x) \in C^{1,2,2,2}([0,T] \times R^{+} \times R^{+} \times R^{+})$ defines the variational operator as

$$\begin{aligned}\mathcal{L}^{\pi} J(t,v,r,x) = \; & J_t + [c - \theta_2\sigma_0^2 q^2 + 2\theta_2\sigma_0^2 q - h_0 - \theta_2\sigma_0^2 + \pi_s(\xi_s v + \xi_v \mu_s \xi_r r) \\ & + \pi_b\sigma_b\xi_r\mu_s r + rx]J_x + (\varphi_r - \kappa_r r)J_r + \kappa_v(\xi_1 - v)J_v + \tfrac{1}{2}\mu_v^2 v J_{vv} \\ & + \tfrac{1}{2}\sigma_r^2 r J_{rr} + \pi_s\mu_v v J_{xv} + \sigma_r^2 r(\pi_s\xi_v + \pi_b\sigma_b)J_{xr} \\ & + \tfrac{1}{2}\left[\sigma_r^2 r(\pi_s\xi_v + \pi_b\sigma_b)^2 + \pi_s^2 v + \sigma_0^2 q^2\right] J_{xx},\end{aligned} \quad (18)$$

where $J_t, J_x, J_r, J_v, J_{vv}, J_{rr}, J_{xx}, J_{xv}, J_{xr}$ represent the first- and second-order partial derivatives with respect to the corresponding variables. The value function $L(t,v,r,x)$ is a convex function, given $z > 0$ as the dyadic variable of the vvariable x, and its Legendre transformation is defined as follows:

$$\hat{L}(t,v,r,x) = \sup_{x>0}\{L(t,v,r,x) - zx\}. \quad (19)$$

Denote $l(t,v,r,x)$ as the optimal value of the variable x and $0 < t < T$, assuming that $l(t,v,r,x)$ satisfies the following equation

$$l(t,v,r,x) = \inf_{x>0}\{x|L(t,v,r,x) \geq zx + \hat{L}(t,v,r,x)\},$$

with the boundary condition

$$l(T,v,r,z) - (U')^{-1}(z), \quad (20)$$

where we then obtain the relation between $l(t,v,r,x)$ and $\hat{L}(t,v,r,x)$:

$$l(t,v,r,x) = -\hat{L}(t,v,r,x). \quad (21)$$

Therefore $l(t,v,r,x)$ and $\hat{L}(t,v,r,x)$ are both pairwise functions of the value function $L(t,v,r,x)$. In solving the optimal reinsurance strategy, the function $l(t,v,r,x)$ is easier to calculate numerically, so the function $l(t,v,r,x)$ is chosen for this study.

Theorem 1. *When an insurance company adopts the HARA utility function as the optimal criterion, the reinsurance–investment problem (13) under the Heston model considering stochastic interest rates has the following optimal reinsurance–investment strategy:*

$$\begin{aligned} q^*(t) &= \frac{\theta_2 L_x}{\theta_2 L_x - L_{xx}} \\ &= \frac{1-n+\theta_2\left(x+\frac{1-n}{m}\gamma g(t,v,r) - G(t,v,r)\right)}{\theta_2\left(x+\frac{1-n}{m}\gamma g(t,v,r) - G(t,v,r)\right)}, \end{aligned}$$

$$\begin{aligned}\pi_s^*(t) &= -\xi_s \tfrac{L_x}{L_{xx}} - \mu_v \tfrac{L_{xv}}{L_{xx}} \\ &= \left(\tfrac{\xi_s}{1-n} - \mu_v\right)\tfrac{1-n}{m}\gamma g(t,v,r) + \left(\tfrac{\xi_s}{1-n} - \mu_v\right)x \\ &\quad -\left(\tfrac{\xi_s}{1-n} + \mu_v \tfrac{f_v}{f(t,v,r)}\right)G(t,v,r) - \tfrac{1-n}{m}\gamma g_v,\end{aligned}$$

$$\begin{aligned}\pi_b^*(t) &= \tfrac{\xi_s\xi_v - \xi_r}{\sigma_b}\tfrac{L_x}{L_{xx}} + \tfrac{\mu_v\xi_v - \xi_r}{\sigma_b}\tfrac{L_{xv}}{L_{xx}} + \tfrac{v}{\sigma_b}\tfrac{L_{xr}}{L_{xx}} \\ &= \left(x + \tfrac{1-n}{m}\gamma g(t,v,r) - G(t,v,r)\right)\left[\tfrac{\xi_r - \xi_s\xi_v}{(1-n)\sigma_b} - \tfrac{v}{\sigma_b}\tfrac{f_r}{f(t,v,r)} - \tfrac{\mu_v\xi_v - \xi_r}{\sigma_b}\tfrac{f_v}{f(t,v,r)}\right] \\ &\quad + \tfrac{1-n}{m}\gamma\left(\tfrac{\mu_v\xi_v - \xi_r}{\sigma_b}g_v + \tfrac{v}{\sigma_b}g_r\right).\end{aligned}$$

Proof. See Appendix A. □

To verify that the result mentioned in Theorem 1 is the optimal reinsurance–investment strategy for the insurance company, we introduce the following verification theorem (Yong and Zhou [35]).

Theorem 2. *(Verification theorem) Suppose that* $L^*_{HARA}(t,v,r,x) \in C^{1,2,2,2}([0,T] \times R^+ \times R^+ \times R^+)$ *given in Equation (A57) is a solution of the HJB Equation (A1); then, for any allowable strategy* $\Pi(t) = \{q(t), \pi_s(t), \pi_b(t) : t \in [0,T]\}$*, there is* $L(t,v,r,x) \leq L^*_{HARA}(t,v,r,x)$*, and*

$$(q(t), \pi_s(t), \pi_b(t)) \in \sup_{\Pi(t)\in\mathcal{L}} L^{\pi,q}(t,v,r,x),$$

When $\Pi(t) = \Pi^*(t)$, we have

$$L(t,v,r,x) = L^*_{HARA}(t,v,r,x).$$

4. Sensitivity Analyses and Numerical Experiments

In this section, we conduct a sensitivity analysis of the parameters related to the optimal reinsurance–investment strategy and match it with the reality in the financial market. The optimal reinsurance–investment strategy obtained in the previous section will be analyzed through numerical calculation experiments to obtain the parameter changes related to the reinsurance ratio, stochastic volatility, stochastic interest rate, and their dynamic impact on the optimal strategy.

The model parameter settings in this section refer to the work of Deelstra et al. (2003) [36], Guan and Liang (2014) [37], and Chang and Chang (2017), and the parameter values are shown in Table 1. Without loss of generality, we take $t = 0$ and only discuss the impact of model parameters on the optimal strategy at the initial moment, as shown in the figures below.

Table 1. Parameter values.

Parameters	Values	Parameters	Values
σ_0	1.5	ξ_1	0.6
φ_r	1.8	h_0	5
κ_r	0.23	κ_v	0.2
ξ_s	0.6	θ_2	0.2
ξ_v	1.7	σ_r	0.083
μ_v	0.4	m	0.05
$X(0)$	100	n	−2
T	1	$r(0)$	0.05
ξ_r	0.8	γ	0.4

In Figure 1, the parameter n is used to measure the degree of risk aversion of an insurance company, that is, the trade-off between the rate of return and the risk it requires when facing the same risk. Specifically, the larger n is, the smaller the absolute risk aversion of the insurance company. Figure 1 shows that the insurance company's reinsurance retention share usually increases when the risk aversion factor rises because the insurance company's aversion to risk decreases and its tolerance to risk increases, so it can reduce reinsurance protection and improve its retained share.

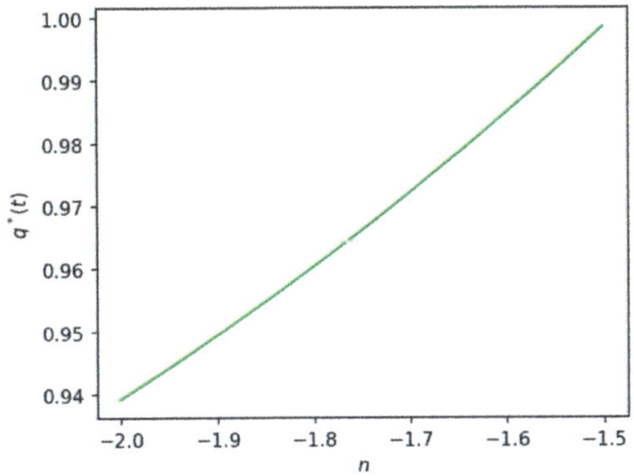

Figure 1. The influence of parameter n on the optimal reinsurance strategy.

Conversely, when n decreases, its reinsurance retention generally decreases. When an insurance company's risk aversion increases, it requires a higher rate of return for the same risk. Therefore, it requires more reinsurance protection to reduce the risk it faces, thereby reducing its retained share.

Figure 2 indicates that the insurance company's optimal retention ratio decreases with the parameter's increase m. The larger m is, the greater the risk aversion of the insurance company. Therefore, if the insurance company chooses to bear less compensation risk, the reinsurance ratio grows and the insurance payment risk the reinsurer bears increases.

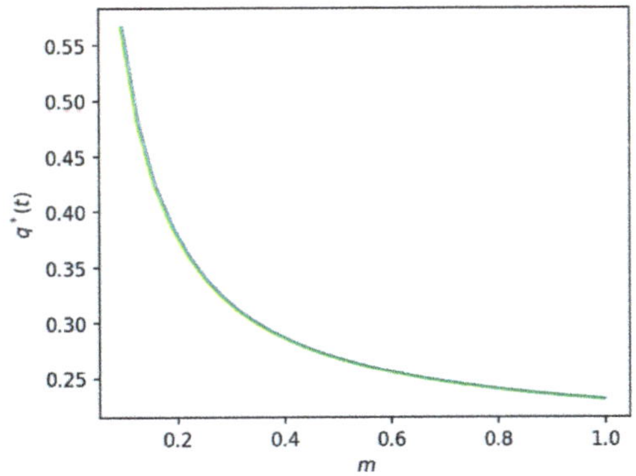

Figure 2. The influence of parameter m on the optimal reinsurance strategy.

In Figure 3, the parameter κ_r represents the average reversion speed of interest rates, which refers to the speed at which market interest rates return from past highs or lows to their long-run average. Typically, the faster interest rates revert to the mean, the more volatile the market. The figure above shows that the optimal retention ratio rises as the parameter κ_r increases. Under the safety load factor condition $\theta_2 = 0.2$, insurance companies may worry that changes in market interest rates will harm their reinsurance asset management and may choose to improve the reinsurance retained share to reduce the risk of their reinsurance asset management. In this case, with faster returns in the interest rate to the average, the insurance company may choose to increase the reinsurance retained share to reduce the risk of its reinsurance asset management.

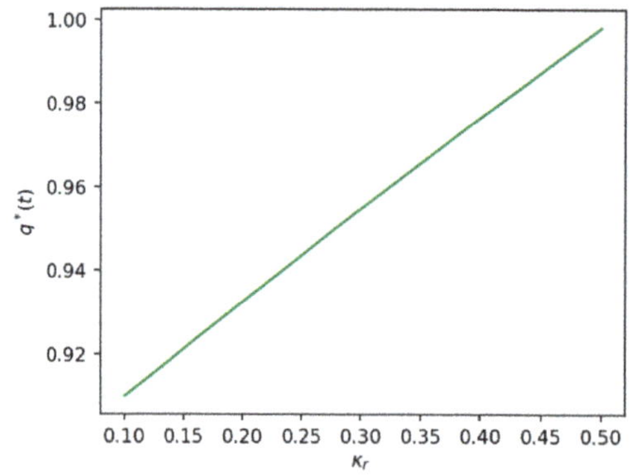

Figure 3. The influence of parameter κ_r on the optimal reinsurance strategy.

In practice, insurance companies usually take some measures to reduce the impact of changes in market interest rates on their reinsurance asset and liability management. For example, insurers can balance interest rate risks between their reinsurance assets and liabilities by holding the assets for longer durations until maturity or by matching liabilities with assets. In addition, insurance companies can also use instruments such as interest rate derivatives to hedge the interest rate risk between their reinsurance assets and liabilities.

In Figure 4, the parameter σ_r represents the interest rate fluctuation. When the parameter σ_r increases, the risk caused by the interest rate fluctuation also grows. The reinsurance strategy of the insurance company is usually more conservative, that is, retaining less self-retained shares and sharing more reinsurance to reduce the impact of interest rate fluctuations on its financial position.

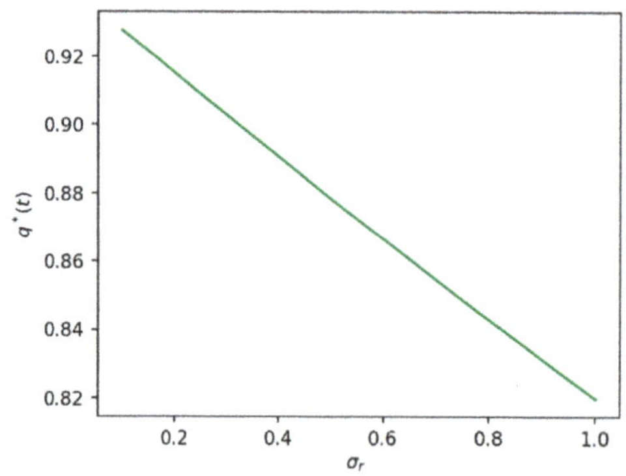

Figure 4. The influence of parameter σ_r on the optimal reinsurance strategy.

Since high-interest rate volatility means that the cash flow risk of insurance companies is more remarkable (unacceptable for insurance companies with a high degree of risk aversion), the insurance company will increase the proportion of reinsurance to reduce its retention and cash flow risk, thereby protecting its financial position. On the other hand, when interest rate volatility is low, insurers typically opt for less reinsurance to obtain a higher rate of return. Low-interest rate volatility means that insurance companies have less of a cash flow risk. Currently, insurance companies can take higher risks in pursuit of higher returns.

Figure 5 gives that as κ_r increases, strategies investing in risky assets $\pi_s(t)$ and strategies $\pi_s(t)$ in risk-free assets grow, while strategies $\pi_b(t)$ in zero-coupon bonds decrease. The high regression speed of the stochastic interest rate in the CIR model means that interest rates change faster, so insurance companies need to adjust their asset allocation more frequently to adapt to changes in the market.

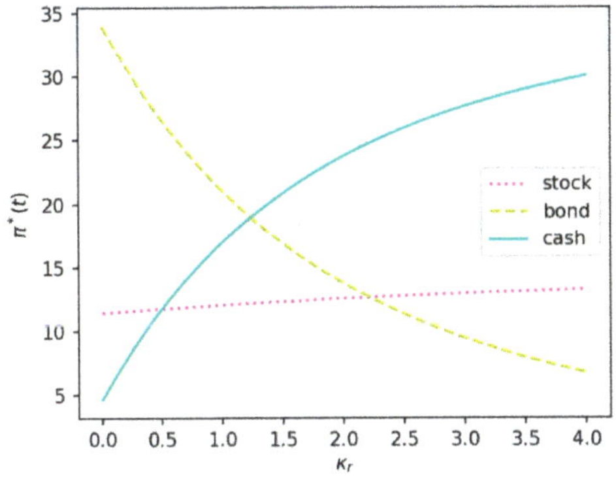

Figure 5. The influence of parameter κ_r on the optimal investment strategy.

In this case, the insurance company will increase its investment in risky assets since they usually have higher yields, which can help improve its return on the investment. At the same time, insurance companies also add their investments in risk-free assets to protect their portfolios from price fluctuations in risky assets.

Instead, insurers reduce their exposure to zero-coupon bonds because these bonds typically have lower yields and their prices are affected by the fluctuations in interest rates. As a result, insurers typically reduce their exposure to zero-coupon bonds to reduce their exposure and raise their returns when the rate of reversion increases.

Figure 6 shows that the optimal investment strategies $\pi_s(t)$ and $\pi_0(t)$ are monotonically decreasing functions of the parameter, while $\pi_b(t)$ is a monotonically increasing function concerning the parameter σ_r. The parameter M determines the volatility of random interest rates. When the volatility of interest rates increases, the uncertainty of risk assets will also improve, making insurance companies invest in risk assets more cautiously. Therefore, in such a situation, insurers may reduce their exposure to risky assets while increasing their exposure to zero-coupon bonds for a more stable return. In addition, since risk-free assets are usually related to interest rates, in the event of increased interest rate volatility, insurance companies may reduce their investment in risk-free assets to avoid the disproportionate impact of interest rate fluctuations on their investments.

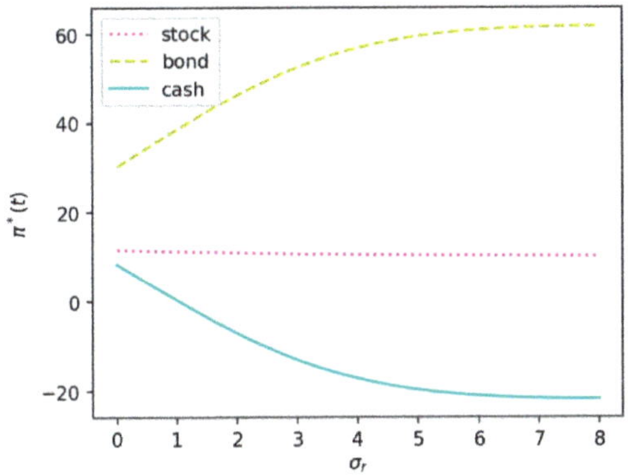

Figure 6. The influence of parameter σ_r on the optimal investment strategy.

Figure 7 shows that as the parameter ξ_r increases, investment $\pi_0(t)$ in risk-free assets decreases, investment $\pi_b(t)$ in zero-coupon bonds goes up, and investment $\pi_s(t)$ in risky assets changes by a small amount. As the parameter ξ_r increases, the market price of random interest rates grows, increasing the uncertainty in future interest rate changes and, in turn, may result in insurance companies reducing their investments in risk-free assets due to the fixed return on such assets yielding lower returns compared to other options when market interest rates rise. Conversely, investments in zero-coupon bonds may increase as they can offer higher returns and serve as a hedge against rising interest rates. Investments in risky assets may change less as insurers strive to achieve higher returns by investing in risky assets to compensate for the reduced returns on risk-free assets and zero-coupon bonds. However, with the increase in stochastic interest rates, the price volatility of risky assets may also increase, leading insurance companies to moderate their investments in risky assets.

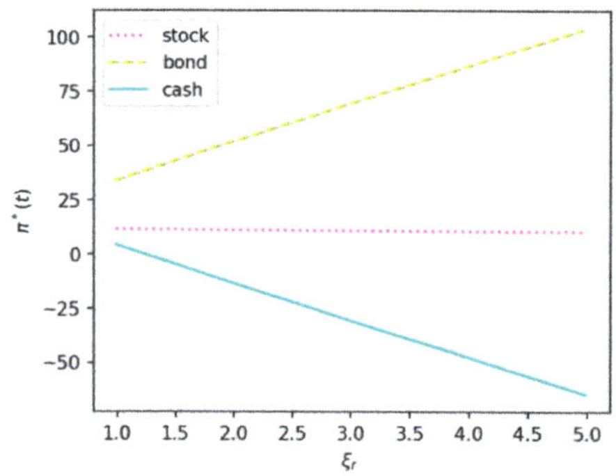

Figure 7. The influence of parameter ξ_r on the optimal investment strategy.

In Figure 8, the optimal strategy $\pi_s(t)$ and zero-coupon bond $\pi_b(t)$ decrease as the parameter κ_v increases, while $\pi_0(t)$ increases. When the average regression speed of risky asset price volatility rises, risky asset price volatility will become more unstable, increasing the risk aversion of insurance companies and leading insurance companies to reduce their investment in risky assets. At the same time, since the price of zero-coupon bonds has an inverse relationship with interest rates, in the event of increased interest rate volatility, insurance companies may reduce their investment in zero-coupon bonds to avoid price falls and losses. On the contrary, risk-free assets like treasury bonds have a lower volatility and more stable returns. Therefore, when the average regression speed of risky asset price volatility goes up, insurance companies may increase investment in these assets.

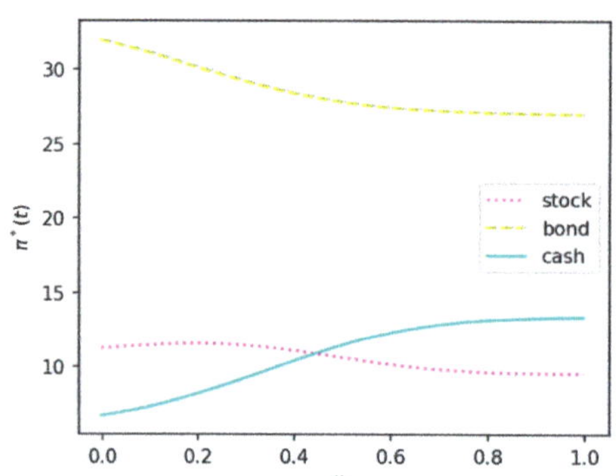

Figure 8. The influence of parameter κ_v on the optimal investment strategy.

Figure 9 indicates that the insurance company's investment $\pi_s(t)$ in risky assets and investment $\pi_0(t)$ in risk-free assets increases as the parameter n goes up. In contrast, its investment $\pi_b(t)$ in zero-coupon bonds decreases as the parameter n increases. The parameter n characterizes the risk aversion factor in the HARA utility function, representing the absolute risk aversion coefficient (ASAC). That is, the larger the value of the parameter, the smaller the absolute risk aversion coefficient.

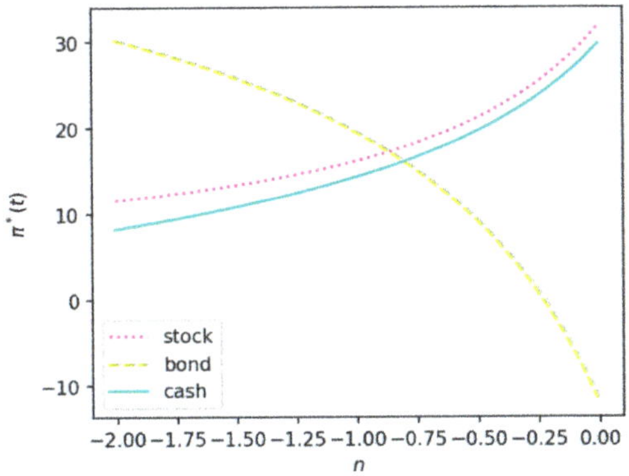

Figure 9. The influence of parameter n on the optimal investment strategy.

Figure 10 shows that investments in a risky asset and a zero-coupon bond decrease as the parameter increases. In contrast, investment in a risk-free asset grows as the parameter m increases because as the parameter goes up, the ASAC also grows. Insurance companies become more risk-averse and invest more in risk-free assets and zero-coupon bonds, reducing investment in risky assets.

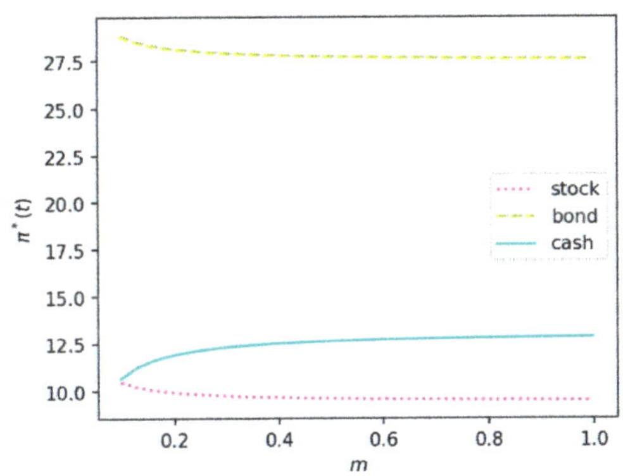

Figure 10. The influence of parameter m on the optimal investment strategy.

We can infer that when risk aversion increases, insurance companies are more inclined to take negligible risks, reducing their investment in risky assets to reduce the risk of their portfolios. In addition, insurers' investments in zero-coupon bonds are usually a good match to their liabilities, thus ensuring sufficient cash flow to cover claims and interest expenses, even at lower yields. With less exposure to risky assets and zero-coupon bonds, insurers may increase exposure to risk-free assets to ensure portfolio liquidity and soundness.

5. Conclusions

In this work, we studied the optimal reinsurance–investment strategy of insurance companies under a stochastic interest rate and stochastic volatility model with the HARA utility function as the criterion. Reinsurance–investment strategies under stochastic volatility models have recently become a hot topic. Assuming that the surplus process of insurance companies obeys the Brownian motion with drift, insurance companies can invest in bank accounts and risky assets by purchasing proportional reinsurance or new business. This paper applied the CIR model to describe the stochastic interest rate, and the Heston model to describe the price process of risky assets. The Legendre transformation and pairwise theory solve the corresponding HJB equations to obtain the analytical expressions for the insurance company's optimal reinsurance–investment strategy and value function. Later, we investigated some sensitivities of the optimal investment strategy. Our results from the numerical example are as follows: the parameters of the financial market in the stochastic interest rate model have an essential impact on the optimal reinsurance strategy; investing in non-performing risky assets with high volatility and low appreciation rates increases the overall risk.

The main contributions of our model are as follows: (1) The risk model considers both insurance and investment risks, and reinsurance is an effective risk management method. (2) We added the random fluctuations of risky and risk-free assets. The premium calculation adopts the variance premium principle, so the random investment of insurance companies is closer to the real financial market than the general geometric model. (3) This work assumes the HARA utility function as the optimal criterion, which has a more general mathematical structure and a broader application.

The modeling framework in this paper is worth extending to other optimal control problems in insurance, such as asset–liability management, optimal pension funds, and optimal life insurance purchases. Further discussions on the reinsurance–investment problem of insurance companies could be made, such as studying the optimal reinsurance–investment problem of investing in multiple risk assets and solving the optimal control problem under different constraints.

Author Contributions: Conceptualization, H.B. and Q.W.; methodology, Y.W.; software, W.W.; validation, H.B. and Y.W.; formal analysis, Q.W. and Y.W.; investigation, W.W.; writing—original draft preparation, Y.W. and Q.W.; writing—review and editing, W.W. and R.M.; visualization, Q.W.; supervision, R.M.; project administration, H.B.; funding acquisition, H.B. All authors have read and agreed to the published version of the manuscript.

Funding: This study has been partly supported by the Scientific Research Funding Project of the Liaoning Province Department of Education (LJKZ0066), the Natural Science Foundation of Liaoning Province (2021-BS-076), the List of Key Science and Technology Projects in Transportation Industry of Ministry of Transport (2022-MS3-102), the Dalian Maritime University Think Tank Special Project (3132023721), the Humanities and Social Science Research General Program of Chinese Ministry of Education (22YJC910011), and the China Postdoctoral Science Foundation Funded Project (2023M733444).

Data Availability Statement: Not applicable.

Conflicts of Interest: The authors declare no conflict of interest.

Appendix A

Proof of Theorem 2.1. According to the standard stochastic optimal control theory, the HJB equation is satisfied by the value function $J(t,v,r,x)$:

$$\begin{aligned}
&\sup_{\Pi(t)\in\mathcal{L}} \Big\{J_t + [c - \theta_2\sigma_0^2 q^2 + 2\theta_2\sigma_0^2 q - h_0 - \theta_2\sigma_0^2 + \pi_s(\xi_s v + \xi_v\mu_s\xi_r r) \\
&+\pi_b\sigma_b\xi_r\mu_s r + rx]J_x + (\varphi_r - \kappa_r r)J_r + \kappa_v(\xi_1 - v)J_v + \tfrac{1}{2}\mu_v^2 v J_{vv} \\
&+\tfrac{1}{2}\sigma_r^2 r J_{rr} + \pi_s\mu_v v J_{xv} + \sigma_r^2 r(\pi_s\xi_v + \pi_b\sigma_b)J_{xr} \\
&+\tfrac{1}{2}[\sigma_r^2 r(\pi_s\xi_v + \pi_b\sigma_b)^2 + \pi_s^2 v + \sigma_0^2 q^2]J_{xx}\Big\} = 0.
\end{aligned} \tag{A1}$$

Assume that $L(t,v,r,x) \in C^{1,2,2,2}([0,T] \times R^+ \times R^+ \times R^+)$ is a solution to the HJB Equation (A1); according to the first-order condition for extremes, look for the derivatives of the HJB equation in Equation (A1) $q(t)$, $\pi_s(t)$ and $\pi_b(t)$; and let the derivatives be zero. Then, the optimal solution can be found as follows:

$$q^*(t) = \frac{\theta_2 L_x}{\theta_2 L_x - L_{xx}}, \tag{A2}$$

$$\pi_s^*(t) = -\xi_s \frac{L_x}{L_{xx}} - \mu_v \frac{L_{xv}}{L_{xx}}, \tag{A3}$$

$$\pi_b^*(t) = \frac{\xi_s \xi_v - \xi_r}{\sigma_b} \frac{L_x}{L_{xx}} + \frac{\mu_v \xi_v - \xi_r}{\sigma_b} \frac{L_{xv}}{L_{xx}} + \frac{v}{\sigma_b} \frac{L_{xr}}{L_{xx}}. \tag{A4}$$

Combining (A2), (A3), and (A4) into the HJB equation, gives

$$\begin{aligned} &L_t + (c - h_0 - \theta_2 \sigma_0^2 + rx)L_x + (\varphi_r - \kappa_r r)L_r + \kappa_v(\xi_1 - v)L_v + \tfrac{1}{2}\mu_v^2 v L_{vv} \\ &+ \tfrac{1}{2}\sigma_r^2 r L_{rr} + \frac{\theta_2^2 \sigma_0^2 L_x^2}{\theta_2 L_x - L_{xx}} - \sigma_r^2 r \frac{(L_{xr} - \xi_r L_x)^2}{2L_{xx}} - v \frac{(\xi_s L_x + \mu_v L_{xv})^2}{2L_{xx}} = 0. \end{aligned} \tag{A5}$$

Equation (A5) is a second-order nonlinear partial differential equation and the form of the solution to Equation (A5) cannot be directly guessed due to the complexity of the HARA utility function and its boundary conditions.

We apply the methods and techniques of the Legendre transformation and pairwise theory to transform Equation (A5) into a second-order linear partial differential equation and ultimately find its shown solution.

Definition A1. *Let $f : R^n \to R$ be a convex function for $z > 0$. Define the Legendre transformation of f as follows:*

$$L(z) = \max_x \{f(x) - zx\}, \tag{A6}$$

which is called the Legendre dual function of function $f(x)$.

If $f(x)$ is a strictly convex function, then there is a unique maximum point in (A6) and its maximum value is marked as x_0, according to the first-order condition

$$\frac{df(x)}{dx} - z = 0,$$

where the unique solution can be obtained as follows:

$$L(z) = f(x_0) - zx_0.$$

According to Gao [38], with the definitions of (A6) and the convexity of the value function $L(t,v,r,x)$, the Legendre transformation is defined as follows:

$$\hat{L}(t,v,r,x) = \sup_{x>0} \{L(t,v,r,x) - zx\}. \tag{A7}$$

Upon denoting $l(t,v,r,x)$ as the optimal value of the variable x and $0 < t < T$, we assume that $l(t,v,r,x)$ satisfies the following equation:

$$l(t,v,r,x) = \inf_{x>0} \{x | L(t,v,r,x) \geq zx + \hat{L}(t,v,r,x)\},$$

where we then obtain the relation between $l(t,v,r,x)$ and $\hat{L}(t,v,r,x)$

$$l(t,v,r,x) = -\hat{L}(t,v,r,x), \tag{A8}$$

Therefore $l(t,v,r,x)$ and $\hat{L}(t,v,r,x)$ are both pairwise functions of the value function $L(t,v,r,x)$. In solving the optimal reinsurance strategy, the function $l(t,v,r,x)$ is more straightforward to calculate numerically, so the function $l(t,v,r,x)$ is chosen for the study. Further calculation gives

$$L_x = z, \tag{A9}$$

$$l(t,v,r,z) = x, \tag{A10}$$

$$\hat{L}(t,v,r,z) = L(t,v,r,l) - zl. \tag{A11}$$

For Equation (A11), calculating the partial derivatives of each other with respect to (t,v,r,z) gives

$$\begin{aligned}
L_t = \hat{L}_t,\ L_{xr} &= -\tfrac{\hat{L}_{rz}}{\hat{L}_{zz}}, \\
L_{xr} = z, L_{xx} &= -\tfrac{1}{\hat{L}_{zz}}, \\
L_r = \hat{L}_r, L_{rr} &= \hat{L}_{rr} - \tfrac{\hat{L}_{rz}^2}{\hat{L}_{zz}}, \\
L_v = \hat{L}_v, L_{vv} &= \hat{L}_{vv} - \tfrac{\hat{L}_{vz}^2}{\hat{L}_{zz}}, \\
L_{xv} = -\tfrac{\hat{L}_{vz}}{\hat{L}_{zz}}, L_{vr} &= \hat{L}_{vr} - \tfrac{\hat{L}_{rz}\hat{L}_{vz}}{\hat{L}_{zz}}.
\end{aligned} \tag{A12}$$

Then, at the terminal moment T, define

$$\hat{L}(T,v,r,z) = \sup_{x>0}\{L(T,v,r,x) - zx\},$$

$$l(T,v,r,z) = \inf_{x>0}\{x \mid L(T,v,r,x) \geq zx + \hat{L}(T,v,r,z)\},$$

where we then have

$$l(T,v,r,z) = (U')^{-1}(z),$$

where $(U')^{-1}(z)$ is the inverse of marginal utility.

Substituting (A12) into (A5) with respect to the value function gives the dyadic function $\hat{L}$:

$$\begin{aligned}
&\hat{L}_t + (c - h_0 - \theta_2\sigma_0^2 + rl)z + (\varphi_r - \kappa_r r)\hat{L}_r + \kappa_v(\xi_1 - v)\hat{L}_v \\
&+\tfrac{1}{2}\mu_v^2 v\left(\hat{L}_{vv} - \tfrac{\hat{L}_{vz}^2}{\hat{L}_{zz}}\right) + \tfrac{1}{2}\sigma_r^2 r\left(\hat{L}_{rr} - \tfrac{\hat{L}_{rz}^2}{\hat{L}_{zz}}\right) + \tfrac{\theta_2^2\sigma_0^2 z^2\hat{L}_{zz}}{\hat{L}_{zz}\theta_2 z+1} \\
&+\sigma_r^2 r\tfrac{\hat{L}_{zz}(z-\xi_r z)^2}{2} + v\tfrac{\left(z\hat{L}_{zz}\xi_s+\mu_v\hat{L}_{vz}\right)^2}{2\hat{L}_{zz}} = 0,
\end{aligned}$$

and further simplification gives

$$\begin{aligned}
&\hat{L}_t + cz - h_0 z - \theta_2\sigma_0^2 z + rlz + (\varphi_r - \kappa_r r)\hat{L}_r + \kappa_v(\xi_1 - v)\hat{L}_v \\
&+\tfrac{1}{2}\mu_v^2 v\hat{L}_{vv} + \tfrac{1}{2}\sigma_r^2 r\hat{L}_{rr} - \tfrac{1}{2}\sigma_r^2 r\tfrac{\hat{L}_{rz}^2}{\hat{L}_{zz}} + \tfrac{1}{2}vz^2\hat{L}_{zz}\xi_s^2 \\
&+z^2\hat{L}_{zz}\left(\tfrac{\theta_2^2\sigma_0^2}{\hat{L}_{zz}\theta_2 z+1} + \sigma_r^2 r\tfrac{(1-\xi_r)^2}{2}\right) + vz\xi_s\mu_v\hat{L}_{vz} = 0.
\end{aligned} \tag{A13}$$

Differentiating z on both sides of Equation (A13) simultaneously yields

$$\begin{aligned}
&\hat{L}_{tz} + c - h_0 - \theta_2\sigma_0^2 + rl + rl_z z + (\varphi_r - \kappa_r r)\hat{L}_{rz} + \kappa_v(\xi_1 - v)\hat{L}_{vz} \\
&+\tfrac{1}{2}\mu_v^2 v\hat{L}_{vvz} - \tfrac{1}{2}\sigma_r^2 r\tfrac{\left(2\hat{L}_{rz}\hat{L}_{rzz}\hat{L}_{zz}+\hat{L}_{rz}^2\hat{L}_{zzz}\right)}{\hat{L}_{zz}^2} \\
&+\tfrac{1}{2}\sigma_r^2 r\hat{L}_{rrz} + z\hat{L}_{zz}\left(\tfrac{2\theta_2^2\sigma_0^2}{\hat{L}_{zz}\theta_2 z+1} + \sigma_r^2 r(1-\xi_r)^2\right) \\
&+z^2\hat{L}_{zzz}\left(\tfrac{\theta_2^2\sigma_0^2}{\hat{L}_{zz}\theta_2 z+1} + \tfrac{\sigma_r^2 r(1-\xi_r)^2}{2}\right) + z^2\hat{L}_{zz}\tfrac{\theta_2^2\sigma_0^2\left(\hat{L}_{zz}\theta_2+\hat{L}_{zzz}\theta_2 z\right)}{\left(\hat{L}_{zz}\theta_2 z+1\right)^2} \\
&+v\xi_s\mu_v\hat{L}_{vz} + vz\xi_s\mu_v\hat{L}_{vzz} + vz\hat{L}_{zz}\xi_s^2 + \tfrac{1}{2}vz^2\hat{L}_{zzz}\xi_s^2 = 0.
\end{aligned}$$

Combining Equation (21) yields a linear differential equation for the dyadic function l:

$$\begin{aligned}&l_t - c + h_0 + \theta_2\sigma_0^2 - rl - rl_z z + (\varphi_r - \kappa_r r)l_r + \kappa_v(\xi_1 - v)l_v \\ &+\tfrac{1}{2}\mu_v^2 v l_{vv} - \tfrac{1}{2}\sigma_r^2 r\tfrac{(2l_r l_{rz} l_z + l_r^2 l_{zz})}{l_z^2} + \tfrac{1}{2}\sigma_r^2 r l_{rr} \\ &+z l_z\left(\tfrac{2\theta_2^2\sigma_0^2}{1-l_z\theta_2 z} + \sigma_r^2 r(1-\xi_r)^2\right) + z^2 l_{zz}\left(\tfrac{\theta_2^2\sigma_0^2}{1-l_z\theta_2 z} + \tfrac{\sigma_r^2 r(1-\xi_r)^2}{2}\right) \\ &-z^2 l_z\tfrac{\theta_2^2\sigma_0^2(l_z\theta_2 + l_{zz}\theta_2 z)}{(1-l_z\theta_2 z)^2} + v\xi_s\mu_v l_v + vz\xi_s\mu_v l_{vz} \\ &+vzl_z\xi_s^2 + \tfrac{1}{2}vz^2 l_{zz}\xi_s^2 = 0.\end{aligned} \tag{A14}$$

The quadratic nonlinear partial differential Equation (21) is transformed into a second-order linear partial differential Equation (A14) utilizing the Legendre transform and the pairwise theory.

By solving Equation (A14), we can obtain the optimal reinsurance–investment strategy for the insurance company. Using the HARA utility as a criterion and using the boundary conditions yields

$$l(T,v,r,z) = (U')^{-1}(z) = \frac{1-n}{m}\left(z^{\frac{1}{n-1}} - \gamma\right). \tag{A15}$$

Based on the idea of equality, it can be conjectured that the solution of Equation (A14) has the following structure:

$$l(t,v,r,x) = \frac{1-n}{m}z^{\frac{1}{n-1}}f(t,v,r) - \frac{1-n}{m}\gamma g(t,v,r) + G(t,v,r), \tag{A16}$$

where the boundary conditions are $f(T,v,r) = 1, g(t,v,r) = 1, G(t,v,r) = 0$.

Calculating the partial derivative for Equation (A16) gives

$$\begin{aligned}&l_t = \tfrac{1-n}{m}z^{\frac{1}{n-1}}f_t - \tfrac{1-n}{m}\gamma g_t + G_t, l_r = \tfrac{1-n}{m}z^{\frac{1}{n-1}}f_r - \tfrac{1-n}{m}\gamma g_r + G_r, \\ &l_{rr} = \tfrac{1-n}{m}z^{\frac{1}{n-1}}f_{rr} - \tfrac{1-n}{m}\gamma g_{rr} + G_{rr}, l_z = \tfrac{1-n}{m}\tfrac{1}{n-1}z^{\frac{1}{n-1}-1}f, \\ &l_{zz} = \tfrac{1-n}{m}\tfrac{2-n}{(n-1)^2}z^{\frac{1}{n-1}-2}f, l_{rz} = \tfrac{1-n}{m}\tfrac{1}{n-1}z^{\frac{1}{n-1}-1}f_r, \\ &l_v = \tfrac{1-n}{m}z^{\frac{1}{n-1}}f_v - \tfrac{1-n}{m}\gamma g_v + G_v,\ l_{vv} = \tfrac{1-n}{m}z^{\frac{1}{n-1}}f_{vv} - \tfrac{1-n}{m}\gamma g_{vv} + G_{vv}, \\ &l_{vz} = \tfrac{1-n}{m}\tfrac{1}{n-1}z^{\frac{1}{n-1}-1}f_v.\end{aligned} \tag{A17}$$

Substituting Equations (A16) and (A17) into Equation (A14) and simplifying gives

$$\begin{aligned}&\tfrac{1-n}{m}z^{\frac{1}{n-1}}[f_t - \tfrac{n}{n-1}rf + (\varphi_r - \kappa_r r)f_r + \kappa_v(\xi_1 - v)f_v + \tfrac{1}{2}\mu_v^2 v f_{vv} + \tfrac{1}{2}\sigma_r^2 r f_{rr} \\ &+\tfrac{n}{n-1}v\xi_s\mu_v f_v + \tfrac{2-n}{2(n-1)^2}f(v\xi_s^2 + \tfrac{2\theta_2^2\sigma_0^2}{v^2} + \sigma_r^2 r(1-\xi_r)^2)] \\ &+\tfrac{1-n}{m}\gamma[-g_t + rg - (\varphi_r - \kappa_r r)g_r - \kappa_v(\xi_1 - v)g_v - \tfrac{1}{2}\mu_v^2 v g_{vv} \\ &-\tfrac{1}{2}\sigma_r^2 r g_{rr} - v\xi_s\mu_v] + G_t - c + h_0 + \theta_2\sigma_0^2 - rG - (\varphi_r - \kappa_r r)G_r \\ &+\kappa_v(\xi_1 - v)G_v + v\xi_s\mu_v G_v + \tfrac{1}{2}\mu_v^2 v G_{vv} + \tfrac{1}{2}\sigma_r^2 r G_{rr} = 0.\end{aligned} \tag{A18}$$

By eliminating the dependence on z and γ in (A18), Equation (A18) can be divided into three parts concerning f, g, and G, where we let each be equal to zero and obtain the following three equations:

$$\begin{cases} f_t - \tfrac{n}{n-1}rf + (\varphi_r - \kappa_r r)f_r + \kappa_v(\xi_1 - v)f_v + \tfrac{1}{2}\mu_v^2 v f_{vv} + \tfrac{1}{2}\sigma_r^2 r f_{rr} \\ +\tfrac{n}{n-1}v\xi_s\mu_v f_v + \tfrac{2-n}{2(n-1)^2}f\left(v\xi_s^2 + \tfrac{2\theta_2^2\sigma_0^2}{v^2} + \sigma_r^2 r(1-\xi_r)^2\right) = 0, \\ f(T,v,r) = 1; \end{cases} \tag{A19}$$

$$\begin{cases} -g_t + rg - (\varphi_r - \kappa_r r)g_r - \kappa_v(\xi_1 - v)g_v - \frac{1}{2}\mu_v^2 v g_{vv} - \frac{1}{2}\sigma_r^2 r g_{rr} \\ -v\xi_s\mu_v g_v = 0, \\ g(T,v,r) = 1; \end{cases} \tag{A20}$$

$$\begin{cases} G_t - c + h_0 + \theta_2\sigma_0^2 - rG - (\varphi_r - \kappa_r r)G_r \\ +\kappa_v(\xi_1 - v)G_v + v\xi_s\mu_v G_v + \frac{1}{2}\mu_v^2 v G_{vv} + \frac{1}{2}\sigma_r^2 r G_{rr} = 0. \\ G(T,v,r) = 0. \end{cases} \tag{A21}$$

Equations (A19)–(A21) will be separately solved below.

Firstly, for the differential Equation (A19), assume that the solution has the following structure

$$f(t,v,r) = e^{A_1(t)+A_2(t)v+A_3(t)r}, \tag{A22}$$

where the boundary condition is $A_1(T) = A_2(T) = A_3(T) = 0$.

Taking the higher-order partial derivatives of each end of Equation (A22) for t, v, and r yields

$$\begin{aligned} f_t &= f(t,v,r)\left(A_1'(t) + A_2'(t)v + A_3'(t)r\right), \\ f_v &= f(t,v,r)A_2(t), f_{vv} = f(t,v,r)A_2^2(t), \\ f_r &= f(t,v,r)A_3(t), f_{rr} = f(t,v,r)A_3^2(t). \end{aligned} \tag{A23}$$

Substituting the above partial derivative result (A23) into Equation (A19) gives

$$\begin{aligned} &f\left[A_1'(t) + \varphi_r A_3(t) + \kappa_v\xi_1 A_2(t) + \tfrac{1}{2}\sigma_r^2 r A_3^2(t) + \tfrac{2-n}{2(n-1)^2}\tfrac{2\theta_2^2\sigma_0^2}{v^2}\right] \\ &+fv\left[A_2'(t) - \kappa_v A_2(t) + \tfrac{1}{2}\mu_v^2 A_2^2(t) + \tfrac{n}{n-1}\xi_s\mu_v A_2(t) + \tfrac{2-n}{2(n-1)^2}\xi_s^2\right] \\ &+fr\left[A_3'(t) - \tfrac{n}{n-1} - \kappa_r A_3(t) + \tfrac{1}{2}\sigma_r^2 r A_3^2(t) + \tfrac{2-n}{2(n-1)^2}\sigma_r^2(1-\xi_r)^2\right] = 0. \end{aligned}$$

Eliminating the dependence on v and r in the above equation gives the following three differential equations:

$$\begin{aligned} &A_1'(t) + \varphi_r A_3(t) + \kappa_v\xi_1 A_2(t) + \tfrac{1}{2}\sigma_r^2 r A_3^2(t) + \tfrac{2-n}{2(n-1)^2}(\xi_s^2 \\ &+\tfrac{2\theta_2^2\sigma_0^2}{v^2} + \sigma_r^2 r(1-\xi_r)^2) = 0, \end{aligned} \tag{A24}$$

$$A_2'(t) + \left(\frac{n}{n-1}\xi_s\mu_v - \kappa_v\right)A_2(t) + \frac{1}{2}\mu_v^2 A_2^2(t) + \frac{2-n}{2(n-1)^2}\xi_s^2 = 0, \tag{A25}$$

$$A_3'(t) + \frac{2-n}{2(n-1)^2}\sigma_r^2(1-\xi_r)^2 - \frac{n}{n-1} - \kappa_r A_3(t) + \frac{1}{2}\sigma_r^2 r A_3^2(t) = 0. \tag{A26}$$

Equations (A25) and (A26) are equations $A_2(t)$ and $A_3(t)$, respectively, that can be solved directly, while Equation (A24) is the equation on $A_1(t)$, $A_2(t)$ and $A_3(t)$. So, we can solve $A_1(t)$, $A_2(t)$ and $A_3(t)$ as follows:

Since Equation (A25) is a Riccati equation, first find the quadratic equation in Equation (A25) for $A_2(t)$ as follows:

$$\frac{1}{2}\mu_v^2 A_2^2(t) + \left(\frac{n}{n-1}\xi_s\mu_v - \kappa_v\right)A_2(t) + \frac{2-n}{2(n-1)^2}\xi_s^2 = 0. \tag{A27}$$

To simplify our calculation later, we can state that

$$a_1 = \frac{1}{2}\mu_v^2, b_1 = \frac{n}{n-1}\xi_s\mu_v - \kappa_v, c_1 = \frac{2-n}{2(n-1)^2}\xi_s^2, \tag{A28}$$

and the discriminant can be obtained as follows:

$$\Delta_1 = b_1^2 - 4a_1c_1 = \left(\frac{n}{n-1}\xi_s\mu_v - \kappa_v\right)^2 - \mu_v^2\frac{2-n}{(n-1)^2}\xi_s^2. \tag{A29}$$

Suppose that $\Delta_1 > 0$; then, Equation (A29) has two distinct roots at this point, denoted as x_1 and x_2 and

$$x_1 = \frac{-b_1 + \sqrt{\Delta_1}}{2a_1}, x_2 = \frac{-b_1 - \sqrt{\Delta_1}}{2a_1}.$$

Then, Equation (A25) can be written in the following form:

$$a_1(A_2(t) - x_1)(A_2(t) - x_2) = -A_2'(t).$$

Separating the variables in the above equation and integrating both sides at the same time gives

$$-a_1(T-t) = \frac{1}{x_1 - x_2}\int_t^T \left(\frac{1}{A_2(t) - x_1} - \frac{1}{A_2(t) - x_2}\right) dA_2(t). \tag{A30}$$

Integrating the two ends of Equation (A25) gives

$$A_2(t) = \frac{x_1x_2\left[1 - e^{-a_1(x_1-x_2)(T-t)}\right]}{x_1 - x_2e^{-a_1(x_1-x_2)(T-t)}}. \tag{A31}$$

The procedure for solving Equation (A25) is similar to that described above. Finding Equation (A25) about $A_3(t)$ of the quadratic equation is as follows:

$$\frac{1}{2}\sigma_r^2 rA_3^2(t) - \kappa_r A_3(t) + \frac{2-n}{2(n-1)^2}\sigma_r^2(1-\xi_r)^2 - \frac{n}{n-1} = 0. \tag{A32}$$

Again, for simplifying purposes, we can have

$$a_2 = \frac{1}{2}\sigma_r^2 r, b_2 = -\kappa_r, c_2 = \frac{2-n}{2(n-1)^2}\sigma_r^2(1-\xi_r)^2 - \frac{n}{n-1}, \tag{A33}$$

then, the discriminant becomes

$$\Delta_2 = b_2^2 - 4a_2c_2 = \kappa_r^2 - \sigma_r^2 r\left(\frac{2-n}{(n-1)^2}\sigma_r^2(1-\xi_r)^2 - \frac{2n}{n-1}\right). \tag{A34}$$

Suppose that $\Delta_2 > 0$; then, the equation has two distinct roots at this point, denoted as x_3 and x_4 respectively, and

$$x_3 = \frac{-b_2 + \sqrt{\Delta_2}}{2a_2}, x_4 = \frac{-b_2 - \sqrt{\Delta_2}}{2a_2}.$$

Then, Equation (A26) can be noted in the following form:

$$a_2(A_3(t) - x_3)(A_3(t) - x_4) = -A_3'(t). \tag{A35}$$

Separating the variables in this equation and integrating both sides at the same time gives

$$-a_2(T-t) = \tfrac{1}{x_3-x_4}\int_t^T \left(\tfrac{1}{A_3(t)-x_3} - \tfrac{1}{A_3(t)-x_4}\right) dA_3(t).$$

Solving this integral equation yields

$$A_3(t) = \frac{x_3 x_4\left[1 - e^{-a_2(x_3-x_4)(T-t)}\right]}{x_3 - x_4 e^{-a_2(x_3-x_4)(T-t)}}.$$

To solve $A_1(t)$, note Equation (A24) in the following form:

$$\begin{aligned} A_1'(t) = {} & A_3'(t) - (\varphi_r + \kappa_r)A_3(t) - \tfrac{2-n}{2(n-1)^2}\left(\xi_s^2 + \tfrac{2\theta_2^2\sigma_0^2}{v^2}\right) \\ & -\tfrac{n}{n-1} - \kappa_v\xi_1 A_2(t). \end{aligned} \tag{A36}$$

Integrating both ends of the above equation from t to T, solves the differential equation and gives $A_1(t)$:

$$\begin{aligned} A_1(t) = {} & A_3(t) + (\varphi_r + \kappa_r)\int_t^T A_3(s)ds + \kappa_v\xi_1\int_t^T A_2(s)ds \\ & + \left[\tfrac{2-n}{2(n-1)^2}\left(\xi_s^2 + \tfrac{2\theta_2^2\sigma_0^2}{v^2}\right) + \tfrac{n}{n-1}\right](T-t). \end{aligned} \tag{A37}$$

At this point, we have obtained the expression in Equation (A37) as

$$f(t,v,r) = e^{A_1(t)+A_2(t)v+A_3(t)r},$$

where the solutions of $A_1(t)$, $A_2(t)$ and $A_3(t)$ are given using (A31), (A36), and (A37), respectively.

Then, we solve Equation (A20), assuming that the solutions have the following structure, where

$$g(t,v,r) = e^{A_4(t)+A_5(t)v+A_6(t)r}, \tag{A38}$$

and taking the high-order partial derivatives of each end of Equation (A38) with respect to t, v, r gives the following:

$$\begin{aligned} & g_t = g(t,v,r)\left(A_4'(t) + A_5'(l)v + A_6'(t)r\right), \\ & g_v = g(t,v,r)A_5(t), g_{vv} = g(t,v,r)A_5^2(t), \\ & g_r = g(t,v,r)A_6(t), g_{rr} = g(t,v,r)A_6^2(t). \end{aligned} \tag{A39}$$

Substituting the partial derivative results into Equation (A20) and simplifying gives

$$\begin{aligned} & g\left(-A_4'(t) - \varphi_r A_6(t) - \kappa_v\xi_1 A_5(t)\right) + gv\left[-A_5'(t) + (\kappa_v - \xi_s\mu_v)A_5(t)\right. \\ & \left.-\tfrac{1}{2}\mu_v^2 A_5^2(t)\right] + gr\left[-A_6'(t) + 1 + \kappa_r A_6(t) - \tfrac{1}{2}\sigma_r^2 A_6^2(t)\right] = 0. \end{aligned} \tag{A40}$$

Eliminating the dependence on v and r in the above equation, we obtained the following three differential equations:

$$-A_4'(t) - \varphi_r A_6(t) - \kappa_v\xi_1 A_5(t) = 0, \tag{A41}$$

$$-A_5'(t) + (\kappa_v - \xi_s\mu_v)A_5(t) - \frac{1}{2}\mu_v^2 A_5^2(t) = 0, \tag{A42}$$

$$-A_6'(t) + 1 + \kappa_r A_6(t) - \frac{1}{2}\sigma_r^2 A_6^2(t) = 0. \tag{A43}$$

where the boundary condition is $A_4(T) = A_5(T) = A_6(T) = 0$.

First, we solve $A_5(t)$. Equation (A42) is a simple first-order linear differential equation, the solution of which can be obtained as follows:

$$A_5(t) = \frac{\xi_s}{2\mu_v}\left(1 - e^{(\kappa_v - \xi_s\mu_v)(T-t)}\right). \tag{A44}$$

Second, we solve Equation (A43), which is a Riccati equation. We first solve the quadratic equation in (A43) with respect to $A_6(t)$:

$$-\frac{1}{2}\sigma_r^2 A_6^2(t) + \kappa_r A_6(t) + 1 = 0. \tag{A45}$$

For simplification of subsequent calculations, we note

$$a_3 = -\frac{1}{2}\sigma_r^2, b_3 = \kappa_r, c_3 = 1,$$

and the discriminant is obtained as

$$\Delta_3 = b_3^2 - 4a_3c_3 = \kappa_r^2 + 2\sigma_r^2 > 0, \tag{A46}$$

where its two dissimilar roots are as follows:

$$x_6 = \frac{-b_3 + \sqrt{\Delta_3}}{2a_3}, x_7 = \frac{-b_3 - \sqrt{\Delta_3}}{2a_3}.$$

Then, Equation (A43) can be written in the following form:

$$a_3(A_6(t) - x_6)(A_6(t) - x_7) = A_6'(t).$$

Separating the variables in the above equation and integrating both sides at the same time gives the following:

$$a_3(T-t) = \tfrac{1}{x_6 - x_7}\int_t^T \left(\tfrac{1}{A_6(s) - x_6} - \tfrac{1}{A_6(s) - x_7}\right) dA_6(t).$$

Solving this integral equation yields $A_6(t)$, as follows:

$$A_6(t) = \frac{x_6x_7\left[1 - e^{a_3(x_6 - x_7)(T-t)}\right]}{x_6 - x_7e^{a_3(x_6 - x_7)(T-t)}}. \tag{A47}$$

Finally, to calculate $A_4(t)$, integrate both ends of Equation (A41):

$$A_4(t) = \int_t^T \varphi_r A_6(s) + \kappa_v\xi_1 A_5(s) ds. \tag{A48}$$

At this point, we obtain the formulation in Equation (A38) as

$$g(t, v, r) = e^{A_4(t) + A_5(t)v + A_6(t)r},$$

where the solutions of $A_4(t)$, $A_5(t)$ and $A_6(t)$ are given using Equations (A44), (A47) and (A48), respectively.

Then, we solve Equation (A21), introducing the following variational operator for the arbitrary function $G(t, v, r)$:

$$\begin{aligned} \nabla G(t, v, r) = &-rG - (\varphi_r - \kappa_r r)G_r + \kappa_v(\xi_1 - v)G_v \\ &+ v\xi_s\mu_v G_v + \tfrac{1}{2}\mu_v^2 v G_{vv} + \tfrac{1}{2}\sigma_r^2 r G_{rr}. \end{aligned} \tag{A49}$$

Then, the differential Equation (A21) can be rewritten as follows:

$$\begin{cases} G_t + \nabla G(t,v,r) - c + h_0 + \theta_2\sigma_0^2 = 0, \\ G(T,v,r) = 0. \end{cases} \tag{A50}$$

On the other hand, the calculation leads to the following:

$$\begin{aligned} G_t &= (-c + h_0 + \theta_2\sigma_0^2)\left(\int_t^T \hat{G}_s ds - \hat{G}(T,v,r)\right), \\ \nabla G(t,v,r) &= (-c + h_0 + \theta_2\sigma_0^2) \int_t^T \nabla\hat{G}(T,v,r)ds. \end{aligned} \tag{A51}$$

Substituting the above equation into Equation (A50) and simplifying it gives

$$\left(-c + h_0 + \theta_2\sigma_0^2\right)\left(\int_t^T (\hat{G}_s + \nabla G(t,v,r)\Big)ds - \hat{G}(t,v,r) + 1\right) = 0, \tag{A52}$$

$$G(t,v,r) = \left(-c + h_0 + \theta_2\sigma_0^2\right)\int_t^T \hat{G}(t,v,r)ds, \tag{A53}$$

and $\hat{G}(t,v,r)$ meets the following partial differential equation:

$$\begin{cases} \hat{G}_t - c + h_0 + \theta_2\sigma_0^2 - r\hat{G} - (\varphi_r - \kappa_r r)\hat{G}_r \\ +\kappa_v(\xi_1 - v)\hat{G}_v + v\xi_s\mu_v\hat{G}_v + \frac{1}{2}\mu_v^2 v\hat{G}_{vv} + \frac{1}{2}\sigma_r^2 r\hat{G}_{rr} = 0, \\ \hat{G}(T,v,r) = 0. \end{cases} \tag{A54}$$

In summary, we solve for $L(t,v,r,x)$:

$$\begin{aligned} \frac{L_x}{L_{xx}} &= -z\hat{L}_{zz} = zl_z = \frac{1-n}{m}\frac{2-n}{(n-1)^2} z^{\frac{1}{n-1}-1} f, \\ &= -\frac{1}{1-n}\left(x + \frac{1-n}{m}\gamma g(t,v,r) - G(t,v,r)\right), \\ \frac{L_{xr}}{L_{xx}} &= \hat{L}_{rz} = -l_r = -\frac{1-n}{m} z^{\frac{1}{n-1}} f_t + \frac{1-n}{m}\gamma g_t - G_t \\ &= -\left(x + \frac{1-n}{m}\gamma g(t,v,r) - G(t,v,r)\right)\frac{f_r}{f(t,v,r)} + \frac{1-n}{m}\gamma g_r, \\ \frac{L_{xv}}{L_{xx}} &= \hat{L}_{vz} = -l_v = -\frac{1-n}{m} z^{\frac{1}{n-1}} f_v + \frac{1-n}{m}\gamma g_v - G_v \\ &= -\left(x + \frac{1-n}{m}\gamma g(t,v,r) - G(t,v,r)\right)\frac{f_v}{f(t,v,r)} + \frac{1-n}{m}\gamma g_v. \end{aligned} \tag{A55}$$

On the other hand, considering $l(t,v,r) = x$ and Equation (A16) leads to the following:

$$z = \frac{m}{1-n}x + \gamma g(t,v,r) - \frac{m}{1-n}G(t,v,r)^{n-1} f^{1-n}(t,v,r). \tag{A56}$$

Since $L_x = z$, the optimal solution of the HJB Equation (A1) is obtained via integration, as follows:

$$L^*_{HARA}(t,v,r,x) = \frac{1-n}{mn}\left(\frac{m}{1-n}x + \gamma g(t,v,r) - \frac{m}{1-n}G(t,v,r)\right)^n f^{1-n}(t,v,r). \tag{A57}$$

In summary, we can obtain the optimal reinsurance–investment strategy under the HARA utility function. The proof is completed.

References

1. Święch, A. Another Approach to the Existence of Value Functions of Stochastic Differential Games. *J. Math. Anal. Appl.* **1996**, *204*, 884–897. [CrossRef]
2. Soner, H.M.; Touzi, N. Stochastic Target Problems, Dynamic Programming, and Viscosity Solutions. *SIAM J. Control Optim.* **2002**, *41*, 404–424. [CrossRef]

3. Rami, M.A.; Moore, J.B.; Zhou, X.Y. Indefinite Stochastic Linear Quadratic Control and Generalized Differential Riccati Equation. *SIAM J. Control Optim. Soc. Ind. Appl. Math.* **2002**, *40*, 1296–1311. [CrossRef]
4. Zhu, J.; Li, S. Time-Consistent Investment and Reinsurance Strategies for Mean-Variance Insurers under Stochastic Interest Rate and Stochastic Volatility. *Mathematics* **2020**, *8*, 2183. [CrossRef]
5. Ali, I.; Khan, S.U. A Dynamic Competition Analysis of Stochastic Fractional Differential Equation Arising in Finance via Pseudospectral Method. *Mathematics* **2023**, *11*, 1328. [CrossRef]
6. Browne, S. Optimal Investment Policies for a Firm With a Random Risk Process: Exponential Utility and Minimizing the Probability of Ruin. *Math. Oper. Res.* **1995**, *20*, 937–958. [CrossRef]
7. Yang, H.; Zhang, L. Optimal investment for insurer with jump-diffusion risk process. *Insur. Math. Econ.* **2005**, *37*, 615–634. [CrossRef]
8. Hipp, C.; Plum, M. Optimal investment for insurers. *Insur. Math. Econ.* **2000**, *27*, 215–228. [CrossRef]
9. David, P.S.; Young, V.R. Minimizing the Probability of Ruin When Claims Follow Brownian Motion with Drift. *N. Am. Actuar. J.* **2005**, *9*, 110–128. [CrossRef]
10. Bai, L.; Zhang, H. Dynamic mean-variance problem with constrained risk control for the insurers. *Math. Methods Oper. Res.* **2008**, *68*, 181–205. [CrossRef]
11. Ramadan, A.T.; Tolba, A.H.; El-Desouky, B.S. A Unit Half-Logistic Geometric Distribution and Its Application in Insurance. *Axioms* **2022**, *11*, 676. [CrossRef]
12. Georgescu, I.; Kinnunen, J. Optimal Saving by Expected Utility Operators. *Axioms* **2020**, *9*, 17. [CrossRef]
13. Jung, E.J.; Kim, J.H. Optimal investment strategies for the HARA utility under the constant elasticity of variance model. *Insur. Math. Econ.* **2012**, *51*, 667–673. [CrossRef]
14. Chang, H.; Chang, K. Optimal consumption–investment strategy under the Vasicek model: HARA utility and Legendre transform. *Insur. Math. Econ.* **2017**, *72*, 215–227. [CrossRef]
15. Zhang, Y.; Zhao, P. Optimal Reinsurance-Investment Problem with Dependent Risks Based on Legendre Transform. *J. Ind. Manag. Optim.* **2020**, *16*, 1457–1479. [CrossRef]
16. Zhang, Y. Optimal Investment Strategies for Asset-Liability Management with Affine Diffusion Factor Processes and Hara Preferences. *J. Ind. Manag. Optim.* **2023**, *19*, 5767–5796. [CrossRef]
17. Cox, J.C. Notes on Option Pricing I: Constant Elasticity of Variance Diffusion. Unpublished Note, Standford University, Graduate School of Business. 1975.
18. Stein, E.M.; Stein, J.C. Stock Price Distributions with Stochastic Volatility: An Analytic Approach. *Rev. Financ. Stud.* **1991**, *4*, 727–752. [CrossRef]
19. Heston, S.L. A Closed-Form Solution for Options with Stochastic Volatility with Applications to Bond and Currency Options. *Rev. Financ. Stud.* **1993**, *6*, 327–343. [CrossRef]
20. Gu, A.; Guo, X.; Li, Z.; Zeng, Y. Optimal control of excess-of-loss reinsurance and investment for insurers under a CEV model. *Insur. Math. Econ.* **2012**, *51*, 674–684. [CrossRef]
21. Wang, S.; Rong, X.; Zhao, H. Optimal time-consistent reinsurance-investment strategy with delay for an insurer under a defaultable market. *J. Math. Anal. Appl.* **2019**, *474*, 1267–1288. [CrossRef]
22. Huang, Y.; Yang, X.; Zhou, J. Robust optimal investment and reinsurance problem for a general insurance company under Heston model. *Math. Methods Oper. Res.* **2017**, *85*, 305–326. [CrossRef]
23. Zhu, H.; Cao, M.; Zhang, C. Time-consistent investment and reinsurance strategies for mean-variance insurers with relative performance concerns under the Heston model. *Financ. Res. Lett.* **2019**, *30*, 280–291. [CrossRef]
24. Zhang, Y.; Zhao, P.; Kou, B. Optimal excess-of-loss reinsurance and investment problem with thinning dependent risks under Heston model. *J. Comput. Appl. Math.* **2021**, *382*, 113082. [CrossRef]
25. Yan, T.; Wong, H. Open-loop equilibrium reinsurance-investment strategy under mean–variance criterion with stochastic volatility. *Insur. Math. Econ.* **2020**, *90*, 105–119. [CrossRef]
26. Sheng, D. Explicit Solution of Reinsurance-Investment Problem for an Insurer with Dynamic Income under Vasicek Model. *Adv. Math. Phys.* **2016**, *2016*, 1967872. [CrossRef]
27. Zhang, X.; Zheng, X. Optimal Investment-Reinsurance Policy with Stochastic Interest and Inflation Rates. *Math. Probl. Eng.* **2019**, *2019*, 5176172. [CrossRef]
28. Yuan, Y.; Mi, H.; Chen, H. Mean-variance problem for an insurer with dependent risks and stochastic interest rate in a jump-diffusion market. *Optimization* **2022**, *71*, 2789–2818. [CrossRef]
29. Guo, C.; Zhuo, X.; Constantinescu, C.; Pamen, O.M. Optimal Reinsurance-Investment Strategy Under Risks of Interest Rate, Exchange Rate and Inflation. *Methodol. Comput. Appl. Probab.* **2018**, *20*, 1477–1502. [CrossRef]
30. Sun, Z.; Guo, J. Optimal mean–variance investment and reinsurance problem for an insurer with stochastic volatility. *Math. Methods Oper. Res.* **2018**, *88*, 59–79. [CrossRef]
31. Wang, H.; Wang, R.; Wei, J. Time-consistent investment-proportional reinsurance strategy with random coefficients for mean–variance insurers. *Insur. Math. Econ.* **2019**, *85*, 104–114. [CrossRef]
32. Guan, G.; Liang, Z. Robust optimal reinsurance and investment strategies for an AAI with multiple risks. *Insur. Math. Econ.* **2019**, *89*, 63–78. [CrossRef]

33. Zhang, Y.; Wu, Y.; Wiwatanapataphee, B.; Angkola, F. Asset liability management for an ordinary insurance system with proportional reinsurance in a CIR stochastic interest rate and Heston stochastic volatility framework. *J. Ind. Manag. Optim.* **2020**, *16*, 71–101. [CrossRef]
34. Grandell, J. *Aspects of Risk Theory*; Springer: New York, NY, USA, 1991.
35. Yong, J.; Zhou, X.Y. *Stochastic Controls: Hamiltonian Systems and HJB Equations*; Springer: New York, NY, USA, 1999; pp. 241–246.
36. Deelstra, G.; Grasselli, M.; Koehl, P.-F. Optimal investment strategies in the presence of a minimum guarantee. *Insur. Math. Econ.* **2003**, *33*, 189–207. [CrossRef]
37. Guan, G.; Liang, Z. Optimal management of DC pension plan in a stochastic interest rate and stochastic volatility framework. *Insur. Math. Econ.* **2014**, *57*, 58–66. [CrossRef]
38. Gao, J. Stochastic optimal control of DC pension funds. *Insur. Math. Econ.* **2008**, *42*, 1159–1164. [CrossRef]

axioms

MDPI

Article

Robust Fisher-Regularized Twin Extreme Learning Machine with Capped L_1-Norm for Classification

Zhenxia Xue [1,2,*] and Linchao Cai [1]

1 School of Mathematics and Information Science, North Minzu University, Yinchuan 750021, China
2 The Key Laboratory of Intelligent Information and Big Data Processing of NingXia Province, North Minzu University, Yinchuan 750021, China
* Correspondence: 2019015@num.edu.cn

Abstract: Twin extreme learning machine (TELM) is a classical and high-efficiency classifier. However, it neglects the statistical knowledge hidden inside the data. In this paper, in order to make full use of statistical information from sample data, we first come up with a Fisher-regularized twin extreme learning machine (FTELM) by applying Fisher regularization into TELM learning framework. This strategy not only inherits the advantages of TELM, but also minimizes the within-class divergence of samples. Further, in an effort to further boost the anti-noise ability of FTELM method, we propose a new capped L_1-norm FTELM (CL_1-FTELM) by introducing capped L_1-norm in FTELM to dwindle the influence of abnormal points, and CL_1-FTELM improves the robust performance of our FTELM. Then, for the proposed FTELM method, we utilize an efficient successive overrelaxation algorithm to solve the corresponding optimization problem. For the proposed CL_1-FTELM, an iterative method is designed to solve the corresponding optimization based on re-weighted technique. Meanwhile, the convergence and local optimality of CL_1-FTELM are proved theoretically. Finally, numerical experiments on manual and UCI datasets show that the proposed methods achieve better classification effects than the state-of-the-art methods in most cases, which demonstrates the effectiveness and stability of the proposed methods.

Keywords: twin extreme learning machine; within-class scatter; fisher regularization; capped L_1-norm; robustness

1. Introduction

Extreme learning machine [1,2], as a remarkable single hidden layer feed-forward neural networks (SLFNs) [3] training method, has been widely studied and applied in many fields such as efficient modeling [4], fashion retailing forecasting [5], fingerprint matching [6], metagenomic taxonomic classification [7], online sequential learning [8], and feature selection [9]. The weights of the input layer and hidden layer offsets are randomly generated. The output weight of the network is calculated effectively by minimizing the training error and the norm of the output weight. In addition, many researchers have tried to extend the extreme learning machine model to the support vector machine (SVM) learning framework to solve the classification problem [10]. Frenay et al. [11] found that the transformation performed by the first layer of ELM can be viewed as a kernel that can be plugged into SVM. Due to solving the support vector machine (SVM) type of optimization method that can be utilized to resolve the ELM model, an extreme learning machine based on the optimization method (OPTELM) was proposed in [12]. For binary classification problems, traditional ELM needs to compute all the sample points of training data at the same time in the training stage, which is time-consuming. The singe hyperplane was trained to perform the classification task in the traditional ELM, which enormously restricts its application prospect and the direction of evolution. Jayadeva et al. [13] proposed twin SVM (TWSVM), which is a famous non-parallel hyper-plane classification algorithm for binary classification. Inspired by TWSVM, Wan et al. [14] proposed the twin extreme learning machine (TELM). Compared with ELM, TELM trains two non-parallel hyperplanes for classification tasks by solving two smaller quadratic programming problems (QPPs). Compared with TWSVM, TELM's optimization problem has fewer constraints, so the training speed is faster and the application prospect is broader. In recent years, researchers have made many improvements to TELM, such as sparse twin extreme learning machine [15], robust twin extreme learning machine [16], time efficient varient of twin extreme learning machine [17], and a generalized adaptive robust distance metric driven smooth regularization learning framework [18], etc.

Although the above ELM-based algorithm has a good classification effect, the statistical knowledge from the data itself is ignored. However, the knowledge of mathematical statistics from the data is very important to construct an efficient classifier. Fisher discriminant analysis (FDA) is an effective discriminant tool by minimizing the intra-class divergence while keeping the inter-class divergence of the data constant. From the above discussion, it can be known that it is necessary to reconstruct a new classification model by combining the characteristics of ELM model and FDA. In recent years, Ma et al. [19] have successfully combined them and proposed a Fisher-regularized extreme learning machine (Fisher-ELM), which not only has the advantages of efficient solution of ELM but also fully considers the statistical knowledge of the data.

Although the above models have good classification performance, most of them consider the L_2-norm. When the data contains noise or outliers, they can not deal with noise and outliers well, which degrades the classification performance of the model. In recent years, researchers have tried to introduce the L_1-norm into various models [20–23] to reduce the impact of outliers. This studies have shown that the L_1-norm was able to reduce the effect of outliers to some extent. However, it was still unsatisfactory when the data contains a large number of outliers. Recently, researchers have introduced the idea of truncation into the L_1-norm, constructed a new capped L_1-norm, and applied it to various models [24–26]. Many studies [27,28] show that the capped L_1-norm not only inherits the advantages of the L_1-norm, but also is bounded. So it is more robust and it approaches the L_0-norm to some degree. For instance, by applying the capped L_1-norm to the twin SVM, Wang et al. [29] proposed a new robust twin support vector machine (CL_1-TWSVM). Based on twin support vector machine with privileged information [30] (TWSVMPI), a new robust TWSVMPI [31] is proposed by replacing the L_2-norm with capped L_1-norm. The new model further improves the anti-noise ability of the pattern.

In order to utilize the advantanges of the twin extreme learning machine and FDA, we first put forward to a novel classifier named Fisher-regularized twin extreme learning machine (FTELM). Also considering the instability of the L_2-norm for the outliers, we introduce the capped L_1-norm into the FTELM model and propose a more robust capped L_1-norm FTELM (CL_1-FTELM) model.

The main contributions of this paper are as follows:

(1) Based on twin extreme learning machine and Fisher-regularization extreme learning machine (FELM), a new Fisher-regularized twin extreme learning machine (FTELM) is proposed. FTELM minimizes intra-class divergence while fixing the inter-class divergence of samples. FTELM takes full account of the statistical information of the sample data, and the training speed is faster than FELM.

(2) Considering the instability of L_2-norm and Hinge loss used by FTELM, we introduce capped L_1-norm instead of them and propose a new capped L_1-norm FTELM model. CL_1-FTELM uses the capped L_1-norm to reduce the influence of noise points, and at the same time utilizes Fisher regularization to consider the statistical knowledge of the data.

(3) Two algorithms are designed by utilizing the successive overrelaxation (SOR) [32] technique and the re-weighted technique [27] to solve the optimization problems of the proposed FTELM and CL_1-FTELM, respectively.

(4) Two theorems about convergence and local optimality of CL_1-FTELM are proved.

The organizational structure of this paper is as follows. In Section 2, we briefly review related work. In Section 3, we describe the FTELM model in detail. The robust capped L_1-norm FTELM learning framework along with related theoretical proofs are described in detail in Section 4. In Section 5, we describes numerical experiments on artificial and benchmark datasets. We summarize this paper in Section 6.

2. Related Work

In this section, we first define some concepts of symbols needed for this paper, and then we briefly review Fisher regularization, Fisher-ELM, TELM and successive overrelaxation algorithm.

2.1. The Concept of Symbols

e is a vector whose components are all ones, an identity matrix is represented by **I**, and a matrix(vector) of zeros is represented by **0**. Then, $||\cdot||_2$ is the L_2 norm, and $||\cdot||_F$ stands for the Frobenius norm.

A binary classification problem in Euclidean space (R^d) can be formulated in the following form:

$$T = \{x_i, y_i\} \in (\mathcal{X}, \mathcal{Y}), (i = 1, ..., m) \tag{1}$$

where $x_i \in \mathcal{X} \subset R^d$ is expressed as an input sample in a d-dimensional Euclidean space. Similarly, $y_i \in \mathcal{Y} = \{-1, +1\}$ is represented as an output label corresponding to an input instance x_i. In addition, m_1 and m_2 represent the number of sample data of the positive class and negative class, respectively, and $m = m_1 + m_2$.

2.2. Fisher Regularization

Fisher regularization has the following form:

$$||f||_F^2 = \mathbf{f}^T\mathbf{N}\mathbf{f} = \sum_{i\in\mathcal{I}_+} (f(x_i) - \bar{f}_+)^2 + \sum_{i\in\mathcal{I}_-} (f(x_i) - \bar{f}_-)^2 \tag{2}$$

where $\mathbf{f} = [f(x_1), f(x_2), \ldots, f(x_m)]^T$, $\mathbf{N} = \mathbf{I} - \mathbf{G}, \mathbf{I} \in R^{m\times m}$ is the identity matrix and $\mathbf{G}$ is the matrix with the elements:

$$\mathbf{G}_{ij} = \begin{cases} \frac{1}{m_1}, for\ i,j \in \mathcal{I}_+ \\ \frac{1}{m_2}, for\ i,j \in \mathcal{I}_- \\ 0, \quad otherwise \end{cases} \tag{3}$$

where $\mathcal{I}_\pm$ are the index sets of positive and negative training data, $m_1 = |\mathcal{I}_+|$, $m_2 = |\mathcal{I}_-|$. The average value of $\mathbf{f}(\mathbf{x})$ over the positive sample set is expressed as $\bar{f}_+$, the average value of $\mathbf{f}(\mathbf{x})$ over the negative sample set is expressed as $\bar{f}_-$. From Equation (2), we can see that the meaning of the Fisher regularization is the intra-class divergence of the data.

The proof of Formula (2) is as follows:

$$\begin{aligned} &\sum_{i\in\mathcal{I}_+} (f(x_i) - \bar{f}_+)^2 = \sum_{i\in\mathcal{I}_+} \left(f^2(x_i) - 2\cdot f(x_i)\cdot \bar{f}_+ + \bar{f}_+^2\right) = \sum_{i\in\mathcal{I}+} f^2(x_i) - m_1\cdot \bar{f}_+^2 \\ &= \mathbf{f}_+^\mathbf{T}\cdot \mathbf{f}_+ - \frac{1}{m_1}\cdot\left(\mathbf{f}_+^\mathbf{T}\cdot\mathbf{e}\cdot\mathbf{e}^\mathbf{T}\cdot\mathbf{f}_+^\mathbf{T}\right) = \mathbf{f}_+^\mathbf{T}\cdot\mathbf{I}_+\mathbf{f}_+ - \mathbf{f}_+^\mathbf{T}\cdot\mathbf{M}_+\cdot\mathbf{f}_+^\mathbf{T} \\ &= \mathbf{f}_+^\mathbf{T}\cdot(\mathbf{I}_+ - \mathbf{M}_+)\cdot\mathbf{f}_+ = \mathbf{f}_+^\mathbf{T}\cdot(\mathbf{N_1})\cdot\mathbf{f}_+ \end{aligned} \tag{4}$$

where $\mathbf{e} = [1, \ldots, 1]^T$ is a vector of m_1 dimensions, $\mathbf{f}_+ = (f(x_1), f(x_2), \ldots, f(x_i), \ldots, f(x_{m_1}))$, $i \in \mathcal{I}_+, \mathbf{I}_+ \in R^{m_1\times m_1}$ is the identity matrix. $\mathbf{M}_+ \in R^{m_1\times m_1}$, and all the entries in the matrix $\mathbf{M}_+$ are $\frac{1}{m_1}$.

Similarly, it can be obtained:

$$\sum_{j\in\mathcal{I}_-}(f(x_i)-\bar{f}_-)^2=\mathbf{f}_-^{\mathbf{T}}\cdot(\mathbf{I}_- - \mathbf{M}_-)\cdot\mathbf{f}_-=\mathbf{f}_-^{\mathbf{T}}\cdot(\mathbf{N_2})\cdot\mathbf{f}_- \tag{5}$$

where $\mathbf{f}_- = (f(x_1), f(x_2), \ldots, f(x_i), \ldots, f(x_{m_2})), i \in \mathcal{I}_-, \mathbf{I}_- \in R^{m_2\times m_2}$ is the identity matrix. $\mathbf{M}_- \in R^{m_2\times m_2}$, and all the entries in the matrix $\mathbf{M}_-$ are $\frac{1}{m_2}$.

Combining Equations (4) and (5), we can get another form of Equation (2):

$$\begin{aligned}
&\mathbf{f}_+^{\mathbf{T}}\cdot(\mathbf{I}_+ - \mathbf{M}_+)\cdot\mathbf{f}_+ + \mathbf{f}_-^{\mathbf{T}}\cdot(\mathbf{I}_- - \mathbf{M}_-)\cdot\mathbf{f}_-\\
&=(\mathbf{f}_+,\mathbf{f}_-)^T\cdot\left[\mathbf{I}-\begin{bmatrix}\mathbf{M}_+ & \mathbf{0_1}\\ \mathbf{0_2} & \mathbf{M}_-\end{bmatrix}\right]\cdot(\mathbf{f}_+,\mathbf{f}_-)\\
&=\mathbf{f}^{\mathbf{T}}\cdot(\mathbf{I}-\mathbf{G})\cdot\mathbf{f}=\mathbf{f}^{\mathbf{T}}\cdot\mathbf{N}\cdot\mathbf{f}
\end{aligned} \tag{6}$$

where $\mathbf{0_1} \in \mathbf{0}^{m_1\times m_2}, \mathbf{0_2} \in \mathbf{0}^{m_2\times m_1}, G = \begin{bmatrix}\mathbf{M}_+ & \mathbf{0_1}\\ \mathbf{0_2} & \mathbf{M}_-\end{bmatrix}$.

2.3. Fisher-Regularized Extreme Learning Machine

The primal problem of Fisher-regularized extreme learning machine (FELM) is as follows:

$$\begin{aligned}
\min_{\alpha,\xi}\quad & \frac{1}{2}\beta^T\cdot\beta + C_1\cdot\mathbf{e}^{\mathbf{T}}\cdot\xi+\frac{1}{2}C_2\cdot\alpha^T\cdot\mathbf{K}_{ELM}\cdot\mathbf{N}\cdot\mathbf{K}_{ELM}.\alpha\\
s.t.\quad & \mathbf{Y}\cdot\mathbf{H}\cdot\beta\geq\mathbf{e}-\xi\\
& \xi\geq\mathbf{0}
\end{aligned} \tag{7}$$

According to the representer theorem $\beta = \sum_{i=1}^{m}\alpha_i\mathbf{h}(x_i) = \mathbf{H}^T\alpha$, problem (7) can be written as problem (8):

$$\begin{aligned}
\min_{\alpha,\xi}\quad & \frac{1}{2}\alpha^T\cdot\mathbf{K}_{ELM}\cdot\alpha + C_1\cdot\mathbf{e}^{\mathbf{T}}\cdot\xi+\frac{1}{2}C_2\cdot\alpha^T\cdot\mathbf{K}_{ELM}\cdot\mathbf{N}\cdot\mathbf{K}_{ELM}.\alpha\\
s.t.\quad & \mathbf{Y}\cdot\mathbf{K_{ELM}}\cdot\alpha\geq\mathbf{e}-\xi\\
& \xi\geq\mathbf{0}
\end{aligned} \tag{8}$$

where $\mathbf{K}_{ELM} \in R^{m\times m}$ is a Gram matrix with elements $k_{ELM}(x_i, x_j), k_{ELM}(x_i, x) = \mathbf{h}(x)^T \cdot \mathbf{h}(x_i)$, $\mathbf{h}(x)$ denotes the output of some hidden node, $\mathbf{Y} \in R^{m\times m}$ is a diagonal matrix with elements y_i, C_1, C_2 are the regularization parameters, and ξ is a nonnegative slack vector.

According to the optimization theory, the dual form of the problem (8) can be obtained as follows:

$$\begin{aligned}
&\min_{\theta}\frac{1}{2}\theta^T\cdot\mathbf{Q}\cdot\theta-\mathbf{e}^T\cdot\theta\\
&s.t.\quad \mathbf{0}\leq\theta\leq C_1\cdot\mathbf{e}
\end{aligned} \tag{9}$$

where $\mathbf{Q} = \mathbf{Y}\cdot\left((\mathbf{I}+C_2\cdot\mathbf{N}\cdot\mathbf{K}_{ELM})^{-1}\right)^T\cdot\mathbf{K}_{ELM}\cdot\mathbf{Y}$.

The decision function of Fisher-regularized extreme learning machine is:

$$f(x)=sign\left(\sum_{i=1}^{m}\alpha_i\cdot k_{ELM}(x_i,x)\right) \tag{10}$$

2.4. Twin Extreme Learning Machine

Similar to the form of TWSVM [13], the primal problem of TELM [14] can be expressed in the following:

$$\begin{aligned} \textbf{Primal} \quad \textbf{TELM}_1: \quad & \min_{\beta_1} \frac{1}{2}\|\mathbf{H}_1 \cdot \beta_1\|_2^2 + C_1 \cdot \mathbf{e_2^T} \cdot \xi \\ & s.t. \quad -\mathbf{H_2} \cdot \beta_1 \geq \mathbf{e_2} - \xi \\ & \qquad \xi \geq \mathbf{0} \end{aligned} \tag{11}$$

$$\begin{aligned} \textbf{Primal} \quad \textbf{TELM}_2: \quad & \min_{\beta_2} \frac{1}{2}\|\mathbf{H}_2 \cdot \beta_2\|_2^2 + C_2 \cdot \mathbf{e_1^T} \cdot \eta \\ & s.t. \quad \mathbf{H_1} \cdot \beta_2 \geq \mathbf{e_1} - \eta \\ & \qquad \eta \geq \mathbf{0} \end{aligned} \tag{12}$$

where $\mathbf{H}_1$ and $\mathbf{H}_2$ respresent the outputs of the hidden layer for positive and negative samples, ξ and η represent the slack vectors, $\mathbf{0}$ is a zero vector, C_1, $C_2 \geq 0$ are penalty parameters, $\mathbf{e}_1 \in R^{m_1}$ and $\mathbf{e}_2 \in R^{m_2}$ are vectors of ones.

By introducing Lagrange multipliers α and ϑ, the dual problem of (11) and (12) can be written as follows:

$$\begin{aligned} \textbf{Dual} \quad \textbf{TELM}_1: \quad & \min_{\alpha} \frac{1}{2}\alpha^T \cdot \mathbf{H}_2\left(\mathbf{H}_1^T \cdot \mathbf{H_1}\right)^{-1} \cdot \mathbf{H}_2^T \cdot \alpha - \mathbf{e_2^T} \cdot \alpha \\ & s.t. \quad \mathbf{0} \leq \alpha \leq C_1 \cdot \mathbf{e}_2 \end{aligned} \tag{13}$$

$$\begin{aligned} \textbf{Dual} \quad \textbf{TELM}_2: \quad & \min_{\vartheta} \frac{1}{2}\vartheta^T \cdot \mathbf{H}_1\left(\mathbf{H}_2^T \cdot \mathbf{H_2}\right)^{-1} \cdot \mathbf{H}_1^T \cdot \vartheta - \mathbf{e_1^T} \cdot \vartheta \\ & s.t. \quad \mathbf{0} \leq \vartheta \leq C_2 \cdot \mathbf{e}_1 \end{aligned} \tag{14}$$

The solution of (13) and (14) are as follows:

$$\beta_1 = -\left(\mathbf{H_1^T} \cdot \mathbf{H_1} + \triangle_1 \mathbf{I}\right)^{-1} \cdot \mathbf{H}_2^T \cdot \alpha \tag{15}$$

$$\beta_2 = -\left(\mathbf{H_2^T} \cdot \mathbf{H_2} + \triangle_2 \mathbf{I}\right)^{-1} \cdot \mathbf{H}_1^T \cdot \vartheta \tag{16}$$

where $\triangle_1$ and $\triangle_2$ are two small positive constants and $\mathbf{I}$ is an identity matrix. The decision function of twin extreme learning machine is:

$$f(x) = arg \min_{k=1,2} d_k(x) = arg \min_{k=1,2}\left|\beta_k^T \cdot \mathbf{h}(\mathbf{x})\right| \tag{17}$$

2.5. Successive Overrelaxation Algorithm

The successive overrelaxation algorithm [32] mainly aims at the following optimization problems:

$$\begin{aligned} & \min_{\mu} \frac{1}{2}\left\|\mathbf{H}^T\mu\right\|_2^2 - \mathbf{e}^T\mu \\ & s.t. \quad \mu \in S = \{\mu | \mathbf{0} \leq \mu \leq C\mathbf{e}\} \end{aligned} \tag{18}$$

Let $\mathbf{HH}^T = \mathbf{L} + \mathbf{E} + \mathbf{L}^T$, the strictly lower triangular matrix of the matrix $\mathbf{HH}^T$ is $\mathbf{L}$, and the diagonal elements of the matrix $\mathbf{HH}^T$ form the diagonal matrix $\mathbf{E}$.

The gradient projection optimality condition is the necessary and sufficient optimality condition for Equation (18):

$$\mu = \left(\mu - \pi\mathbf{E}^{-1}\left(\mathbf{HH}^T\mu - \mathbf{e}\right)\right)_{\#}, \pi \geq 0$$

where the 2-norm projection onto the feasible region of Equation (18) is denoted by $(\cdot)_{\#}$, that is:

$$((\mu)_{\#})_i = \begin{cases} 0, if \quad \mu_i \le 0, i = 1,2,\ldots,m \\ \mu_i, if \quad 0 < \mu_i < C, i = 1,2,\ldots,m \\ C, if \quad \mu_i \ge C, i = 1,2,\ldots,m \end{cases} \tag{19}$$

The matrix $\mathbf{HH}^T$ is expressed in the following form:

$$\begin{aligned} &\mathbf{HH}^T = \pi^{-1}\mathbf{E}(\mathbf{B}+\mathbf{C}) \\ &s.t.\ \mathbf{B}-\mathbf{C}\ is\ positive\ definite \end{aligned} \tag{20}$$

Here:

$$\mathbf{B} = \left(\mathbf{I} + \pi\mathbf{E}^{-1}\mathbf{L}\right), \mathbf{C} = \left((\pi-1)\mathbf{I} + \pi\mathbf{E}^{-1}\mathbf{L}^T\right), 0 < \pi < 2 \tag{21}$$

According to the [33], the matrix splitting algorithm is as follows:

$$\mu^{i+1} = \left(\mu^{i+1} - \mathbf{B}\mu^{i+1} - \mathbf{C}\mu^i + \pi\mathbf{E}^{-1}\mathbf{e}\right)_{\#} \tag{22}$$

Substituting Equation (21) into Equation (22), it can be obtained:

$$\mu^{i+1} = \left(\mu^i - \pi\mathbf{E}^{-1}\left(\mathbf{HH}^T\mu^i - \mathbf{e} + \mathbf{L}\left(\mu^{i+1} - \mu^i\right)\right)\right)_{\#} \tag{23}$$

3. Fisher-Regularized Twin Extreme Learning Machine

3.1. Model Formulation

As mentioned above, TELM solves two smaller QPPs, which can get the solution quickly. However, it ignores the prior statistical knowledge from data. FELM minimizes the within-class scatter while controlling the between-class scatter of samples, but FELM needs to solve a large-scale quadratic programming problems which is time-consuming. In this paper, by combining the advantages of FELM and TELM, we first propose the Fisher-regularized twin extreme learning machine (FTELM) by introducing the Fisher regularization into the TELM feature space. FTELM only needs to solve two smaller quadratic programming problems and meanwhile utilizes the prior statistical knowledge from data. The pair of FTELM primal problems is as follows:

$$\begin{aligned} \textbf{Primal}\quad \textbf{FTELM}_1: \quad & \min_{\beta_1,\xi} \ \frac{1}{2}\|\mathbf{H}_1\cdot\beta_1\|^2 + C_1\cdot\mathbf{e}_2^T\cdot\xi + \frac{C_2}{2}\cdot\mathbf{f}_1(x)^T\cdot\mathbf{N}_1\cdot\mathbf{f}_1(x) \\ & s.t.\quad -\mathbf{H}_2\cdot\beta_1 + \xi \ge \mathbf{e}_2 \\ & \xi \ge \mathbf{0} \end{aligned} \tag{24}$$

$$\begin{aligned} \textbf{Primal}\quad \textbf{FTELM}_2: \quad & \min_{\beta_2,\eta} \ \frac{1}{2}\|\mathbf{H}_2\cdot\beta_2\|^2 + C_3\cdot\mathbf{e}_1^T\cdot\eta + \frac{C_4}{2}\cdot\mathbf{f}_2(x)^T\cdot\mathbf{N}_2\cdot\mathbf{f}_2(x) \\ & s.t.\quad \mathbf{H}_1\cdot\beta_2 + \eta \ge \mathbf{e}_1 \\ & \eta \ge \mathbf{0} \end{aligned} \tag{25}$$

From the Equations (4) and (5), we can know that $\mathbf{N}_1 = \mathbf{I}_+ - \mathbf{M}_+$ and $\mathbf{N}_2 = \mathbf{I}_- - \mathbf{M}_-$, C_1, C_2, C_3, $C_4 > 0$ are regularization parameters, ξ and η are the error vectors, and all the elements in vectors $\mathbf{e}_1 \in R^{m_1}$ and $\mathbf{e}_2 \in R^{m_2}$ are one. FTELM first inherits the advantage of the classical twin extreme learning machine, which computes two non-parallel hyperplanes to solve the classification problem. Secondly, FTELM takes full account of the statistical information of the samples and further improves the classification accuracy of the classifier. The optimization objective function in (24) of FTELM mainly has three terms: minimizing the distance from the positive class sample points to the positive class hyperplane, minimizing empirical loss, and minimizing the intra-class divergence from the samples. The constraint condition in (24) of the optimization objective function is that the distance between the negative class sample points and the positive class hyperplane is greater than or equal to one. In a word, FTELM makes the positive class sample points closer to the positive class hyperplane, and the negative class sample points far away from the positive class hyperplane. At the same time, the positive class sample points are more concentrated in the center of the positive class sample points. There is a similar explanation for the model (25).

According to the representer theorem $\beta = \sum_{i=1}^{m} \alpha_i \mathbf{h}(x_i) = \mathbf{H}^T \alpha$, then $\beta_1 = \mathbf{H}_1^T \cdot \alpha_1$ and $\beta_2 = \mathbf{H}_2^T \cdot \alpha_2$. We know that $\mathbf{f} = \mathbf{H} \cdot \beta$. Therefore, the problem (24) and (25) can be written in the following forms:

$$\begin{aligned} \min_{\alpha_1,\xi} \quad & \frac{1}{2}\alpha_1^T \cdot \mathbf{K}_{ELM1} \cdot \mathbf{K}_{ELM1} \cdot \alpha_1 + C_1 \cdot \mathbf{e}_2^T \cdot \xi + \frac{C_2}{2}\alpha_1^T \cdot \mathbf{K}_{ELM1} \cdot \mathbf{N}_1 \cdot \mathbf{K}_{ELM1} \cdot \alpha_1 \\ s.t. \quad & -\mathbf{H_2} \cdot \mathbf{H}_1^T \cdot \alpha_1 + \xi \geq \mathbf{e_2} \\ & \xi \geq \mathbf{0} \end{aligned} \tag{26}$$

$$\begin{aligned} \min_{\alpha_2,\eta} \quad & \frac{1}{2}\alpha_2^T \cdot \mathbf{K}_{ELM2} \cdot \mathbf{K}_{ELM2} \cdot \alpha_2 + C_3 \cdot \mathbf{e}_1^T \cdot \eta + \frac{C_4}{2}\alpha_2^T \cdot \mathbf{K}_{ELM2} \cdot \mathbf{N}_2 \cdot \mathbf{K}_{ELM2} \cdot \alpha_2 \\ s.t. \quad & \mathbf{H_1} \cdot \mathbf{H}_2^T \cdot \alpha_2 + \eta \geq \mathbf{e_1} \\ & \eta \geq \mathbf{0} \end{aligned} \tag{27}$$

where $\mathbf{K}_{ELM1} = \mathbf{H}_1 \cdot \mathbf{H_1^T}$ and $\mathbf{K}_{ELM2} = \mathbf{H}_2 \cdot \mathbf{H_2^T}$ are Gram matrices.

3.2. Model Solution

Introducing Lagrange multipliers $\theta = (\theta_1, \ldots, \theta_{m_2})^T$ and $\vartheta = (\vartheta_1, \ldots, \vartheta_{m_2})^T$, the Lagrange function of (26) can be written as follows:

$$\begin{aligned} \mathcal{L}(\alpha_1, \xi, \theta, \vartheta) = & \frac{1}{2}\alpha_1^T \cdot \mathbf{K}_{ELM1} \cdot (\mathbf{I}_1 + C_2 \cdot \mathbf{N}_1) \cdot \mathbf{K}_{ELM1} \cdot \alpha_1 + C_1 \cdot \mathbf{e}_2^T \cdot \xi \\ & - \theta^T \cdot \left(-\mathbf{H}_2 \cdot \mathbf{H}_1^T \cdot \alpha_1 + \xi - \mathbf{e}_2\right) - \vartheta^T \cdot \xi \end{aligned} \tag{28}$$

According to the KKT conditions, we get:

$$\frac{\partial \mathcal{L}}{\partial \alpha_1} = \mathbf{K}_{ELM1} \cdot (\mathbf{I}_1 + C_2 \cdot \mathbf{N}_1) \cdot \mathbf{K}_{ELM1} \cdot \alpha_1 + \mathbf{H}_1 \cdot \mathbf{H_2^T} \cdot \theta = \mathbf{0} \tag{29}$$

$$\frac{\partial \mathcal{L}}{\partial \xi} = C_1 \cdot \mathbf{e}_2 - \theta - \vartheta = \mathbf{0} \tag{30}$$

$$\theta^T \cdot \left(-\mathbf{H}_2 \cdot \mathbf{H}_1^T \cdot \alpha_1 + \xi - \mathbf{e}_2\right) = \mathbf{0} \tag{31}$$

$$\vartheta^T \cdot \xi = \mathbf{0} \tag{32}$$

$$\theta \geq \mathbf{0} \tag{33}$$

$$\vartheta \geq \mathbf{0} \tag{34}$$

From (29) and (30), we can get:

$$\alpha_1^* = -(\mathbf{K}_{ELM1} \cdot (\mathbf{I}_1 + C_2 \cdot \mathbf{N}_1) \cdot \mathbf{K}_{ELM1})^{-1} \cdot \mathbf{H}_1 \cdot \mathbf{H}_2^T \cdot \theta \tag{35}$$

$$\mathbf{0} \leq \theta \leq C_1 \cdot \mathbf{e}_2 \tag{36}$$

By substituting (29)–(34) into (28), the dual optimization problem for (26) can be written in the following form:

$$\begin{aligned} \textbf{Dual} \quad \textbf{FTELM}_1 : \min_{\theta} \quad & \frac{1}{2}\theta^T \cdot \mathbf{Q}_1 \cdot \theta - \mathbf{e}_2^{\mathbf{T}} \cdot \theta \\ s.t. \quad & \mathbf{0} \le \theta \le C_1 \cdot \mathbf{e}_2 \end{aligned} \tag{37}$$

Here $\mathbf{Q}_1 = \mathbf{H}_2 \cdot \mathbf{H}_1^T \cdot (\mathbf{K}_{ELM1} \cdot (\mathbf{I}_1 + C_2 \cdot \mathbf{N}_1) \cdot \mathbf{K}_{ELM1})^{-1} \cdot \mathbf{H}_1 \cdot \mathbf{H}_2^T$. Similarly, we can obtain the dual of (27) as:

$$\begin{aligned} \textbf{Dual} \quad \textbf{FTELM}_2 : \min_{\lambda} \quad & \frac{1}{2}\lambda^T \cdot \mathbf{Q}_2 \cdot \lambda - \mathbf{e}_1^{\mathbf{T}} \cdot \lambda \\ s.t. \quad & \mathbf{0} \le \lambda \le C_3 \cdot \mathbf{e}_1 \end{aligned} \tag{38}$$

Here $\lambda = (\lambda_1, \ldots, \lambda_{m_1})^T$ is the vector of Lagrange multipliers and we can get: $\mathbf{Q}_2 = \mathbf{H}_1 \cdot \mathbf{H}_2^T \cdot (\mathbf{K}_{ELM2} \cdot (\mathbf{I}_2 + C_4 \cdot \mathbf{N}_2) \cdot \mathbf{K}_{ELM2})^{-1} \cdot \mathbf{H}_2 \cdot \mathbf{H}_1^T$.

We use the successive overrelaxation (SOR) [32] technique to solve the convex quadratic optimization problems of (37) and (38) (The SOR-FTELM algorithm is summarized as Algorithm 1). We can get θ and λ. Therefore, we can obtain the solution for problems of (24) and (25) in the following :

$$\beta_1 = -\mathbf{H}_1^T \cdot (\mathbf{K}_{ELM1} \cdot (\mathbf{I}_1 + C_2 \cdot \mathbf{N}_1) \cdot \mathbf{K}_{ELM1} + \delta_1 \cdot \mathbf{I}_1)^{-1} \cdot \mathbf{H}_1 \cdot \mathbf{H}_2^T \cdot \theta \tag{39}$$

$$\beta_2 = \mathbf{H}_2^T \cdot (\mathbf{K}_{ELM2} \cdot (\mathbf{I}_2 + C_4 \cdot \mathbf{N}_2) \cdot \mathbf{K}_{ELM2} + \delta_2 \cdot \mathbf{I}_2)^{-1} \cdot \mathbf{H}_2 \cdot \mathbf{H}_1^T \cdot \lambda \tag{40}$$

The decision function of FTELM is:

$$f(x) = arg \min_{k=1,2} \left| \beta_k^T \cdot \mathbf{h}(\mathbf{x}) \right| \tag{41}$$

Algorithm 1 The procedure of SOR-FTELM.

Input:
Training set $T = \{x_i, y_i\}_{i=1}^m$, where $x_i \in R^d$, $y_i = \pm 1$, the number of hidden node number L, tolerance ε, regularization parameters C_1, C_2, C_3, C_4.
Output:
β_1, β_2, and the decision function of FTELM.
1: Compute the graph matrix $\mathbf{N}_1, \mathbf{N}_2$ by Equations (4) and (5).
2: Choose an activation function such as $G(x) = \frac{1}{1+e^{-x}}$ and compute the hidden layer output matrix $\mathbf{H}_1, \mathbf{H}_2$ by $\mathbf{h}(x_i) = G\left(\sum_{j=1}^d \omega_{ji} x_j + b_i\right)$ and compute $\mathbf{K}_{ELM1}$=$\mathbf{H}_1\mathbf{H}_1^T$ and $\mathbf{K}_{ELM2}$=$\mathbf{H}_2\mathbf{H}_2^T$.
3: Choose $t \in (0,2)$, start with any $\theta^0 \in R^{m_2}$,Having θ^i, compute θ^{i+1} as follows:

$$\theta^{i+1} = \left(\theta^i - t\mathbf{E}_1\left(\mathbf{Q}_1\theta^i - \mathbf{e}_2 + \mathbf{L}_1\left(\theta^{i+1} - \theta^i\right)\right)\right)_\#$$

until $\left|\theta^{i+1} - \theta^i\right| \le \varepsilon$, where $\mathbf{e}_2$ is a vector of ones of appropriate dimensions. $\mathbf{L}_1 \in R^{m_2 \times m_2}$ is the strictly lower triangular matrix, where $l_{ij} = q_{ij}, i > j$. $\mathbf{E}_1 \in R^{m_2 \times m_2}$ is the diagonal matrix, where $e_{ij} = q_{ij}, i > j$.
Then, given any $\lambda^0 \in R^{m_1}$, Having λ^i, compute λ^{i+1} as follows

$$\lambda^{i+1} = \left(\lambda^i - t\mathbf{E}_2\left(\mathbf{Q}_2\lambda^i - \mathbf{e}_1 + \mathbf{L}_2\left(\lambda^{i+1} - \lambda^i\right)\right)\right)_\#$$

4: Compute the output weights β_1, β_2 using Equations (39) and (40).
5: Construct the following decision functions:

$$f(x) = arg \min_{k=1,2} \left| \beta_k^T \cdot \mathbf{h}(\mathbf{x}) \right|$$

4. Capped L_1-Norm Fisher-Regularized Twin Extreme Learning Machine

4.1. Model Formulation

The Fisher-regularized twin extreme learning machine proposed in the previous section not only inherits the advantages of the twin extreme learning machine but also makes full use of the statistical information of the samples. However, due to the use of the squared L_2-norm distance and hinge loss function, the Fisher-regularized twin extreme learning machine is not robust enough when noisy points are present, which often enlarges the impact of abnormal values. In order to reduce the influence of outliers and improve the robustness of the FTELM, we propose a capped L_1-norm Fisher twin extreme machine (CL_1-FTELM) by replacing the L_2-norm and hinge loss in the FTELM with capped L_1-norm. The primal CL_1-FTELM is in the following:

Primal CL_1-FTELM$_1$:

$$\begin{aligned}\min_{\alpha_1,\xi}\sum_{i=1}^{m_1}\min\left(\left\|\mathbf{h}^T(x_i)\cdot\mathbf{H_1}^T\cdot\alpha_1\right\|_1,\varepsilon_1\right)+C_1\cdot\sum_{j=1}^{m_2}\min\left(\|\xi_j\|_1,\varepsilon_2\right)\\+\frac{C_2}{2}\cdot\alpha_1^T\cdot\mathbf{K}_{ELM1}\cdot\mathbf{N}_1\cdot\mathbf{K}_{ELM1}\cdot\alpha_1\\s.t.\quad-\mathbf{H}_2\cdot\mathbf{H}_1^T\cdot\alpha_1+\xi\geq\mathbf{e}_2\end{aligned}\tag{42}$$

Primal CL_1-FTELM$_2$:

$$\begin{aligned}\min_{\alpha_2,\eta}\sum_{j=1}^{m_2}\min\left(\left\|\mathbf{h}^T(x_j)\cdot\mathbf{H_2}^T\cdot\alpha_2\right\|_1,\varepsilon_3\right)+C_3\cdot\sum_{i=1}^{m_1}\min(\|\eta_i\|_1,\varepsilon_4)\\+\frac{C_4}{2}\cdot\alpha_2^T\cdot\mathbf{K}_{ELM2}\cdot\mathbf{N}_2\cdot\mathbf{K}_{ELM2}\cdot\alpha_2\\s.t.\quad\mathbf{H}_1\cdot\mathbf{H}_2^T\cdot\alpha_2+\eta\geq\mathbf{e}_1\end{aligned}\tag{43}$$

where $C_1, C_2, C_3, C_4 > 0$ are regularization parameters, $\varepsilon_1, \varepsilon_2, \varepsilon_3, \varepsilon_4$ are thresholding parameters.

CL_1-FTELM uses the capped L_1-norm to reduce the influence of noise points, and at the same time utilizes Fisher regularization to consider the statistical knowledge of the data. Based on FTELM, CL_1-FTELM changes the L_2-norm metric and Hinge loss function of the original model to the capped L_1-norm. The capped L_1-norm is bounded and can constrain the impact of noise within a certain range. Therefore, the anti-noise ability of the model can be improved. The optimization objective function in (42) of CL_1-FTELM also contains three terms: minimizing the distance between the positive class sample points and the positive class hyperplane by using capped L_1-norm metric, minimizing empirical loss by using capped L_1-norm loss function, and minimizing the within-class scatter of the samples. The constraints in (42) of CL_1-FTELM are as follows: the distance between the negative class sample points and the positive class hyperplane is greater than or equal to one. In summary, CL_1-FTELM inherits the advantages of FTELM, while further improving the noise immunity of the model by replacing the metric and loss function with the capped L_1-norm. However, the CL_1-FTELM is a non-convex and non-smooth problem. Here, we use the reweighting technique [27] to solve the problem corresponding to the CL_1-FTELM model, which is shown below:

CL_1-FTELM$_1$:

$$\begin{aligned}\min_{\alpha_1,\xi}\quad\frac{1}{2}\alpha_1^T\cdot\mathbf{K}_{ELM1}\cdot\mathbf{F}\cdot\mathbf{K}_{ELM1}\cdot\alpha_1+\frac{C_1}{2}\cdot\xi^T\cdot\mathbf{D}\cdot\xi\\+\frac{C_2}{2}\cdot\alpha_1^T\cdot\mathbf{K}_{ELM1}\cdot\mathbf{N}_1\cdot\mathbf{K}_{ELM1}\cdot\alpha_1\\s.t.\quad-\mathbf{H}_2\cdot\mathbf{H}_1^T\cdot\alpha_1+\xi\geq\mathbf{e}_2\end{aligned}\tag{44}$$

where $\mathbf{F}$ and $\mathbf{D}$ are two diagonal matrices with i-th and j-th diagonal elements as:

$$f_i=\begin{cases}\frac{1}{\left|\mathbf{h}^T(x_i)\cdot\mathbf{H}_1^T\cdot\alpha_1\right|},\left|\mathbf{h}^T(x_i)\cdot\mathbf{H}_1^T\cdot\alpha_1\right|\leq\varepsilon_1,i\in(1,\ldots,m_1)\\\sigma_1,\quad otherwise\end{cases}\tag{45}$$

$$d_j = \begin{cases} \frac{1}{|\xi_j|}, |\xi_j| \leq \varepsilon_2, j \in (1, \dots, m_2) \\ \\ \sigma_2, \quad otherwise \end{cases} \tag{46}$$

Here σ_1, σ_2 are two small constants.

CL_1-FTELM$_2$:

$$\begin{aligned} \min_{\alpha_2, \eta} \quad & \frac{1}{2}\alpha_2^T \cdot \mathbf{K}_{ELM2} \cdot \mathbf{R} \cdot \mathbf{K}_{ELM2} \cdot \alpha_2 + \frac{C_3}{2} \cdot \eta^T \cdot \mathbf{S} \cdot \eta \\ & + \frac{C_4}{2} \cdot \alpha_2^T \cdot \mathbf{K}_{ELM2} \cdot \mathbf{N}_2 \cdot \mathbf{K}_{ELM2} \cdot \alpha_2 \\ & s.t. \quad \mathbf{H}_1 \cdot \mathbf{H}_2^T \cdot \alpha_2 + \eta \geq \mathbf{e}_1 \end{aligned} \tag{47}$$

where **R** and **S** are two diagonal matrices with j-th and i-th diagonal elements as:

$$r_j = \begin{cases} \frac{1}{\left|\mathbf{h}^T(x_j) \cdot \mathbf{H}_2^T \cdot \alpha_2\right|}, \left|\mathbf{h}^T(x_j) \cdot \mathbf{H}_2^T \cdot \alpha_2\right| \leq \varepsilon_3, j \in (1, \dots, m_2) \\ \\ \sigma_3, \quad otherwise \end{cases} \tag{48}$$

$$s_i = \begin{cases} \frac{1}{|\eta_i|}, |\eta_i| \leq \varepsilon_4, i \in (1, \dots, m_1) \\ \\ \sigma_4, \quad otherwise \end{cases} \tag{49}$$

Here σ_3, σ_4 are two small constants.

4.2. Model Solution

Introducing Lagrange multipliers α, the Lagrange function of (44) can be written as follows:

$$\begin{aligned} \mathcal{L}(\alpha_1, \xi, \alpha) = & \frac{1}{2}\alpha_1^T \cdot \mathbf{K}_{ELM1} \cdot (\mathbf{F} + C_2 \cdot \mathbf{N}_1) \cdot \mathbf{K}_{ELM1} \cdot \alpha_1 + \frac{C_1}{2} \cdot \xi^T \cdot \mathbf{D} \cdot \xi \\ & - \alpha^T \cdot \left(-\mathbf{H}_2 \cdot \mathbf{H}_1^T \cdot \alpha_1 + \xi - \mathbf{e}_2\right) \end{aligned} \tag{50}$$

According to the KKT conditions, we can get the following formula:

$$\frac{\partial \mathcal{L}}{\partial \alpha_1} = \mathbf{K}_{ELM1} \cdot (\mathbf{F} + C_2 \cdot \mathbf{N}_1) \cdot \mathbf{K}_{ELM1} \cdot \alpha_1 + \mathbf{H}_1 \cdot \mathbf{H}_2^T \cdot \alpha = 0 \tag{51}$$

$$\frac{\partial \mathcal{L}}{\partial \xi} = C_1 \cdot \mathbf{D} \cdot \xi - \alpha = 0 \tag{52}$$

$$\alpha^T \cdot \left(-\mathbf{H}_2 \cdot \mathbf{H}_1^T \cdot \alpha_1 + \xi - \mathbf{e}_2\right) = 0 \tag{53}$$

$$\alpha \geq 0 \tag{54}$$

From Equations (51) and (52), we can get:

$$\begin{aligned} \alpha_1 &= -(\mathbf{K}_{ELM1} \cdot (\mathbf{F} + C_2 \cdot \mathbf{N}_1) \cdot \mathbf{K}_{ELM1})^{-1} \cdot \mathbf{H}_1 \cdot \mathbf{H}_2^T \cdot \alpha \\ \xi &= \frac{1}{C_1} \cdot \mathbf{D}^{-1} \cdot \alpha \end{aligned}$$

Similarly, we can get:

$$\begin{aligned} \alpha_2 &= (\mathbf{K}_{ELM2} \cdot (\mathbf{R} + C_4 \cdot \mathbf{N}_2) \cdot \mathbf{K}_{ELM2})^{-1} \cdot \mathbf{H}_2 \cdot \mathbf{H}_1^T \cdot \lambda \\ \eta &= \frac{1}{C_3} \cdot \mathbf{S}^{-1} \cdot \lambda \end{aligned}$$

Thus, we can get the dual problem of (44) as follows:
Dual CL_1-FTELM$_1$

$$\min_{\alpha\geq 0}\frac{1}{2}\alpha^T\cdot\left(\left(\mathbf{H}_2\mathbf{H}_1^T\right)\mathbf{Q}_1^{-1}\left(\mathbf{H}_1\mathbf{H}_2^T\right)+\frac{1}{C_1}\mathbf{D}^{-1}\right)\cdot\alpha-\mathbf{e}_2^T\cdot\alpha \tag{55}$$

where $\mathbf{Q}_1=\mathbf{K}_{ELM1}\cdot(\mathbf{F}+C_2\cdot\mathbf{N}_1)\cdot\mathbf{K}_{ELM1}$.

In the same way, we can obtain the dual problem of the Equation (47) as follows:
Dual CL_1-FTELM$_2$

$$\min_{\lambda\geq 0}\frac{1}{2}\lambda^T\cdot\left(\left(\mathbf{H}_1\mathbf{H}_2^T\right)\mathbf{Q}_2^{-1}\left(\mathbf{H}_2\mathbf{H}_1^T\right)+\frac{1}{C_3}\mathbf{S}^{-1}\right)\cdot\lambda-\mathbf{e}_1^T\cdot\lambda \tag{56}$$

where $\mathbf{Q}_2=\mathbf{K}_{ELM2}\cdot(\mathbf{R}+C_4\cdot\mathbf{N}_2)\cdot\mathbf{K}_{ELM2}$.

After solving (55) and (56), α and λ are derived, and then α_1 and α_2 are obtained. So, the decision function of CL_1-FTELM is as follows:

$$y=arg\min_{k=1,2}\left|\alpha_k^T\cdot\mathbf{H}_k\cdot\mathbf{h}(\mathbf{x})\right|=arg\min_{k=1,2}\sum_{i=1}^{m_k}\alpha_{k_i}\cdot k_{ELM_k}(x,x_i) \tag{57}$$

Based on the above discussion, our algorithm will be presented in Algorithm 2. Next, we give the convergence analysis of Algorithm 2.

Algorithm 2 The procedure of CL_1-FTELM.

Input:
Training set $T=\{x_i,y_i\}_{i=1}^m$, where $x_i\in R^d$, $y_i=\pm1$, the number of hidden node number L, regularization parameters $C_1,C_2,C_3,C_4>0$, $\varepsilon_1,\varepsilon_2,\varepsilon_3,\varepsilon_4>0$, $\rho_1,\rho_2,\sigma_1,\sigma_2,\sigma_3,\sigma_4$.
Output:
α_1^*,α_2^* and the decision function of CL_1-FTELM.
1: Initialize $\mathbf{F}_0\in R^{m_1\times m_1}$, $\mathbf{D}_0\in R^{m_2\times m_2}$, $\mathbf{R}_0\in R^{m_2\times m_2}$, $\mathbf{S}_0\in R^{m_1\times m_1}$.
2: Compute the graph matrix $\mathbf{N}_1$, $\mathbf{N}_2$ by Equations (4) and (5).
3: Choose an activation function such as $G(x)=\frac{1}{1+e^{-x}}$ and compute the hidden layer output matrix $\mathbf{H}_1$, $\mathbf{H}_2$ by $\mathbf{h}(x_i)=G\left(\sum_{j=1}^d\omega_{ji}x_j+b_i\right)$ and compute $\mathbf{K}_{ELM1}=\mathbf{H}_1\mathbf{H}_1^T$ and $\mathbf{K}_{ELM2}=\mathbf{H}_2\mathbf{H}_2^T$.
4: Set t = 0.
5: **While**
Solving (55) and (56), the α^t and λ^t can be obtained.
Then get the solution $\alpha_1^t,\alpha_2^t,\xi^t$, and η^t by

$$\alpha_1^t=-(\mathbf{K}_{ELM1}\cdot(\mathbf{F}_t+C_2\cdot\mathbf{N}_1)\cdot\mathbf{K}_{ELM1})^{-1}\cdot\mathbf{H}_1\cdot\mathbf{H}_2^T\cdot\alpha^t,\xi^t=\frac{1}{C_1}\cdot\mathbf{D}_t^{-1}\cdot\alpha^t$$

$$\alpha_2^t=(\mathbf{K}_{ELM2}\cdot(\mathbf{R}_t+C_4\cdot\mathbf{N}_2)\cdot\mathbf{K}_{ELM2})^{-1}\cdot\mathbf{H}_2\cdot\mathbf{H}_1^T\cdot\lambda^t,\eta^t=\frac{1}{C_3}\cdot\mathbf{S}_t^{-1}\cdot\lambda^t$$

Update the matrices F_{t+1}, D_{t+1}, R_{t+1}, and S_{t+1} by (45), (46), (48) and (49), respectively.
Compute the objective function values J_1^{t+1} and J_2^{t+1}, by

$$J_1^{t+1}=\frac{1}{2}(\alpha_1^t)^T\cdot\mathbf{K}_{ELM1}\cdot\mathbf{F}_{t+1}\cdot\mathbf{K}_{ELM1}\cdot\alpha_1^t+\frac{C_1}{2}\cdot(\xi^t)^T\cdot\mathbf{D}_{t+1}\cdot\xi^t+\frac{C_2}{2}\cdot(\alpha_1^t)^T\cdot\mathbf{K}_{ELM1}\cdot\mathbf{N}_1\cdot\mathbf{K}_{ELM1}\cdot\alpha_1^t \tag{58}$$

$$J_2^{t+1}=\frac{1}{2}(\alpha_2^t)^T\cdot\mathbf{K}_{ELM2}\cdot\mathbf{R}_{t+1}\cdot\mathbf{K}_{ELM2}\cdot\alpha_2^t+\frac{C_3}{2}\cdot(\eta^t)^T\cdot\mathbf{S}_{t+1}\cdot\eta^t+\frac{C_4}{2}\cdot(\alpha_2^t)^T\cdot\mathbf{K}_{ELM2}\cdot\mathbf{N}_2\cdot\mathbf{K}_{ELM2}\cdot\alpha_2^t \tag{59}$$

if $\left|J_1^{t+1}-J_1^t\right|\leq\rho_1$ and $\left|J_2^{t+1}-J_2^t\right|\leq\rho_2$.
break
else
t=t+1
6: **end while**
7: Stop the iteration process and get the solution of α_1^*,α_2^*.

4.3. Convergence Analysis

Before we prove the convergence of the iterative algorithm, we first review two lemmas [34].

Lemma 1. *For any non-zeros vectors* $x, y \in R^n$, *if* $f(x) = \|x\|_1 - \frac{\|x\|_1^2}{2\|y\|_1}$, *then the following inequalities* $f(x) \le f(y)$ *hold.*

Lemma 2. *For any non-zeros vectors* $x, y, p, q \in R^n$, *if* $f(x,p) = \|x\|_1 - \frac{\|x\|_1^2}{2\|y\|_1} + C\left(\|p\|_1 - \frac{\|p\|_1^2}{2\|q\|_1}\right)$, $C \in R^+$, *then the following inequalities* $f(x,p) \le f(y,q)$ *hold.*

The proof of two lemmas is detailed in [34].

Theorem 1. *Algorithm 2 monotonically decreases the objectives of problems (42) and (43) in each iteration until it converges.*

Proof. Here, we only use problem (42) as an example to prove Theorem 1.

$$J(\alpha_1, \xi) = \min_{\alpha_1, \xi} \sum_{i=1}^{m_1} \min\left(\left\|\mathbf{h}^T(x_i) \cdot \mathbf{H_1}^T \cdot \alpha_1\right\|_1, \varepsilon_1\right) + C_1 \cdot \sum_{j=1}^{m_2} \min\left(\|\xi_j\|_1, \varepsilon_2\right) + \frac{C_2}{2} \cdot \alpha_1^T \cdot \mathbf{K}_{ELM1} \cdot \mathbf{N}_1 \cdot \mathbf{K}_{ELM1} \cdot \alpha_1 \tag{60}$$

when $\left\|\mathbf{h}^T(x_i) \cdot \mathbf{H}_1^T \cdot \alpha_1\right\|_1 < \varepsilon_1$ and $\|\xi_j\|_1 < \varepsilon_2$,we have:

$$J(\alpha_1, \xi) = \min_{\alpha_1, \xi} \sum_{i=1}^{m_1} \left\|\mathbf{h}^T(x_i)\mathbf{H}_1^T\alpha_1\right\|_1 + C_1 \sum_{j=1}^{m_2} \|\xi_j\|_1 + \frac{C_2}{2} \cdot \alpha_1^T \cdot \mathbf{K}_{ELM1} \cdot \mathbf{N}_1 \cdot \mathbf{K}_{ELM1} \cdot \alpha_1 \tag{61}$$

We take the derivative of Equation (61) with respect to α_1 and ξ separately and then obtain that:

$$\begin{cases} \sum_{i=1}^{m_1} \frac{\mathbf{H}_1\mathbf{h}(x_i)\mathbf{h}^T(x_i)\mathbf{H}_1^T\alpha_1}{\left|\mathbf{h}^T(x_i)\mathbf{H}_1^T\alpha_1\right|} + C_2 \cdot \mathbf{K}_{ELM1} \cdot \mathbf{N_1} \cdot \mathbf{K}_{ELM1} \cdot \alpha_1 = 0 \\ C_1 \cdot \sum_{j=1}^{m_2} \frac{\xi_j}{|\xi_j|} = 0 \end{cases} \tag{62}$$

by the above Equation (62), we can get:

$$\sum_{i=1}^{m_1} \frac{\mathbf{H}_1\mathbf{h}(x_i)\mathbf{h}^T(x_i)\mathbf{H}_1^T\alpha_1}{\left|\mathbf{h}^T(x_i)\mathbf{H}_1^T\alpha_1\right|} + C_1 \cdot \sum_{j=1}^{m_2} \frac{\xi_j}{|\xi_j|} + C_2 \cdot \mathbf{K}_{ELM1} \cdot \mathbf{N_1} \cdot \mathbf{K}_{ELM1} \cdot \alpha_1 = 0 \tag{63}$$

We define $f_i = \frac{1}{\left|\mathbf{h}^T(x_i) \cdot \mathbf{H}_1^T \cdot \alpha_1\right|}$ and $d_j = \frac{1}{|\xi_j|}$ as the diagonal entries of $\mathbf{F}$ and $\mathbf{D}$, respectively. Thus we can rewrite Equation (63) as follows:

$$\mathbf{H}_1 \cdot \mathbf{H}_1^T \cdot \mathbf{F} \cdot \mathbf{H}_1^T \cdot \mathbf{H}_1 \cdot \alpha_1 + C_1 \cdot \mathbf{D} \cdot \xi + C_2 \cdot \mathbf{K}_{ELM1} \cdot \mathbf{N_1} \cdot \mathbf{K}_{ELM1} \cdot \alpha_1 = 0 \tag{64}$$

Obviously, Equation (64) is the optimal solution to the following problem:

$$\min_{\alpha_1, \xi} \ \frac{1}{2}\alpha_1^T \cdot \mathbf{K}_{ELM1} \cdot \mathbf{F} \cdot \mathbf{K}_{ELM1} \cdot \alpha_1 + \frac{C_1}{2} \cdot \xi^T \cdot \mathbf{D} \cdot \xi + \frac{C_2}{2} \cdot \alpha_1^T \cdot \mathbf{K}_{ELM1} \cdot \mathbf{N}_1 \cdot \mathbf{K}_{ELM1} \cdot \alpha_1 \tag{65}$$

Now, assume that $\bar{\alpha}_1$ and $\bar{\xi}$ denote the updated α_1 and ξ of Algorithm 2, respectively. Thus we can get:

$$\begin{aligned}
&\frac{1}{2}\bar{\alpha}_1^T \cdot \mathbf{K}_{ELM1} \cdot \mathbf{F} \cdot \mathbf{K}_{ELM1} \cdot \bar{\alpha}_1 + \frac{C_1}{2} \cdot \bar{\xi}^T \cdot \mathbf{D} \cdot \bar{\xi} \\
&+ \frac{C_2}{2} \cdot \bar{\alpha}_1^T \cdot \mathbf{K}_{ELM1} \cdot \mathbf{N}_1 \cdot \mathbf{K}_{ELM1} \cdot \bar{\alpha}_1 \\
&\leq \frac{1}{2}\alpha_1^T \cdot \mathbf{K}_{ELM1} \cdot \mathbf{F} \cdot \mathbf{K}_{ELM1} \cdot \alpha_1 + \frac{C_1}{2} \cdot \xi^T \cdot \mathbf{D} \cdot \xi \\
&+ \frac{C_2}{2} \cdot \alpha_1^T \cdot \mathbf{K}_{ELM1} \cdot \mathbf{N}_1 \cdot \mathbf{K}_{ELM1} \cdot \alpha_1
\end{aligned} \tag{66}$$

we have rewritten Equation (66) as follows

$$\begin{aligned}
&\sum_{i=1}^{m_1} \frac{(\mathbf{K}_{ELM1}\bar{\alpha}_1)^T(\mathbf{K}_{ELM1}\bar{\alpha}_1)}{2|\mathbf{h}^T(x_i)\mathbf{H}_1^T\alpha_1|} + \sum_{j=1}^{m_2} \frac{C_1(\bar{\xi}_j)^2}{2|\xi_j|} \\
&+ \frac{C_2}{2}\bar{\alpha}_1^T \cdot \mathbf{K}_{ELM1} \cdot \mathbf{N}_1 \cdot \mathbf{K}_{ELM1} \cdot \bar{\alpha}_1 \\
&\leq \sum_{i=1}^{m_1} \frac{(\mathbf{K}_{ELM1}\alpha_1)^T(\mathbf{K}_{ELM1}\alpha_1)}{2|\mathbf{h}^T(x_i)\mathbf{H}_1^T\alpha_1|} + \sum_{j=1}^{m_2} \frac{C_1(\xi_j)^2}{2|\xi_j|} \\
&+ \frac{C_2}{2}\alpha_1^T \cdot \mathbf{K}_{ELM1} \cdot \mathbf{N}_1 \cdot \mathbf{K}_{ELM1} \cdot \alpha_1
\end{aligned} \tag{67}$$

Here, we let $x = \mathbf{K}_{ELM1}\bar{\alpha}_1$, $y = \mathbf{K}_{ELM1}\alpha_1$, $C = C_1$, $p = \bar{\xi}_j$, $q = \xi_j$. Based on Lemma 2, we have

$$\begin{aligned}
&|\mathbf{K}_{ELM1} \cdot \bar{\alpha}_1| - \frac{|\mathbf{K}_{ELM1} \cdot \bar{\alpha}_1|^2}{2|\mathbf{K}_{ELM1} \cdot \alpha_1|} + C_1 \cdot \left(|\bar{\xi}_j| - \frac{|\bar{\xi}_j|^2}{2|\xi_j|}\right) \\
&\leq |\mathbf{K}_{ELM1} \cdot \alpha_1| - \frac{|\mathbf{K}_{ELM1} \cdot \alpha_1|^2}{2|\mathbf{K}_{ELM1} \cdot \alpha_1|} + C_1 \cdot \left(|\xi_j| - \frac{|\xi_j|^2}{2|\xi_j|}\right)
\end{aligned} \tag{68}$$

then we can get

$$\begin{aligned}
&\sum_{i=1}^{m_1}\left(\left|\mathbf{h}^T(x_i) \cdot \mathbf{H}_1^T \cdot \bar{\alpha}_1\right| - \frac{|\mathbf{K}_{ELM1} \cdot \bar{\alpha}_1|^2}{2|\mathbf{K}_{ELM1} \cdot \alpha_1|}\right) + C_1 \sum_{j=1}^{m_2}\left(|\bar{\xi}_j| - \frac{|\bar{\xi}_j|^2}{2|\xi_j|}\right) \\
&\leq \sum_{i=1}^{m_1}\left(\left|\mathbf{h}^T(x_i) \cdot \mathbf{H}_1^T \cdot \alpha_1\right| - \frac{|\mathbf{K}_{ELM1} \cdot \alpha_1|^2}{2|\mathbf{K}_{ELM1} \cdot \alpha_1|}\right) + C_1 \sum_{j=1}^{m_2}\left(|\xi_j| - \frac{|\xi_j|^2}{2|\xi_j|}\right)
\end{aligned} \tag{69}$$

combining (67) and (69), we can get the following inequalities

$$\begin{aligned}
&\sum_{i=1}^{m_1}\left(\left|\mathbf{h}^T(x_i) \cdot \mathbf{H}_1^T \cdot \bar{\alpha}_1\right|\right) + C_1 \sum_{j=1}^{m_2}(|\bar{\xi}_j|) \\
&+ \frac{C_2}{2}\bar{\alpha}_1^T \cdot \mathbf{K}_{ELM1} \cdot \mathbf{N}_1 \cdot \mathbf{K}_{ELM1} \cdot \bar{\alpha}_1 \\
&\leq \sum_{i=1}^{m_1}\left(\left|\mathbf{h}^T(x_i) \cdot \mathbf{H}_1^T \cdot \alpha_1\right|\right) + C_1 \sum_{j=1}^{m_2}(|\xi_j|) \\
&+ \frac{C_2}{2}\alpha_1^T \cdot \mathbf{K}_{ELM1} \cdot \mathbf{N}_1 \cdot \mathbf{K}_{ELM1} \cdot \alpha_1
\end{aligned} \tag{70}$$

further, we can get

$$\begin{aligned}&\sum_{i=1}^{m_1}\min\left(\left|\mathbf{h}^T(x_i)\cdot\mathbf{H}_1^T\cdot\bar{\alpha}_1\right|\right)+C_1\sum_{j=1}^{m_2}\min(|\bar{\xi}_j|)\\&+\frac{C_2}{2}\bar{\alpha}_1^T\cdot\mathbf{K}_{ELM1}\cdot\mathbf{N}_1\cdot\mathbf{K}_{ELM1}\cdot\bar{\alpha}_1\\&\leq\sum_{i=1}^{m_1}\min\left(\left|\mathbf{h}^T(x_i)\cdot\mathbf{H}_1^T\cdot\alpha_1\right|\right)+C_1\sum_{j=1}^{m_2}\min(|\xi_j|)\\&+\frac{C_2}{2}\alpha_1^T\cdot\mathbf{K}_{ELM1}\cdot\mathbf{N}_1\cdot\mathbf{K}_{ELM1}\cdot\alpha_1\end{aligned} \tag{71}$$

Therefore, we have $J(\bar{\alpha}_1,\bar{\xi})\leq J(\alpha_1,\xi)$. Similarly, when $\left\|\mathbf{h}^T(x_i)\mathbf{H}_1^T\alpha_1\right\|_1\leq\varepsilon_1$ and $\left\|\xi_j\right\|\geq\varepsilon_2$, or $\left\|\mathbf{h}^T(x_i)\mathbf{H}_1^T\alpha_1\right\|_1\geq\varepsilon_1$ and $\left\|\xi_j\right\|\leq\varepsilon_2$, or $\left\|\mathbf{h}^T(x_i)\mathbf{H}_1^T\alpha_1\right\|_1\geq\varepsilon_1$ and $\left\|\xi_j\right\|\geq\varepsilon_2$, we can obviously get $J(\bar{\alpha}_1,\bar{\xi})\leq J(\alpha_1,\xi)$. Thus, the inequality $J(\bar{\alpha}_1,\bar{\xi})\leq J(\alpha_1,\xi)$ holds. The three terms in Equation (60) are equal to or greater than 0. Meaning that Algorithm 2 decreases objective of problem (42) until convergence. □

Theorem 2. *Algorithm 2 will converge to a local optimum to the problem in (42).*

Proof. Here, we only use (42) as an example to prove Theorem 2.

When $\left\|\mathbf{h}^T(x_i)\mathbf{H}_1^T\alpha_1\right\|_1\leq\varepsilon_1$ and $\left\|\xi_j\right\|_1\leq\varepsilon_2$, we write out the formula of (42) Lagrange function:

$$\begin{aligned}\mathcal{L}_1(\alpha_1,\xi,\lambda)&=\sum_{i=1}^{m_1}\left(\left\|\mathbf{h}^T(x_i)\mathbf{H}_1^T\alpha_1\right\|_1\right)+C_1\sum_{j=1}^{m_2}\left(\left\|\xi_j\right\|_1\right)\\&+\frac{C_2}{2}\alpha_1^T\cdot\mathbf{K}_{ELM1}\cdot\mathbf{N}_1\cdot\mathbf{K}_{ELM1}\cdot\alpha_1-\lambda^T\sum_{j=1}^{m_2}\left(\mathbf{h}^T(x_j)\mathbf{H}_1^T\alpha_1+\xi_j-1\right)\end{aligned} \tag{72}$$

Then, we take the derivative of $\mathcal{L}(\alpha_1,\xi,\lambda)$ with respect to α_1

$$\begin{aligned}\frac{\partial\mathcal{L}_1}{\partial\alpha_1}&=\sum_{i=1}^{m_1}\frac{\mathbf{H}_1\mathbf{h}(x_i)\mathbf{h}^T(x_i)\mathbf{H}_1^T\alpha_1}{\left|\mathbf{h}^T(x_i)\mathbf{H}_1^T\alpha_1\right|}+C_2\cdot\mathbf{K}_{ELM1}\cdot\mathbf{N}_1\cdot\mathbf{K}_{ELM1}\cdot\alpha_1\\&+\mathbf{H}_1\cdot\mathbf{H}_2^T\cdot\lambda=\mathbf{K}_{ELM1}\cdot(\mathbf{F}+C_2\cdot\mathbf{N}_1)\cdot\mathbf{K}_{ELM1}\cdot\alpha_1+\mathbf{H}_1\cdot\mathbf{H}_2^T\cdot\lambda=\mathbf{0}\end{aligned} \tag{73}$$

Similarly, we get the Lagrangian function of problem (44):

$$\begin{aligned}\mathcal{L}_2(\alpha_1,\xi,\alpha)&=\frac{1}{2}\alpha_1^T\cdot\mathbf{K}_{ELM1}\cdot(\mathbf{F}+C_2\cdot\mathbf{N}_1)\cdot\mathbf{K}_{ELM1}\cdot\alpha_1+\frac{C_1}{2}\cdot\xi^T\cdot\mathbf{D}\cdot\xi\\&-\lambda^T\cdot\left(-\mathbf{H}_2\cdot\mathbf{H}_1^T\cdot\alpha_1+\xi-\mathbf{e}_2\right)\end{aligned} \tag{74}$$

Taking the derivative of $\mathcal{L}_2(\alpha_1,\xi,\alpha)$ with respect to α_1:

$$\frac{\partial\mathcal{L}_2}{\partial\alpha_1}=\mathbf{K}_{ELM1}\cdot(\mathbf{F}+C_2\cdot\mathbf{N}_1)\cdot\mathbf{K}_{ELM1}\cdot\alpha_1+\mathbf{H}_1\cdot\mathbf{H}_2^T\cdot\lambda=\mathbf{0} \tag{75}$$

The other three cases are similar. From the discussion above, we may safely draw that Equations (73) and (75) are equivalent, so we can use problem (44) instead of problem (42) to solve CL_1-FTELM, which further illustrates that Algorithm 2 can converge to a local optimal solution. □

5. Experiments

Description of the four comparison algorithms:

OPTELM: The optimization function of the model consists of minimizing the L_2-norm of the weight vector and minimizing empirical loss. It neither consider the establishment of two non-parallel hyperplanes to deal with classification tasks, nor consider the statistical information of samples. At the same time, since it uses L_2-norm metric and Hinge loss, it has weak anti-noise ability.

TELM: The optimization function of the model consists of minimizing the distance from the sample points to the hyperplane as well as minimizing empirical loss. TELM does not fully consider the statistical information of the sample. At the same time, its metric uses the L_2-norm metric and the loss function uses the Hinge loss. When there is noise in the data set, the influence of noise data will be amplified and the accuracy of classification will be reduced.

FELM: The optimization function of the model includes minimizing the L_2-norm of the weight vector, minimizing empirical loss, and minimizing the within-class scatter of the number sample data. Although FELM takes into account the statistics of the sample, it has to deal with a much larger optimization problem than the twin extreme learning machines, which is time-consuming. At the same time, FELM still continues the metric and loss used by OPTELM, so its anti-noise ability is weak.

CL_1-TWSVM: CL_1-TWSVM is formed on the basis of twin support vector machines by changing the model's metric and loss to capped L_1-norm. Although CL_1-TWSVM has the ability to resist noise, it does not fully take into account the statistics of the data. Meanwhile, CL_1-TWSVM not only needs to solve the weight vector of the hyperplane, but also needs to solve the bias of the hyperplane, so it is time-consuming.

We systematically compare our algorithm above advanced algorithms (OPTELM [12], TELM [14], FELM [19], and CL_1-TWSVM [29]) on artificial synthetic datasets and UCI real datasets to verify the effectiveness of our FTELM and CL_1-FTELM. In Section 5.1, we describe the relevant experimental setting in detail. We describe their performance in different cases in Sections 5.2 and 5.3, respectively. In Section 5.4, we use the one-versus-rest multi-classification method to perform data classification tasks in four image datasets: Yale "http://www.cad.zju.edu.cn/home/dengcai/Data/FaceData.html (accessed on 15 February 2023)", ORL "http://www.cad.zju.edu.cn/home/dengcai/Data/FaceData.html (accessed on 15 February 2023)", USPS "http://www.cad.zju.edu.cn/home/dengcai/Data/MLData.html (accessed on 15 February 2023)" handwritten digit dataset and MNIST "http://www.cad.zju.edu.cn/home/dengcai/Data/MLData.html (accessed on 15 February 2023)" dataset.

5.1. Experimental Setting

All experiments were implemented in MATLAB R2020a installed in a personal computer (PC) with an AMD Radeon Graphics processor (3.2 GHz), and 16 GB random-access memory (RAM). For CL_1-TWSVM, and CL_1-FTELM, we take the maximum number of iterations to be 100 and the iteration stopping threshold to be 0.001. The activation functions used in a total of five models (OPTELM, TELM, FELM, FTELM, and CL_1-FTELM) are $G(x) = \frac{1}{1+e^{-x}}$. The Gaussian kernel function $K(x,z) = e^{-\frac{\|x-z\|^2}{2\sigma^2}}$ was used for CL_1-TWSVM. The parameters selected by all the above algorithms are as follows: ε_1, ε_2, ε_3, ε_4 were selected from $\{10^i | -6,-5,-4\}$, C_1, C_2, C_3, C_4 were selected from $\{10^i | -5,-4,\dots,4,5\}$, σ was chosen from $\{2^i | -3,-2,\dots,2,3\}$, and the hidden layer node number L was chosen from $\{50,100,200,500,1000,2000,5000,10{,}000\}$. The optimal parameters used by the model are selected by 10-fold cross-validation and grid search. Normalization was performed for both artificial and UCI datasets. For image datasets, we randomly select 20% of the data as the test set to get the classification accuracy of the algorithm. All experimental processes are repeated 10 times and the average of the 10 test results is used as the performance measure, and the evaluation criterion selected in this paper is classification accuracy (ACC).

5.2. *Experiments on Artificial Datasets*

We first do experiments on the Banana, Circle, Two spirals, and XOR datasets which are generated by trigonometric function(sine, cosine), two circle lines, two spirals lines, and two intersecting lines, respectively. The two-dimensional distributions of the four synthetic datasets are shown in Figure 1. Dark blue '+' represents class 1, and cyan '∘' represents class 2. Figure 2 illustrates the experimental results of four twin algorithms namely TELM, FTELM, CL_1-TWSVM, and CL_1-FTELM for four datasets with 0%, 20%, and 25% noise in terms of accuracy. From Figure 2a, we can observe that the classification accuracy of our FTELM and CL_1-FTELM in Banana and Two spirals datasets is higher than the other two methods. In the Circle and XOR datasets, the classification accuracy of the four methods is similar. The experimental results show that fully considering the statistical information of the data can effectively improve the classification accuracy of the classifier, which shows that our CL_1-FTELM method is effective. From Figure 2b,c, we can see that the overall effect of FTELM is better than TELM. This shows the importance of fully considering the statistical information of the sample. At the same time, we can see that CL_1-FTELM has the best effect, followed by CL_1-TWSVM. It shows that the capped L_1-norm can control the influence of noise on the model in a certain range, and further shows the effectiveness of using the capped L_1-norm. In summary, Figure 2 illustrates the effectiveness of considering sample statistics information and changing the distance metric and loss of the model into capped L_1-norm at the same time.

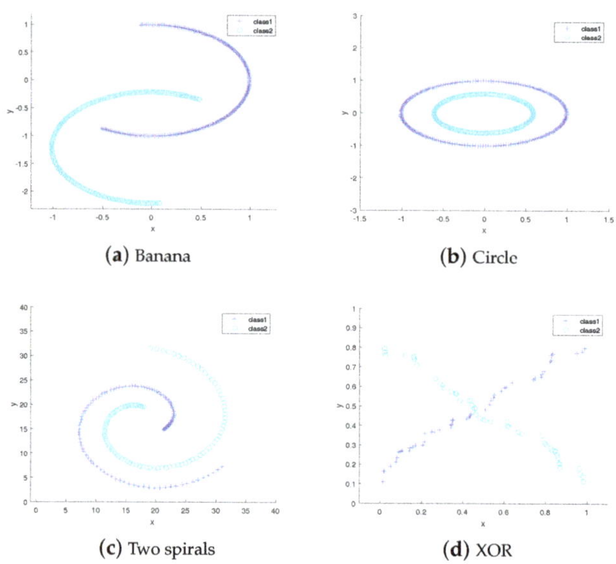

(**a**) Banana (**b**) Circle

(**c**) Two spirals (**d**) XOR

Figure 1. Four types of data without noise.

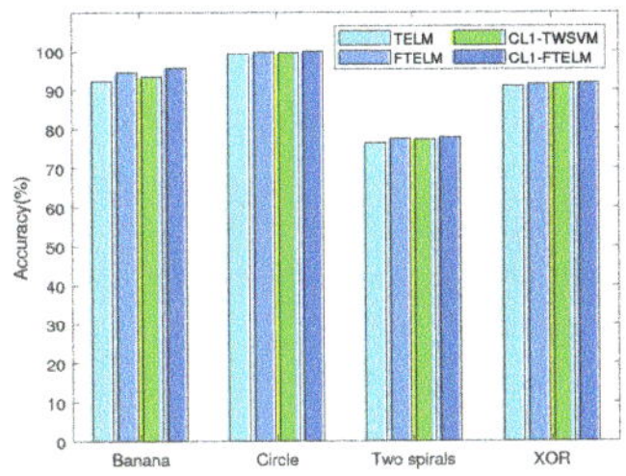

(a) Accuracy for four algorithms on four types of data without noise.

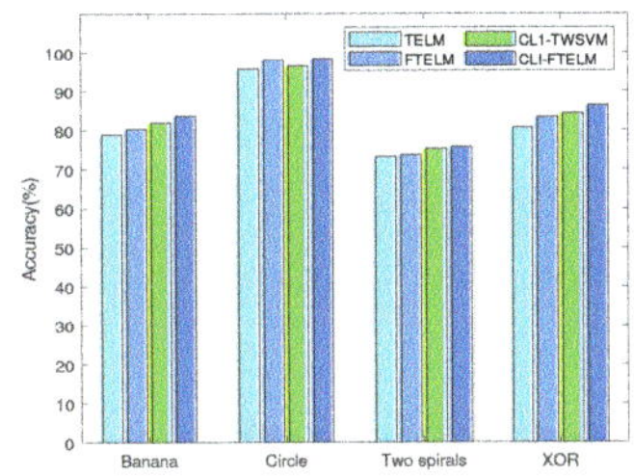

(b) Accuracy for four algorithms on four types of data with 20% noise.

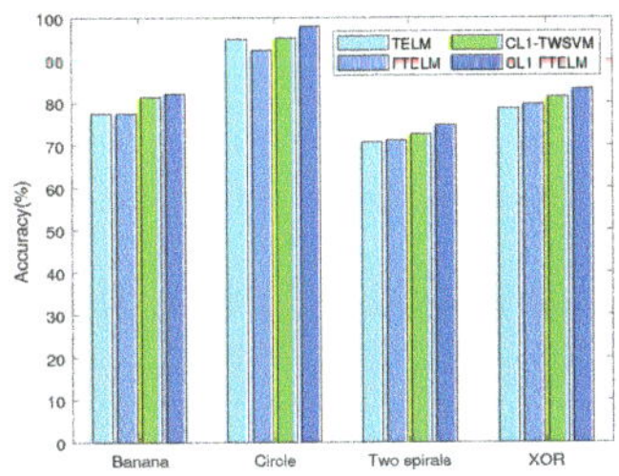

(c) Accuracy for four algorithms on four types of data with 25% noise.

Figure 2. Accuracy for TELM, FTELM, CL_1-TWSVM, and CL_1-FTELM on four types of data with 0%, 20%, and 25% noise.

To further show the robustness of CL_1-FTELM, we add noise with different ratios to the Circle dataset. Figure 3 shows the accuracy of TELM, FTELM, CL_1-TWSVM, and CL_1-FTELM algorithms on the Circle dataset in different noises ratios. The ratio is set in the range of $\{0.1, 0.15, 0.2, 0.25\}$. We plot the accuracy results of ten experiments with different noise ratios in a box-shaped plot. By observing the median of the four subgraphs, we can find that the median of CL_1-FTELM algorithm is much higher than the other three algorithms. And CL_1-FTELM method in four different noise ratios results is relatively concentrated. In other words, the variance of ten experimental results obtained by the CL_1-FTELM algorithm is smaller and the mean value is larger. The above results show that our CL_1-FTELM has better stability and better classification effect in environments containing noise. This shows the effectiveness and noise resistance of the distance metric and loss functions of the model using the capped L_1-norm.

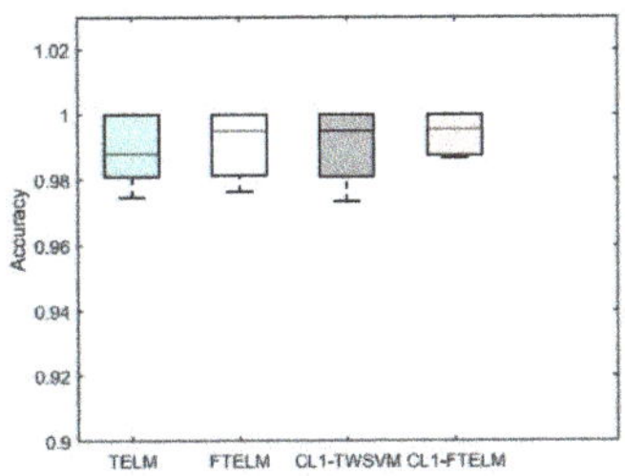

(a) Accuracy for four algorithms on Circle dataset with 10% noise.

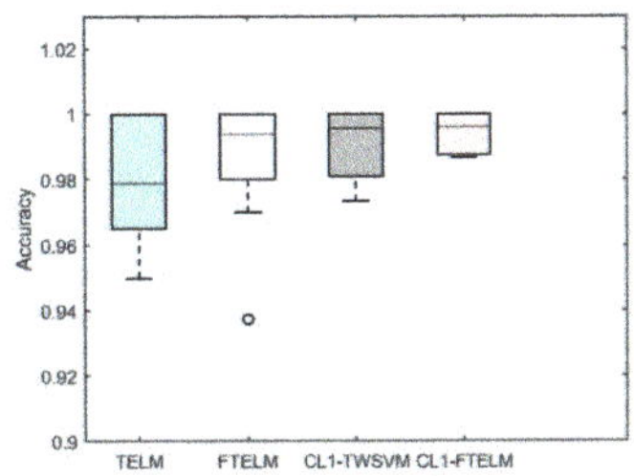

(b) Accuracy for four algorithms on Circle dataset with 15% noise.

Figure 3. *Cont.*

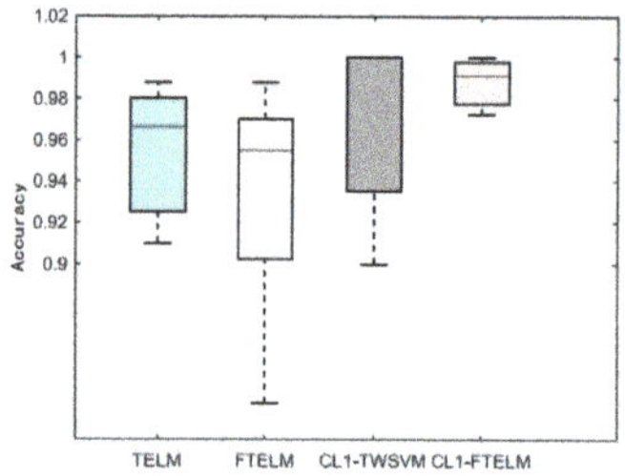

(c) Accuracy for four algorithms on Circle dataset with 20% noise.

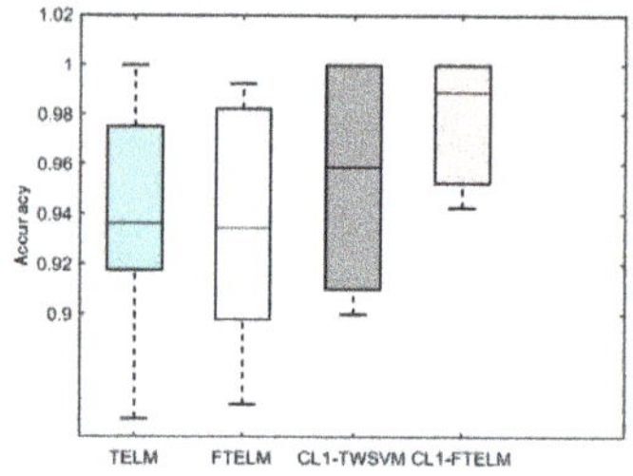

(d) Accuracy for four algorithms on Circle dataset data with 25% noise.

Figure 3. Accuracy for TELM, FTELM, CL_1-TWSVM, and CL_1-FTELM on Circle dataset with noise in different ratios.

5.3. Experiments on UCI Datasets

In this section, we conduct the numerical simulation on UCI datasets. Table 1 describes the features of the UCI datasets used in detail. We also added two algorithms (OPTELM, FELM) to verify the classification performance of FTELM and CL_1-FTELM in ten UCI data sets.

Table 1. Characteristics of UCI datasets.

Datasets	Instances	Attributes	Datasets	Instances	Attributes
Australian	690	14	Vote	432	16
German	1000	24	Ionosphere	351	35
Breast cancer	699	9	Pima	768	8
WDBC	569	30	QSAR	1055	41
Wholesale	440	7	Spam	4601	57

All experimental results obtained based on the optimal parameters are shown in Table 2. Here, the average running time according to the optimal parameters is denoted by Times(s), and the average classification plus or minus standard deviation is denoted by $ACC\pm$. From Table 2, we can see that FTELM performs better than OPTELM, TELM, and FELM on all ten datasets. This indicates that adding Fisher regularization term on the basis of TELM framework can significantly improve the accuracy of model classification. In addition, the average training time of FTELM algorithm on most data sets is smaller than that of FELM algorithm, which indicates that FTELM has inherited the advantages of TELM's short training time. In addition, we also can draw our CL_1-FTELM in most data sets has achieved the highest classification accuracy besides the WDBC data set. Through the analysis of the above results, we can conclude that the Fisher regularization and capped L_1-norm added to the TELM learning framework can effectively improve the performance of the classifier. It is shown that the proposed FTELM and CL_1-FTELM are efficient algorithms.

In order to more significantly verify the robustness of CL_1-FTELM to outliers, we added 20% and 25% Gaussian noise to 10 data sets, respectively. All experimental results are presented in Tables 3 and 4. From Tables 3 and 4, we find that the classification accuracy of all six algorithms decreases after adding noise. However, the classification accuracy of our algorithm CL_1-FTELM is the highest of the eight datasets, which further reveals the effectiveness of our method using capped L_1-norm instead of Hinge loss and L_2-norm distance metric. Compared with the other five algorithms, our CL_1-FTELM algorithm is more time-consuming. This is due to that CL_1-FTELM requires a lot of time in the process of training to iterative calculation, eliminating outliers, and computing graph matrices. In addition, we used different noise factor values (0.1, 0.15, 0.2, 0.25, 0.3) on the Cancer,

German, Ionosphere, and WDBC for the six algorithms. The experimental results are given in Figure 4. It can be seen from Figure 4a that when the Breast Cancer dataset contains 10% noise, the effects of our FTELM and CL_1-FTELM are comparable. This shows that it is important to consider the statistical information of the sample. As the ratio of noise increases, the classification accuracy of all methods decreases, but our CL_1-FTELM still has the highest accuracy. This illustrates the effectiveness of our using the capped L_1-norm. Figure 4b shows that with the increase of noise ratio, the decline trend of accuracy of CL_1-TWSVM and CL_1-FTELM is similar, but CL_1-FTELM is still the most stable among the six methods when facing the influence of noise. From both Figure 4c,d, we can clearly observe that the anti-noise effect of our CL_1-FTELM is the best. This illustrates the effectiveness of using the Fisher regularization term as well as the capped L_1-norm.

Table 2. Experimental results on UCI datasets, The best results are marked in bold.

Datasets	OPTELM ACC $\pm$ S (%) Times (s)	TELM ACC $\pm$ S (%) Times (s)	FELM ACC $\pm$ S (%) Times (s)	FTELM ACC $\pm$ S (%) Times (s)	CL_1-TWSVM ACC $\pm$ S (%) Times (s)	CL_1-FTELM ACC $\pm$ S (%) Times (s)
Australian	85.31 $\pm$ 0.34	85.60 $\pm$ 0.44	85.46 $\pm$ 0.19	86.79 $\pm$ 0.33	85.82 $\pm$ 0.28	**87.13 $\pm$ 0.52**
	0.682	0.593	1.698	**0.456**	1.676	2.533
German	76.26 $\pm$ 0.52	76.40 $\pm$ 0.16	76.50 $\pm$ 0.42	76.56 $\pm$ 0.47	76.70 $\pm$ 0.25	**77.15 $\pm$ 1.18**
	1.182	0.979	4.555	**0.474**	5.318	7.006
Breast cancer	95.70 $\pm$ 0.24	96.35 $\pm$ 0.15	96.45 $\pm$ 0.09	97.07 $\pm$ 0.15	96.39 $\pm$ 0.13	**97.32 $\pm$ 0.53**
	0.601	0.668	1.646	**0.505**	4.011	3.902
WDBC	96.71 $\pm$ 0.27	97.13 $\pm$ 0.48	97.55 $\pm$ 0.17	**98.55 $\pm$ 0.26**	97.09 $\pm$ 0.25	97.86 $\pm$ 0.21
	0.416	0.605	1.144	0.578	3.618	4.551
Wholesale	87.35 $\pm$ 0.93	89.86 $\pm$ 0.84	90.26 $\pm$ 0.12	90.56 $\pm$ 0.33	89.89 $\pm$ 0.30	**90.70 $\pm$ 0.56**
	0.278	2.091	0.665	0.359	1.246	1.377
Vote	95.31 $\pm$ 0.16	95.56 $\pm$ 0.30	96.04 $\pm$ 0.24	96.12 $\pm$ 0.31	95.21 $\pm$ 0.54	**96.43 $\pm$ 0.35**
	0.256	0.502	0.651	0.445	1.077	0.992
Ionosphere	90.59 $\pm$ 0.84	91.38 $\pm$ 0.52	92.32 $\pm$ 0.32	92.74 $\pm$ 0.83	92.56 $\pm$ 0.54	**93.32 $\pm$ 1.21**
	0.184	0.476	0.421	0.268	1.128	2.237
Pima	76.83 $\pm$ 0.73	77.51 $\pm$ 0.08	77.79 $\pm$ 0.10	78.24 $\pm$ 0.49	77.49 $\pm$ 0.37	**78.82 $\pm$ 0.98**
	0.858	**0.795**	2.099	0.932	1.743	4.708
QSAR	83.91 $\pm$ 0.66	86.56 $\pm$ 0.19	87.12 $\pm$ 0.18	87.35 $\pm$ 0.23	85.72 $\pm$ 0.59	**87.50 $\pm$ 0.56**
	1.442	**0.979**	2.489	2.864	2.665	14.288
Spam	85.57 $\pm$ 0.65	91.38 $\pm$ 0.52	89.67 $\pm$ 0.21	91.94 $\pm$ 1.23	90.56 $\pm$ 1.23	**92.27 $\pm$ 0.54**
	125.498	**64.314**	488.251	108.232	158.145	170.261

Table 3. Experimental results on UCI datasets with 20% noise, The best results are marked in bold.

Datasets	OPTELM ACC $\pm$ S (%) Times (s)	TELM ACC $\pm$ S (%) Times (s)	FELM ACC $\pm$ S (%) Times (s)	FTELM ACC $\pm$ S (%) Times (s)	CL_1-TWSVM ACC $\pm$ S (%) Times (s)	CL_1-FTELM ACC $\pm$ S (%) Times (s)
Australian	79.68 $\pm$ 1.75	80.37 $\pm$ 0.56	79.06 $\pm$ 1.36	80.44 $\pm$ 1.34	81.98 $\pm$ 0.87	**82.78 $\pm$ 0.57**
	0.621	0.728	1.756	**0.224**	1.708	3.224
German	69.67 $\pm$ 0.97	73.57 $\pm$ 1.85	71.99 $\pm$ 1.35	72.76 $\pm$ 0.88	73.86 $\pm$ 1.35	**74.32 $\pm$ 1.12**
	1.318	0.981	4.102	**0.398**	5.673	6.764
Breast cancer	70.60 $\pm$ 0.45	76.97 $\pm$ 0.42	70.32 $\pm$ 0.37	77.81 $\pm$ 0.56	79.84 $\pm$ 0.37	**80.14 $\pm$ 0.91**
	0.803	0.706	1.552	**0.315**	4.572	5.034
WDBC	82.98 $\pm$ 0.15	84.38 $\pm$ 1.01	83.29 $\pm$ 0.68	89.43 $\pm$ 1.15	89.98 $\pm$ 0.30	**93.77 $\pm$ 0.32**
	0.419	**0.204**	0.992	0.376	3.899	4.861
Wholesale	73.40 $\pm$ 0.93	73.77 $\pm$ 0.69	73.74 $\pm$ 0.76	74.77 $\pm$ 0.56	78.74 $\pm$ 0.91	**79.47 $\pm$ 2.58**
	0.275	0.543	0.659	0.404	0.849	1.420
Vote	93.48 $\pm$ 0.62	**94.36 $\pm$ 0.60**	94.24 $\pm$ 0.82	94.10 $\pm$ 0.94	93.90 $\pm$ 0.44	94.29 $\pm$ 0.61
	0.277	0.619	0.549	**0.114**	1.048	1.398
Ionosphere	80.79 $\pm$ 2.88	82.71 $\pm$ 2.09	81.00 $\pm$ 3.11	86.06 $\pm$ 1.67	85.76 $\pm$ 1.58	**87.74 $\pm$ 1.08**
	0.159	**0.021**	0.456	0.737	0.391	2.081
Pima	65.79 $\pm$ 0.23	67.07 $\pm$ 0.56	66.12 $\pm$ 0.12	66.30 $\pm$ 1.34	70.25 $\pm$ 1.57	**71.42 $\pm$ 0.94**
	0.873	**0.649**	2.051	1.492	1.758	3.968
QSAR	68.32 $\pm$ 2.48	68.80 $\pm$ 0.95	68.54 $\pm$ 2.50	72.28 $\pm$ 2.18	71.09 $\pm$ 2.02	**72.31 $\pm$ 1.98**
	1.534	3.089	4.578	**0.892**	1.828	9.151
Spam	83.16 $\pm$ 0.57	87.38 $\pm$ 2.31	85.66 $\pm$ 0.65	**87.98 $\pm$ 0.87**	85.77 $\pm$ 2.21	86.75 $\pm$ 0.45
	128.798	**60.565**	432.257	106.267	147.365	160.231

Table 4. Experimental results on UCI datasets with 25% noise, The best results are marked in bold.

Datasets	OPTELM ACC ± S (%) Times (s)	TELM ACC ± S (%) Times (s)	FELM ACC ± S (%) Times (s)	FTELM ACC ± S (%) Times (s)	CL_1-TWSVM ACC ± S (%) Times (s)	CL_1-FTELM ACC ± S (%) Times (s)
Australian	73.68 ± 2.20	75.41 ± 1.52	74.25 ± 2.01	76.40 ± 1.19	80.56 ± 1.07	**81.63 ± 0.71**
	0.585	0.673	1.627	**0.206**	2.205	2.261
German	69.72 ± 0.13	72.87 ± 0.82	71.41 ± 0.88	73.15 ± 0.87	73.13 ± 1.16	**73.25 ± 0.76**
	1.565	0.871	3.855	**0.342**	5.233	6.798
Breast cancer	67.59 ± 0.18	70.43 ± 0.79	67.23 ± 0.24	71.65 ± 0.58	70.93 ± 0.52	**72.71 ± 0.49**
	0.654	0.513	1.438	**0.309**	4.476	5.124
WDBC	79.61 ± 0.78	81.66 ± 0.84	79.83 ± 0.72	87.96 ± 1.13	88.50 ± 0.74	**92.43 ± 0.76**
	0.417	**0.197**	0.887	0.334	3.675	4.861
Wholesale	71.79 ± 1.03	71.63 ± 0.89	69.63 ± 0.38	71.60 ± 1.02	75.53 ± 1.02	**75.74 ± 3.48**
	0.570	2.021	0.623	**0.338**	1.147	1.387
Vote	92.62 ± 0.88	92.95 ± 0.50	93.12 ± 0.80	93.21 ± 0.80	93.21 ± 0.68	**93.50 ± 1.00**
	0.252	0.503	0.514	**0.121**	1.213	1.390
Ionosphere	78.15 ± 2.94	78.79 ± 3.01	76.62 ± 3.67	83.59 ± 1.49	82.94 ± 2.90	**85.03 ± 2.28**
	0.229	**0.058**	0.313	0.737	0.576	1.987
Pima	65.67 ± 0.12	65.45 ± 1.55	65.89 ± 0.12	65.79 ± 0.14	**69.01 ± 1.55**	68.51 ± 2.75
	0.803	0.761	2.182	**0.471**	5.532	4.012
QSAR	67.49 ± 3.08	67.81 ± 1.63	70.30 ± 2.33	**71.53 ± 3.00**	70.49 ± 2.13	69.72 ± 2.14
	2.067	2.730	4.251	**0.849**	1.783	12.564
Spam	71.77 ± 1.05	75.35 ± 0.72	70.89 ± 1.23	76.43 ± 1.16	83.56 ± 0.26	**84.75 ± 0.78**
	99.541	**61.254**	462.221	116.267	142.365	165.214

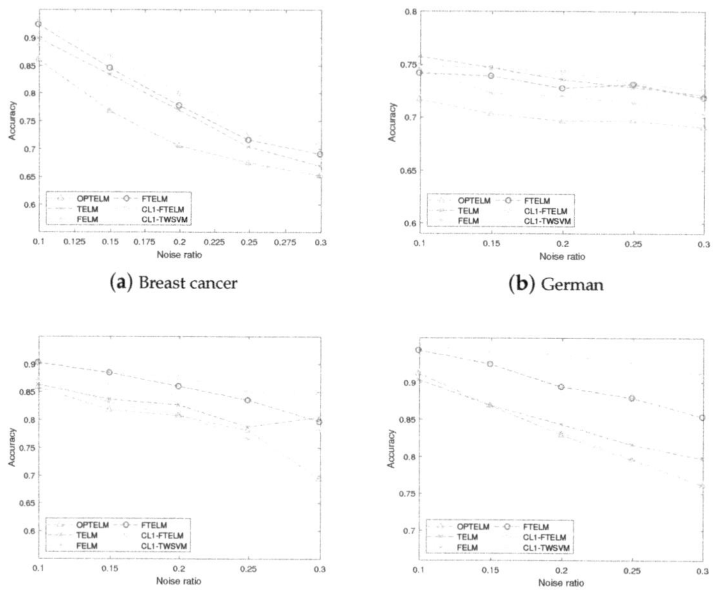

(**a**) Breast cancer (**b**) German

(**c**) Ionosphere (**d**) WDBC

Figure 4. Accuracies of six algorithms via different noises factors.

We also conduct experiments on four data sets (Breast cancer, QSAR, WDBC, and Vote) to verify the convergence of the proposed Algorithm 2. As shown in Figure 5, we plot the objective function value of each iteration. It can be seen that the objective function value converges to a fixed value rapidly with the increase in the number of iterations. This shows that our algorithm can make the objective function value can converge to a local optimal value within a limited number of iterations. The effectiveness and convergence of the Algorithm 2 are demonstrated.

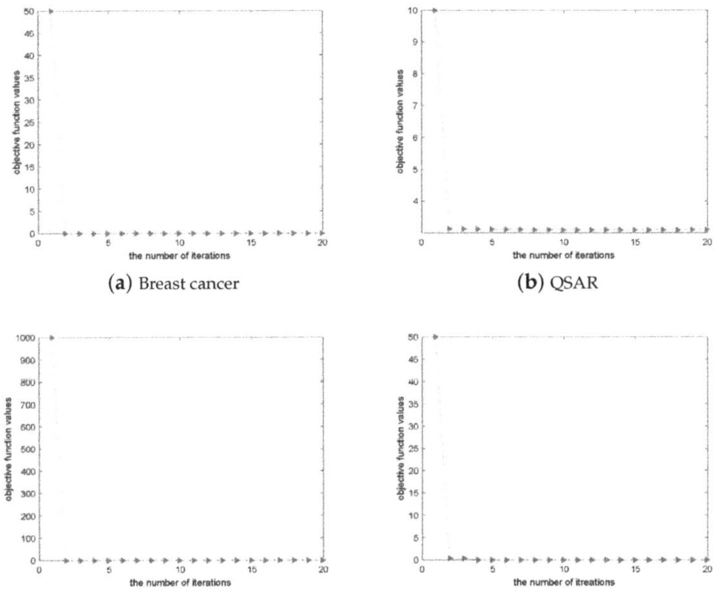

(a) Breast cancer **(b)** QSAR **(c)** WDBC **(d)** Vote

Figure 5. Objective values of CL_1-FTELM on four datasets.

5.4. Experiments on Image Datasets

The image datasets include Yale, ORL, USPS, and MNIST. Figure 6 illustrates examples of four high-dimensional image datasets. The number of samples and characteristics of the four image datasets are shown in Table 5. These four image datasets are used to investigate the performance of our FTELM and CL_1-FTELM for multi-classification. Specifically, for the MNIST dataset, we only select the first 2000 samples to participate in the experiment.

Table 5. Characteristics of image datasets.

Datasets	Instances	Attributes	Datasets	Instances	Attributes
Yale	165	1024	ORL	400	1024
USPS	9298	256	MNIST	70,000	784

Table 6 shows the specific experimental results. As can be seen from the results of the experiment, our CL_1-FTELM and CL_1-TWSVM have similar training times. This is because this paper uses an iterative algorithm to solve non-convex optimization problem of CL_1-FTELM , which is time-consuming. Simultaneously, the CL_1- FTELM at Yale, ORL, USPS, and MNIST four datasets classification accuracy is highest among the six algorithms. In addition, the classification accuracy of our FTELM algorithm on the four image datasets is the second highest after our CL_1-FTELM. The above results fully show the effectiveness of our two algorithms in dealing with multi-classification tasks.

Table 6. Experimental results on images and handwritten digits datasets. The best results are marked in bold.

Datasets	OPTELM ACC ± S (%) Times (s)	TELM ACC ± S (%) Times (s)	FELM ACC ± S (%) Times (s)	FTELM ACC ± S (%) Times (s)	CL_1-TWSVM ACC ± S (%) Times (s)	CL_1-FTELM ACC ± S (%) Times (s)
Yale	89.39 ± 2.85 0.126	91.44 ± 1.58 **0.101**	90.54 ± 2.01 0.262	92.23 ± 1.29 0.136	91.54 ± 1.07 0.135	**93.12 ± 1.71** 0.492
ORL	87.72 ± 1.53 1.169	90.87 ± 0.52 **0.483**	90.41 ± 0.78 3.064	92.45 ± 0.67 0.529	92.32 ± 1.16 1.338	**93.25 ± 0.46** 2.695
USPS	98.76 ± 0.18 118.729	98.83 ± 0.69 17.536	98.23 ± 0.24 134.438	99.65 ± 0.68 **6.795**	99.23 ± 0.42 358.368	**99.89 ± 0.89** 355.762
MNIST	89.61 ± 0.58 8.723	90.66 ± 0.74 1.237	89.83 ± 0.75 41.656	91.26 ± 1.13 **0.868**	90.88 ± 0.14 14.258	**91.53 ± 0.56** 14.973

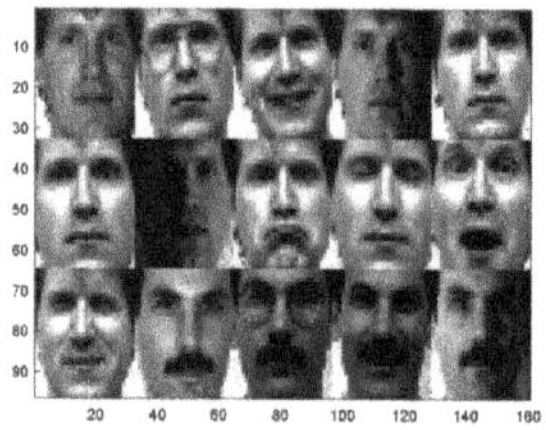

(**a**) Yale

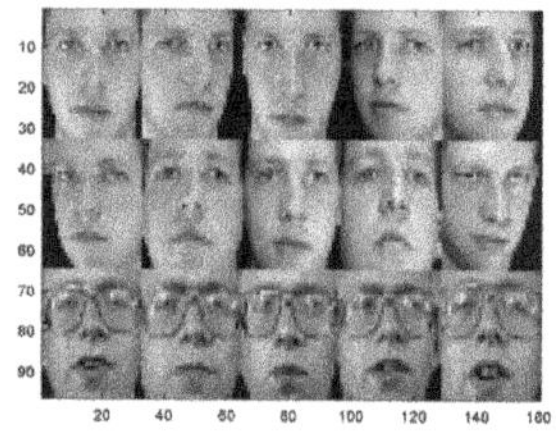

(**b**) ORL

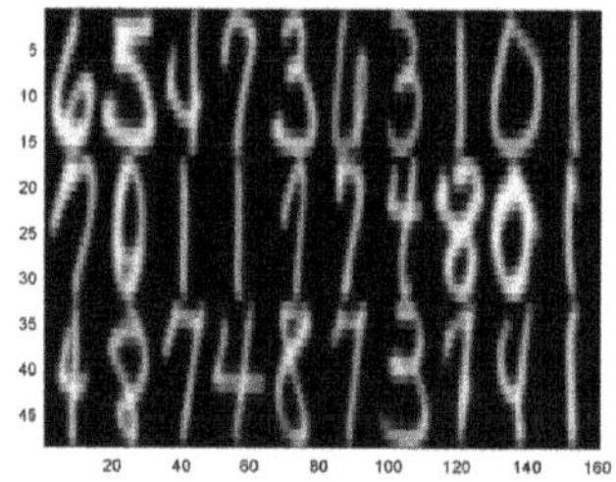

(**c**) USPS

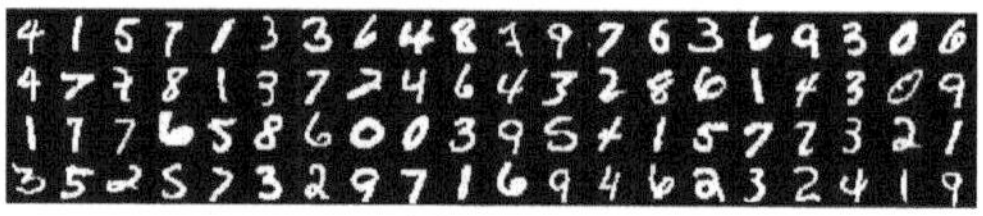

(**d**) MINST

Figure 6. Examples of four high-dimensional image datasets.

6. Conclusions

In this paper, we have proposed FTELM and CL_1-FTELM. FTELM not only inherits the advantages of TELM but also takes full account of the statistical information of samples, so as to further improve the classification performance of the classifier. Specifically, when there is no noise in the data or the ratio of noise is very small, our FTELM algorithm can deal with the classification problem very well, not only time-saving but also with high classification accuracy. CL_1-FTELM further improves the anti-noise ability of the model by replacing the L_2-norm and hinge loss in FTELM with capped L_1-norm. It not only utilizes the distribution information of the data but also improves the anti-noise ability of the model. Furthermore, we have designed two algorithms to solve the problems of FTELM and CL_1-FTELM. In addition, we present two theorems to prove the convergence of our CL_1-FTELM. However, in terms of computational cost, FTELM is better than CL_1-FTELM to some extent. Therefore, in future work, we will propose some new tricks to accelerate the computation of the CL_1-FTELM. In addition, trying to extend FTELM and CL_1-FTELM from supervised learning to semi-supervised learning framework is also a future research focus.

Author Contributions: Z.X., conceptualization, methodology, validation, investigation, project administration, writing—original draft. L.C., methodology, software, validation, formal analysis, investigation, data curation, writing—original draft. All authors have read and agreed to the published version of the manuscript.

Funding: The authors wish to acknowledge the financial support of the National Nature Science Youth Foundation of China (No. 61907012), the Start-up Funds of Scientific Research for Personnel Introduced by North Minzu University (No. 2019KYQD41), the Special project of North Minzu University (No. FWNX01), the Basic Research Plan of Key Scientific Research Projects of Colleges and Universities in Henan Province (No. 19A120005), the Construction Project of First-Class Disciplines in Ningxia Higher Education (NXYLXK2017B09), the Young Talent Cultivation Project of North Minzu University (No. 2021KYQD23), the Natural Science Foundation of Ningxia Provincial of China (No. 2022A0950), the Fundamental Research Funds for the Central Universities (No. 2022XYZSX03).

Informed Consent Statement: The authors declare that they have no known competing financial interests or personal relationships that could have appeared to influence the work reported in this paper.

Data Availability Statement: The UCI machine learning repository is available at "http://archive.ics.uci.edu/ml/datasets.php (accessed on 15 February 2023)". The image data are available at "http://www.cad.zju.edu.cn/home/dengcai/Data/FaceData.html (accessed on 15 February 2023)".

Acknowledgments: The authors thank the anonymous reviewers for their constructive comments.

Conflicts of Interest: The authors declare no conflict of interest.

References

1. Huang, G.B.; Zhu, Q.Y.; Siew, C.K. Extreme learning machine: A new learning scheme of feedforward neural networks. In Proceedings of the 2004 IEEE International Joint Conference on Neural Networks (IEEE Cat. No. 04CH37541), Budapest, Hungary, 25–29 July 2004; Volume 2, pp. 985–990.
2. Huang, G.B.; Zhu, Q.Y.; Siew, C.K. Extreme learning machine: Theory and applications. *Neurocomputing* **2006**, *70*, 489–501. [CrossRef]
3. Huang, G.B.; Chen, Y.Q.; Babri, H.A. Classification ability of single hidden layer feedforward neural networks. *IEEE Trans. Neural Networks* **2000**, *11*, 799–801. [CrossRef] [PubMed]
4. Chen, X.; Cui, B. Efficient modeling of fiber optic gyroscope drift using improved EEMD and extreme learning machine. *Signal Process.* **2016**, *128*, 1–7.
5. Xia, M.; Zhang, Y.; Weng, L.; Ye, X. Fashion retailing forecasting based on extreme learning machine with adaptive metrics of inputs. *Knowl.-Based Syst.* **2012**, *36*, 253–259. [CrossRef]
6. Yang, J.; Xie, S.; Yoon, S.; Park, D.; Fang, Z.; Yang, S. Fingerprint matching based on extreme learning machine. *Neural Comput. Appl.* **2013**, *22*, 435–445. [CrossRef]
7. Rasheed, Z.; Rangwala, H. Metagenomic Taxonomic Classification Using Extreme Learning Machines. *J. Bioinform. Comput. Biol.* **2012**, *10 5*, 1250015. [CrossRef]
8. Zou, Q.Y.; Wang, X.J.; Zhou, C.J.; Zhang, Q. The memory degradation based online sequential extreme learning machine. *Neurocomputing* **2018**, *275*, 2864–2879.
9. Fu, Y.; Wu, Q.; Liu, K.; Gao, H. Feature Selection Methods for Extreme Learning Machines. *Axioms* **2022**, *11*, 444. [CrossRef]
10. Liu, Q.; He, Q.; Shi, Z. Extreme support vector machine classifier. In Proceedings of the Advances in Knowledge Discovery and Data Mining: 12th Pacific-Asia Conference, PAKDD 2008, Osaka, Japan, 20–23 May 2008; pp. 222–233.
11. Frénay, B.; Verleysen, M. Using SVMs with randomised feature spaces: An extreme learning approach. In Proceedings of the 18th European Symposium on Artificial Neural Networks, ESANN 2010, Bruges, Belgium, 28–30 April 2010.
12. Huang, G.B.; Ding, X.; Zhou, H. Optimization method based extreme learning machine for classification. *Neurocomputing* **2010**, *74*, 155–163. [CrossRef]
13. Khemchandani, R.; Chandra, S. Twin support vector machines for pattern classification. *IEEE Trans. Pattern Anal. Mach. Intell.* **2007**, *29*, 905–910.
14. Wan, Y.; Song, S.; Huang, G.; Li, S. Twin extreme learning machines for pattern classification. *Neurocomputing* **2017**, *260*, 235–244. [CrossRef]
15. Shen, J.; Ma, J. Sparse Twin Extreme Learning Machine with ε-Insensitive Zone Pinball Loss. *IEEE Access* **2019**, *7*, 112067–112078. [CrossRef]

16. Yuan, C.; Yang, L. Robust twin extreme learning machines with correntropy-based metric. *Knowl.-Based Syst.* **2021**, *214*, 106707. [CrossRef]
17. Anand, P.; Bharti, A.; Rastogi, R. Time efficient variants of Twin Extreme Learning Machine. *Intell. Syst. Appl.* **2023**, *17*, 200169. [CrossRef]
18. Ma, J.; Yu, G. A generalized adaptive robust distance metric driven smooth regularization learning framework for pattern recognition. *Signal Process.* **2023**, *211*, 109102. [CrossRef]
19. Ma, J.; Wen, Y.; Yang, L. Fisher-regularized supervised and semi-supervised extreme learning machine. *Knowl. Inf. Syst.* **2020**, *62*, 3995–4027. [CrossRef]
20. Gao, S.; Ye, Q.; Ye, N. 1-Norm least squares twin support vector machines. *Neurocomputing* **2011**, *74*, 3590–3597. [CrossRef]
21. Yan, H.; Ye, Q.L.; Zhang, T.A.; Yu, D.J. Efficient and robust TWSVM classifier based on L1-norm distance metric for pattern classification. In Proceedings of the 2017 4th IAPR Asian Conference on Pattern Recognition (ACPR), Nanjing, China, 26–29 November 2017; pp. 436–441.
22. Ye, Q.; Yang, J.; Liu, F.; Zhao, C.; Ye, N.; Yin, T. L1-norm distance linear discriminant analysis based on an effective iterative algorithm. *IEEE Trans. Circuits Syst. Video Technol.* **2016**, *28*, 114–129. [CrossRef]
23. Wu, Q.; Wang, F.; An, Y.; Li, K. L-1-Norm Robust Regularized Extreme Learning Machine with Asymmetric C-Loss for Regression. *Axioms* **2023**, *12*, 204. [CrossRef]
24. Wu, M.J.; Liu, J.X.; Gao, Y.L.; Kong, X.Z.; Feng, C.M. Feature selection and clustering via robust graph-laplacian PCA based on capped L 1-norm. In Proceedings of the 2017 IEEE International Conference on Bioinformatics and Biomedicine (BIBM), Kansas City, MO, USA, 13–16 November 2017; pp. 1741–1745.
25. Nie, F.; Huang, H.; Cai, X.; Ding, C. Efficient and robust feature selection via joint L2, 1-norms minimization. *Adv. Neural Inf. Process. Syst.* **2010**, *23*, 1813–1821.
26. Ma, J.; Yang, L.; Sun, Q. Capped L1-norm distance metric-based fast robust twin bounded support vector machine. *Neurocomputing* **2020**, *412*, 295–311. [CrossRef]
27. Jiang, W.; Nie, F.; Huang, H. Robust Dictionary Learning with Capped L1-Norm. In Proceedings of the 24th International Conference on Artificial Intelligence, Buenos Aires, Argentina, 25–31 July 2015; pp. 3590–3596.
28. Nie, F.; Huo, Z.; Huang, H. Joint Capped Norms Minimization for Robust Matrix Recovery. In Proceedings of the 26th International Joint Conference on Artificial Intelligence, Melbourne, Australia, 19–25 August 2017; pp. 2557–2563.
29. Wang, C.; Ye, Q.; Luo, P.; Ye, N.; Fu, L. Robust capped L1-norm twin support vector machine. *Neural Netw.* **2019**, *114*, 47–59. [CrossRef]
30. Pal, A.; Khemchandani, R.R.n. Learning TWSVM using Privilege Information. In Proceedings of the 2018 IEEE Symposium Series on Computational Intelligence (SSCI), Bangalore, India, 18–21 November 2018; pp. 1548–1554.
31. Li, Y.; Sun, H.; Yan, W.; Cui, Q. R-CTSVM+: Robust capped L1-norm twin support vector machine with privileged information. *Inf. Sci.* **2021**, *574*, 12–32. [CrossRef]
32. Mangasarian, O.; Musicant, D. Successive overrelaxation for support vector machines. *IEEE Trans. Neural Netw.* **1999**, *10*, 1032–1037. [CrossRef] [PubMed]
33. Luo, Z.Q.; Tseng, P. Error bounds and convergence analysis of feasible descent methods: A general approach. *Ann. Oper. Res.* **1993**, *46*, 157–178. [CrossRef]
34. Yang, Y.; Xue, Z.; Ma, J.; Chang, X. Robust projection twin extreme learning machines with capped L1-norm distance metric. *Neurocomputing* **2023**, *517*, 229–242. [CrossRef]

axioms

MDPI

Article

Analysis of Water Infiltration under Impermeable Dams by Analytical and Boundary Element Methods in Complex

Elena Corina Cipu

Department of Applied Mathematics, Centre for Research and Training in Innovative Techniques of Applied Mathematics in Engineering "Traian Lalescu" (CiTi), Faculty of Applied Sciences, University Politehnica of Bucharest, 313 Splaiul Independentei, 060042 Bucharest, Romania; corina.cipu@upb.ro

Abstract: The boundary element method (BEM) is used by applying Cauchy's formula to the boundary of the water movement domain under a dam. By approximating the border with a polygon through linear interpolation, the relationships between the complex velocities on each edge of the polygon are analytically deduced. For the case of the flow domain described by a semi- circular closed contours, the numerical values of the velocity are computed and compared with those obtained only analytically. Conclusions on the analytical and numerical context are drawn.

Keywords: potential theory; BEM; complex analysis; estimations

MSC: 65N38; 30-04; 76-05; 31-00; 68W50

1. Introduction

Analysis of water infiltration under impermeable dams has important applications, and it deals with the study of how water seeps into the ground through permeable channels and how this affects the groundwater recharge and the stormwater management. Water infiltration is the most important way to replenish groundwater in the dam land. Groundwater is a vital source of freshwater for many ecosystems and human activities.

Permeable channels are unlined or lined with flexible materials that allow part of the runoff to infiltrate through their boundaries while conveying the rest of the runoff. Permeable channels can reduce the volume of runoff and lessen the effort needed to control it in the downstream basin. However, water infiltration also affects the hydraulic behavior of the flow in permeable channels, such as the water depth, velocity, and discharge. Therefore, analytic methods are needed to model and predict the infiltration capacity of permeable channels under different flow conditions and channel characteristics.

Cases of planar movement of groundwater are very frequently encountered in practice. They can be solved by exact methods, for simple cases, or through approximation methods, using simplified assumptions and numerical approximations (FEM, BEM). The movement of groundwater is a potential movement, and, if it is also planar, its study can be completed with the help of analytic functions of a complex variable (see [1,2]).

In a general case, for a potential flow, with the velocity potential φ the equation of equipotential lines is $\varphi = const$ and the velocity is $u = \dfrac{\partial \varphi}{\partial x}, v = \dfrac{\partial \varphi}{\partial y}$. For a harmonic function φ, the complex potential could be considered through Cauchy-Riemann conditions. Denoting the analytic function that expresses the complex potential with $f(z) = \varphi + i\psi$, then $\dfrac{\partial \varphi}{\partial x} = \dfrac{\partial \psi}{\partial y}, \dfrac{\partial \varphi}{\partial y} = -\dfrac{\partial \psi}{\partial x}$ and it's derivative

$$w(z) = \frac{df}{dz} = \frac{\partial \varphi}{\partial x} + i\frac{\partial \psi}{\partial x} = \frac{\partial \psi}{\partial y} - i\frac{\partial \varphi}{\partial y} = u - iv,$$

the complex velocity is expressed, and ψ is the current function with $\psi = const$ the equation of current lines.

Among the classic types of plane fluid flows that can be expressed by a complex potential we can enumerate: uniform flow; stagnation point flow; source and sink; vortex. The complex potential $f(z) = Ue^{-i\alpha}z$ corresponds to uniform flow at speed U in a direction making an angle α with the x-axis. The stream function is $\psi = V(y\cos\alpha - x\sin\alpha)$. Here we are interested in finding the velocity field $\mathbf{v} = (u(x,y), v(x,y)) = V(\cos\alpha, \sin\alpha)$. Furthermore, the complex potential $f(z) = \frac{k}{2}z^2$ corresponds to stagnation point flow with strength $k \geq 0$.

For an arbitrary point (a,b) in the complex plane and $c = a + ib$, the complex potential $f(z) = \frac{Q}{2\pi}\log(z-c)$ represents a source of strength $Q > 0$ and a sink for $Q < 0$.

A vortex of strength C at the origin is represented by the complex potential $f(z) = \frac{-iC}{2\pi}\log z$. This is again a multi-valued function, but we consider the principal form. For $C > 0$, rotation is anticlockwise, and for $C < 0$ rotation is clockwise.

Terzaghi's theory is a classical method for analyzing seepage in earth dams. It involves the assumption of steady-state, two-dimensional flow through an isotropic, homogeneous soil medium. The theory uses Darcy's law and provides a basic understanding of seepage patterns and flow velocities (see [3–7]). In some cases, simplified analytical solutions can be employed to estimate seepage quantities. We can assume a potential flow, meaning that the flow is irrotational and the streamlines are parallel to the dam surface.

The paper is organized as follows. In Section 2, analytical methods for water infiltration under an impermeable dam are discussed, and two cases are highlighted: semicircular and half plane water infiltration zone. The main results are then given in Section 3, in which Cauchy's formula and the polygon decomposition of a curve are used for the analysis of water infiltration under an impermeable Dam. The solution of the system obtained leads to complex potential and complex velocity. At the end of the section, the numerical solution for the semicircular boundary is graphically represented. Section 4 end the paper.

2. Analytical Methods for Water Infiltration under an Impermeable Dam

The mathematical physics governing water infiltration under impermeable dams can be described by Darcy's Law, the Richards and Laplace's equation (see [3–7]). We consider a planar potential flow with x the spatial variable and elevation y.

Darcy's Law relates the flow rate of water through a porous medium to the hydraulic gradient and the hydraulic conductivity. It can be written as: then $q = -kA\nabla h$ or $q = -k(\nabla h + \gamma\nabla y)$, where: q is the volumetric flow rate of water per unit area (debit); K is the hydraulic conductivity of the soil; A is the cross-sectional area; ∇h is the hydraulic gradient in the direction of flow; h is the hydraulic head (water table elevation); and γ is the specific gravity of water.

The Richards Equation extends Darcy's Law by also considering the unsaturated flow of water through porous media. It considers the change in water content and hydraulic head with respect to time and space. The one-dimensional form of the Richards Equation for water infiltration can be expressed as:

$$\frac{\partial\theta}{\partial t} = \nabla\cdot(k\nabla \mathrm{h}) + \mathrm{S} \text{ or } \frac{\partial\theta}{\partial t} = \frac{\partial}{\partial \mathrm{y}}[\mathrm{k}(\theta)\frac{\partial \mathrm{h}}{\partial \mathrm{y}}] + \mathrm{S},$$

where: θ is the volumetric water content of the soil and $k(\theta)$ is the unsaturated hydraulic conductivity of the soil, which is a function of θ; S represents source/sink terms, such as precipitation or extraction. This equation describes the movement of water into and through the soil as a function of time, hydraulic conductivity, and the hydraulic head gradient.

The continuity equation ensures the conservation of mass during water flow. It's expression, $\partial\theta/\partial t + \nabla\cdot(\theta q) = 0$, with $(\nabla\cdot)$ the divergence operator. It can be written, in the case of water infiltration, as $\nabla \cdot \mathrm{q} = \nabla \cdot (-k\nabla h) = \mathrm{S}$, where S is the source/sink term representing any external water sources or sinks.

Laplace's equation is derived from combining Darcy's law and the continuity equation. For steady-state conditions without any external sources or sinks $(S = 0)$, it simplifies to $\nabla^2 h = 0$. This equation describes the potential distribution of hydraulic head throughout the soil domain.

Boundary conditions are essential to solving the problem. For impermeable dam surfaces, the hydraulic head at the dam surface is constant and equal to the elevation of the dam crest. Furthermore, the hydraulic head is known or prescribed at the ground surface, often determined by the initial conditions or external factors. Depending on the specific problem, appropriate boundary conditions need to be assigned at the lateral boundaries of the computational domain, such as no flow or a specified hydraulic head. Boundary conditions and initial conditions must be specified to solve the Richards Equation. The boundary conditions typically involve the hydraulic head or water content at the soil surface and at the interface with the impermeable dam. Solving the Richards Equation numerically, often using numerical methods such as finite difference or finite element techniques, allows for the prediction of water infiltration patterns and the assessment of factors such as seepage rates, water table variations, and potential risks to dam stability caused by water infiltration.

A linearized problem of the two-dimensional steady potential flow could be used for analyzing the water infiltration under an impermeable dam using complex analysis and BEM (see [8,9]), considering a closed domain for the water flow. To mathematically describe the potential complex of water infiltration under impermeable dams, we can use the concept of potential theory, in which case the governing equation for the potential function φ and for the stream function ψ, is Laplace's equation:

$$\nabla^2\varphi = \partial^2\varphi/\partial x^2 + \partial^2\varphi/\partial y^2 = 0; \nabla^2\psi = \partial^2\psi/\partial x^2 + \partial^2\psi/\partial y^2 = 0.$$

Suppose that an impermeable dam separates two accumulations of water, according to Figure 1. In one of the accumulations (the one on the left) upstream, the water rises to the level h_1, and in the other one (the one on the right) downstream, the water rises to the level h_2. The curves AB and CD (dam sole) are waterproof lines. Using the notation q for the debit, the conditions imposed on them are

$$\psi|_{AB} = c,\ c = \text{ const } \ \psi|_{CD} = c + q, \tag{1}$$

usually $c = 0$.

The curves BC and DA are power lines. As the potential calculus (both the complex and the real) is given through its derivatives, we can impose the boundary conditions by adding an arbitrary constant to the velocity potential (same on all the parts of the border). So we will put

$$\varphi|_{DA} = -kh_1,\ \varphi|_{BC} = -kh_2. \tag{2}$$

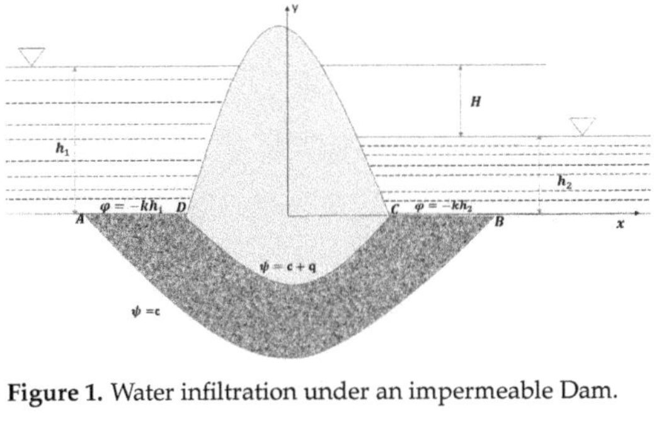

Figure 1. Water infiltration under an impermeable Dam.

We have mentioned that we do not know the value of the constant q in advance, which is why this method is often not used. Finding this constant is particularly important because the debit characterizes the flow of water infiltrated under the dam. Indeed, noting with $\mathbf{n}$ the external normal vector at the boundary, the infiltration rate is

$$\int_A^D \mathbf{v}\cdot(-\mathbf{n})\,ds = -\int_A^D \frac{\partial\varphi}{\partial n}ds = \int_A^D \frac{\partial\psi}{\partial s}\,ds = \psi|_D - \psi|_A = q. \tag{3}$$

In a problem of infiltration, the debit describes the seepage flow, meaning the amount of water that seeps or is lost through soil permeability or through cracks in the dam in this context ([10]). The seepage rate depends on the hydraulic pressure difference and the hydraulic characteristics of the medium through which the water flows, as stated before. If the dam is not impermeable, the infiltration area is considered as $A = LH$ with L length of the dam and the complex potential take the form $f(z) = C\left(e^{i\theta}z + \log z\right)$ with $C = \dfrac{k\gamma H^2}{4i}$ and θ the angle of inclination of the water surface. In Figure 2, the infiltration speed and the seepage flow are depicted.

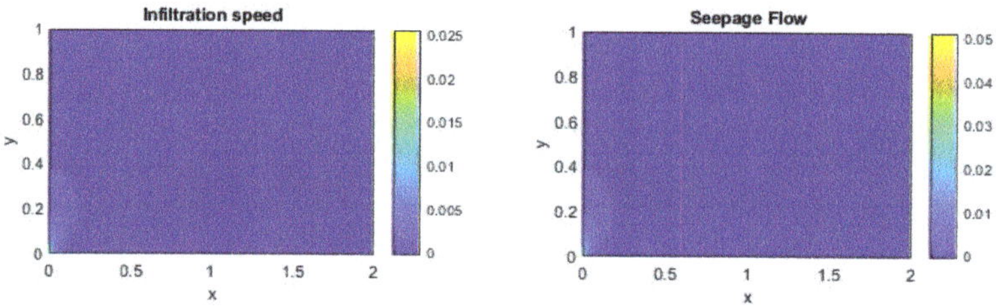

Figure 2. Infiltration speed and seepage flow: L = 2, H = 1, k = 0.1, $\theta = 0$.

In Figures 3 and 4 the potential and the stream function dependence of spatial variables is plotted, in case with inclination of water surface and without.

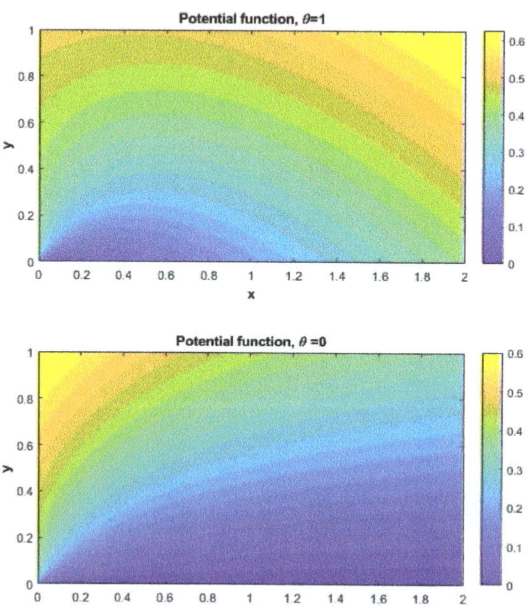

Figure 3. Potential function for different inclination angles (L = 2, H = 1).

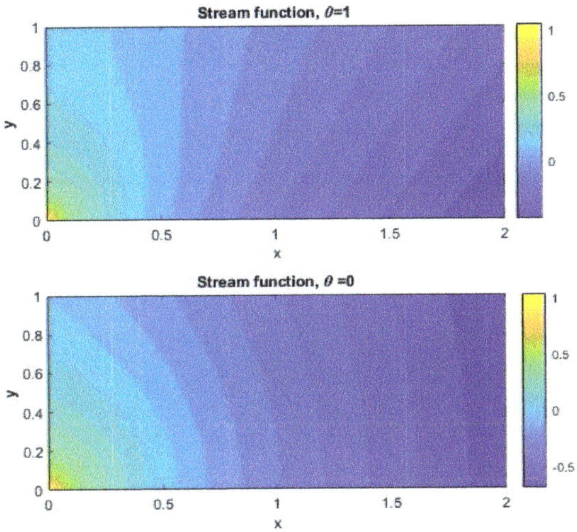

Figure 4. Stream function for different inclination angles (L = 2, H = 1, k = 0.1).

2.1. Semicircular Water Infiltration Zone

We consider now the case in which the flow of the infiltrated fluid is in a semicircular domain.

We assume that the waterproof lines are

$$\begin{aligned} AB : z = & \ R_2 e^{i\theta},\ \theta \in [-\pi, 0], R_2 > R_1, \\ DC : z = & \ R_1 e^{i\theta},\ \theta \in [-\pi, 0], \end{aligned} \tag{4}$$

and the power lines

$$\begin{aligned} AD: \ & y = 0,\ x \in [-R_2, -R_1], \\ CB: \ & y = 0,\ x \in [R_1, R_2]. \end{aligned} \tag{5}$$

Choosing the complex potential under the form

$$f(z) = \frac{k(h_2 - h_1)}{\pi} i \log z + k(h_2 - 2h_1), C = -2k(h_2 - h_1) > 0, \tag{6}$$

using the principal form of the logarithm, we have boundary conditions (2) as well as the conditions

$$\psi|_{DC} = \frac{k(h_2 - h_1)}{\pi} \log R_1,\ \psi|_{AB} = \frac{k(h_2 - h_1)}{\pi} \log R_2. \tag{7}$$

The infiltrated water flow rate is

$$q = \psi|_{DC} - \psi|_{AB} = \frac{k(h_2 - h_1)}{\pi} \log \frac{R_1}{R_2}. \tag{8}$$

The complex velocity is

$$u - iv = -\frac{ikH}{\pi z},\ H = h_1 - h_2. \tag{9}$$

In Figure 5, the velocity field for $h_1 - h_2 = 1, R_2 = 2, R_1 = 1, k = 1$ parameters is presented.

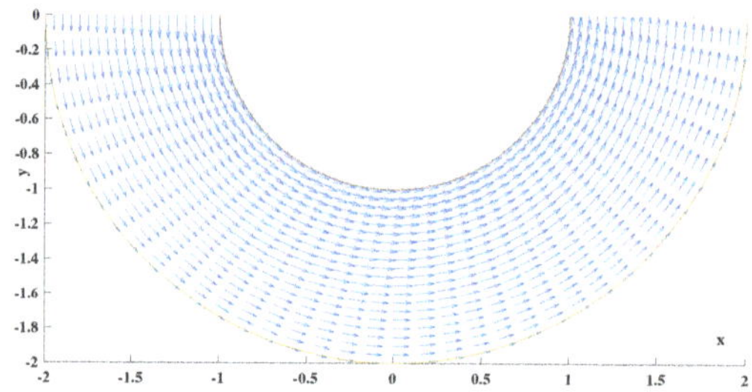

Figure 5. Velocity field for semicircular case.

2.2. The Lower Half Plane Water Infiltration Zone

The infiltrated fluid flows in the half-plane $y < 0$ and the affixes of the points in this half-plane are $z = re^{i\theta}$, $0 < r < \infty$, $-\pi < \theta < 0$.

We assume that the segment $y = 0, x \in (-R, R)$ represents the waterproof sole of the dam, where $\psi = c$ and the half-lines $y = 0, x \in (-\infty, -R)$ and $y = 0, x \in (R, \infty)$ represent power lines, on which $\varphi = -kh_1 + c$ respectively $\varphi = -kh_2 + c$. From where

$$v\big|_{y\to 0-,x\in[-R,R]} = -\frac{\partial \psi}{\partial x} = 0 \tag{10}$$

$$u\big|_{y=0,x\in(-\infty,-R)} = u\big|_{y=0,x\in(R,\infty)} = \frac{\partial \varphi}{\partial x} = 0 \tag{11}$$

because the function $\dfrac{ia}{\sqrt{z^2 - R^2}}, a > 0$, defined on the inferior half-plane is vanishing at infinity and has the following values on the boundary:

$$\frac{ia}{\sqrt{z^2 - R^2}} = \begin{cases} \dfrac{ia}{\sqrt{x^2 - R^2}}, y = 0,\ x \in (R, \infty), \\ \dfrac{-a}{\sqrt{R^2 - x^2}}, y \to 0-,\ x \in (-R, R), \\ \dfrac{-ia}{\sqrt{x^2 - R^2}}, y = 0,\ x \in (-\infty, -R), \end{cases} \tag{12}$$

we shall consider for the complex velocity the following expression

$$w(z) = u(x, y) - iv(x, y) = \frac{ia}{\sqrt{z^2 - R^2}} \tag{13}$$

from where we obtain the complex potential

$$f(z) = ia \log\left(z + \sqrt{z^2 - R^2}\right) + K, K = k(h_2 - 2h_1) \tag{14}$$

that on the real axis becomes

$$f(z) = \begin{cases} ia \log(x + \sqrt{x^2 - R^2}), y = 0, x \in (R, \infty), \\ ia \log R - \arg\left(x - i\sqrt{R^2 - x^2}\right), y \to 0-, x \in (-R, R), \\ ia \log\left(-x + \sqrt{x^2 - R^2}\right) + a\pi, y = 0, x \in (-\infty, -R). \end{cases} \tag{15}$$

In Figure 6, for water infiltration under a dam with segment $[-R, R]$ as an impermeable base, the velocity field for parameters $h_1 - h_2 = 1, R = 1$ is presented.

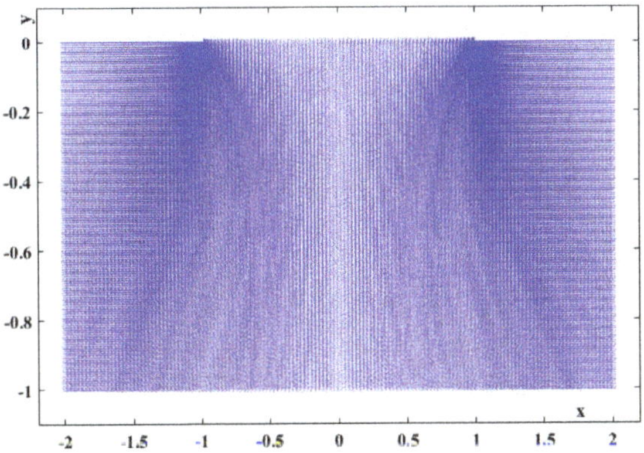

Figure 6. Velocity field for half-plane case.

In the vicinity of the points $z = -R$ and $z = R$ the speed suddenly changes direction and becomes infinite. To visualize this, in Figure 7 the streamlines of the velocity on the dependence of $r \in [0, R_2]$ and $\theta \in [-\pi, 0]$ are plotted, which describe part of the half-plane. Also, for the same case, the potential function and stream function are depicted in in Figure 8.

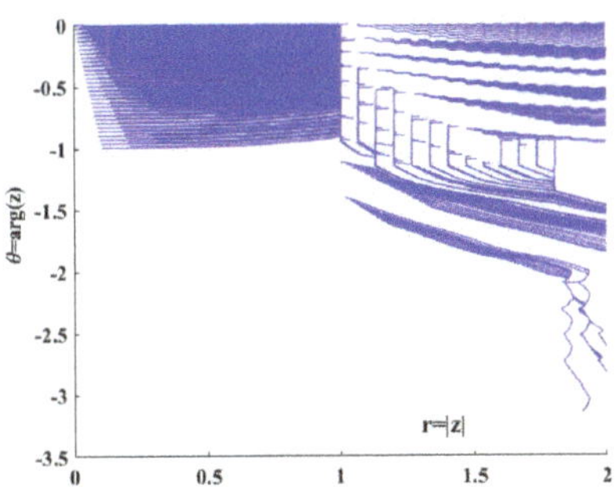

Figure 7. Velocity streamlines for half-plane case.

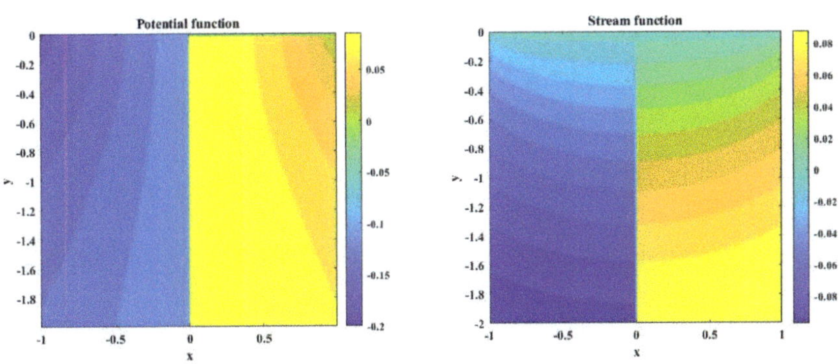

Figure 8. Potential function and stream function for half-plane case.

3. BEM in Complex Analysis

Water infiltration can affect the stability of an impermeable dam. BEM (see [11–15]) can help evaluate the uplift pressure distribution on the dam foundation, which is caused by water infiltration. By modeling the dam and its surrounding soil as boundary elements, BEM can analyze the uplift pressures and assess their impact on the dam's stability. Likewise, the seepage patterns and rates of water infiltration under an impermeable dam could be computed at various locations by discretizing the dam and the surrounding soil region into boundary elements and solving the Dirichlet problem expressed in Figure 1.

For each point z_0 under the boundary $\Gamma = AB \cup BC \cup CD \cup DA$, we shall use the Cauchy's formula, $f(z_0) = \frac{1}{2\pi i}\int_\Gamma \frac{f(z)}{z-z_0}dz$, $z_0 \in D$, the domain determined by Γ, to compute the value of $f(z_0)$ through the values of the function on the boundary of the domain, Γ.

Within the boundary element method, the boundary Γ is approximated by a polygon consisting of $N = 2n + 2m$ sections $\Gamma_j = [z_j, z_{j+1}], j = 1,2,\ldots,N$; having the peaks $z_j = x_j + iy_j$, called nodes or control points located on Γ. With linear interpolation for $f(\zeta)$

$$f(z)|_{\Gamma_j} = f(z_j)\frac{z - z_{j+1}}{z_j - z_{j+1}} + f(z_{j+1})\frac{z_j - z}{z_j - z_{j+1}} \tag{16}$$

from where

$$\int_\Gamma \frac{f(z)}{z-z_0}dz = \sum_{j=1}^{N}\left[f(z_j)\int_{\Gamma_j}\frac{z-z_{j+1}}{z_j-z_{j+1}}\frac{dz}{z-z_0} + f(z_{j+1})\int_{\Gamma_j}\frac{z_j-z}{z_j-z_{j+1}}\frac{dz}{z-z_0}\right]. \tag{17}$$

Analytically computing the integrals of (17) results:

$$\begin{aligned} f(z) &= \sum_{j=1}^{N} f(z_j)g_j(z), \\ 2\pi i\, g_j(z) &= \frac{z-z_{j-1}}{z_j-z_{j-1}}\log\left(\frac{z-z_j}{z-z_{j-1}}\right) + \frac{z-z_{j+1}}{z_j-z_{j+1}}\log\left(\frac{z-z_{j+1}}{z-z_j}\right) \end{aligned} \tag{18}$$

relations in which $z_0 \in D$ was renamed with z, that is the variable of functions $(g_j(z))_{j\in\{1,\ldots,N\}}$ and f. For each $z := z_k = x_k + iy_k, j = 1,2,\ldots,N$, we introduce the coefficients $G_{kj} = g_j(z_k)$. These coefficients are calculated using (18) except of $G_{(j-1)j}$, G_{jj}, $G_{(j+1)j}$ which have the expressions:

$$\begin{aligned} 2\pi i G_{(j-1)j} &= 2\pi i \lim_{z\to z_{j-1}} g_j(z) = \frac{z_{j-1}-z_{j+1}}{z_j-z_{j+1}}\log\frac{z_{j-1}-z_{j+1}}{z_{j-1}-z_j}, \\ 2\pi i G_{jj} &= 2\pi i \lim_{z\to z_j} g_j(z) = \log\frac{z_j-z_{j+1}}{z_j-z_{j-1}} \\ 2\pi i G_{(j+1)j} &= 2\pi i \lim_{z\to z_{j+1}} g_j(z) = \frac{z_{j+1}-z_{j-1}}{z_j-z_{j-1}}\log\frac{z_{j+1}-z_j}{z_{j+1}-z_{j-1}}. \end{aligned} \tag{19}$$

From (18) we obtain the algebraic system

$$f(z_k) = \sum_{j=1}^{N} f(z_j)G_{kj}. \tag{20}$$

With notations

$$\begin{aligned} M_{kj} &= \operatorname{Re} G_{kj}, \quad N_{kj} = \operatorname{Im} G_{kj}, \\ \varphi_k &= \operatorname{Re} f(z_k), \quad \psi_k = \operatorname{Im} f(z_k), \end{aligned} \tag{21}$$

separating the real terms from the imaginary ones in (20)

$$\begin{aligned}&\sum_{j=1}^{N}\left(\delta_{kj}-M_{kj}\right)\varphi_j+\sum_{j=1}^{N}N_{kj}\psi_j=0,k=1,2,\ldots,N\\&-\sum_{j=1}^{N}N_{kj}\varphi_j+\sum_{j=1}^{N}\left(\delta_{kj}-M_{kj}\right)\psi_j=0,k=1,2,\ldots,N\end{aligned}\tag{22}$$

with δ_{ij} the Kronocker symbol, that us one for $i=j$.

The equations of the system (22) are not independent, and below we will choose among them accordingly a number of $N=2n+2m$ independent equations. The choosing criterion for the equations is the following: we will look for the elements of the matrix with which the vector of the unknowns is multiplied to have diagonal elements of the form $1-M_{jj}$. Accordingly, the diagonal of the matrix of unknown coefficients will be dominant, and the matrix will be well conditioned. The system becomes

$$\begin{aligned}&\sum_{j=1}^{n}\left(\delta_{lj}-M_{lj}\right)\varphi_j+\sum_{j=n+1}^{n+m}N_{lj}\psi_j-\sum_{j=n+m+1}^{2n+m}M_{lj}\varphi_j+\sum_{j=2n+m+1}^{2n+2m}N_{lj}\psi_j+(\sum_{j=1}^{n}N_{lj})q=\\&=kH\sum_{j=2n+m+1}^{2n+2m}M_{lj},\qquad l=1,\ldots,n\end{aligned}\tag{23}$$

$$\begin{aligned}&-\sum_{j=1}^{n}N_{lj}\varphi_j+\sum_{j=n+1}^{n+m}\left(\delta_{lj}-M_{lj}\right)\psi_j-\sum_{j=n+m+1}^{2n+m}N_{lj}\varphi_j-\sum_{j=2n+m+1}^{2n+2m}M_{lj}\psi_j-(\sum_{j=1}^{n}M_{lj})q=\\&=kH\sum_{j=2n+m+1}^{2n+2m}N_{lj},\qquad l=n+1,\ldots,n+m\end{aligned}\tag{24}$$

$$\begin{aligned}&-\sum_{j=1}^{n}M_{lj}\varphi_j+\sum_{j=n+1}^{n+m}N_{lj}\psi_j+\sum_{j=n+m+1}^{2n+m}\left(\delta_{lj}-M_{lj}\right)\varphi_j+\sum_{j=2n+m+1}^{2n+2m}N_{lj}\psi_j+(\sum_{j=1}^{n}N_{lj})q=\\&=kH\sum_{j=2n+m+1}^{2n+2m}M_{lj},l=n+m+1,\ldots,2n+m\end{aligned}\tag{25}$$

$$\begin{aligned}&-\sum_{j=1}^{n}N_{kj}\varphi_j-\sum_{j=n+1}^{n+m}M_{kj}\psi_j-\sum_{j=n+m+1}^{2n+m}N_{kj}\varphi_j-\sum_{j=2n+m+1}^{2n+2m}\left(\delta_{kj}-M_{kj}\right)\psi_j-(\sum_{j=1}^{n}M_{lj})q=\\&-kH\sum_{j=2n+m+1}^{2n+2m}N_{lj},l=2n+m+1,\ldots,2n+2m.\end{aligned}\tag{26}$$

Using the Cauchy theorem $\int_\Gamma f(z)dz=0$ and based on (16) approximation, one obtain

$$\sum_{j=1}^{2n+2m}\int_{\Gamma_j}\left[f\left(z_j\right)\frac{z-z_{j+1}}{z_j-z_{j+1}}+f\left(z_{j+1}\right)\frac{z_j-z}{z_j-z_{j+1}}\right]dz=0\tag{27}$$

that is

$$\sum_{j=1}^{N}\left(\int_{\Gamma_j}\frac{f(z_{j+1})z_j-f(z_j)z_{j+1}}{z_j-z_{j+1}}dz+\int_{\Gamma_j}\frac{f(z_j)-f(z_{j+1})}{z_j-z_{j+1}}zdz\right)=0$$

and after integration

$$\sum_{j=1}^{N}f(z_j)\left(z_j-z_{j+1}\right)+f\left(z_{j+1}\right)\left(z_j-z_{j+1}\right)=0,z_{N+1}=z_1$$

from where, separating the imaginary part and taking into account the boundary conditions described in Table 1, results

$$\begin{aligned}&\sum_{j=1}^{n}(y_{j+1}-y_{j-1})\varphi_j+\sum_{j=n+1}^{n+m}(x_{j+1}-x_{j-1})\psi_j+\sum_{j=n+m+1}^{2n+m}(y_{j+1}-y_{j-1})\varphi_j+\\&\sum_{j=2n+m+1}^{2n+2n}(x_{j+1}-x_{j-1})\psi_j+q\sum_{j=1}^{n}(x_{j+1}-x_{j-1})=kH\sum_{j=2n+m+1}^{2n+2n}(y_{j+1}-y_{j-1})\end{aligned} \tag{28}$$

equation that closes the system (23)–(26) in a matriceal form $AX=B$ with the vector of the unknowns expressed by

$$X=[(\varphi_j)_{j=1,\dots,n},(\psi_j)_{j=n+1,\dots,n+m},(\varphi_j)_{j=n+m+1,\dots,2n+m},(\psi_j)_{j=2n+m+1,\dots,2n+2m},q]^t,$$

where

$$\begin{aligned}B_l&=kH\sum_{j=2n+m+1}^{2n+2m}M_{lj},\ l\in\{1,\dots,n\},\\B_l&=kH\sum_{j=2n+m+1}^{2n+2m}N_{lj},\ l\in\{n+1,\dots,n+m\},\\B_l&=kH\sum_{j=2n+m+1}^{2n+2m}M_{lj},\ l\in\{n+m+1,\dots,2n+m\},\\B_l&=kH\sum_{j=2n+m+1}^{2n+2m}N_{lj},l\in\{2n+m+1,\dots,2n+2m\}.\end{aligned} \tag{29}$$

Using (19), that for $j=1$ and $j=N$ becomes

$$\begin{aligned}&2\pi iG_{11}=\log\left(\frac{z_1-z_2}{z_1-z_N}\right),\ 2\pi iG_{NN}=\log\left(\frac{z_N-z_1}{z_N-z_{N-1}}\right)\\&2\pi iG_{1N}=\frac{z_N-z_2}{z_1-z_2}\log\left(\frac{z_N-z_2}{z_N-z_1}\right),\ 2\pi iG_{N1}=\frac{z_1-z_N}{z_1-z_{N-1}}\log\left(\frac{z_1-z_N}{z_1-z_{N-1}}\right),\end{aligned} \tag{30}$$

and $(21)_1$ leads to

$$\begin{aligned}N_{11}&=-\frac{1}{2\pi}\log\left|\frac{z_1-z_2}{z_1-z_N}\right|;M_{11}=\frac{1}{2\pi}\arg\left(\frac{z_1-z_2}{z_1-z_N}\right)\\N_{jj}&=-\frac{1}{2\pi}\log\left|\frac{z_j-z_{j+1}}{z_j-z_{j-1}}\right|;M_{jj}=\frac{1}{2\pi}\arg\left(\frac{z_j-z_{j+1}}{z_{ji}-z_{j-1}}\right),j\in\{2,\dots,N-1\}\\N_{NN}&=-\frac{1}{2\pi}\log\left|\frac{z_N-z_1}{z_N-z_{N-1}}\right|;M_{NN}=\frac{1}{2\pi}\arg\left(\frac{z_N-z_1}{z_N-z_{N-1}}\right).\end{aligned} \tag{31}$$

Furthermore, for $j\in\{2,\dots,N-1\}$

$$\begin{aligned}G_{(j-1)j}&=\frac{-i}{2\pi}\frac{z_{j-1}-z_{j+1}}{z_j-z_{j+1}}\log\left(\frac{z_{j-1}-z_{j+1}}{z_{j-1}-z_j}\right),\\G_{(j+1)j}&=\frac{-i}{2\pi}\frac{z_{j+1}-z_{j-1}}{z_j-z_{j-1}}\log\left(\frac{z_{j+1}-z_j}{z_{j+1}-z_{j-1}}\right),\\G_{kj}&=\frac{-i}{2\pi}\frac{z_k-z_{j-1}}{z_j-z_{j-1}}\log\left(\frac{z_k-z_j}{z_k-z_{j-1}}\right)+\\&\quad\frac{(-i)}{2\pi}\frac{z_k-z_{j+1}}{z_j-z_{j+1}}\log\left(\frac{z_k-z_{j+1}}{z_k-z_j}\right),k\neq j-1,j,j+1,\end{aligned} \tag{32}$$

further, the complex velocity in a point $z_0 \in D$ with $\Gamma = \partial D$ is determined from

$$w(z_0) = \frac{df}{dz}(z_0) = \frac{1}{2\pi i}\int_{\Gamma} \frac{f(z)}{(z-z_0)^2}dz \tag{33}$$

and using (16)

$$w(z_0) = \sum_{j=1}^{2n+2m} h_j(z_0)\, f(z_j) \tag{34}$$

with

$$\begin{aligned} h_j(z_0) &= \frac{1}{2\pi i}\int_{z_j}^{z_{j+1}} \left[f(z_j)\frac{z-z_{j+1}}{z_j-z_{j+1}} + f(z_{j+1})\frac{z_j-z}{z_j-z_{j+1}} \right] \frac{dz}{(z-z)^2} = \\ &= \frac{1}{2\pi i}\int_{z_j}^{z_{j+1}} \frac{z-z_{j+1}}{z_j-z_{j+1}}\frac{dz}{(z-z_0)^2} + \frac{1}{2\pi i}\int_{z_{j-1}}^{z_j} \frac{z_{j-1}-z}{z_{j-1}-z_j}\frac{dz}{(z-z_0)^2} = \\ &= \frac{1}{2\pi i}\left(\frac{1}{z_j-z_{j-1}}\log\left(\frac{z_j-z_0}{z_{j-1}-z_0}\right) - \frac{1}{z_{j+1}-z_j}\log\left(\frac{z_{j+1}-z_0}{z_j-z_0}\right) \right). \end{aligned} \tag{35}$$

Table 1. Boundary conditions specifying.

Boundary Γ	Nodes z_j	Unknowns	Conditions
AB: waterproof bed	$j = 1,\ldots,n$	φ_j	$\psi_j = q$
BC: feeding surface	$j = n+1,\ldots,n+m$	ψ_j	$\varphi_j = 0$
CD: bottom dam	$j = n+m+1,\ldots,2n+m$	φ_j	$\psi_j = 0$
DA: feeding surface	$j = 2n+m+1,\ldots,2n+2m$	ψ_j	$\varphi_j = -kH$

Semicircular Water Infiltration Zone

For the semicircular boundary, we shall compare the results with those obtained through analytical methods.

As expressed in Table 2, for the nodes in Cartesian coordinates, we have

$$\begin{aligned} &z_j \in AB,\, x_j = R_2\cos\left(\frac{(n+1-j)\pi}{n}\right),\; y_j = -R_2\sin\left(\frac{(n+1-j)\pi}{n}\right) \\ &z_j \in BC,\; x_j = R_2 - \frac{(R_2-R_1)(j-n-1)}{m},\; y_j = 0 \\ &z_j \in CD,\, x_j = R_1\cos\left(\frac{(j-n-m-1)\pi}{n}\right),\, y_j = -R_1\sin\left(\frac{(j-n-m-1)\pi}{n}\right) \\ &z_j \in DA,\; x_j = -R_1 - \frac{(R_2-R_1)(j-2n-m-1)}{m},\; y_j = 0. \end{aligned} \tag{36}$$

We consider $z_0 \in D$, with $x_0 = r\cos(\theta_0), y_0 = r\sin(\theta_0)$, case in which $R_1 < r = |z_0| < R_2, \theta_0 \in [-\pi, 0]$.

Table 2. Boundary parametrization for semicircular case.

Boundary Γ	Nodes z_j	Nodes Values
AB	$j = 1,\ldots,n$	$z_j = R_2\exp(-i(n+1-j)\pi/n)$
BC	$j = n+1,\ldots,n+m$	$z_j = R_2 - \frac{(R_2-R_1)(j-n-1)}{m}$
CD	$j = n+m+1,\ldots,2n+m$	$z_j = R_1\exp(-i(j-n-m-1)\pi/n)$
DA	$j = 2n+m+1,\ldots,2n+2m$	$z_j = -R_1 - \frac{(R_2-R_1)(j-2n-m-1)}{m}$

In Figure 9, the velocity field for parameters $h_1 - h_2 = 1, R_2 = 2, R_1 = 1, k = 1$ in case of a semicircular water infiltration zone, is presented.

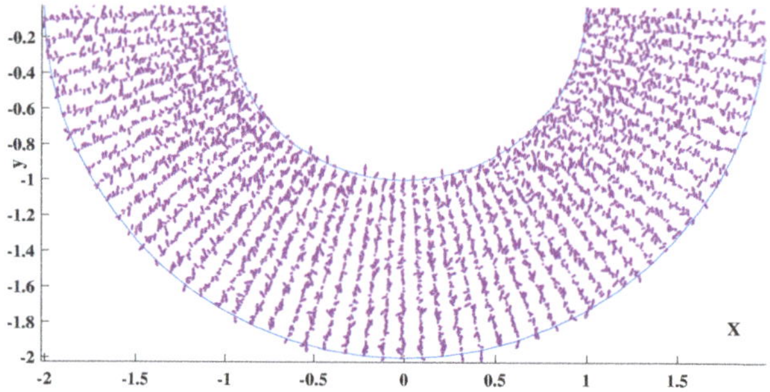

Figure 9. Velocity field for a semicircular water infiltration zone, numerical result.

4. Conclusions

The infiltration process of check dams is complex and is affected by many factors such as rainfall, soil characteristics, land cover, slope, and evapotranspiration. Analytical methods based on potential theory and complex analysis can help to simulate and predict the process of water infiltration from dams, allowing for more precise and effective control than empirical models (see [16]). This can provide a theoretical basis for the optimal use of soil water and the design of permeable channels for stormwater management (see [17]).

Different types of complex potentials expressed in literature were used to simulate the water infiltration, and the quantities derived from knowing the potential were determined using the original MatLab R2022b codes. A detailed determination of complex potential for particular cases, such as semicircular crowns and lower half-plane water infiltration zones were considered. The velocity field for both cases was precised.

Based on the analytical calculus made through the boundary element method in Section 3, it is possible to obtain the numerical values for the complex potential and the stream function as well as for the flow rate (debit constant q) using the (23)–(26) system in the matriceal form. The solution could be used if the boundary Γ of the flow domain is known, such as in the semicircular case. Using the two functions, the complex velocity is analytically obtained through Cauchy's formula.The system could be used for any smooth, closed curve describing the boundary of the flow domain when the parameterization of the curve is known.

If only the correspondences of the points (x_j, y_j) are known through experimental measurements then curve fitting could be used to improve the accuracy of the results more than obtained with the linearization used in (16). The accuracy of the original solution of the Dirichlet problem proposed in Figure 1 obtained in Section 3 can be improved by replacing the linear interpolation, at least with Spline functions whose analytical form can be used. Other studies, such as ([18]), are made using artificial neural networks instead of BEM ([19]).

Funding: The work has been founded through the University Politehnica of Bucharest, "PubArt" program.

Data Availability Statement: Not applicable.

Acknowledgments: The work has been founded through the University Politehnica of Bucharest, "PubArt" program.

Conflicts of Interest: The authors declare no conflict of interest.

References

1. Fetter, C.W. *Applied Hydrogeology*, 4th ed.; Prentice-Hall, Inc.: Upper Saddle River, NJ, USA, 2001; ISBN 0-13-088239-9.
2. Mateescu, C. *Hidraulica, Hydraulics*; Didactica si Pedagogica: Bucharest, Romania, 1961.
3. Bear, J.; Cheng, A.H.D. Seepage Drainage and Flow Nets. *Rev. Geophys. Space Phys.* **1980**, *18*, 729. [CrossRef]
4. Barry, D.A.; Chandler, J.H.; Groenevelt, J.P.E. Analytic Elements in the Solution of Laplace's Equation: A Review. *Adv. Water Resour.* **2004**, *27*, 931–947. [CrossRef]
5. Rubin, Y.; Langevin, C.D.; Wolfsberg, A.W. MODFLOW-2000, the U.S. Geological Survey Modular Ground-Water Model—User Guide to the LMT6 Package. In *Techniques and Methods*, 6th ed.; U.S. Geological Survey: Reston, VA, USA, 2003.
6. Salas, J.D.; Hite, R.A.; Bausch, R.E. Two-Dimensional Flow in Heterogeneous Aquifers: A Review of Analytical Methods. *Adv. Water Resour.* **1991**, *14*. [CrossRef]
7. van Genuchten, M.T. A Closed-Form Equation for Predicting the Hydraulic Conductivity of Unsaturated Soils. *Soil Sci. Soc. Am. J.* **1980**, *44*, 892–898. [CrossRef]
8. Carabineanu, A.; Dinu, A.; Oprea, I. The Application of the Boundary Element Method to the mAgnetohydrodynamic Duct Flow. *Z. Für Angew. Math. Und Phys.* **1995**, *46*, 971–981. [CrossRef]
9. Carabineanu, A. The study of the potential flow past a submerged hydrofoil by the complex boundary element method. *Eng. Anal. Bound. Elem.* **2014**, *39*, 23–35. [CrossRef]
10. Saffman, P.G. *Vortex Dynamics*; Cambridge University Press: Cambridge, UK, 1992.
11. Brebbia, C.A.; Dominguez, J. *Boundary Elements: An Introductory Course*; WIT Press: Billerica, MA, USA, 1992; ISBN 978-1-85312-349-8.
12. Beskos, A.; Kolmogorov, K. *Boundary Element Methods in Engineering Science*; Springer Science and Business Media: Berlin/Heidelberg, Germany; Imperial College Press: London, UK, 2008; ISBN 978-1-84816-579-3.
13. Huang, Y.S.; Ling, P.J. The Application of Boundary Element Method to the Seepage Analysis of Water Conservation Dams. *J. Hydraul. Res.* **1992**, *30*. [CrossRef]
14. Leung, C.M.; Tse, P.W. Application of the Boundary Element Method to Flow through Anisotropic Porous Media. *Eng. Anal. Bound. Elem.* **1995**, *15*. [CrossRef]
15. Willis, J.R.; Brebbia, C.A.; Santos, G.D. *Boundary Element Techniques: Theory and Applications in Engineering*; Springer Science and Business Media: Berlin/Heidelberg, Germany, 2008.
16. Scrădeanu, D.; Gheorghe, A. *Hidrogeologie Generală, General Hydrogeology*; Bucharest University Press: Bucharest, Romania, 2007; ISBN 978-973-737-367-0.
17. Song, Z.; Zhao, F.; Cui, Q.H.; Wang, J. Stability Analysis of Tailings Dam under Muddy Water Infiltration. In Proceedings of the 2015 International Conference on Architectural, Civil and Hydraulics Engineering (ICACHE 2015), Guangzhou, China, 28–29 November 2015; pp. 279–283.
18. Zhang, H.; Song, Z.; Peng, P.; Sun, Y.; Ding, Z.; Zhang, X. Research on seepage field of concrete dam foundation based on artificial neural network. *Alex. Eng. J.* **2021**, *60*, 1–14. [CrossRef]
19. Carabineanu, A.; Dinu, A. The study of the incompressible flow past a smooth obstacle in a channel by the boundary element method. *Rev. Roum. Sci. Techn. Mec. Appl.* **1993**, *38*, 601–616.

axioms

MDPI

Article

Join Operation for Semantic Data Enrichment of Asynchronous Time Series Data

Eloi Garcia [1], Mohammad Peyman [2], Carles Serrat [1] and Fatos Xhafa [1,*]

[1] Department of Mathematics, Barcelona School of Building Construction, Universitat Politècnica de Catalunya-BarcelonaTECH, 08028 Barcelona, Spain
[2] Department of Computer Science, Multimedia and Telecommunication, Universitat Oberta de Catalunya, 08018 Barcelona, Spain
* Correspondence: fatos@cs.upc.edu

Abstract: In this paper, we present a novel framework for enriching time series data in smart cities by supplementing it with information from external sources via semantic data enrichment. Our methodology effectively merges multiple data sources into a uniform time series, while addressing difficulties such as data quality, contextual information, and time lapses. We demonstrate the efficacy of our method through a case study in Barcelona, which permitted the use of advanced analysis methods such as windowed cross-correlation and peak picking. The resulting time series data can be used to determine traffic patterns and has potential uses in other smart city sectors, such as air quality, energy efficiency, and public safety. Interactive dashboards enable stakeholders to visualize and summarize key insights and patterns.

Keywords: join operation; data standardization; spatial data distribution; lagged cross-correlations; time series data; semantic data enrichment; Open Data Barcelona; Smart City

MSC: 62H11; 62M30; 62M10; 37M10; 68P05; 68P20

1. Introduction

In today's data-driven world, the amount of data generated and collected is increasing at an exponential rate, making it difficult to make sense of it and extract valuable insights from large amounts of data. Since raw data cannot provide an accurate representation of the underlying information and its relationships to other data points, adding context and meaning to data is becoming increasingly important, because it helps to improve the accuracy and value of data analysis [1]. Enriching data with semantic information aids in the clarification of relationships between data points, the identification of patterns, and the extraction of insights that would, otherwise, be missed. In other words, semantic enrichment is the process of enhancing raw data with semantic annotations or metadata to make it more meaningful, machine-readable, and usable. Semantic enrichment aims to convert unstructured, or poorly structured, data into structured, semantically rich, data that humans and computers can easily understand, and process, leading to improved results in tasks, such as information retrieval, text classification, and sentiment analysis [2,3].

Figure 1 illustrates the comprehensive process of semantic data enrichment, which begins with the collection of raw data from various sources. Following that, the raw data must be acquired by accessing and importing it into a suitable data management system. After that, the pertinent data is extracted from the acquired dataset, utilizing an array of techniques, such as data mining, text analysis, etc. Following data extraction, the data preprocessing phase begins, which involves cleaning and normalizing the data, resulting in the organization of the extracted data into a standardized and consistent format. This standardization makes data comparison and analysis more straightforward.

The normalized data is then supplemented with metadata or labels to provide additional information about the data type, structure, and semantics.

Subsequently, ontology languages are used to create a formal representation of the domain-specific concepts and relationships found in the enriched data. To provide a more comprehensive understanding of the data, the enriched data is linked with other relevant datasets, either within the same system or from external sources. The final step is to integrate the enriched data with existing data systems and applications, making it more accessible and useful to end-users.

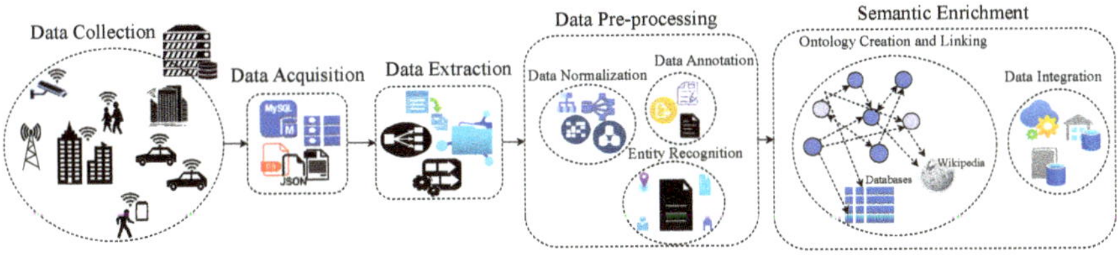

Figure 1. Semantic Data Enrichment.

Improving interoperability is another significant advantage of semantic data enrichment. When different systems and applications share a common understanding of the data being used, they can work more effectively together. This can result in better data exchange and more efficient data use, reducing the need for manual data entry and the risk of errors. For instance, Bouaicha and Ghemmaz [4] proposes a method for integrating and harmonizing data from various IoT sources in order to facilitate the exchange and processing of meteorological data. The approach makes use of semantic technologies to provide a common understanding of the data and to solve any semantic inconsistencies that may exist between various IoT sources. The authors conducted tests to determine the efficacy of the proposed solution and reported positive results. Additionally, semantic data enrichment can lead to increased data reuse. Organizations can reuse data more effectively by improving data quality and understanding. Bassier et al. [5] describes a process for transforming existing building geometry data into linked data, which is a form of semantic enrichment. The linked data contains additional information about the geometry of the building, making it more meaningful and usable for a variety of applications. The authors increase the value and reuse potential of the building geometry data by converting it to linked data. Furthermore, semantic data enrichment can be used in a variety of industries (i.e., healthcare, finance, logistics, manufacturing, telecommunications, government, etc.), to improve performance by providing a better understanding of data and the relationships between data points [6].

However, despite its numerous advantages, implementing semantic data enrichment is not without difficulties. Data quality, scalability, and security are three major challenges. To provide a clear understanding of the data, semantic annotations must be accurate, complete, and consistent. The process of identifying, extracting, and validating semantic annotations is time-consuming and resource-intensive, making improved data quality a difficult task. Another challenge is scalability, because, as the amount of data generated and collected grows, the ability to process and enrich large amounts of data in real-time becomes increasingly difficult. Even though sensitive information may be included in the enriched data, security is a challenge. Maintaining trust in data requires a delicate balance in ensuring the privacy and security of sensitive data while still allowing its use for analysis. Furthermore, smart cities can improve their data collection, management, and analysis by leveraging this technology. This data can then be used to improve the quality of life for citizens, increase efficiency and sustainability, and improve the overall functioning of the city. Semantic data enrichment is, thus, a critical component of the smart city ecosystem, serving as a foundation for advanced applications, such as traffic management, environmental monitoring, public safety, and many others [7,8].

Motivation and Context: Barcelona Smart City Research Project

With the rise of urbanization around the world, and the increasing demand for sustainable and efficient city transport and mobility operations, it has become essential for cities to develop projects that take into account new available technologies and possibilities opening up in the global market, such as services on-demand and online accessible products. Furthermore, zero-emission vehicles are increasingly common in cities (e.g.,: electric vehicles, unmanned aerial vehicles, autonomous vehicles, etc.) and new sensibilities from public institutions for sustainable, transparent, and effective development have created an urge from these entities to rethink and redevelop how public transportation, and its interaction with its users, is established.

Having all these needs as end goals, Barcelona City Council –Ajuntament de Barcelona– has been developing different initiatives that aim to meet the new needs that Barcelona's citizens have inquired about over the past years. One of them is the Open Data Barcelona initiative [9], a project that started in 2010, and which fosters a "pluralistic digital economy" and develops a "new model of urban innovation based on the transformation and digital innovation of the public sector and the implication among companies, administrations, the academic world, organizations, communities, and people, with a clear public and citizen leadership". The Open Data Barcelona service is transversal to several of the pillars of the city's planning strategy, giving citizens access to all data available from the main administrative departments of the city council.

Another initiative taken by the city council is the Optimizing Carsharing and Ridesharing Mobility in Smart Sustainable Cities project within the Barcelona Science Plan 2020–2023 [10], which analyzes the possible impact that carsharing and ridesharing strategies can have in the Greater Barcelona Metropolitan area, together with intelligent systems that redistribute the available resources for optimal and sustainable performance, using mainly Open Data Barcelona assets for its development. These new strategies can directly impact the cost reduction of carsharing and ridesharing operations, an aspect that would have, indirectly, an impact on the final cost for citizens of many products and services. Moreover, its final aim is to promote universal user-friendly access to cost-effective transport and mobility options without compromising safety and security. Thus, these new strategies could reduce direct and indirect costs. In addition, these concepts and solutions facilitate new carsharing and ridesharing business models that contribute to more sustainable transport and mobility practices.

This project presents research findings that use different data sources, such as empirical time-series data and various algorithms, predictive models, and simulations, to simulate traffic flows in a city. However, these data sources may have heterogeneity in their definitions and structures, which can limit their interoperability and usefulness. To address this issue, this paper proposes a common framework that homogenizes and merges all available data sources into a single, semantically enriched database. The resulting database can be used to support real-time decision-making in city transport and mobility operations for carsharing and ridesharing. This paper introduces a new framework for enriching time series data quality in smart city applications. The framework supplements time series data with external data sources using semantic data processing techniques to improve data quality and provide contextual information. This paper also demonstrates the effectiveness of the proposed framework by using traffic density data from Open Data Barcelona in a case study in the context of Barcelona's smart city.

The primary objective of this article is to present and develop an application of semantic technology in order to create a data semantic model that can effectively enrich time series data, specifically within the context of a smart city. By leveraging the semantic data model developed, several notable contributions are made by this article, which are outlined in detail below.

- The first contribution is the enhancement of data quality for asynchronous time series data, which is crucial for ensuring that accurate and reliable insights can be drawn from the information.

- Secondly, the article showcases the ability to integrate and unify data that originates from various, heterogeneous sources, thus facilitating a more comprehensive understanding of the smart city ecosystem.
- Another key aspect of this work is the increased availability of data, which can be used to support a wide range of smart city applications and initiatives aimed at improving urban living conditions. By making data more accessible, the article contributes to the advancement of smart city technologies and the development of innovative solutions to address the challenges faced by urban communities.
- Lastly, the article generates a methodology for handling all sorts of smart city data, making it possible for different actors and stakeholders involved in smart city applications to effectively utilize and benefit from the insights provided. This methodology ensures that the semantic data model can be applied to a broad range of scenarios and contexts, thereby increasing its overall value and impact.

Overall, the article emphasizes the importance of semantic technology in the context of smart cities and demonstrates its potential to significantly enhance the quality, availability, and utility of time series data. By doing so, the article contributes to ongoing efforts to harness the power of data and technology to create more sustainable, efficient, and livable urban environments.

The rest of the paper is organized as follows. We discuss related work on semantic data enrichment in Section 2. Next, in Section 3, we introduce our data semantic enrichment model and its implementation. To demonstrate the effectiveness of our approach, we present a case study and computational results in Section 4. In Section 5, we summarize our main findings. Finally, in Section 6, we conclude with an outlook on future research directions.

2. Related Work

The use of semantic technologies has received a lot of attention in recent years. In the context of the Internet of Things (IoT), Honti and Abonyi [11] summarized recent advances in the application of semantic sensor technologies, and investigates the various approaches and techniques used for the semantic enrichment of sensor data, as well as the field's challenges and future directions. The review provides a comprehensive overview of the research in this area, emphasizing the significance of semantic sensor technologies in improving interoperability and data quality in IoT systems. Xhafa et al. [12] assessed the performance of an edge computing layer for IoT stream processing, with a particular emphasis on semantic data enrichment. The findings indicated that edge computing is a promising solution to improve the efficiency and effectiveness of semantic data enrichment by lowering latency and increasing data processing reliability. The study sheds light on the potential of edge computing in supporting the growth of IoT and improving the quality of semantic data across multiple domains. Chen et al. [13] investigated the design and implementation of a data infrastructure that supports urban analytics using semantics. To provide a comprehensive view of the urban environment, the authors propose a semantic-enabled infrastructure that integrates multiple data sources. The infrastructure makes use of ontologies to represent data relationships and provide a common understanding of the data. The authors describe the infrastructure's implementation in practice and assess its effectiveness in supporting urban analytics tasks. They demonstrated that the semantic-enabled infrastructure could effectively integrate and analyze data from multiple sources, providing valuable insights for urban decision-making. In the field of semantic models for the analysis of data from IoT sensors, Zappatore et al. [14] proposed a system that extracts relevant data from IoT sensors using semantic models and then analyzes the data to infer relationships between environmental factors and human well-being. According to the study, the use of semantic models can lead to a more accurate and efficient analysis of IoT sensor data and valuable insights into how environmental factors impact human health and well-being.

Additionally, Buchmann and Karagiannis [15] discusses a method for transforming diagrammatic conceptual models into a more semantically rich Web of Data representation. The authors presented a pattern-based approach for converting these models into a format that computers can better understand and process, allowing for easier integration and interoperability between various data sources on the web. This approach aims to improve web data interoperability and make it easier for computers to understand and process information.

To facilitate the integration of multiple data sources in smart cities, Djenouri et al. [16] proposed a method for matching different ontologies. To match ontologies and resolve semantic mismatches between them, the method employs a combination of techniques, such as semantic similarity, instance-based matching, and domain knowledge. The authors assessed the proposed method's performance in a case study involving the integration of multiple data sources for smart city applications. Xu et al. [17] proposed a system for annotating data in the IoT ecosystem that uses both domain-specific and general ontologies, as well as a hybrid approach to semantic annotation. According to the study, using semantic annotations can improve the efficiency and accuracy of data processing in IoT ecosystems, as well as the interoperability of different IoT devices. Xue et al. [18] describe recent advances in the semantic enrichment of building and city information models. The authors investigated the various approaches and techniques used for semantic enrichment, as well as the field's challenges and future directions. The review spanned ten years and provides an in-depth look at the research in this field. The findings showed that semantic enrichment has been widely adopted in the field of building and city information modeling, resulting in improved data interoperability, data quality, and data usability. According to the authors, semantic enrichment continues to play an important role in the development of smart cities and the built environment.

The application of semantic technologies is not limited to these sectors, as similar studies have been conducted in the field of semantic sensor technologies, wherein Amato et al. [19] proposed a semantically enriched data model for improving sensor network interoperability. The authors presented a semantic enrichment technique that combines metadata with raw data to make it more meaningful and machine-readable. The method relies on ontologies and vocabularies to represent the meaning and relationships between data elements. The authors evaluated the proposed approach's performance in a real-world scenario and demonstrated that it can effectively improve sensor network interoperability. The study provides valuable insights into the potential of semantic enrichment for improving data quality in sensor networks and offers a promising solution for overcoming data interoperability challenges in this domain. Furthermore, Jiang et al. [20] discuss the use of neural networks to represent computer code in an hierarchical, semantically-aware manner. The authors proposed a method for improving computer code representation in order to better capture its meaning and structure. This is accomplished by incorporating semantic information into the code representation, which allows the neural network to comprehend the relationships between various parts of the code. The resulting code representation is hierarchical, allowing for the effective representation of complex code structures, and it can be used for tasks like code summarizing, completion, and search. The authors assessed their method and demonstrated that it outperformed existing methods in a variety of tasks.

Ataei Nezhad et al. [21] presented a secure IoT data aggregation method that utilizes an authentication mechanism to ensure data integrity and confidentiality. The proposed methodology uses a two-tier architecture, in which data is aggregated locally by trusted nodes before being sent to a central aggregator for processing. The authentication mechanism is built on a symmetric key encryption scheme that ensures secure communication between nodes, while also preventing unauthorized data access. The authors also conducted simulation experiments to evaluate the proposed method's performance and compared it to other existing methods, demonstrating its effectiveness in terms of data accuracy, security, and energy efficiency. Iatrellis et al. [22] proposed a new approach to managing smart city-related competencies that makes use of cloud computing and semantic web technologies. The authors discuss the increasing complexity of smart cities necessitating a more efficient method of managing competencies across multiple domains and stakeholders. They describe a system that uses a cloud-based platform to integrate competency management, learning management, and assessment tools, all while utilizing semantic web technologies to ensure interoperability and accuracy. The system is intended to be flexible, adaptable, and scalable, and the authors believe it has the potential to revolutionize the way we manage competencies in smart city contexts.

Furthermore, Ribeiro and Braghetto [23] provides a scalable data integration architecture for smart cities, which allows for the integration of heterogeneous data from various sources. The architecture is composed of three layers: data collection, data processing, and data analysis. According to the authors, the proposed architecture can address the challenges associated with integrating and analyzing large amounts of data generated by smart city systems. The article also includes a case study that used real-world data from a smart city project to assess the performance of the proposed architecture. The study's findings showed that the proposed architecture is effective and scalable for integrating and analyzing data from multiple sources. The authors in Tao [24] proposed a framework based on semantic ontologies for modeling, retrieval, and inference of incomplete mobile trajectory data. To represent domain knowledge and improve the accuracy of trajectory data analysis, the framework employs semantic ontology. It also uses a probabilistic model to handle missing data in trajectories and a graph-based retrieval method to search for trajectory similarity. The experimental results showed that the proposed framework is effective and efficient in dealing with incomplete trajectory data and improving trajectory retrieval accuracy.

Psyllidis et al. [25] described a platform for urban analytics and the integration of semantic data in city planning. The platform aims to facilitate collaboration among various stakeholders involved in urban planning by providing tools for collecting, analyzing, and visualizing data from various sources in an intuitive and interactive manner. The platform makes data from various domains accessible to both experts and non-experts by utilizing semantic technologies. According to the authors, this platform can help cities become more responsive to their citizens' needs and more sustainable in the long run.

The authors in Costa and Santos [26] proposed SusCity, a big data warehousing approach for smart cities that aims to address the challenges of managing and analyzing the large and diverse data generated by smart city systems. The approach is built on a three-layer architecture that includes a data ingestion layer, a data warehousing layer, and an analytics layer. The data ingestion layer includes tools for data collection, cleansing, and transformation, whereas the data warehousing layer includes a data model and storage system optimized for big data. The analytics layer includes data analysis and visualization tools, as well as machine learning algorithms for predictive analytics.

Table 1 summarizes the various approaches of the reviewed literature, as well as the area of study and specific methods used.

Despite the extensive research conducted in this field, none of the papers discussed have addressed the issue of combining asynchronous spatial data collected from different coordinates and moments in time. This problem can arise when dealing with the geographical, physical, and logistical complexities involved in smart city monitoring. However, our paper introduces an innovative approach that incorporates information from external sources through semantic data enrichment to augment smart city time series data. Our technique effectively unifies multiple data sources into a consistent time series, addressing challenges such as data quality, context, and time gaps.

Table 1. Summarized reviewed work.

Article	Year	Area of Study	Methods	Contributions
[11]	2019	IoT, & Semantic sensor technologies	Literature review	Semantic sensor technologies improve interoperability and data quality in IoT systems.
[12]	2020	IoT, & Edge computing	Experimental study	Edge computing is a promising solution for improving the efficiency and effectiveness of semantic data enrichment.
[13]	2020	Urban Analytics & Semantic-enabled infrastructure	Case study	Semantic-enabled infrastructure can effectively integrate and analyze data from multiple sources, providing valuable insights for urban decision-making.
[14]	2023	IoT & Semantic models for data analysis	System proposal	Semantic models can lead to a more accurate and efficient analysis of IoT sensor data and valuable insights into how environmental factors impact human well-being.
[15]	2015	Web of Data & Diagrammatic conceptual models	Pattern-based approach	Pattern-based approach improves web data interoperability.
[16]	2020	Smart cities & Ontology matching	Case study	Proposed method effectively matches ontologies and resolves semantic mismatches between them.
[17]	2023	IoT & Semantic annotation	System proposal	Semantic annotations can improve the efficiency and accuracy of data processing in IoT ecosystems and the interoperability of different IoT devices.
[18]	2021	Building and city information modeling & Semantic enrichment	Literature review	Semantic enrichment improves data interoperability, data quality, and data usability.
[19]	2021	Semantic sensor technologies & Semantically enriched data model	Experimental study	Semantically enriched data model effectively improves sensor network interoperability.
[20]	2022	Hierarchical & semantically-aware code representation	System proposal	Incorporating semantic information into code representation improves comprehension of code structure.
[21]	2022	IoT	Authentication-based secure data aggregation	Proposed a two-tier architecture for secure data aggregation in IoT using symmetric key encryption.
[22]	2021	Smart Cities	Cloud-based platform, Semantic web technologies, Competency management, Learning management, Assessment tools	Proposed system is flexible, adaptable, and scalable, and has the potential to revolutionize the way we manage competencies in smart city contexts.

Table 1. *Cont.*

Article	Year	Area of Study	Methods	Contributions
[23]	2022	Smart Cities	Scalable data integration architecture, Three-layer architecture for data collection, processing, and analysis, Case study using real-world data	Proposed architecture is effective and scalable for integrating and analyzing data from multiple sources.
[24]	2023	Mobile Trajectory Data	Semantic ontology, Probabilistic model for handling missing data, Graph-based retrieval method	Proposed framework is effective and efficient in dealing with incomplete trajectory data and improving trajectory retrieval accuracy.
[25]	2015	Urban Analytics	Platform for urban analytics and integration of semantic data in city planning	Platform facilitates collaboration among various stakeholders involved in urban planning by providing tools for collecting, analyzing, and visualizing data.
[26]	2017	Smart Cities	Big data warehousing approach, Three-layer architecture for data ingestion, warehousing, and analytics, Machine learning algorithms for predictive analytics	Approach addresses the challenges of managing and analyzing the large and diverse data generated by smart city systems.

3. Data Semantic Enrichment Model and Implementation

3.1. Model

In this section, we provide a detailed description of the model used to associate an initial set of values with the closest available measurements based on geographical proximity and minimum difference in timestamps, while considering the availability of additional data. This model is designed to provide an accurate representation of the predefined conditions in different sections of a city, based on the closest measurements available. In the following section, we describe the model in detail, including the inputs, outputs, and the development of the data enrichment process.

3.1.1. Input

Let C be the set of sections of the city, and let T be the set of timestamps. For each section $c \in C$, let D_c be a dataset of initial values for c at different timestamps $t \in T$. Let S be a set of geographic locations associated with each dataset D_c. For each timestamp $t \in T$, let M_t be a set of measurements taken at different locations $s \in S_t$ at time t. Each measurement $m \in M_t$ has a geographic location s_m and a timestamp t_m, and may be associated with additional data D'_m that is available only at s_m.

3.1.2. Output

For each section $c \in C$ and timestamp $t \in T$, find the closest measurement $m_{c,t}$ in M_t to the initial values dataset D_c, based on both geographical proximity and minimum difference on timestamps. If additional data D'_m is available for $m_{c,t}$, associate it with the corresponding initial dataset value in D_c.

3.1.3. Semantic Data Model

For each section $c \in C$ and timestamp $t \in T$, we can compute the closest measurement $m_{c,t}$ in M_t as follows:

STEP 1. Compute the geographic distances $d(s, D_c)$ between each location $s \in S$ associated with D_c and each location $s' \in S_t$ in M_t:

$$d(s, D_c) = \min_{s' \in S_t}\{\text{distance}(s, s')\}, \tag{1}$$

where $\text{distance}(s, s')$ is the geographical distance between s and s'.

STEP 2. Find the measurement $m_{c,t}$ that minimizes the sum of the geographic distance and the absolute time difference with D_c:

$$m_{c,t} = \arg\min_{m \in M_t}\{d(s_m, D_c) + |\min_{m' \in M_t}\{|t_m - t_{m'}|\} - t|\}. \tag{2}$$

In other words, we find the measurement m in M_t that has the minimum sum of geographic distance with D_c and the absolute time difference with the closest measurement in M_t to t. The closest measurement in M_t to t is obtained by computing the minimum time difference between all pairs of measurements in M_t.

STEP 3. If additional data D'_m is available for $m_{c,t}$, associate it with the corresponding initial set value in D_c:

$$\text{initial set}(c, t) = \begin{cases} (\text{initial set}(c, t), \text{value}(m_{c,t})) & \text{if } D'_m \nexists \text{ for } m_{c,t}, \\ (\text{initial set}(c, t), \text{value}(m_{c,t}), D'_m) & \text{otherwise.} \end{cases} \tag{3}$$

In other words, if additional data is not available for $m_{c,t}$, we simply associate the initial dataset value from the closest measurement in M_t to D_c. Otherwise, we associate both the initial set value and the additional data D'_m.

3.2. Implementation

The implementation of our proposed methodology involves the use of an algorithm that associates initial dataset values with measurements and additional data, considering both geographical proximity and the availability of additional data. The algorithm aims to find the closest measurement to each section of the city and associates it with the corresponding initial dataset value. By implementing this algorithm, we can efficiently associate traffic density values with the closest and most relevant measurements, while ensuring the accuracy and reliability of the results.

Algorithm 1 associates the initial values with measurements and additional data, as depicted on the Figure 2, by first looping through each section of the city and each dataset, and finding the closest measurement in the dataset to the section of the city based on geographical proximity and the minimum time difference between the measure and the subset (s, t). The closest measurement is identified as the one with the shortest distance to the section of the city. Once the closest measurement is identified, the algorithm checks if there is any additional data available for the measurement in the corresponding dataset. If additional data is available, the algorithm associates the traffic density value for the section of the city with the corresponding measurement and additional data.

Algorithm 1: The methodology for associating initial geographical values in time with asynchronous measurements and additional data

```
for each initial section s do
    generate geographical coordinates and associate them with the location
    for each timestamp measurement t do
        for each dataset d do
            min_d = min_{d∈D}(m_{c,t})
            Associate s with min_d
            if D'_m ∃ for min_d then
                Associate D'_m with s
            end
        end
    end
end
```

Following Algorithm 1, we can estimate the complexity cost by analyzing each of the steps defined and their implications. That is:

- Initializing geographical coordinates for each initial section has a computational cost of $\mathcal{O}(|C|)$.
- The computation of the distance $d(s, D_c)$ between each location associated with D_c and each location in S_t, following the definition of the step where we have two sets of locations, requires iterating over them. This step has a time complexity of $\mathcal{O}(|C||S_t|)$.
- Finding the measurement $m_{c,t}$ that minimizes the sum of geographic distances and absolute time differences involves finding minimum values across data points. This step in the worst-case complexity is $\mathcal{O}(|M_t|^2)$.
- If additional data is available for a measurement, we need to associate it with its corresponding initial dataset value. This step incurs an extra cost if there exist additional data; otherwise, it adds no extra computational expense. The association process requires constant time which can be achieved using hash tables or similar structures.

Therefore, the overall running time can be expressed as:

$$T(n) = \mathcal{O}(|C||S_t| \cdot |M_t|^2) \tag{4}$$

where:

n : represents the input size.
$|C|$: denotes number of sections in city C.
$|S_t|$: denotes number of locations within timestamp set.
$|M_t|^2$: denotes evaluation of all possible pairs from measurements at given timestamps t.

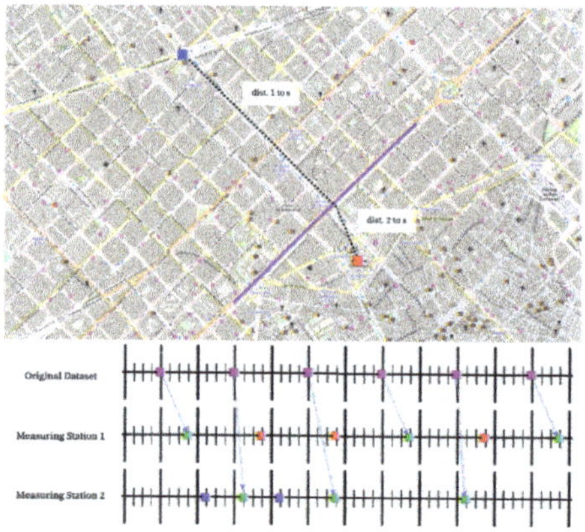

Figure 2. Graphical representation of the flow on the Algorithm 1 for a given dataset with two different measure stations and a section s.

The implementation of Algorithm 1 is performed in Python using the libraries `pandas` and `geopandas` (see Code Listing A1) in Appendix A. `pandas` is a popular data manipulation library that provides data structures and functions to work with time-series data, as well as tools for data cleaning, exploration, and visualization. On the other hand, `geopandas` extends the functionality of `pandas` by adding support for geospatial data, which is essential for analyzing and visualizing the spatial distribution of traffic density and pollution. The main reasons behind the usage of `pandas` as the main library for data manipulation and structuring are the following:

- Efficient data manipulation: Pandas provides efficient data structures like DataFrame and Series, making it easy to manipulate large datasets.
- Time-series support: Pandas offers built-in functionality for handling time-series data, which is useful for analyzing temporal patterns in data.
- Data cleaning and exploration: Pandas provides tools for handling missing data, filtering, and transforming data, which are essential for preparing datasets for analysis.
- Visualization: Pandas integrates with popular visualization libraries, allowing for easy creation of plots and charts to explore data patterns.
- Geospatial data handling: Geopandas extends pandas by adding support for geospatial data types, which is crucial when working with spatial information like coordinates and geometries.
- Spatial analysis: Geopandas offers spatial operations and functions that enable the analysis of spatial relationships, distances, and intersections between geospatial objects.
- Geospatial visualization: Geopandas integrates with visualization libraries to create maps and other spatial visualizations, which help in understanding spatial patterns and distributions.

Using these libraries, we were able to preprocess and analyze the original collected data by cleaning, merging, and organizing it in a way that made it easier to work with. The data was then transformed into a format that could be used to generate maps, graphs, and other visualizations that aided in handling the data for geographical distances. The use of

Python and the pandas and geopandas libraries provided the necessary tools to generate a comprehensive dataset that covered variations on data availability, while also considering asynchronous data collection and different geographical points for the measurements.

The asynchronous_join, as shown at Code Listing function A1 in Appendix A. performs an asynchronous geospatial join operation between an initial dataset and an extra dataset using the methodology described above. The function finds the station with the minimum combined distance, in terms of both geographic distance and time difference, from each location in the initial dataset, and extracts the desired measure and any additional measures from the selected station.

For this code implementation we defined the following inputs and outputs and analyzed its overall performance.

3.2.1. Inputs

The correct function of this implementation needs a set of variables with a predefined structure:

- initial_dataset: A pandas DataFrame containing the initial dataset to join. It should be structured accordingly with the following description of parameters:
  - Column Coordinates: Column with GeoPandas geometry objects.
  - Column Timestamp: Column with datetime objects representing timestamps.
- extra_dataset: A GeoDataFrame containing the extra dataset to join. It should be structured accordingly with the following description of parameters:
  - Column Coordinates: Column with GeoPandas geometry objects representing spaces with real coordinates
  - Column Timestamp: Column with datetime objects representing timestamps.
  - Columns for measurements: One or more columns with structured values that are associated with the two previous columns.
- measure: A string representing the measure to extract from the GeoDataFrame extra_dataset. It should match the name of the column being extracted.
- extra_values: A Boolean, indicating whether to extract additional measures from the GeoDataFrame extra_dataset.
- names_extra_measures: A list of strings representing the additional measures to extract from the GeoDataFrame extra_dataset. They have to match the name of the columns being extracted.

3.2.2. Outputs

The expected output of this implementation is a GeoDataFrame containing the joined data in the following structure:

- Column original_index: indices from the original dataset are stored here to make it easier to perform joins with other data.
- Column section: Column with GeoPandas geometry objects.
- Column timestamp: Column with datetime objects representing timestamps.
- Column geography: Column with GeoPandas geometry objects representing spaces with real coordinates.

3.3. Computational Complexity and Performance

We denote n as the number of rows in the *initial_dataset* input variable and m as the number of rows in the *extra_dataset* input variable. Since the initial definition of the algorithm contains nested loops that search for the closest measuring station and timestamp for each point in the initial dataset, the computational complexity is defined as $O(n^3)$. This means that the running time increases significantly as the size of the dataset grows.

Due to this limitation on scalability, improvements were made on the final implementation bringing the complexity down to $O(nm^2)$, with the use of two main improvements that sped up the search for the closest station and timestamp shown at Code Listing A2, in Appendix A. This resulted in a significant improvement in performance, especially for large datasets.

The `asyncronous_join` function has a loop that iterates over every point in the initial dataset, having a size proportional to n. For each point, the function must calculate the distance to every point in the extra dataset, which has a size proportional to m. The calculation of normalized distances between the initial point and every point in the extra dataset has a time complexity of $O(m)$, as it must loop over every point in the extra dataset. Similarly, the normalization of the timestamps has a time complexity of $O(m)$ as it also must loop over every point in the extra dataset. After normalization, the function must combine the two measures into a single distance value for each point in the extra dataset. This operation has a time complexity of $O(m)$, as it involves element-wise addition of two arrays of length m. Finally, the function must find the point in the extra dataset that has the minimum combined distance from the current initial point. This operation has a time complexity of $O(m)$, as it must loop over every point in the extra dataset to find the minimum distance.

Therefore, the total time complexity of the `asynchronous_join()` function is $O(nm^2)$. This is because for every point in the initial dataset, the function must perform $O(m^2)$ calculations to find the point in the extra dataset with the minimum distance. Any other computational improvement had to be discarded, since the complexity of the possible geographical references could not be supported by the definition of the implementation.

In terms of space complexity, the function creates a new GeoDataFrame to store the output, which has a size proportional to n. Additionally, the function creates a spatial index for the extra dataset, which has a size proportional to m. With this, we can state that the total space complexity of the function is $O(n+m)$.

4. Case Study: From Time Series Data to Semantically Enriched Data

The growth of urban areas has brought about a significant increase in the number of vehicles on the roads, resulting in an unprecedented level of traffic congestion. As a result, it has become increasingly important for city planners and transportation authorities to gain insights into traffic patterns and trends, in order to optimize traffic flow and reduce congestion. In this case study, we explore the use of an algorithm for associating traffic density values with measurements and additional data, as a means of moving from time series data to semantically enriched data. By applying this algorithm to a real-world dataset, we aim to demonstrate the potential of this approach in improving the accuracy and reliability of traffic analysis, and in supporting the development of more effective traffic management strategies.

4.1. Challenges of the Real Life Problem of Car Traffic in the City

In order to study alternatives to car traffic in the city of Barcelona, the Optimizing Carsharing and Ridesharing Mobility in Smart Sustainable Cities project [9] requires geographical data with a timestamp component, like traffic density and air pollution, among others. Consequently, the need to study the relationship between these variables led to the demand for datasets that provide a comprehensive understanding of the issue. However, generating such datasets comes with two main challenges that can impede the research process.

The first challenge faced when generating a dataset about traffic density, pollution, and other variables is the asynchronous data collection. Traffic density and pollution are collected at different times and depend on physical devices that measure the data in an open environment, making them susceptible to damage and downtime. As a result, generating a comprehensive dataset that covers these variations requires a robust data collection method that captures the fluctuations in traffic density and pollution levels, while accounting for the unavailability and potential downtime of the measuring devices. The method defined above includes a predefined merge structure that allows the data to be paired with a logic that considers these external situations to ensure the accuracy and completeness of the resulting dataset.

The other significant challenge in generating these homogeneous datasets is the different geographical points for the measurements. Each measurement is taken from different locations, making it necessary to collect data from different geographical points, generating a logic that decides which data better represents the reality for each section of the city. Standardized protocols can help ensure that data is collected consistently and in a compatible format, making integration and management more straightforward.

4.2. Definition of Requirements and State of the Original Data

The motivation behind this case study was driven by the need for traffic-related data from the Open Data Barcelona portal, as well as the need to study relevant time series data with different coordinate ranges and periodicity of measure, all of which are included within the same source. In particular, the data requires a comprehensive analysis of traffic flow in Barcelona, along with additional measures, such as pollution levels and alternative transportation capacities.

To facilitate an in-depth analysis of different sections of the city, it is essential to incorporate geographic filters for all the data provided. This enables the study of individual neighborhoods, streets, and other relevant city subdivisions, enabling more targeted and effective urban planning strategies.

One of the main challenges in working with Open Data Barcelona is the lack of standardization in the original data. Some datasets, particularly those that rely on a limited number of measuring stations spread across the city, often include two columns labeled 'Longitude' and 'Latitude' that indicate the location of the measurements. Other datasets may relate to specific sections of streets or districts within the city, and may not contain direct geographic data. In these cases, additional preprocessing may be necessary to add geographic data to the dataset. The heterogeneous presentation of the data can make it difficult for the public to access the information, as well as hinder efforts to interconnect and create a comprehensive picture of the city. This challenge underscores the importance of preprocessing the data to ensure standardization and consistency, enabling more effective data analysis and visualization.

4.3. Preprocessing, Feature Engineering and Standardization

A preprocessing method is defined with the ultimate goal of standardization and interoperability, with the adoption of time and space filters, and it involves several key steps (see processing workflow in Figure 3).

In the first step, the user selects a dataset of interest from the Open Data Barcelona portal, specifying a specific time and geographic range. Subsequently, built-in methods request the data through an API, returning the raw dataset in its original form. It is important to emphasize that each chosen dataset requires a unique preprocessing and cleaning method due to the differences in data sources and structures.

To ensure the necessary treatment for each dataset, we developed a modular approach that involves the removal of invalid and redundant data, identification and elimination of duplicate entries, and standardization of geographical and temporal properties. Special emphasis was given to generating `GeoPandasDataframes` with geometries derived from the coordinates provided in the original data, which could be `Points`, `Linestrings`, or `Polygons`, depending on the nature of the data. Moreover, after cleaning and standardizing the data, we restructured the initial dataset to ensure that the data was presented in a consistent format for further analysis.

Finally, this method employed built-in predefinitions of different sections of the city to extract the selected period and section of data chosen by the user. This facilitated targeted analysis of specific neighborhoods, streets, and other relevant city subdivisions. In summary, the proposed preprocessing method plays a crucial role in enabling the analysis of Open Data Barcelona datasets by providing clean and standardized data that is readily available for further exploration and analysis.

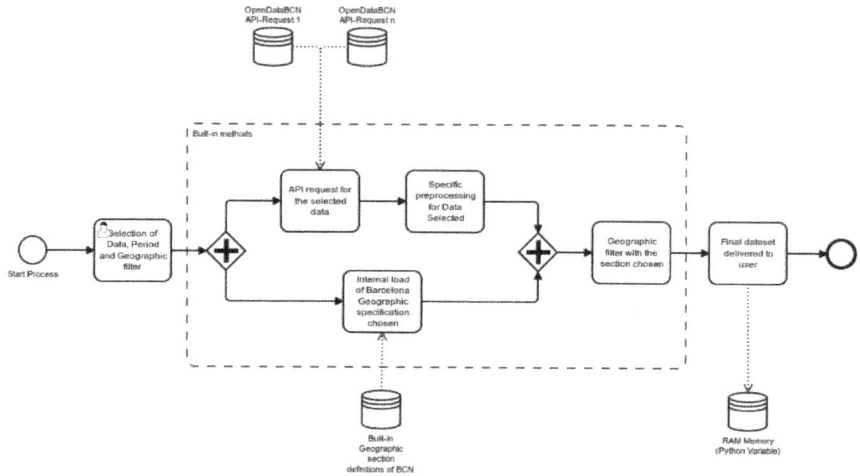

Figure 3. Preprocessing flow diagram designed for the use case.

4.4. Open Data Barcelona Data Selection and Geographic Sections Definition

In Table 2 we present the datasets included in the case study for the asynchronous join process. The table includes information on the number of different geographical locations contained in each dataset, their geographic definitions, and the types of information that can be retrieved from them. Additionally, the estimated update rate and periodicity in which the data was updated was in accordance with what Open Data Barcelona stated in each dataset metadata.

Table 2. Datasets used in the case study.

Dataset	Geographical Locations	Information	Periodicity
Traffic Density (Geographic definition: Lines)	534 sections of streets defined in the city map of Barcelona	Traffic Density values and Initial Locations in a categorical internal system (from no traffic to jam).	Every 15 min (when there is data available)
Pollutants (Geographic definition: Points)	Eight pollution sensors coordinates (points) spread out on Barcelona city	Pollutant Values: • SO_2 (μg/m^3), • NO (μg/m^3), • NO_2 (μg/m^3), • $PM_{2.5}$ (μg/m^3), • NOx (μg/m^3), • O_3 (μg/m^3), • CO (μg/m^3), • PM_{10} (μg/m^3), • C (μg/m^3), • $Biomass_C$ (%).	Every hour (when there is data available)
Public Bike Availability (Geographic definition: Points)	519 public bike system stations	Bike availability number by type: • Mechanic Bikes, • Electric Bikes, • Parking spots.	Every 20 to 40 s (when there is data available)

To establish the formal definitions for the geographic filter, we referred to the definitions provided by the Barcelona City Council—*Ajuntament de Barcelona*, which are made available to the final user as a parameter for geographic filtering. These definitions are illustrated in Figure 4, and can be narrowed down to:

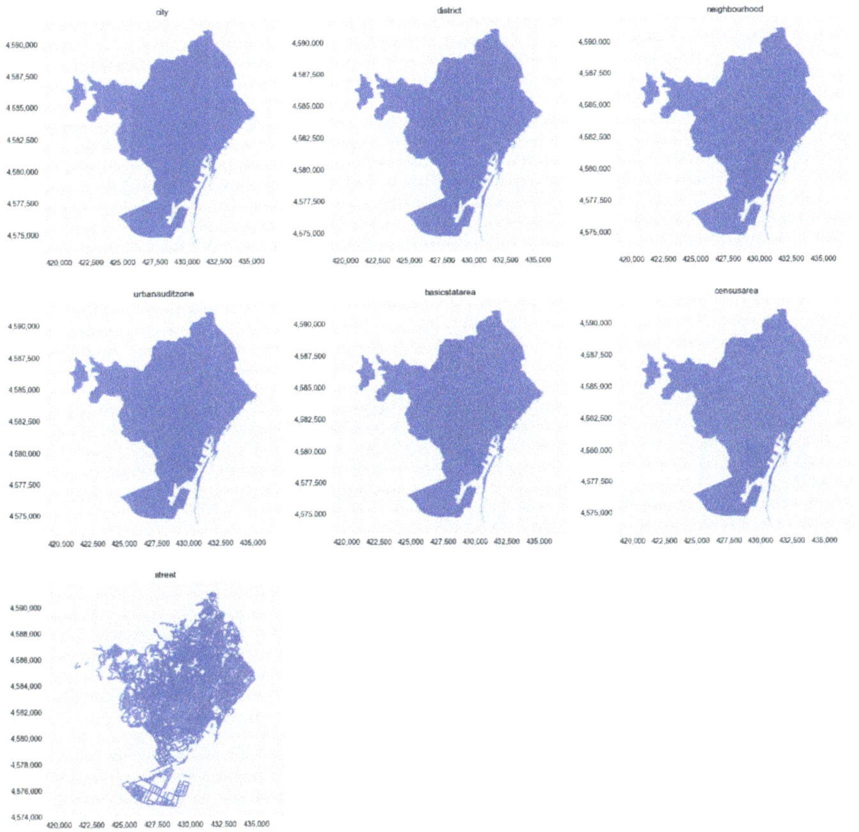

Figure 4. Geographic sections defined for Barcelona city.

- `city`: This filter includes the entire city of Barcelona. This is the largest geographic area and encompasses all of the neighborhoods and districts within the city.
- `district`: Barcelona city is divided into 10 administrative districts, for which some data is only available on this division.
- `neighbourhood`: Each district in Barcelona city is further subdivided into neighborhoods.
- `urbanauditzone`: The Urban Audit project is a European-wide initiative that aims to provide comparative urban statistics. This filter allows focus to be directed on data from specific zones defined by the Urban Audit project.
- `basicstatarea`: These areas are used by the Barcelona City Council for statistical purposes only, and there are 233 different areas. This filter allows focus to be directed on data from a specific area that is relevant to the statistical analysis being performed.
- `censusarea`: These areas are defined by the Spanish National Institute of Statistics (INE) for census purposes. This filter allows focus to be directed on data from a specific area that is relevant to the census analysis being performed.
- `street`: This filter allows focus to be directed on data from specific street segments within the Barcelona city. This can be useful for analyzing data that is related to traffic patterns, foot traffic, and other street-level activities.

4.5. Computational Results

In this section, we present the computational results obtained from using the methodologies and implementations discussed in this study, including the `asynchronous_join` method, to merge the selected data into a homogeneous time series for the different street sections in Barcelona, while keeping the original objective of providing a comprehensive view of the traffic data in Barcelona and presenting unified time series data that incorporate the information from all three data sources.

Combining data from different sources provides a broader perspective of the city's traffic and helps in identifying trends and patterns that may not have been apparent in individual datasets, as shown in Figure 5. The resulting time series provides a valuable resource for analyzing and understanding the traffic patterns in Barcelona. For example, correlations between certain pollution levels and areas of the city that are more prone to traffic congestion can now be evaluated, along with tracking changes in traffic patterns over time based on the availability of other methods of public transportation.

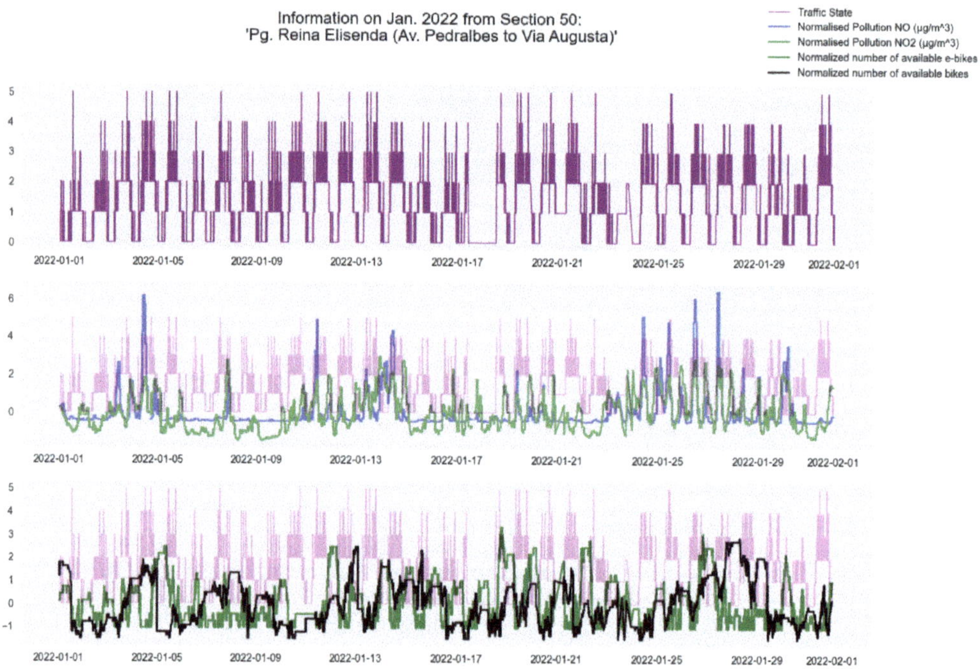

Figure 5. Comparison of three time series: original traffic density (**top**), generated normalized NO/NO_2 pollution (**middle**), and generated normalized public bike availability in Barcelona (**bottom**).

One significant advantage of the proposed methodology is that it enables the application of more advanced analysis methods, like windowed cross-correlation [27], a time series analysis technique used to identify correlations and time lags between different time series data points. With this kind of tool now available, users can identify time lags between two time series that came from different sources. For example, Figure A1, in Appendix B, displays the windowed cross-correlation and its rolling variate between traffic density and pollution levels over time. It is possible to identify the effects of different dimensions in which the original data was defined on the resulting dataset. In sources with a less frequent update rate, the results show a more static output than their counterparts.

With the proposed methodology, it is also possible to perform another time series analysis technique to identify correlations, like peak picking data points from different sources. This enables users to identify local maxima in their time series correlation by the changes in the offsets. For example, one could calculate the Pearson correlation between traffic density and pollution levels over time, as shown in Figure A2 in Appendix B. By doing so, it would be possible to determine the strength of the relationship between the two variables and potentially identify periods and offsets of high correlation, or even discard correlations.

The use of `asynchronous_join` also allows for the creation of interactive dashboards that can be used to display the time series data in a more comprehensible format with compatibility between `geopandas` packages and `folium`, a Python library for creating interactive maps and visualizations using Leaflet.js. These dashboards can provide visualizations and summaries of the key insights and patterns identified in the data, making it easier for stakeholders to understand and act upon the information. An example can be observed in Figure 6, where pollution data and traffic density data are shown on a synchronous interactive display code, whereby a dashboard displays real-time pollution data from multiple monitoring stations across a city and represents them in the closer street sections, so they provide a better understanding of the original issue.

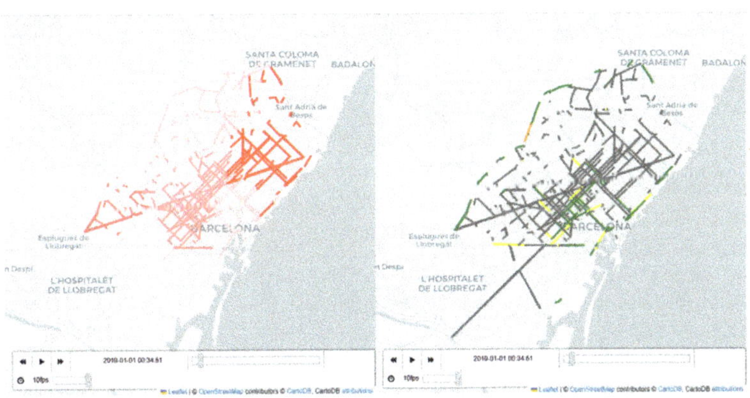

Figure 6. Dashboard for interactivemaps and visualizations. (**Right**) NO_2 Pollution rates ($\mu g/m^3$). (**Left**) Traffic Density (scalar scale).

Overall, the use of the `asynchronous_join` method, along with other methodologies presented in this study, allows us to merge data from multiple sources into a unified time series, providing a comprehensive view of traffic data in Barcelona. This approach enables the identification of trends and patterns in the data, and provides a valuable resource for developing more advanced analyses and predictive models.

5. Summative Evaluation

The use of semantic data enrichment, merging and processing techniques, such as `asynchronous_join`, have proven to be powerful tools for enriching, homogenizing and merging different and multiple data sources into a unified time series. A more comprehensive view of the data can be achieved that enables identification of patterns and trends that may not have been visible in individual datasets.

In the case of traffic data in Barcelona city, merging data from multiple sources allowed us to identify correlations between traffic density and pollution levels, as well as to identify patterns in the availability of public bicycles and traffic congestion. By applying time series analysis techniques, such as windowed cross-correlation and peak picking, it is possible to go further and explore the correlations and patterns, providing valuable insights for city officials and other stakeholders. The use of interactive dashboards and visualizations can also facilitate communication of the insights, making it easier for stakeholders to understand and act upon the information. This has potential benefits for urban planning, infrastructural development, and public health policies.

It should be noted, however, that the process of merging data from multiple sources does not come without challenges. One significant challenge is the lack of synchronization between datasets. This might result in missing data, outliers, and other inconsistencies that can affect the accuracy of the results. The use of data cleaning and processing techniques, as well as careful selection of compatible datasets, is crucial to mitigate these issues.

In summary, the integration of data from multiple sources through techniques such as `asynchronous_join`, provides a powerful tool for analyzing and understanding complex phenomena, such as traffic patterns in urban areas. By leveraging time series analysis techniques and interactive dashboards, we can obtain valuable insights and communicate these insights effectively to stakeholders. However, care must be taken to address the challenges of data synchronization and cleaning to ensure the accuracy and reliability of the results.

6. Conclusions and Future Works

In this article, we proposed a semantically based enrichment methodology for merging data from multiple sources even when the original data collection datasets are not synchronized. We started by discussing a methodology that effectively merges these different datasets from multiple sources by creating a unified time series. We explained how this method works by identifying the geospatial and temporal similarities between datasets. We applied the methodology to different datasets from the Barcelona city public data service, like traffic densities, public bicycle availability, and pollution monitoring stations to create a unified time series that provides a comprehensive view of traffic patterns in the city. We also discussed how combining data from different sources enables us to identify correlations and patterns that may not have been apparent in individual datasets. The obtained computational results showed the usefulness of the proposed approach to analyze complex datasets, and to identify trends and patterns, while the creation of interactive dashboards to display the time series data in a more comprehensible format can support stakeholders (urban planners, policymakers, etc.) in understanding and acting upon the information. The proposed approach can be applied to a wide range of fields where data from multiple sources needs to be merged and analyzed, such as healthcare, finance, and environmental studies. Furthermore, while this approach has been applied specifically to traffic patterns and pollution levels in Barcelona, it has the potential to be utilized in other domains and cities with multiple sources of data. For instance, this method could be employed to study public transportation usage and its relationship to urban development, or to investigate patterns of energy consumption and their associations with climate change.

Although the asynchronous geospatial join function presented has a number of strengths, there are also several potential weaknesses to consider.

One potential weakness is the reliance on Euclidean distance as a measure of proximity between points. While this is a common approach in geospatial analysis, it may not always be the most appropriate measure, particularly when dealing with datasets that span large geographic areas or have complex spatial structures. In these cases, other distance measures, such as geodesic distance or network distance, may be more appropriate.

Another potential weakness is the assumption that the time difference between two points is proportional to the distance between them. While this may be a reasonable assumption in some cases, it may not hold true in all situations. For example, the relationship between distance and travel time may vary depending on factors such as mode of transportation, traffic conditions, and topography.

Future work could explore the use of alternative distance measures and time normalization techniques to improve the accuracy of the function. Additionally, incorporating uncertainty measures and error propagation into the geospatial join operation could improve the reliability of the results.

Another direction for future work could be the integration of machine learning algorithms into the geospatial join process. For example, clustering algorithms could be used to group similar points together before performing the geospatial join operation, or regression models could be used to predict missing values or correct errors in the input datasets.

Overall, while the asynchronous geospatial join function presented has its strengths, there are also potential weaknesses to consider and areas for future research and improvement.

Author Contributions: Conceptualization, F.X. and C.S.; methodology, E.G. and F.X.; implementation, E.G.; validation, F.X. and C.S.; literature review, E.G. and M.P.; writing—original draft preparation, E.G., M.P. and F.X; writing—review and editing, E.G., F.X. and C.S.; supervision, F.X. and C.S. All authors have read and agreed to the published version of the manuscript.

Funding: This work was partially funded by the Spanish Ministry of Science (PID2019-111100RB-C21 /AEI/ 10.13039/501100011033), as well as by the Barcelona City Council and Fundació "la Caixa" under the framework of the Barcelona Science Plan 2020-2023 (grant 21S09355-001).

Institutional Review Board Statement: Not applicable.

Informed Consent Statement: Not applicable.

Data Availability Statement: The data used in this study were obtained from Open Data Barcelona.

Acknowledgments: This research was supported by Departament de Recerca i Universitats de la Generalitat de Catalunya (Spain) (2021 SGR 01421 (GRBIO)).

Conflicts of Interest: The authors declare no conflict of interest.

Appendix A. Python Code

Listing A1. Python code for the implementation of the Algorithm 1.

```
import geopandas as gpd
import numpy as np

def asynchronous_join(initial_dataset, extra_dataset, measure, extra_values=
                                        False, names_extra_measures=None):
"""
A function that performs an asynchronous geospatial join operation between an
initial dataset and an extra dataset using a specified measure.
"""
if names_extra_measures is None:
names_extra_measures = ['']

# Create a spatial index for the extra dataset
extra_dataset_sindex = extra_dataset.sindex

# Create a GeoDataFrame to store the output
output_columns = gpd.GeoDataFrame(columns=['original_index', measure, '
                                        geometry'], geometry='geometry')
output_columns = output_columns.set_crs(epsg=4326)

for i in range(len(initial_dataset)):
# Get the current location
location = initial_dataset.iloc[i]

# Calculate the normalized distances and time differences between the current
                                        location and all stations
normalized_distances = calculate_normalized_distances(extra_dataset.geometry.
                                        iloc[:].values[i], extra_dataset.
                                        geometry.x.iloc[:].values[i],
                                        extra_dataset.geometry.y.iloc[:].
                                        values[i])
normalized_timestamps = normalize_timestamps(extra_dataset.timestamp.values -
                                        location.timestamp)

# Find the station with the minimum combined distance
combined_distance = normalized_distances + normalized_timestamps
selected_station_index = np.argmin(combined_distance)
selected_station_data = extra_dataset.iloc[selected_station_index]

# Extract the desired measure and any additional measures from the selected
                                        station
output_columns.loc[i] = [i, selected_station_data[measure],
                                        selected_station_data['geometry']]

# Extract additional measures, if requested
if extra_values:
for extra_measure in names_extra_measures:
output_columns.loc[i, extra_measure] = selected_station_data[extra_measure]

return output_columns
```

Listing A2. Auxiliary Python methods for performance improvement.

```
def normalize_timestamps(timestamps):
"""
A function that normalizes a series of timestamps to the range [0, 1].
"""
min_ts, max_ts = timestamps.min(), timestamps.max()
return (timestamps - min_ts) / (max_ts - min_ts)

@jit(nopython=True)
def calculate_normalized_distances(geometry, x, y):
"""
A JIT-compiled function that calculates the normalized distance between
two arrays of points, lines, or polygons using Euclidean distance.
"""
if geometry.type == 'Point':
min_x, max_x, min_y, max_y = np.min(x), np.max(x), np.min(y), np.max(y)
distance_x = (x - min_x) / (max_x - min_x)
distance_y = (y - min_y) / (max_y - min_y)
return np.sqrt(distance_x ** 2 + distance_y ** 2)

elif geometry.type == 'LineString' or geometry.type == 'MultiLineString':
distances = []
for i in range(len(x)):
distances.append(np.sum(np.sqrt(np.sum(np.diff(np.vstack((x[i], y[i])).T,
                                          axis=0) ** 2, axis=1))))
min_distance = np.min(distances)
max_distance = np.max(distances)
return (distances - min_distance) / (max_distance - min_distance)

elif geometry.type == 'Polygon' or geometry.type == 'MultiPolygon':
distances = []
for i in range(len(x)):
poly = geometry.buffer(0.00001) # buffer to ensure polygons are valid
dist = poly.exterior.distance(Point(x[i], y[i]))
distances.append(dist)
min_distance = np.min(distances)
max_distance = np.max(distances)
return (distances - min_distance) / (max_distance - min_distance)
```

Appendix B. Computational Results

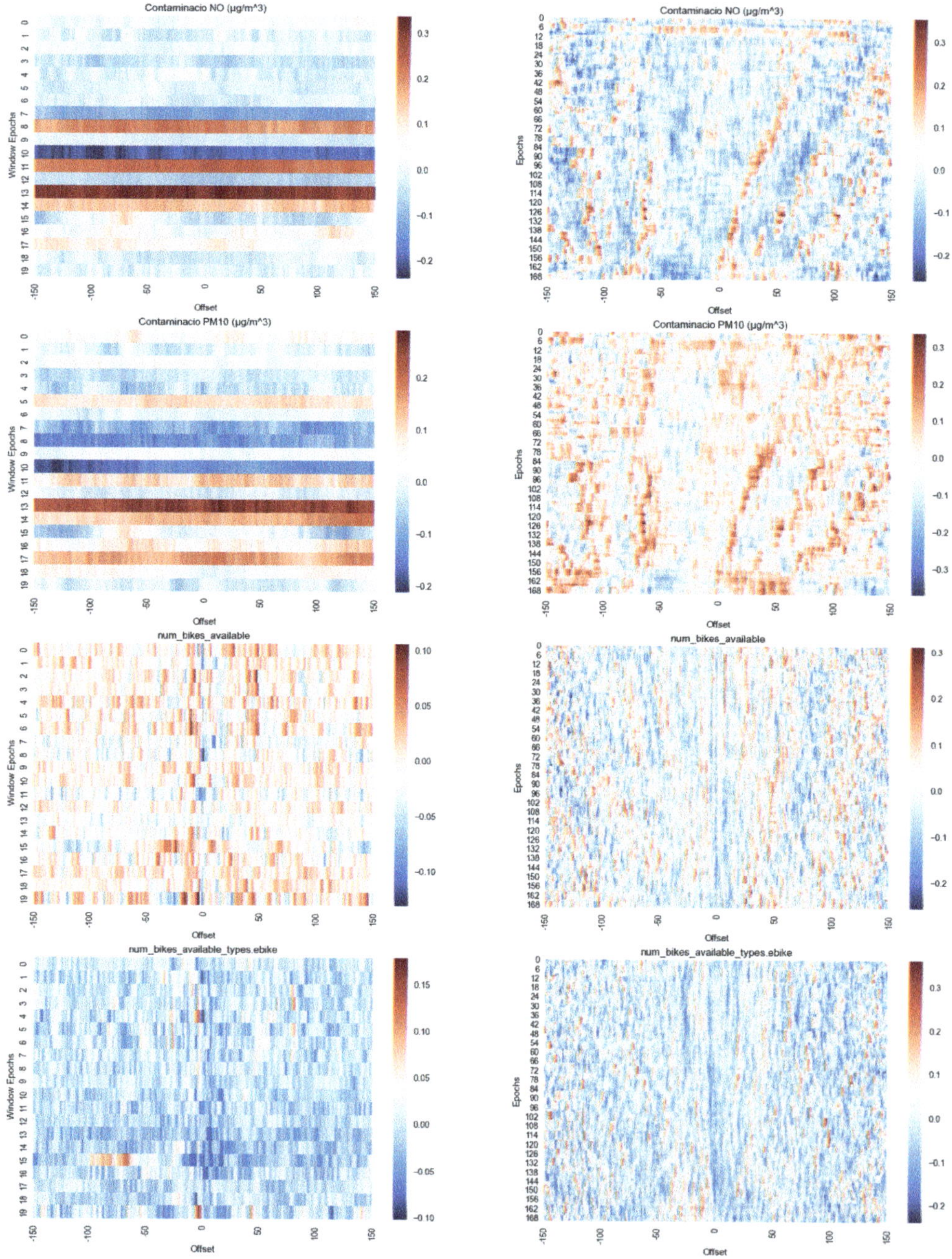

Figure A1. Windowed Time Lagged Cross Correlation (**Right**) and Rolling Windowed Time Lagged Cross Correlation (**Left**) for a subset of variables compared to traffic density.

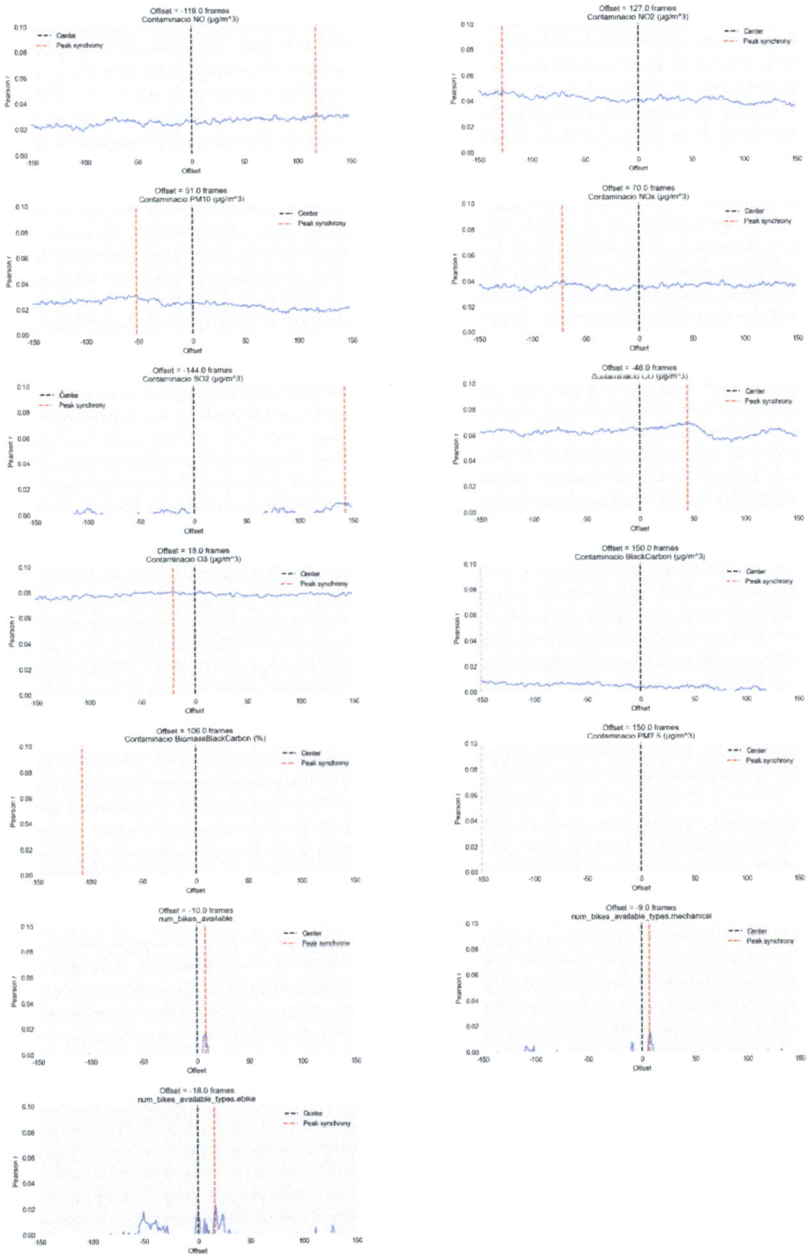

Figure A2. Overall lagged cross-correlations for different variables in the resulting dataset compared to traffic density.

References

1. Azad, S.A.; Wasimi, S.; Ali, A.S. Business data enrichment: Issues and challenges. In Proceedings of the 2018 5th Asia-Pacific World Congress on Computer Science and Engineering (APWC on CSE), Nadi, Fiji, 10–12 December 2018; pp. 98–102.
2. Clarke, M.; Harley, P. How smart is your content? Using semantic enrichment to improve your user experience and your bottom line. *Science* **2014**, *37*, 41.

3. Belsky, M.; Sacks, R.; Brilakis, I. Semantic enrichment for building information modeling. *Comput. Aided Civ. Infrastruct. Eng.* **2016**, *31*, 261–274. [CrossRef]
4. Bouaicha, S.; Ghemmaz, W. A Semantic Interoperability Approach for Heterogeneous Meteorology Big IoT Data. In *Proceedings of the 12th International Conference on Information Systems and Advanced Technologies "ICISAT 2022" Intelligent Information, Data Science and Decision Support System*; Springer: Berlin/Heidelberg, Germany, 2023; pp. 214–225.
5. Bassier, M.; Bonduel, M.; Derdaele, J.; Vergauwen, M. Processing existing building geometry for reuse as Linked Data. *Autom. Constr.* **2020**, *115*, 103180. [CrossRef]
6. Palavalli, A.; Karri, D.; Pasupuleti, S. Semantic internet of things. In Proceedings of the 2016 IEEE Tenth International Conference on Semantic Computing (ICSC), Laguna Hills, CA, USA, 4–6 February 2016; pp. 91–95.
7. Zhang, L.; Liu, K. Semantic Modeling for Supporting Planning Decision Making toward Smart Cities. In Proceedings of the Construction Research Congress 2022, Arlington, VA, USA, 9–12 March 2022; pp. 272–280.
8. Božić, B.; Winiwarter, W. A showcase of semantic time series processing. *Int. J. Web Inf. Syst.* **2013**, *9*, 117–141. [CrossRef]
9. Ajuntament de Barcelona. Open Data BCN. Available online: https://opendata-ajuntament.barcelona.cat/en/open-data-bcn (accessed on 13 February 2023).
10. Ajuntament de Barcelona. Barcelona Science Plan 2020–2023. Available online: https://www.barcelona.cat/barcelonaciencia/en/who-we-are/city-science-and-knowledge/barcelona-science-plan-2020-2023 (accessed on 13 February 2023).
11. Honti, G.M.; Abonyi, J. A review of semantic sensor technologies in internet of things architectures. *Complexity* **2019**, *2019*, 6473160. [CrossRef]
12. Xhafa, F.; Kilic, B.; Krause, P. Evaluation of IoT stream processing at edge computing layer for semantic data enrichment. *Future Gener. Comput. Syst.* **2020**, *105*, 730–736. [CrossRef]
13. Chen, Y.; Sabri, S.; Rajabifard, A.; Agunbiade, M.E.; Kalantari, M.; Amirebrahimi, S. The design and practice of a semantic-enabled urban analytics data infrastructure. *Comput. Environ. Urban Syst.* **2020**, *81*, 101484. [CrossRef]
14. Zappatore, M.; Longo, A.; Martella, A.; Di Martino, B.; Esposito, A.; Gracco, S.A. Semantic models for IoT sensing to infer environment–wellness relationships. *Future Gener. Comput. Syst.* **2023**, *140*, 1–17. [CrossRef]
15. Buchmann, R.A.; Karagiannis, D. Pattern-based transformation of diagrammatic conceptual models for semantic enrichment in the Web of Data. *Procedia Comput. Sci.* **2015**, *60*, 150–159. [CrossRef]
16. Djenouri, Y.; Belhadi, H.; Akli-Astouati, K.; Cano, A.; Lin, J.C.W. An ontology matching approach for semantic modeling: A case study in smart cities. *Comput. Intell.* **2022**, *38*, 876–902. [CrossRef]
17. Xu, Y.; Xiao, W.; Yang, X.; Li, R.; Yin, Y.; Jiang, Z. Towards effective semantic annotation for mobile and edge services for Internet-of-Things ecosystems. *Future Gener. Comput. Syst.* **2023**, *139*, 64–73. [CrossRef]
18. Xue, F.; Wu, L.; Lu, W. Semantic enrichment of building and city information models: A ten-year review. *Adv. Eng. Inform.* **2021**, *47*, 101245. [CrossRef]
19. Amato, F.; Casola, V.; Gaglione, A.; Mazzeo, A. A semantic enriched data model for sensor network interoperability. *Simul. Model. Pract. Theory* **2011**, *19*, 1745–1757. [CrossRef]
20. Jiang, Y.; Su, X.; Treude, C.; Wang, T. Hierarchical semantic-aware neural code representation. *J. Syst. Softw.* **2022**, *191*, 111355. [CrossRef]
21. Ataei Nezhad, M.; Barati, H.; Barati, A. An Authentication-Based Secure Data Aggregation Method in Internet of Things. *J. Grid Comput.* **2022**, *20*, 29. [CrossRef] [PubMed]
22. Iatrellis, O.; Panagiotakopoulos, T.; Gerogiannis, V.C.; Fitsilis, P.; Kameas, A. Cloud computing and semantic web technologies for ubiquitous management of smart cities-related competences. *Educ. Inf. Technol.* **2021**, *26*, 2143–2164. [CrossRef]
23. Ribeiro, M.B.; Braghetto, K.R. A Scalable Data Integration Architecture for Smart Cities: Implementation and Evaluation. *J. Inf. Data Manag.* **2022**, *13*. [CrossRef]
24. Tao, M. Semantic ontology enabled modeling, retrieval and inference for incomplete mobile trajectory data. *Future Gener. Comput. Syst.* **2023**, *145*, 1–11. [CrossRef]
25. Psyllidis, A.; Bozzon, A.; Bocconi, S.; Titos Bolivar, C. A platform for urban analytics and semantic data integration in city planning. In Proceedings of the Computer-Aided Architectural Design Futures. The Next City-New Technologies and the Future of the Built Environment: 16th International Conference, CAAD Futures 2015, São Paulo, Brazil, 8–10 July 2015; Selected Papers 16; Springer: Berlin/Heidelberg, Germany, 2015; pp. 21–36.
26. Costa, C.; Santos, M.Y. The SusCity big data warehousing approach for smart cities. In Proceedings of the 21st International Database Engineering & Applications Symposium, Bristol, UK, 12–14 July 2017; pp. 264–273.
27. Boker, S.; Xu, M.; Rotondo, J.; King, K. Windowed cross-correlation and peak picking for the analysis of variability in the association between behavioral time series. *Psychol. Methods* **2002**, *7*, 338–355. [CrossRef] [PubMed]

axioms

MDPI

Article

Interval Valued Pythagorean Fuzzy AHP Integrated Model in a Smartness Assessment Framework of Buildings

Mimica R. Milošević [1,*], Dušan M. Milošević [2], Dragan M. Stević [3] and Miljan Kovačević [3]

1 Faculty of Informatics and Computer Science, University Union-Nikola Tesla, Cara Dušana 62-64, 11158 Belgrade, Serbia
2 Department of Mathematics, Faculty of Electronic Engineering, University of Niš, Aleksandra Medvedeva 14, 18104 Niš, Serbia
3 Faculty of Technical Sciences, University of Priština, Knjaza Miloša 7, 38220 Kosovska Mitrovica, Serbia
* Correspondence: mmilosevic@unionnikolatesla.edu.rs

Abstract: Buildings can be made more user-friendly and secure by putting "smart" design strategies and technology processes in place. Such strategies and processes increase energy efficiency, make it possible to use resources rationally, and lower maintenance and construction costs. In addition to using wireless technologies and sensors to improve thermal, visual, and acoustic comfort, "smart" buildings are known for their energy, materials, water, and land management systems. Smart buildings use wireless technologies and sensors to improve thermal, visual, and acoustic comfort. These systems are known for managing energy, materials, water, and land. The task of the study is to consider the indicators that form the basis of the framework for evaluating intelligent buildings. The indicators for the development of "smart" buildings are classified into six categories in this paper: green building construction, energy management systems, safety and security management systems, occupant comfort and health, building automation and control management systems, and communication and data sharing. The paper aims to develop a scoring model for the smartness of public buildings. In developing the scoring system, the decision-making process requires an appropriate selection of the optimal solution. The contents of the research are the methods known as the Pythagorean Fuzzy Analytic Hierarchy Process (PF-AHP), Interval Valued Pythagorean Fuzzy AHP with differences (IVPF-AHP d), and the proposed method Interval Valued Pythagorean Fuzzy AHP (IVPF-AHP p). The research focuses on the IVPF-AHP as one of the methods of Multi-Criteria Decision-Making (MCDM) and its implementation. The comparative analysis of the three presented methods indicates a significant degree of similarity in the ranking, which confirms the ranking similarity. The results highlight the importance of bioclimatic design, smart metering, ecological materials, and renewable energy systems.

Keywords: Pythagorean Fuzzy Analytic Hierarchy Process; Interval Valued Pythagorean Fuzzy Analytic Hierarchy Process; smartness; buildings

MSC: 90B50

1. Introduction

Many facets of sustainable cities are the focus of fashionable urban development initiatives. According to earlier studies, 70% of the world's population will live in cities by 2050 [1]. The correlation between sustainability and the requirement for urban places to be livable, robust to global issues, and responsive to their residents was stressed by many researchers who spoke about the creation of forthcoming cities [2]. Future urban planning should prioritize ecological comfort, energy efficiency, and minimal negative environmental impact. The construction sector is developing rapidly and will continue to grow—the equivalent of the size of Paris—every week [3]. Considering that the built environment affects a large part of global greenhouse gas emissions, necessary planned actions had to be taken in this area. For the European construction sector, all new buildings must henceforth be buildings with near-zero energy consumption, as a significant reduction of greenhouse gas emissions in the built environment is necessary.

The vision of a "smart city", which is emerging as a result of the fourth industrial revolution in recent decades, is developing by utilizing cutting-edge Information and Communications (IC) technology to improve people's quality of life. It makes the current environment more robust and self-sufficient to sustainably meet the above listed requirements by transforming it on an ecological, economic, cultural, and social level [4]. The idea of a "smart city" has permeated many further elements of urban life, including the economy, transportation, environment, society, and living conditions [5]. Strenuous changes in city life, which occur daily, have prompted us to consider ways to build a more sustainable society that can withstand the rapid development of our environment [6]. Through the use of data sensors, public platforms for e-government and e-commerce, the ongoing development of traffic, the digitization of cultural heritage, and virtual tours, cutting-edge technologies based on big data, Internet of Things platforms, and remote sensing images have become part of people's everyday lives in modern and advanced urban infrastructure [7,8]. The new Building Management System (BMS) will significantly contribute to the market's growth through the proliferation of the Internet of Things (IoT), Artificial Intelligence (AI), Virtual Reality (VR), and Business Information Modeling (BIM). The advancement of the construction industry as a consequence of the use of IC technologies has an impact on the development of the idea of "smart buildings". Sustainable buildings are attractive and healthy for building users, while at the same time, they have a low environmental impact during their lifetime and fulfil their social and cultural potential. At the same time, another concept of the so-called smart or intelligent building has emerged, driven by the rapid growth of technology connected to the IoT. Awareness of the importance of developing smart buildings has increased in the last few decades. Modern smart buildings have their roots in the mechanical engineering development of self-regulating ecological systems in the 18th and 19th centuries. However, it was not until the end of the 20th century, with the use of digital computers and inventions, that the concept of smart buildings expanded to integrate technologies into various building systems. Buildings with cutting-edge Heating, Ventilation, and Air-Conditioning (HVAC) systems, enhanced materials, and significant energy savings are now considered "smart buildings". Facilities in the EU account for 40% of energy use, according to the European Commission [9]; therefore, the "smart buildings" idea is heavily centered on energy minimization with the enhancement of user experience.

A standard, widely acknowledged definition of a "smart building" does not exist. Numerous theoretical and empirical findings from academics and industry professionals have helped clarify the transformation of conventional buildings into more adaptable and efficient ones. Buildings are increasingly required to adapt to climate change to meet environmental performance standards and advance "smart" solutions [10]. A "smart building" integrates and considers intelligence, enterprise, control, and materials, as well as construction, as a whole building system, according to Buckman et al. [11]. For supervision and control, these facilities have centralized automation and control systems. Sound and light data can be collected using sensors and tracks to minimize energy use in different microclimate conditions [12]. The European Performance of Buildings Directive (EPBD), which was revised to include "smart" readiness indicators to enable rating of the smartness of the structures, established the idea of "smart" buildings. The Global e-Sustainability Initiative's SMARTer2030 report also provides a technology outlook for "smart" buildings in 2030, highlighting the influence of IC technologies to reach better levels of energy efficiency [13]. A green building includes construction plans, production, transportation, and use of sustainable materials, with minimal waste and maintenance [14]. With green building certification systems, a wide range of smart building technologies are now available to create more sustainable and intelligent buildings. Smart buildings imply the use of innovative technologies and processes, as well as design solutions, for the development of buildings that are comfortable and safe for their tenants and, at the same time, economical for their owners [15]. Thermal comfort, visual comfort, and indoor air quality are three fundamental variables that assess the standard of living inside a building environment [16]. Energy evaluation is essential for owners and tenants, as it can reveal how much energy is used. As a result, energy evaluation ought to serve as inspiration to find possible savings. Hence, the smart use of energy in buildings can assist in lowering both energy use and costs [17]. "Smart" decisions in this area reduce energy costs and carbon emissions from the building sector [18–20].

New challenges are emerging, and whether it is called "green building", "sustainable building", or "smart building", it is clear that we are living in the era of information technology and that old-fashioned, disconnected, and unsustainable buildings are no longer sustainable. Smart performance development in architectural object design and construction influences smart cities' development as urban environments. Evaluating the smartness of architectural objects, regardless of their purpose, is significant for creating the possibility to compare their performance from the aspect of sustainable construction. The concept defined by the indicators in the paper has an extensive impact on the aspect of financial construction and the maintenance of buildings, the comfort of staying in the building, and the degree of energy consumption, and the proposed evaluation system would have practical application when making decisions about the choice of the most optimal design solution before its development to the executive project.

When we talk specifically about buildings of public purpose, in contrast to residential architecture, they are characterized by the functional plan complexity, the significant area they occupy, and their contents (cultural facilities, educational facilities, health facilities, commercial facilities, and business facilities, catering facilities). The evaluation of the proposed performance is vital when selecting satisfying office space for rent or purchase, in the case of already built facilities for business purposes, or in the construction of facilities for the accommodation of guests (hotels, hostels, resorts, etc.). In the case of museums and galleries, the evaluation of the smartness of buildings is vital due to the maintenance of adequate HVAC conditions in the case of educational facilitie, schools, kindergartens, colleges, etc. It is crucial to select a design solution that could provide users with a comfortable stay and low energy consumption.

Speaking specifically about buildings of public purpose, in contrast to residential architecture, they are characterized by the complexity of the practical plan and the significant area they occupy, depending on the process of creating smart cities, a notable role played by state-initiated projects and strategies, investment programs for new construction and programs for sustainable renovation and energy rehabilitation, which are often aimed primarily at facilities intended for the youngest (kindergartens and elementary schools), facilities of health institutions and gerontological centers, as objects of public purpose.

The research started by reviewing the existing definitions and frameworks of the smart building to gain the key features and understanding of concepts, resulting in a concise definition that can describe the new building concept and a list of indicators to form the basis of an assessment framework. The assessment of a building's architectural smartness is a complex question. It is connected to the newly developed technologies that have been used, but it also depends on how the technologies are combined and the kind of system they enhance. The most recent machine learning algorithms can be used and applied as a decision support system for various assessments in construction [21]. This paper examines the issue of rating the smartness of public buildings using multi-criteria decision-making. The proposed study would prioritize the requirements for "smart" building development using the IVPF-AHP to identify the best indicators for transforming conventional public buildings into smart ones. A total of 34 indicators are selected for six capital sustainability and smartness dimensions, representing a holistic approach. The outcomes of three methods—two IVPF-AHP and one PF-AHP—are compared and discussed.

The structure of the paper is as follows. After the Introduction, Section 2 illustrates the assessment of the smartness of buildings by defining indicators and provides a hierarchical structure and the methodology of IVPF-AHP. Section 3 provides results with the PF-AHP and two approaches of IVPF-AHP methods, and the obtained results discussion related to the ranking of sub-criteria. The study is concluded in Section 4, which also suggests some areas for further research.

2. Materials and Methods

The steps in the research framework are as follows, because of the complexity of the intended study goal and the wide range of factors that affect the creation of "smart" buildings:

- Defining and implementing the indicators connected to the construction of "smart" public buildings;
- Formulating and utilizing the Pythagorean Fuzzy Analytic Hierarchy Process (PF-AHP);
- Pythagorean Fuzzy Analytic Hierarchy Process (PF–AHP)
    - Preliminaries
    - Interval Valued Pythagorean Fuzzy AHP with differences (IVPF-AHP d)
    - Proposed Interval Valued Pythagorean Fuzzy AHP (IVPF-AHP p);
- Ranking indicators as a foundation for creating a scoring system for the smartness of public buildings.

Multi-criteria decision-making methods are applied in many research areas [22,23]. The evaluative role of experts in complex decision-making problems requires a fuzzy logic theory when dealing with various uncertainties. A significant and challenging issue that also arises when devising solutions to the concerns covered in this study is the subjectivity and uncertainty of the evaluators' assessments of the evaluation criteria. The Fuzzy Set Theory (FST), presented by Zadeh [24], is applied to solving many decision-making problems. This theory's various iterations have been developed over a long period and successfully applied to resolve various decision-making problems.

Pythagorean Fuzzy Sets (PFS), a brand-new intuitionistic fuzzy sets extension, is one of these additions [25,26].

There are numerous studies in the construction industry employing the AHP for ranking alternatives for the selection of construction contractors and subcontractors [27], the choice of the project implementation process [28], or the selection of architectural consultants [29]. In addition, the AHP has been used for determining selection criteria weights for the choice of bridge elements for maintenance [30], dispute resolution methodology [31], project selection based on risk assessment [32], and more recently, for the choice of contract types [33] and project procurement systems [34]. An overview of the application of the AHP in construction is given in [35].

The use of Interval methods facilitates the work of experts in the sense of facile determination in the classification of the performed grades, as was performed in existing research [36,37]. It is easier for an expert to choose an interval membership (non-membership) than a corresponding crisp value.

2.1. Building Smartness Assessment: Defining Indicators

Understanding the characteristics and specific criteria that comprise smart buildings is quite challenging, given the development of new technologies and is, therefore, the subject of much research [36–40]. A literature review is carried out to select criteria and sub-criteria for determining the smart buildings indicators more systematically at the beginning of the research. Indicators have been divided into six main groups, as suggested by Gunatilaka et al. [36]. Existing tools for evaluating buildings have focused mainly on environmental aspects [41], so the applicability of such a criterion in determining the building's smartness level is questioned. Most of the green building evaluation schemes that are widely used (Globes, Leadership in Energy and Environmental Design, Building Research Establishment Environmental Assessment Method, Green Rating for Integrated Habitat Assessment, Green Mark, Comprehensive Assessment System for Built Environment Efficiency, and Green Star) are highly focused on assessing the entire life cycle and ensuring long-term environmental benefits, but at the same time, can be criticized for their unequal treatment of the three pillars of sustainability [42]. Table 1 lists and describes the major criteria categories and the literature review findings. The table indicates the most significant factors that examine different perspectives of the smartness assessment framework from which the system of classification criteria has been created.

Table 1. Outline of the evaluation criteria for "smart" buildings.

Criterion and Description	Literature Review Findings
Green buildings construction	
Criterion applies to green and ecologically friendly processes in different aspects of building, from urban planning to material selection. Guidelines for creating sub-criteria are land management, bioclimatic design, use of ecological materials, and Renewable Energy Systems (RES), including waste management.	[36–38,41,43–48]
Energy Management System	
Criterion is related to increasing energy efficiency systems and minimizing energy use, enabling buildings to adapt to weather conditions. Guidelines for creating sub-criteria are smart metering, advanced HVAC control systems, and energy storage systems with the use of dynamic building envelope systems.	[36,37,39,43,49]
Occupancy comfort & health	
Criterion applies to the different user's thermal aspects and visual and acoustic comfort. Guidelines for creating sub-criteria are well being and health, such as indoor air quality and personalized control of appliances.	[36,37,41,43,50]
Safety & Security Management System	
Criterion is related to the safety of people's lives and assets with disaster security support and privacy policies. Guidelines for creating sub-criteria are control of access and movement detection, fire prevention, detection, protection, and cyber security.	[36–38,41]
Communication & data sharing	
Criterion is related to the use of different innovative smart technologies that enable communication between other systems in buildings: cloud base data storage and IoT. Besides, data protection, wireless communication, and cyber systems are guidelines for creating sub-criteria.	[36–39,43,51–56]
Building automation & control system	
Indicators are connected to automated data monitoring and control systems and changeable conditions. Guidelines for sub-criteria are data-gathering devices with sensors, software implementation, and asset tracking.	[36–39,43,50,57]

The design and development of smart buildings is a complex task. Every smart building is unique, and achieving reliability and real-time adaptations to environmental conditions are some of the challenges in developing smart buildings [58]. Different domains and constituent variables associated with building smartness are identified in Table 1 by the literature review. In the selection of indicators, an agreement is reached based on the given literature. Twenty-eight experts participated in the selection of indicators and evaluation. The proposed literature was the basis for the sub-criteria selection. The professional profile of experts is in Figure 1a and work experience is in Figure 1b.

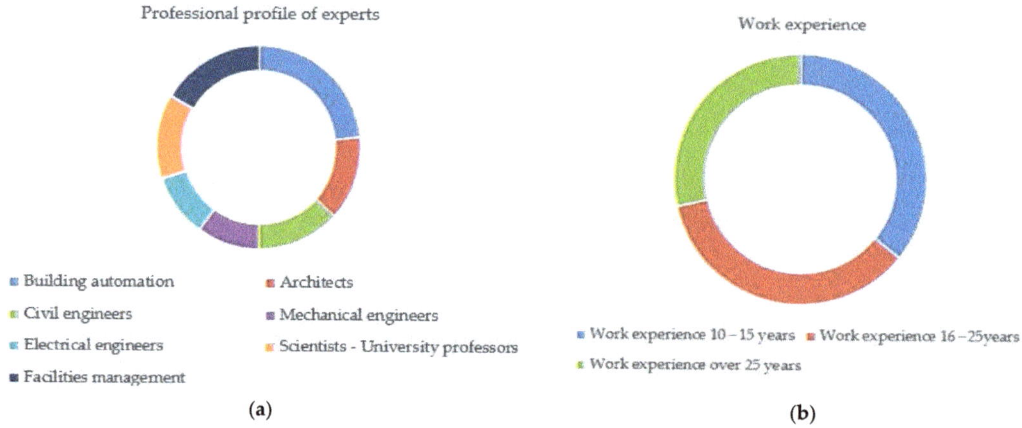

Figure 1. Background analysis of experts: (**a**) Professional profile; (**b**) Work experience.

The hierarchy structure of the indicators affecting the smartness assessment framework of buildings is presented in Figure 2. The experts answered the question: "How much more important is criterion x compared to criterion y for achieving satisfactory Green Buildings Construction?". The criteria used in a decision problem are compared for each level, and the the obtained values are saved in matrix form.

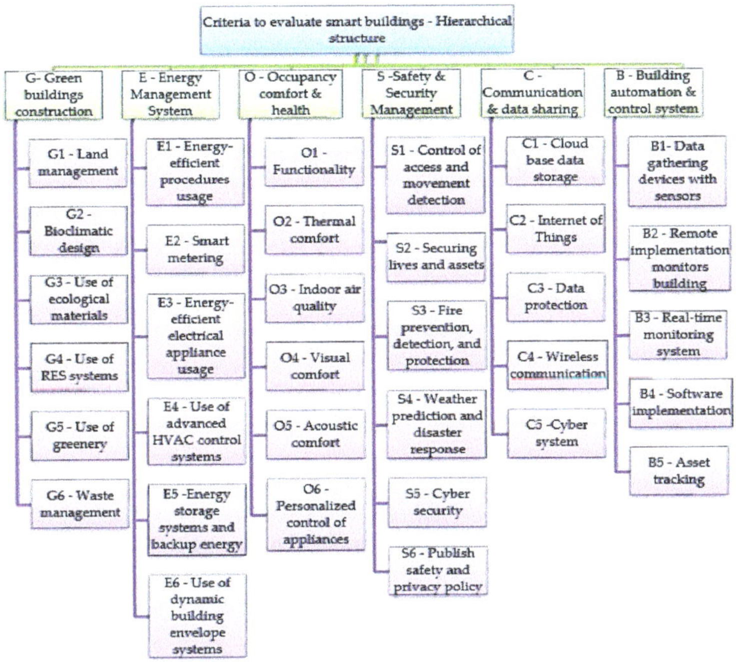

Figure 2. Hierarchy structure.

2.2. Implementing the Pythagorean Fuzzy Analytic Hierarchy Process

Atannasov [59] proposed intuitionistic type-2 fuzzy sets, which were later upgraded to Pythagorean Fuzzy Sets (PFS) by Yager [60]. Although the membership degree and non-membership degree assigned by experts in PFS may add up to more than 1 (Figure 3), their squares' sum must be less than or equal to 1 [61]. The AHP method, with Pythagorean fuzzy sets, can be used to eliminate uncertainty and ambiguity.

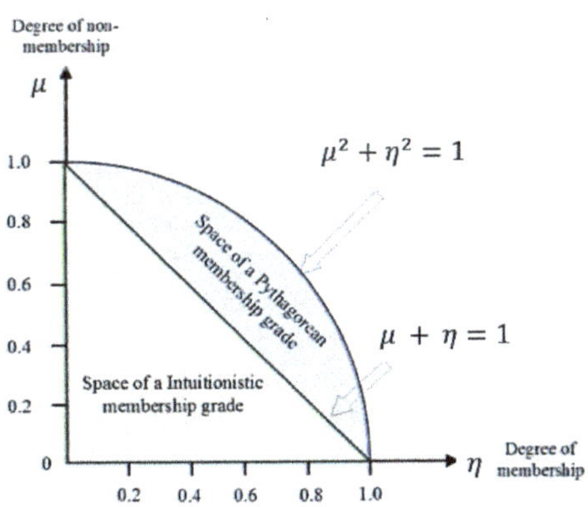

Figure 3. Space of Pythagorean membership grade.

With PFS, when creating comparison matrices, the comparison is made on two aspects—membership and non-membership, unlike the AHP method, where the comparison is made only by one aspect—significance. The field of application of PFS has increased compared to the intuitionistic approach.

2.2.1. Preliminaries

Definition 1. *Let X be the universal set. A Pythagorean fuzzy set Π is an object having the form [62], as in Equation (1)*

$$\Pi = \{\langle x, \mu_{\Pi}(x), \eta_{\Pi}(x)\rangle; x \in X\}, \tag{1}$$

where the function $\mu_{\Pi}(x) : X \to [0, 1]$ defines the degree of membership and $\eta_{\Pi}(x) : X \to [0, 1]$ defines the degree of non-membership of the element $x \in X$ to Π respectively, and, for every $x \in X$, it holds the Equation (2)

$$0 \leq \mu_{\Pi}(x)^2 + \eta_{\Pi}(x)^2 \leq 1. \tag{2}$$

The degree of hesitancy condition is Equation (3)

$$\pi_{\tilde{\Pi}}(x) = \sqrt{1 - \mu_{\Pi}(x)^2 + \eta_{\Pi}(x)^2}. \tag{3}$$

For a PFS Π, the pair $\langle \mu_{\Pi}, \eta_{\Pi}\rangle$ is called a Pythagorean Fuzzy Number (PFN). For convenience, the pair $\langle \mu_{\Pi}, \eta_{\Pi}\rangle$ is often denoted by $\langle \mu, \eta\rangle$, where $\mu \in [0,1], \eta \in [0,1]$, $0 \leq \mu^2 + \eta^2 \leq 1$.

Definition 2. *For two PFNs $\Pi_1 = \langle \mu_1, \eta_1\rangle$, $\Pi_2 = \langle \mu_2, \eta_2\rangle$ and scalar $\lambda > 0$, the elementary operations are defined [63] by Equations (4)–(7):*

$$\Pi_1 \bigoplus \Pi_2 = \left\langle \sqrt{\mu_1^2 + \mu_2^2 - \mu_1^2\mu_2^2}, \eta_1\eta_2 \right\rangle, \tag{4}$$

$$\Pi_1 \bigoplus \Pi_2 = \left\langle \mu_1\mu_2, \sqrt{\eta_1^2 + \eta_2^2 - \eta_1^2\eta_2^2} \right\rangle, \tag{5}$$

$$\lambda\Pi_1 = \left\langle \sqrt{1 - (1 - \mu_1^2)^{\lambda}}, \eta_1^{\lambda} \right\rangle, \tag{6}$$

$$\Pi_1^{\lambda} = \left\langle \mu_1^{\lambda}, \sqrt{1 - (1 - \eta_1^2)^{\lambda}} \right\rangle. \tag{7}$$

Definition 3. *Let $\Pi_i = \langle \mu_i, \eta_i\rangle$, $i = 1, \ldots, n$ be a collection of PFNs. Then, their aggregated value using Pythagorean Fuzzy Weighted Averaging (PFWA) operator is performed [64] by Equation (8)*

$$PFWA(\Pi_1, \Pi_2, \ldots, \Pi_n) = \left\langle \sqrt{1 - \prod_{i=1}^{n} (1 - \mu_i^2)^{w_i}}, \prod_{i=1}^{n} \eta_i^{w_i} \right\rangle, \tag{8}$$

where $w_i = (w_1, w_2, \ldots, w_n)$ is the weight vector of Π_i, $i = 1, \ldots, n$ with $w_i \in [0,1]$ and $\sum_{i=1}^{n} w_i = 1$.

Definition 4. *The defuzzification formula for a Singular Value Pythagorean Fuzzy Number (SV-PFN) $\Pi = \langle \mu_1, \eta_1\rangle$ is given by Equation (9), as in [65].*

$$def(\Pi) = \frac{1 - \eta_1^2}{2 - \eta_1^2 - \mu_1^2} \tag{9}$$

The alternatives are ranked based on alternative scores using Equation (9).

The next few definitions can be seen in the papers [66,67].

Definition 5. *An Interval-Value Pythagorean Fuzzy Set (IV-PFS) $\widetilde{\Pi}$, on the universal set X, is defined by Equation (10)*

$$\widetilde{\Pi} = \left\{ \left\langle x, \left[\mu^L_{\widetilde{\Pi}}(x), \mu^U_{\widetilde{\Pi}}(x)\right], \left[\eta^L_{\widetilde{\Pi}}(x), \eta^U_{\widetilde{\Pi}}(x)\right] \right\rangle \middle| x \in X \right\}, \tag{10}$$

where $0 \le \mu^L_{\widetilde{\Pi}}(x) \le \mu^U_{\widetilde{\Pi}}(x) \le 1, 0 \le \eta^L_{\widetilde{\Pi}}(x) \le \eta^U_{\widetilde{\Pi}}(x) \le 1$ *and* $\left(\mu^U_{\widetilde{\Pi}}(x)\right)^2 + \left(\eta^U_{\widetilde{\Pi}}(x)\right)^2 \le 1.$

Similar to PFSs, for each element $x \in X$, its hesitation interval relative to $\widetilde{\Pi}$ is given by Equation (11) as

$$\pi_{\widetilde{\Pi}}(x) = \langle \pi^L_{\widetilde{\Pi}}(x), \pi^U_{\widetilde{\Pi}}(x) \rangle = \left\langle \sqrt{1 - \left(\mu^U_{\widetilde{\Pi}}(x)\right)^2 - \left(\eta^U_{\widetilde{\Pi}}(x)\right)^2}, \sqrt{1 - \left(\mu^L_{\widetilde{\Pi}}(x)\right)^2 - \left(\eta^L_{\widetilde{\Pi}}(x)\right)^2} \right\rangle. \tag{11}$$

Especially, for every $x \in X$, if $\mu_{\widetilde{\Pi}}(x) = \mu^L_{\widetilde{\Pi}}(x) = \mu^U_{\widetilde{\Pi}}(x)$, $\eta_{\widetilde{\Pi}}(x) = \eta^L_{\widetilde{\Pi}}(x) = \eta^U_{\widetilde{\Pi}}(x)$ then, IVPFS $\widetilde{\Pi}$ reduces to an ordinary PFS.

For an IV-PFS $\widetilde{\Pi}$, the pair $\left\langle \left[\mu^L_{\widetilde{\Pi}}, \mu^U_{\widetilde{\Pi}'}\right], \left[\eta^L_{\widetilde{\Pi}}, \eta^U_{\widetilde{\Pi}'}\right] \right\rangle$ is called an Interval Valued Pythagorean Fuzzy Number (IV-PFN). For convenience, the pair $\left\langle \left[\mu^L_{\widetilde{\Pi}}, \mu^U_{\widetilde{\Pi}'}\right], \left[\eta^L_{\widetilde{\Pi}}, \eta^U_{\widetilde{\Pi}'}\right] \right\rangle$ is often denoted by $\langle [\mu^L, \mu^U], [\eta^L, \eta^U] \rangle$, where $\langle [\mu^L, \mu^U] \rangle \subset [0,1], [\eta^L, \eta^U] \subset [0,1], (\mu^U)^2 + (\eta^U)^2 \le 1.$

Definition 6. *Let $\widetilde{\Pi} = \langle [\mu_L, \mu_U], [\eta_L, \eta_U] \rangle$ be an interval-valued PF. The hesitancy degree of the lower and upper points of $\widetilde{\Pi}$, π_L and π_U, respectively, can be calculated by Equations (12) and (13)*

$$\pi_L = \sqrt{1 - (\mu_U^2 + \eta_U^2)} \tag{12}$$

$$\pi_U = \sqrt{1 - (\mu_L^2 + \eta_L^2)}. \tag{13}$$

Definition 7. *Let $\widetilde{\Pi}_1 = \langle [\mu_1^L, \mu_1^U], [\eta_1^L, \eta_1^U] \rangle$ and $\widetilde{\Pi}_2 = \langle [\mu_2^L, \mu_2^U], [\eta_2^L, \eta_2^U] \rangle$ be any two Interval Valued Pythagorean Fuzzy Numbers (IV-PFNs) and $\lambda > 0$. Then, the arithmetic operations are defined as follows in Equations (14)–(17)*

$$\widetilde{\Pi}_1 \bigoplus \widetilde{\Pi}_2 = \left\langle \left[\sqrt{(\mu_1^L)^2 + (\mu_2^L)^2 - (\mu_1^L)^2(\mu_2^L)^2}, \sqrt{(\mu_1^U)^2 + (\mu_2^U)^2 - (\mu_1^U)^2(\mu_2^U)^2} \right], \left[\eta_1^L\eta_2^L, \eta_1^U\eta_2^U \right] \right\rangle, \tag{14}$$

$$\widetilde{\Pi}_1 \bigoplus \widetilde{\Pi}_2 = \left\langle \left[\mu_1^L\mu_2^L, \mu_1^U\mu_2^U \right], \left[\sqrt{(\eta_1^L)^2 + (\eta_2^L)^2 - (\eta_1^L)^2(\eta_2^L)^2}, \sqrt{(\eta_1^U)^2 + (\eta_2^U)^2 - (\eta_1^U)^2(\eta_2^U)^2} \right] \right\rangle, \tag{15}$$

$$\lambda\widetilde{\Pi}_1 = \left\langle \left[\sqrt{1 - \left(1 - (\mu_1^L)^2\right)^\lambda}, \sqrt{1 - \left(1 - (\mu_1^U)^2\right)^\lambda} \right], \left[\left(\eta_1^L\right)^\lambda, \left(\eta_1^U\right)^\lambda \right] \right\rangle, \tag{16}$$

$$\widetilde{\Pi}_1^\lambda = \left\langle \left[\left(\mu_1^L\right)^\lambda, \left(\mu_1^U\right)^\lambda \right], \left[\sqrt{1 - \left(1 - (\eta_1^L)^2\right)^\lambda}, \sqrt{1 - \left(1 - (\eta_1^U)^2\right)^\lambda} \right] \right\rangle. \tag{17}$$

Definition 8. *Let $\widetilde{\Pi}_i = \langle [\mu_1^L, \mu_1^U], [\eta_1^L, \eta_1^U] \rangle$, $i = 1, \ldots, n$, be any collection of IV-PFNs and $w_i = (w_1, w_2, \ldots, w_n)$ be the weight vector of $\widetilde{\Pi}_i$ such that $w_i \in [0,1]$ and $\sum_{i=1}^n w_i = 1$. Then, Interval Valued Pythagorean Fuzzy Averaging (IV-PFA) operator is defined by (18)*

$$IVPFA\left(\widetilde{\Pi}_1, \widetilde{\Pi}_2, \ldots, \widetilde{\Pi}_n\right) = \left\langle \left[\sqrt{1 - \prod_{i=1}^n \left(1 - (\mu_i^L)^2\right)^{w_i}}, \sqrt{1 - \prod_{i=1}^n \left(1 - (\mu_i^U)^2\right)^{w_i}} \right], \left[\prod_{i=1}^n \left(\eta_i^L\right)^{w_i}, \prod_{i=1}^n \left(\eta_i^U\right)^{w_i} \right] \right\rangle. \tag{18}$$

where $w_i = \frac{1}{n}$.

Definition 9. *Let* $\widetilde{\Pi}_1 = \langle [\mu_1^L, \mu_1^U], [\eta_1^L, \eta_1^U] \rangle$ *and* $\widetilde{\Pi}_2 = \langle [\mu_2^L, \mu_2^U], [\eta_2^L, \eta_2^U] \rangle$ *be interval valued PFNs and* π_1^L, π_1^U, π_2^L *and* π_2^U *are the hesitancy degrees of lower and upper points of the* $\widetilde{\Pi}_1$ *and* $\widetilde{\Pi}_2$*, respectively. The distance between* $\widetilde{\Pi}_1$ *and* $\widetilde{\Pi}_2$ *can be calculated by (19), as in [68]*

$$d\left(\widetilde{\Pi}_1, \widetilde{\Pi}_2\right) = \frac{\sqrt{\left(\left(\mu_1^L\right)^2 - \left(\mu_2^L\right)^2\right)\left(1 - \frac{\pi_1^L - \pi_2^L}{2}\right) + \sqrt{\left(\left(\mu_1^U\right)^2 - \left(\mu_2^U\right)^2\right)\left(1 - \frac{\pi_1^U - \pi_2^U}{2}\right)}}}{2} \quad (19)$$

Definition 10. *Let* $\widetilde{\Pi} = \langle [\mu_L, \mu_U], [\eta_L, \eta_U] \rangle$ *be an interval-valued PFN and* π_L *and* π_U *are the hesitancy degree of the lower and upper points of* $\widetilde{\Pi}$*, then, the defuzzifying procedure of this number is calculated by (20), as in [69]*

$$def\left(\widetilde{\Pi}\right) = \frac{1}{6}\left(\mu_L^2 + \mu_U^2 + \left(1 - \pi_L^4 - \eta_L^2\right) + \left(1 - \pi_U^4 - \eta_U^2\right) + \mu_L\mu_U + \sqrt[4]{\left(1 - \pi_L^4 - \eta_L^2\right)\left(1 - \pi_U^4 - \eta_U^2\right)}\right). \quad (20)$$

2.2.2. Pythagorean Fuzzy Analytic Hierarchy Process (PF–AHP)

The classic AHP method compares only according to the importance of indicators. In the PF-AHP method, the comparison is made for two criteria: membership and non-membership. Figure 4 shows the steps of PF–AHP.

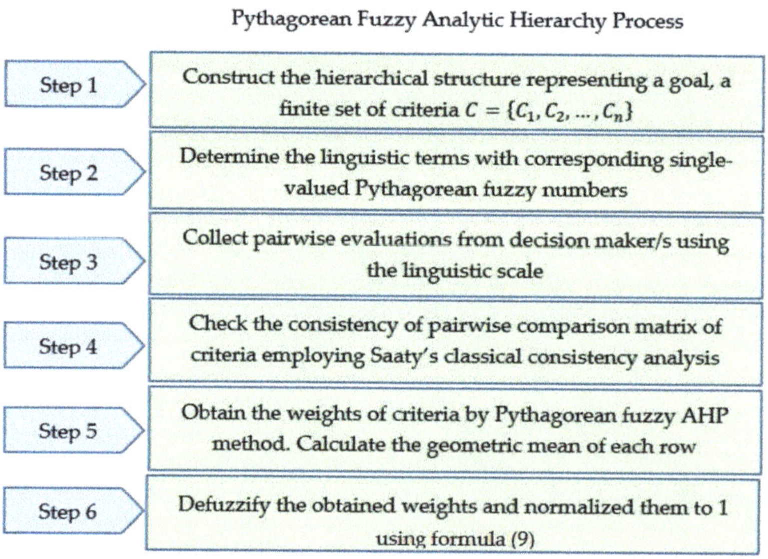

Figure 4. The steps of PF–AHP.

2.2.3. Interval Valued Pythagorean Fuzzy AHP (IVPF-AHP) with Differences (IVPF-AHP d)

The IVPF-AHP provides an additional possibility of using intervals, giving more freedom to experts in creating comparison matrices. The IVPF-AHP d method, in which defuzzification is performed using differences (see Step 5), consists of the following steps, shown in Figure 5:

First, the experts are expected to express their opinion and give ratings concerning the identified indicators according to the problem in pairs. The language variables are shown in Table 2. Pythagorean Linguistic Scales of Fuzzy Numbers are defined by two parameters of PFN: membership and non-membership functions.

Table 2. Rating scale in PFS, Interval PFS, linguistic terms, and crisp values.

Rating Scale in PFS	Rating Scale in Interval PFS	Linguistic Terms (LT)	Crisp Values
$\langle 0.1, 0.9\rangle$	$\langle [0, 0.1], [0.8, 0.9]\rangle$	Absolutely weak dominance (AW)	1
$\langle 0.2, 0.8\rangle$	$\langle [0.1, 0.2], [0.7, 0.8]\rangle$	Extremely weak dominance (EW)	2
$\langle 0.3, 0.7\rangle$	$\langle [0.2, 0.3], [0.6, 0.7]\rangle$	Very weak dominance (VW)	3
$\langle 0.4, 0.6\rangle$	$\langle [0.3, 0.4], [0.5, 0.6]\rangle$	Fairly weak dominance (FW)	4
$\langle 0.5, 0.4\rangle$	$\langle [0.5, 0.5], [0.5, 0.5]\rangle$	Equal importance (E)	5
$\langle 0.6, 0.4\rangle$	$\langle [0.5, 0.6], [0.3, 0.4]\rangle$	Fairly strong dominance (FS)	6
$\langle 0.7, 0.3\rangle$	$\langle [0.6, 0.7], [0.2, 0.3]\rangle$	Very strong dominance (VS)	7
$\langle 0.8, 0.2\rangle$	$\langle [0.7, 0.8], [0.1, 0.2]\rangle$	Extremely strong dominance (ES)	8
$\langle 0.9, 0.1\rangle$	$\langle [0.8, 0.9], [0, 0.1]\rangle$	Absolutely strong dominance (AS)	9

The expert assessment aggregation is obtained by the averaging method. First, the corresponding crisp value m_i for each expert has been attached based on the linguistic assessments. Since each expert has weights w_i, $\sum_{i=1}^{k} w_i = 1$, the aggregated value has been obtained by the formula $\frac{1}{k}\sum_{i=1}^{k} w_i m_i$. According to this value, by rounding to the nearest integer, the corresponding value of the fuzzy number is obtained.

The decimal scale used in the PF-AHP method, instead of the integer values used in the AHP method, is necessary to satisfy the inequality that the sum of the squares of the membership and non-membership functions must be less than 1.

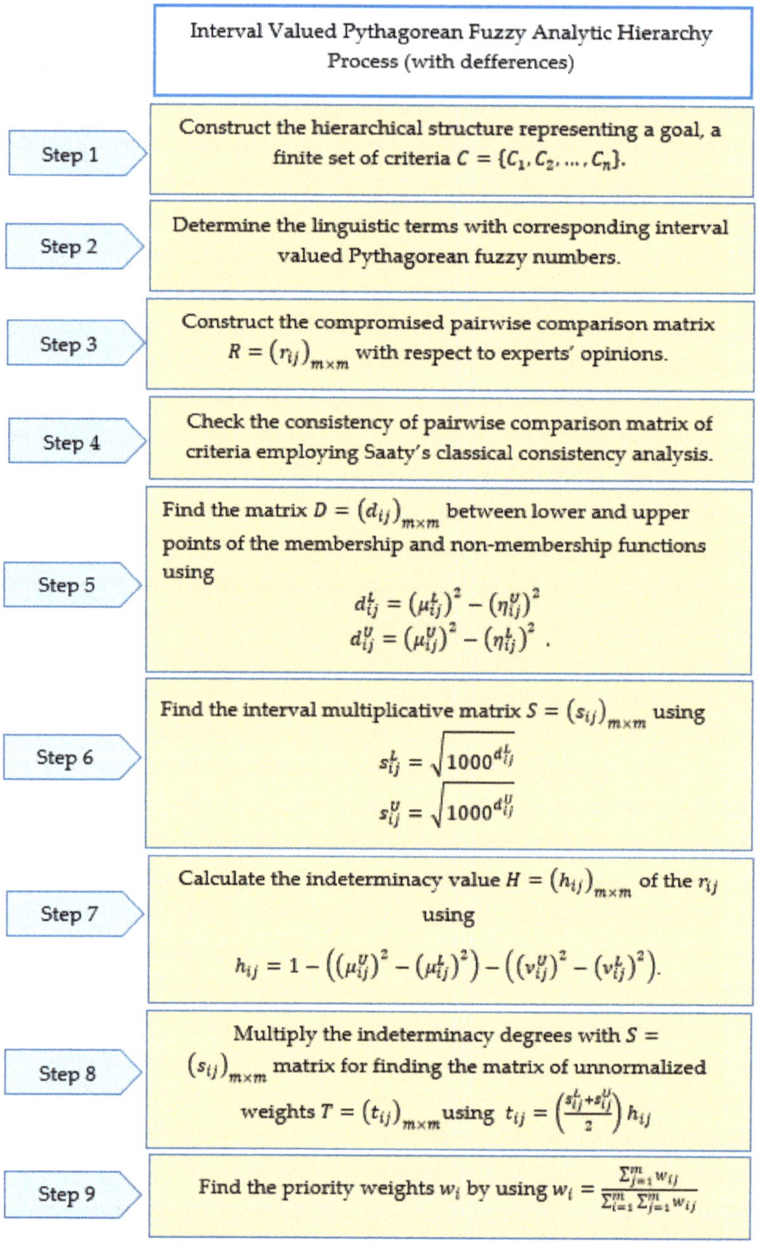

Figure 5. The steps of IVPF-AHP d.

2.2.4. Proposed Interval Valued Pythagorean Fuzzy AHP (IVPF-AHP p)

Following the PF-AHP steps presented in Section 2.2.1, we have developed a suitable IVPF-AHP p, whose steps are given as follows:

- Step 1. Define the goal, the final set of criteria $C = \{C_1, C_2, \ldots, C_n\}$, and sub-criteria and form a hierarchical structure
- Step 2. Define linguistic expressions using Interval Valued Pythagorean Fuzzy numbers.

- Step 3. Create Interval Valued Pythagorean Fuzzy comparison matrices from decision makers using linguistic expressions.
- Step 4. Check the consistency of the Interval Valued Pythagorean Fuzzy comparison matrices of criteria employing Saaty's classical consistency analysis. The method is consistent if the corresponding AHP method is consistent.
- Step 5. Use the IVPF-AHP approach to determine the criteria weights. Determine each row's geometric mean. The procedure is carried out in two steps. Before obtaining root values, Pythagorean values for each criterion are multiplied.
- Step 6. Defuzzify the obtained weights and normalize them to 1. In the defuzzification procedure, we use Equation (20).
- The proposed method is a natural extension of PF-AHP to IVPF-AHP.

3. Results and Discussion

The algorithms outlined in Sections 2.2.2–2.2.4 are applied in this section. Matrices of pairwise comparison PFNs and interval IVPFNs are made respecting experts' opinions. The corresponding Pythagorean fuzzy comparison matrices are created following the markings in Table 2. The hierarchy of problems is defined under the goal based on the indicators given in Figure 1. Based on Saaty's classical consistency analysis, one calculates matrix consistency index $CI = \frac{\lambda_{max}-n}{n-1}$ and consistency index $CR = \frac{CI}{RI}$, where λ_{max} is the greatest eigenvalue of the matrix of dimensions n, and RI is the random index given by:

$$(n,\ RI) = \{(1,0),(2,0),(3,0,58),(4,0.90),(5,1.12),(6,1.24),(7,1.32),(8,1.41)\ \}$$

The values of $CR < 0.1$ indicate that the comparison matrices are consistent. Pythagorean fuzzy pairwise comparison matrices of main criteria and sub-criteria in the PF-AHP method are shown in Tables 3–9.

Table 3. Aggregated decision matrix in PF–AHP for the main criteria (CI = 0.0196675, CR = 0.0158609).

	G	E	S	O	B	C
G	⟨0.5, 0.5⟩	⟨0.5, 0.4⟩	⟨0.7, 03⟩	⟨0.7, 0.3⟩	⟨0.7, 0.3⟩	⟨0.8, 0.2⟩
E	⟨0.5, 0.6⟩	⟨0.5, 0.5⟩	⟨0.7, 0.3⟩	⟨0.7, 0.3⟩	⟨0.7, 0.3⟩	⟨0.8, 0.2⟩
S	⟨0.3, 0.7⟩	⟨0.3, 0.7⟩	⟨0.5, 0.5⟩	⟨0.5, 0.4⟩	⟨0.5, 0.4⟩	⟨0.6, 0.4⟩
O	⟨0.3, 0.7⟩	⟨0.3, 0.7⟩	⟨0.5, 0.6⟩	⟨0.5, 0.5⟩	⟨0.5, 0.4⟩	⟨0.6, 0.4⟩
B	⟨0.3, 0.7⟩	⟨0.3, 0.7⟩	⟨0.5, 0.6⟩	⟨0.5, 0.6⟩	⟨0.5, 0.5⟩	⟨0.6, 0.4⟩
C	⟨0.2, 0.8⟩	⟨0.2, 0.8⟩	⟨0.4, 0.6⟩	⟨0.4, 0.6⟩	⟨0.4, 0.6⟩	⟨0.5, 0.5⟩

Table 4. Aggregated decision matrix in PF–AHP for the sub-criteria G (CI = 0.0312977, CR = 0.0252401).

	G_2	G_3	G_4	G_1	G_5	G_6
G_2	⟨0.5, 0.5⟩	⟨0.6, 0.4⟩	⟨0.6, 0.4⟩	⟨0.7, 0.3⟩	⟨0.8, 0.2⟩	⟨0.8, 0.2⟩
G_3	⟨0.4, 0.6⟩	⟨0.5, 0.5⟩	⟨0.5, 0.4⟩	⟨0.6, 0.4⟩	⟨0.7, 0.3⟩	⟨0.7, 0.3⟩
G_4	⟨0.4, 0.6⟩	⟨0.5, 0.6⟩	⟨0.5, 0.5⟩	⟨0.6, 0.4⟩	⟨0.7, 0.3⟩	⟨0.7, 0.3⟩
G_1	⟨0.3, 0.7⟩	⟨0.4, 0.6⟩	⟨0.4, 0.6⟩	⟨0.5, 0.5⟩	⟨0.6, 0.4⟩	⟨0.6, 0.4⟩
G_5	⟨0.2, 0.8⟩	⟨0.3, 0.7⟩	⟨0.3, 0.7⟩	⟨0.4, 0.6⟩	⟨0.5, 0.5⟩	⟨0.5, 0.4⟩
G_6	⟨0.2, 0.8⟩	⟨0.3, 0.7⟩	⟨0.3, 0.7⟩	⟨0.4, 0.6⟩	⟨0.5, 0.6⟩	⟨0.5, 0.5⟩

Table 5. Aggregated decision matrix in PF–AHP for the sub-criteria E (CI = 0.0116255, CR = 0.00937541).

	E_1	E_2	E_3	E_4	E_5	E_6
E_1	⟨0.5, 0.5⟩	⟨0.6, 0.4⟩	⟨0.6, 0.4⟩	⟨0.7, 0.3⟩	⟨0.7, 0.3⟩	⟨0.7, 0.3⟩
E_2	⟨0.4, 0.6⟩	⟨0.5, 0.5⟩	⟨0.5, 0.4⟩	⟨0.6, 0.4⟩	⟨0.6, 0.4⟩	⟨0.6, 0.4⟩
E_3	⟨0.4, 0.6⟩	⟨0.5, 0.6⟩	⟨0.5, 0.5⟩	⟨0.6, 0.4⟩	⟨0.6, 0.4⟩	⟨0.6, 0.4⟩
E_4	⟨0.3, 0.7⟩	⟨0.4, 0.6⟩	⟨0.4, 0.6⟩	⟨0.5, 0.5⟩	⟨0.5, 0.4⟩	⟨0.5, 0.4⟩
E_5	⟨0.3, 0.7⟩	⟨0.4, 0.6⟩	⟨0.4, 0.6⟩	⟨0.5, 0.6⟩	⟨0.5, 0.5⟩	⟨0.5, 0.4⟩
E_6	⟨0.3, 0.7⟩	⟨0.4, 0.6⟩	⟨0.4, 0.6⟩	⟨0.5, 0.6⟩	⟨0.5, 0.6⟩	⟨0.5, 0.5⟩

Table 6. Aggregated decision matrix in PF–AHP for the sub-criteria S ($CI = 0.0426034$, $CR = 0.0343576$).

	S_1	S_2	S_3	S_4	S_5	S_6
S_1	⟨0.5, 0.5⟩	⟨0.6, 0.4⟩	⟨0.6, 0.4⟩	⟨0.8, 0.2⟩	⟨0.8, 0.2⟩	⟨0.9, 0.1⟩
S_2	⟨0.4, 0.6⟩	⟨0.5, 0.5⟩	⟨0.5, 0.4⟩	⟨0.7, 0.3⟩	⟨0.7, 0.3⟩	⟨0.8, 0.2⟩
S_3	⟨0.4, 0.6⟩	⟨0.5, 0.6⟩	⟨0.5, 0.5⟩	⟨0.7, 0.3⟩	⟨0.7, 0.3⟩	⟨0.8, 0.2⟩
S_4	⟨0.2, 0.8⟩	⟨0.3, 0.7⟩	⟨0.3, 0.7⟩	⟨0.5, 0.5⟩	⟨0.5, 0.4⟩	⟨0.6, 0.4⟩
S_5	⟨0.2, 0.8⟩	⟨0.3, 0.7⟩	⟨0.3, 0.7⟩	⟨0.5, 0.6⟩	⟨0.5, 0.5⟩	⟨0.6, 0.4⟩
S_6	⟨0.1, 0.9⟩	⟨0.2, 0.8⟩	⟨0.2, 0.8⟩	⟨0.4, 0.6⟩	⟨0.4, 0.6⟩	⟨0.5, 0.5⟩

Table 7. Aggregated decision matrix in PF–AHP for the sub-criteria O ($CI = 0.0234898$, $CR = 0.0209731$).

	O_1	O_2	O_3	O_4	O_5	O_6
O_1	⟨0.5, 0.5⟩	⟨0.6, 0.4⟩	⟨0.7, 0.3⟩	⟨0.7, 0.3⟩	⟨0.8, 0.2⟩	⟨0.8, 0.2⟩
O_2	⟨0.4, 0.6⟩	⟨0.5, 0.5⟩	⟨0.6, 0.4⟩	⟨0.6, 0.4⟩	⟨0.7, 0.3⟩	⟨0.7, 0.3⟩
O_3	⟨0.3, 0.7⟩	⟨0.4, 0.6⟩	⟨0.5, 0.5⟩	⟨0.5, 0.4⟩	⟨0.6, 0.4⟩	⟨0.6, 0.4⟩
O_4	⟨0.3, 0.7⟩	⟨0.4, 0.6⟩	⟨0.5, 0.6⟩	⟨0.5, 0.5⟩	⟨0.6, 0.4⟩	⟨0.6, 0.4⟩
O_5	⟨0.2, 0.8⟩	⟨0.3, 0.7⟩	⟨0.4, 0.6⟩	⟨0.4, 0.6⟩	⟨0.5, 0.5⟩	⟨0.5, 0.4⟩
O_6	⟨0.2, 0.8⟩	⟨0.3, 0.7⟩	⟨0.4, 0.6⟩	⟨0.4, 0.6⟩	⟨0.5, 0.6⟩	⟨0.5, 0.5⟩

Table 8. Aggregated decision matrix in PF–AHP for the sub-criteria B ($CI = 0.0312977$, $CR = 0.0252401$).

	B_1	B_2	B_3	B_4	B_5
B_1	⟨0.5, 0.5⟩	⟨0.6, 0.4⟩	⟨0.6, 0.4⟩	⟨0.8, 0.2⟩	⟨0.8, 0.2⟩
B_2	⟨0.4, 0.6⟩	⟨0.5, 0.5⟩	⟨0.5, 0.4⟩	⟨0.7, 0.3⟩	⟨0.7, 0.3⟩
B_3	⟨0.4, 0.6⟩	⟨0.5, 0.6⟩	⟨0.5, 0.5⟩	⟨0.7, 0.3⟩	⟨0.7, 0.3⟩
B_4	⟨0.2, 0.8⟩	⟨0.3, 0.7⟩	⟨0.3, 0.7⟩	⟨0.5, 0.5⟩	⟨0.5, 0.4⟩
B_5	⟨0.2, 0.8⟩	⟨0.3, 0.7⟩	⟨0.3, 0.7⟩	⟨0.5, 0.6⟩	⟨0.5, 0.5⟩

Table 9. Aggregated decision matrix in PF–AHP for the sub-criteria C ($CI = 0.0317228$, $CR = 0.0283239$).

	C_1	C_2	C_3	C_4	C_5
C_1	⟨0.5, 0.5⟩	⟨0.6, 0.4⟩	⟨0.6, 0.4⟩	⟨0.7, 0.3⟩	⟨0.8, 0.2⟩
C_2	⟨0.4, 0.6⟩	⟨0.5, 0.5⟩	⟨0.5, 0.4⟩	⟨0.6, 0.4⟩	⟨0.7, 0.3⟩
C_3	⟨0.4, 0.6⟩	⟨0.5, 0.6⟩	⟨0.5, 0.5⟩	⟨0.6, 0.4⟩	⟨0.7, 0.3⟩
C_4	⟨0.3, 0.7⟩	⟨0.4, 0.6⟩	⟨0.4, 0.6⟩	⟨0.5, 0.5⟩	⟨0.6, 0.4⟩
C_5	⟨0.2, 0.8⟩	⟨0.3, 0.7⟩	⟨0.3, 0.7⟩	⟨0.4, 0.6⟩	⟨0.5, 0.5⟩

Figure 6 gives a graphic representation of the weights of criteria and sub-criteria. It can be seen that the weight values of the proposed IVPF-AHP method (IVPF-AHP p) given in Section 2.2.4 are between the PF-AHP method and IVPF-AHP method, with differences (IVPF-AHP d) given in Section 2.2.3.

Aggregated decision interval matrices of criteria and sub-criteria in the PF-AHP method are shown in Tables 10–16.

Final weights of sub-criteria in the smartness assessment of buildings are shown in Figure 7 for all three observed methods.

The obtained results indicate the dominance of two sub-criteria in the algorithm, G2 and E2. Additionally, the first three indicators are the same for all three methods, and two interval methods have overlaps in the order of the first seven indicators. The final ranking results, obtained by the consistent application, are shown in Table 17.

The rankings of the "smart" building-related indicators presented in Table 17 are the basis for creating a mechanism for a scoring system for the smartness of public buildings. The main criteria level indicators under groups G (green building construction) and E (energy management systems) are recognized by experts as a requirement for the development of "smart" buildings for public use. The obtained results show that bio-climatic design of the building (G_2), smart metering (E_2), use of ecological materials (G_3), use of renewable energy sources (G_4), energy-efficient procedures usage (E_1), use of advanced HVAC control systems (E_4), data gathering devices with sensors (B_1) and securing lives and assets (S_2) possess an essential influence on the creation of "smart" buildings for public use. The ranks of the last-ranked indicators differ for all three methods. It turned out that the publish safety and privacy policy (S_6) and cyber system (C_5) were ranked worst.

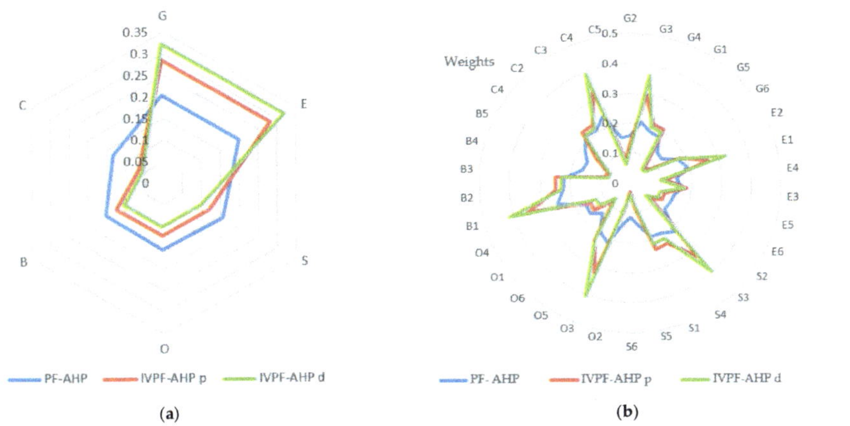

Figure 6. Graphic representation of (**a**) criteria weights and (**b**) sub-criteria weights.

Table 10. Aggregated decision interval matrix in IVPF–AHP for the main criteria (CI = 0.0317228, CR = 0.0283239).

	E	**G**	**S**	**O**	**B**	**C**
G	$\langle [0.5,0.5], [0.5,0.5] \rangle$	$\langle [0.5,0.5], [0.5,0.5] \rangle$	$\langle [0.6,0.7], [0.2,0.3] \rangle$	$\langle [0.6,0.7], [0.2,0.3] \rangle$	$\langle [0.6,0.7], [0.2,0.3] \rangle$	$\langle [0.7,0.8], [0.1,0.2] \rangle$
E	$\langle [0.5,0.5], [0.5,0.5] \rangle$	$\langle [0.5,0.5], [0.5,0.5] \rangle$	$\langle [0.6,0.7], [0.2,0.3] \rangle$	$\langle [0.6,0.7], [0.5,0.5] \rangle$	$\langle [0.6,0.7], [0.5,0.5] \rangle$	$\langle [0.7,0.8], [0.1,0.2] \rangle$
S	$\langle [0.2,0.3], [0.5,0.5] \rangle$	$\langle [0.2,0.3], [0.5,0.5] \rangle$	$\langle [0.5,0.5], [0.5,0.5] \rangle$	$\langle [0.5,0.5], [0.5,0.5] \rangle$	$\langle [0.5,0.5], [0.5,0.5] \rangle$	$\langle [0.5,0.5], [0.3,0.4] \rangle$
O	$\langle [0.2,0.3], [0.5,0.5] \rangle$	$\langle [0.2,0.3], [0.5,0.5] \rangle$	$\langle [0.5,0.5], [0.5,0.5] \rangle$	$\langle [0.5,0.5], [0.5,0.5] \rangle$	$\langle [0.5,0.5], [0.5,0.5] \rangle$	$\langle [0.5,0.6], [0.3,0.4] \rangle$
B	$\langle [0.2,0.3], [0.5,0.5] \rangle$	$\langle [0.2,0.3], [0.5,0.5] \rangle$	$\langle [0.5,0.5], [0.5,0.5] \rangle$	$\langle [0.5,0.5], [0.5,0.5] \rangle$	$\langle [0.5,0.5], [0.5,0.5] \rangle$	$\langle [0.5,0.6], [0.3,0.4] \rangle$
C	$\langle [0.1,0.2], [0.7,0.8] \rangle$	$\langle [0.1,0.2], [0.7,0.8] \rangle$	$\langle [0.3,0.4], [0.5,0.6] \rangle$	$\langle [0.3,0.4], [0.5,0.6] \rangle$	$\langle [0.3,0.4], [0.5,0.6] \rangle$	$\langle [0.5,0.5], [0.5,0.5] \rangle$

Table 11. Aggregated decision interval matrix in IVPF–AHP for the sub-criteria G (CI = 0.0312977, CR = 0.0252401).

	G_2	G_3	G_4	G_1	G_5	G_6
G_2	$\langle [0.5,0.5], [0.5,0.5] \rangle$	$\langle [0.5,0.6], [0.3,0.4] \rangle$	$\langle [0.5,0.6], [0.3,0.4] \rangle$	$\langle [0.6,0.7], [0.2,0.3] \rangle$	$\langle [0.7,0.8], [0.1,0.2] \rangle$	$\langle [0.7,0.8], [0.1,0.2] \rangle$
G_3	$\langle [0.3,0.4], [0.5,0.6] \rangle$	$\langle [0.5,0.5], [0.5,0.5] \rangle$	$\langle [0.5,0.5], [0.5,0.5] \rangle$	$\langle [0.5,0.6], [0.3,0.4] \rangle$	$\langle [0.6,0.7], [0.2,0.3] \rangle$	$\langle [0.6,0.7], [0.2,0.3] \rangle$
G_4	$\langle [0.3,0.4], [0.5,0.6] \rangle$	$\langle [0.5,0.5], [0.5,0.5] \rangle$	$\langle [0.5,0.5], [0.5,0.5] \rangle$	$\langle [0.5,0.6], [0.3,0.4] \rangle$	$\langle [0.6,0.7], [0.2,0.3] \rangle$	$\langle [0.6,0.7], [0.2,0.3] \rangle$
G_1	$\langle [0.2,0.3], [0.6,0.7] \rangle$	$\langle [0.3,0.4], [0.5,0.6] \rangle$	$\langle [0.3,0.4], [0.5,0.6] \rangle$	$\langle [0.5,0.5], [0.5,0.5] \rangle$	$\langle [0.5,0.6], [0.3,0.4] \rangle$	$\langle [0.5,0.6], [0.3,0.4] \rangle$
G_5	$\langle [0.1,0.2], [0.7,0.8] \rangle$	$\langle [0.2,0.3], [0.6,0.7] \rangle$	$\langle [0.2,0.3], [0.6,0.7] \rangle$	$\langle [0.3,0.4], [0.5,0.6] \rangle$	$\langle [0.5,0.5], [0.5,0.5] \rangle$	$\langle [0.5,0.5], [0.5,0.5] \rangle$
G_6	$\langle [0.1,0.2], [0.7,0.8] \rangle$	$\langle [0.2,0.3], [0.6,0.7] \rangle$	$\langle [0.2,0.3], [0.6,0.7] \rangle$	$\langle [0.3,0.4], [0.5,0.6] \rangle$	$\langle [0.5,0.5], [0.5,0.5] \rangle$	$\langle [0.5,0.5], [0.5,0.5] \rangle$

Table 12. Aggregated decision interval matrix in IVPF–AHP for the sub-criteria E (CI = 0.0116255, CR = 0.00937541).

	E_2	E_1	E_4	E_3	E_5	E_6
E_2	$\langle[0.5,0.5],[0.5,0.5]\rangle$	$\langle[0.5,0.6],[0.3,0.4]\rangle$	$\langle[0.5,0.6],[0.3,0.4]\rangle$	$\langle[0.6,0.7],[0.2,0.3]\rangle$	$\langle[0.6,0.7],[0.2,0.3]\rangle$	$\langle[0.6,0.7],[0.2,0.3]\rangle$
E_1	$\langle[0.3,0.4],[0.5,0.6]\rangle$	$\langle[0.5,0.5],[0.5,0.5]\rangle$	$\langle[0.5,0.5],[0.5,0.5]\rangle$	$\langle[0.5,0.6],[0.3,0.4]\rangle$	$\langle[0.5,0.6],[0.3,0.4]\rangle$	$\langle[0.5,0.6],[0.3,0.4]\rangle$
E_4	$\langle[0.3,0.4],[0.5,0.6]\rangle$	$\langle[0.5,0.5],[0.5,0.5]\rangle$	$\langle[0.5,0.5],[0.5,0.5]\rangle$	$\langle[0.5,0.6],[0.3,0.4]\rangle$	$\langle[0.5,0.6],[0.3,0.4]\rangle$	$\langle[0.5,0.6],[0.3,0.4]\rangle$
E_3	$\langle[0.2,0.3],[0.6,0.7]\rangle$	$\langle[0.3,0.4],[0.5,0.6]\rangle$	$\langle[0.3,0.4],[0.5,0.6]\rangle$	$\langle[0.5,0.5],[0.5,0.5]\rangle$	$\langle[0.5,0.5],[0.5,0.5]\rangle$	$\langle[0.5,0.5],[0.5,0.5]\rangle$
E_5	$\langle[0.2,0.3],[0.7,0.8]\rangle$	$\langle[0.3,0.4],[0.5,0.6]\rangle$	$\langle[0.3,0.4],[0.5,0.6]\rangle$	$\langle[0.5,0.5],[0.5,0.5]\rangle$	$\langle[0.5,0.5],[0.5,0.5]\rangle$	$\langle[0.5,0.5],[0.5,0.5]\rangle$
E_6	$\langle[0.2,0.3],[0.6,0.7]\rangle$	$\langle[0.3,0.4],[0.5,0.6]\rangle$	$\langle[0.3,0.4],[0.5,0.6]\rangle$	$\langle[0.5,0.5],[0.5,0.5]\rangle$	$\langle[0.5,0.5],[0.5,0.5]\rangle$	$\langle[0.5,0.5],[0.5,0.5]\rangle$

Table 13. Aggregated decision interval matrix in IVPF–AHP for the sub-criteria S (CI = 0.0426034, CR = 0.0343576).

	S_2	S_3	S_4	S_1	S_5	S_6
S_2	$\langle[0.5,0.5],[0.5,0.5]\rangle$	$\langle[0.5,0.6],[0.3,0.4]\rangle$	$\langle[0.5,0.6],[0.3,0.4]\rangle$	$\langle[0.7,0.8],[0.1,0.2]\rangle$	$\langle[0.7,0.8],[0.1,0.2]\rangle$	$\langle[0.7,0.8],[0.1,0.2]\rangle$
S_3	$\langle[0.3,0.4],[0.5,0.6]\rangle$	$\langle[0.5,0.5],[0.5,0.5]\rangle$	$\langle[0.5,0.5],[0.5,0.5]\rangle$	$\langle[0.6,0.7],[0.2,0.3]\rangle$	$\langle[0.6,0.7],[0.2,0.3]\rangle$	$\langle[0.7,0.8],[0.1,0.2]\rangle$
S_4	$\langle[0.3,0.4],[0.5,0.6]\rangle$	$\langle[0.5,0.5],[0.5,0.5]\rangle$	$\langle[0.5,0.5],[0.5,0.5]\rangle$	$\langle[0.6,0.7],[0.2,0.3]\rangle$	$\langle[0.6,0.7],[0.2,0.3]\rangle$	$\langle[0.7,0.8],[0.1,0.2]\rangle$
S_1	$\langle[0.1,0.2],[0.7,0.8]\rangle$	$\langle[0.2,0.3],[0.6,0.7]\rangle$	$\langle[0.2,0.3],[0.6,0.7]\rangle$	$\langle[0.5,0.5],[0.5,0.5]\rangle$	$\langle[0.5,0.5],[0.5,0.5]\rangle$	$\langle[0.5,0.6],[0.3,0.4]\rangle$
S_5	$\langle[0.1,0.2],[0.7,0.8]\rangle$	$\langle[0.2,0.3],[0.6,0.7]\rangle$	$\langle[0.2,0.3],[0.6,0.7]\rangle$	$\langle[0.5,0.5],[0.5,0.5]\rangle$	$\langle[0.5,0.5],[0.5,0.5]\rangle$	$\langle[0.5,0.6],[0.3,0.4]\rangle$
S_6	$\langle[0,0.1],[0.8,0.9]\rangle$	$\langle[0.1,0.2],[0.7,0.8]\rangle$	$\langle[0.1,0.2],[0.7,0.8]\rangle$	$\langle[0.3,0.4],[0.5,0.6]\rangle$	$\langle[0.1,0.2],[0.7,0.8]\rangle$	$\langle[0.5,0.5],[0.5,0.5]\rangle$

Table 14. Aggregated decision interval matrix in IVPF–AHP for the sub-criteria O (CI = 0.0312977, CR = 0.0252401).

	O_2	O_3	O_5	O_6	O_1	O_4
O_2	$\langle[0.5,0.5],[0.5,0.5]\rangle$	$\langle[0.5,0.6],[0.3,0.4]\rangle$	$\langle[0.6,0.7],[0.2,0.3]\rangle$	$\langle[0.6,0.7],[0.2,0.3]\rangle$	$\langle[0.7,0.8],[0.1,0.2]\rangle$	$\langle[0.7,0.8],[0.1,0.2]\rangle$
O_3	$\langle[0.3,0.4],[0.5,0.6]\rangle$	$\langle[0.5,0.5],[0.5,0.5]\rangle$	$\langle[0.5,0.6],[0.3,0.4]\rangle$	$\langle[0.5,0.6],[0.3,0.4]\rangle$	$\langle[0.6,0.7],[0.2,0.3]\rangle$	$\langle[0.6,0.7],[0.2,0.3]\rangle$
O_5	$\langle[0.2,0.3],[0.6,0.7]\rangle$	$\langle[0.3,0.4],[0.5,0.6]\rangle$	$\langle[0.5,0.5],[0.5,0.5]\rangle$	$\langle[0.5,0.5],[0.5,0.5]\rangle$	$\langle[0.5,0.6],[0.3,0.4]\rangle$	$\langle[0.5,0.6],[0.3,0.4]\rangle$
O_8	$\langle[0.2,0.3],[0.6,0.7]\rangle$	$\langle[0.3,0.4],[0.5,0.6]\rangle$	$\langle[0.5,0.5],[0.5,0.5]\rangle$	$\langle[0.5,0.5],[0.5,0.5]\rangle$	$\langle[0.5,0.6],[0.3,0.4]\rangle$	$\langle[0.5,0.6],[0.3,0.4]\rangle$
O_1	$\langle[0.1,0.2],[0.7,0.8]\rangle$	$\langle[0.2,0.3],[0.6,0.7]\rangle$	$\langle[0.3,0.4],[0.5,0.6]\rangle$	$\langle[0.3,0.4],[0.5,0.6]\rangle$	$\langle[0.5,0.5],[0.5,0.5]\rangle$	$\langle[0.5,0.5],[0.5,0.5]\rangle$
O_4	$\langle[0.1,0.2],[0.7,0.8]\rangle$	$\langle[0.2,0.3],[0.6,0.7]\rangle$	$\langle[0.3,0.4],[0.5,0.6]\rangle$	$\langle[0.3,0.4],[0.5,0.6]\rangle$	$\langle[0.5,0.5],[0.5,0.5]\rangle$	$\langle[0.5,0.5],[0.5,0.5]\rangle$

The performance defined by the indicators in the paper has an impact on the financial aspect of construction and maintenance of buildings, the comfort of staying in the building, and the degree of energy consumption, and the proposed evaluation system would have practical application when making decisions about the choice of the most optimal design solution before its development in the executive project.

In the process of creating smart cities, an important role is played by state-initiated projects and strategies, investment programs for new construction, and programs for sustainable renovation and energy rehabilitation, which are often aimed primarily at facilities intended for the youngest (kindergartens and elementary schools), facilities of health institutions and gerontological centers, as objects of public purpose.

Table 15. Aggregated decision interval matrix in IVPF–AHP for the sub-criteria B (CI = 0.0234898, CR = 0.0209731).

	B_1	B_2	B_3	B_4	B_5
B_1	$\langle [0.5,0.5], [0.5,0.5] \rangle$	$\langle [0.5,0.6], [0.3,0.4] \rangle$	$\langle [0.5,0.6], [0.3,0.4] \rangle$	$\langle [0.7,0.8], [0.1,0.2] \rangle$	$\langle [0.7,0.8], [0.1,0.2] \rangle$
B_2	$\langle [0.3,0.4], [0.5,0.6] \rangle$	$\langle [0.5,0.5], [0.5,0.5] \rangle$	$\langle [0.5,0.5], [0.5,0.5] \rangle$	$\langle [0.6,0.7], [0.2,0.3] \rangle$	$\langle [0.6,0.7], [0.2,0.3] \rangle$
B_3	$\langle [0.3,0.4], [0.5,0.6] \rangle$	$\langle [0.5,0.5], [0.5,0.5] \rangle$	$\langle [0.5,0.5], [0.5,0.5] \rangle$	$\langle [0.6,0.7], [0.2,0.3] \rangle$	$\langle [0.6,0.7], [0.2,0.3] \rangle$
B_4	$\langle [0.1,0.2], [0.7,0.8] \rangle$	$\langle [0.2,0.3], [0.6,0.7] \rangle$	$\langle [0.2,0.3], [0.6,0.7] \rangle$	$\langle [0.5,0.5], [0.5,0.5] \rangle$	$\langle [0.5,0.6], [0.3,0.4] \rangle$
B_5	$\langle [0.1,0.2], [0.7,0.8] \rangle$	$\langle [0.2,0.3], [0.6,0.7] \rangle$	$\langle [0.2,0.3], [0.6,0.7] \rangle$	$\langle [0.5,0.5], [0.5,0.5] \rangle$	$\langle [0.5,0.5], [0.5,0.5] \rangle$

Table 16. Aggregated decision interval matrix in IVPF–AHP for the sub-criteria C (CI = 0.0317228, CR = 0.0283239).

	C_4	C_2	C_3	C_1	C_5
C_4	$\langle [0.5,0.5], [0.5,0.5] \rangle$	$\langle [0.5,0.6], [0.3,0.4] \rangle$	$\langle [0.5,0.6], [0.3,0.4] \rangle$	$\langle [0.6,0.7], [0.2,0.3] \rangle$	$\langle [0.7,0.8], [0.1,0.2] \rangle$
C_2	$\langle [0.3,0.4], [0.5,0.6] \rangle$	$\langle [0.5,0.5], [0.5,0.5] \rangle$	$\langle [0.5,0.5], [0.5,0.5] \rangle$	$\langle [0.5,0.6], [0.3,0.4] \rangle$	$\langle [0.6,0.7], [0.2,0.3] \rangle$
C_3	$\langle [0.3,0.4], [0.5,0.6] \rangle$	$\langle [0.5,0.5], [0.5,0.5] \rangle$	$\langle [0.5,0.5], [0.5,0.5] \rangle$	$\langle [0.5,0.6], [0.3,0.4] \rangle$	$\langle [0.6,0.7], [0.2,0.3] \rangle$
C_1	$\langle [0.2,0.3], [0.6,0.7] \rangle$	$\langle [0.3,0.4], [0.5,0.6] \rangle$	$\langle [0.3,0.4], [0.5,0.6] \rangle$	$\langle [0.5,0.5], [0.5,0.5] \rangle$	$\langle [0.5,0.6], [0.3,0.4] \rangle$
C_5	$\langle [0.1,0.2], [0.7,0.8] \rangle$	$\langle [0.2,0.3], [0.6,0.7] \rangle$	$\langle [0.2,0.3], [0.6,0.7] \rangle$	$\langle [0.3,0.4], [0.5,0.6] \rangle$	$\langle [0.5,0.5], [0.5,0.5] \rangle$

Table 17. Final ranking of indicators.

Rank	PF-AHP	IVPF-AHP p	IVPF-AHP d	Rank	PF-AHP	IVPF-AHP p	IVPF-AHP d
1.	G2	G2	G2	18.	E6	O3	S4
2.	E2	E2	E2	19.	O3	G5	C4
3.	G3	G3	G3	20.	G5	G6	G5
4.	B1	G4	G4	21.	C2	C4	G6
5.	G4	E1	E1	22.	G6	O5	O5
6.	E1	E4	E4	23.	C3	O6	O6
7.	E4	B1	B1	24.	O5	C2	C2
8.	S2	S2	O2	25.	O6	C3	C3
9.	B2	O2	S2	26.	B4	S1	B4
10.	O2	G1	G1	27.	Cl	S5	B5
11.	G1	E3	E3	28.	B5	O1	O1
12.	B3	E5	E5	29.	S1	O4	O4
13.	C4	E6	E6	30.	S5	B4	S1
14.	E3	B2	B2	31.	O1	B5	S5
15.	S3	B3	B3	32.	O4	Cl	Cl
16.	E5	S3	O3	33.	C5	C5	S6
17.	S4	S4	S3	34.	S6	S6	C5

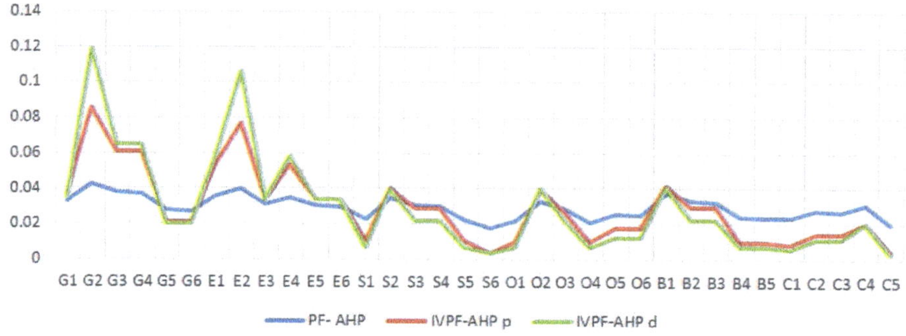

Figure 7. Graphic representation of the final weights ranking of sub-criteria.

To compare the lists of ranked criteria, using the three mentioned methods, we use Spearman's rank correlation coefficient [70] by Equation (21)

$$\mathrm{R_s} = 1 - \frac{6\sum_{k=1}^{N}\left(\mathcal{R}_{a_k} - \mathcal{R}_{b_k}\right)^2}{N(N^2-1)}. \tag{21}$$

A total of N elements are ranked, and $\mathcal{R}_{a_k}$ and $\mathcal{R}_{b_k}$ are ranks of the element k in the compared rankings. The comparison of similarities used a WS coefficient was introduced to analyze the ranking similarity [71] by Equation (22), where

$$\mathrm{WS} = 1 - \sum_{k=1}^{N}\left(2^{-\mathcal{R}_{a_k}}\frac{\left|\mathcal{R}_{a_k} - \mathcal{R}_{b_k}\right|}{\max\left\{\left|1-\mathcal{R}_{a_k}\right|, \left|n-\mathcal{R}_{b_k}\right|\right\}}\right). \tag{22}$$

By applying Equations (21) and (22), all compared results are presented in Table 18, and since min{$\mathrm{R_s}$, WS} = 0.95783, it may be said that all rankings have a notable similarity.

Table 18. Ranking similarity.

Method	PF-AHP	IVPF-AHP d	IVPF-AHP p
PF-AHP		Rs = 0.966081 WS = 0.994832	Rs = 0.95783 WS = 0.995135
IVPF-AHP d	Rs = 0.966081 WS = 0.991096		Rs= 0.987777 WS = 0.99977
IVPF-AHP p	Rs = 0.95783 WS = 0.991277	Rs = 0.987777 WS = 0.999769	

The scoring system applies only to public purpose buildings, which means that for other types of buildings—residential or industrial—a new ranking would have to be created, with the same and(or) partially changed indicators, depending on the purpose of the buildings. Previous research on the adoption indicators has been performed, and the division of indicators in this way more or less exists and is the result of scientific research. In this paper, unlike others, they are ranked exclusively for public purpose objects, and their ranking is universal for all types of public buildings.

The scoring system for assessing the level of smartness of public-use buildings is directly obtained from the weights. For ease of use, it can be multiplied by 100 and rounded to the nearest whole number. To avoid the narrow scale range of PF-AHP and the too-wide range in IVPF-AHP d, we create a scoring model by the arithmetic mean of the three methods presented. The scoring results are in Table 19.

Table 19. Scoring of indicators.

PF-AHP	Score	IVPF-AHP p	Score	IVPF-AHP d	Score	Scoring Method	Score
G2	42	G2	85	G2	118	G2	82
E2	39	E2	76	E2	105	E2	74
G3	37	G3	60	G3	65	G4	55
B1	37	G4	60	G4	65	G3	54
G4	37	E1	53	E1	58	E1	49
E1	35	E4	53	E4	58	E4	48
E4	34	B1	42	B1	40	B1	40
S2	34	S2	40	O2	40	S2	38
B2	33	O2	39	S2	39	O2	37
O2	32	G1	36	G1	34	G1	34
G1	32	E3	33	E3	33	E3	33
B3	32	E5	33	E5	33	E5	32
C4	31	E6	33	E6	33	E6	32
E3	31	B2	29	B2	22	B2	28
S3	30	B3	29	B3	22	B3	28
E5	30	S3	28	O3	21	S3	27
S4	30	S4	28	S3	21	S4	27
E6	29	O3	27	S4	21	O3	25
O3	28	G5	21	C4	20	C4	24
G5	27	G6	21	G5	20	G5	23
C2	27	C4	20	G6	20	G6	22
G6	27	O5	17	O5	12	O5	18
C3	27	O6	17	O6	12	O6	18
O5	25	C2	14	C2	11	C2	17
O6	24	C3	14	C3	11	C3	17
B4	24	S1	10	B4	7	S1	13
Cl	23	S5	10	B5	7	B4	13
B5	23	O1	10	O1	6	B5	13
S1	22	O4	10	O4	6	S5	13
S5	22	B4	10	S1	6	O4	12
O1	21	B5	10	S5	6	O1	12
O4	21	Cl	8	Cl	6	C1	12
C5	19	C5	4	S6	3	C5	9
S6	17	S6	3	C5	3	S6	8

Table 19 presents the framework for the implementation of the scoring system. First, the evaluator must check whether the building meets the criteria and sub-criteria from the scoring system. The sum of all the points given for the indicators is the final result, indicating the level of smartness of the building, based on which, decisions can be reached regarding strategies to improve or maintain the level of smartness.

It can be seen from the final scoring in Table 19 that the points assigned to the indicators obtained using the IVPF-AHP p method are between the scores of PF-AHP and IVPF-AHP d. The practical interpretation is that the scores are in a smaller range, and there is less difference in the scoring of the indicators of the PF-AHP method. On the other hand, the scores of the IVPF-AHP method belong to a widening range and favor the key indicators. The application of the proposed method is more compromised.

Based on the received final rankings, we created an integrated model of a smartness assessment framework of buildings, shown in Figure 8. The model is based on the identification of influential factors.

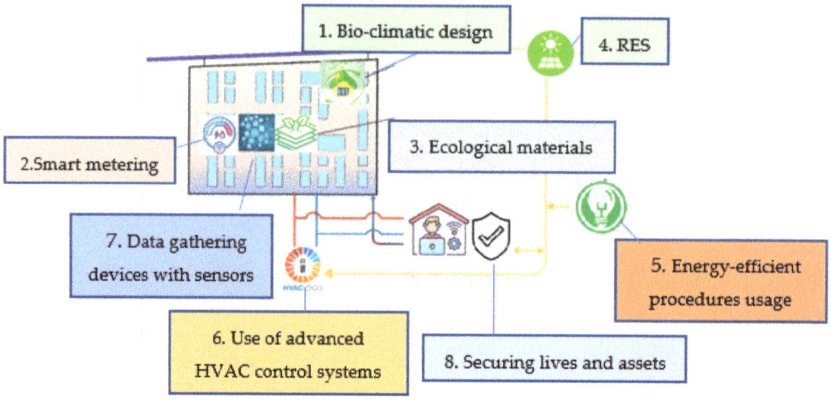

Figure 8. Influential factors in the smartness assessment framework of public buildings.

4. Conclusions

Measuring the smartness of a building is complex because there are many issues to consider and, in addition, perceptions differ depending on the roles of the project participants. This study proposes a new decision algorithm IVPF-AHP p based on PF-AHP, and provides comparative results with IVPF-AHP d based on defuzzification with differences, and provides all three methods' results simultaneously. In this study, the relevant indicators ranking the development of Smart Buildings in the context of the broader Smart City concept are implemented by applying these methods. The comparative analysis obtained by applying the proposed method IVPF-AHP p and PF-AHP as well as IVPF-AHP d indicates a significant degree of similarity in the rank, confirmed by the Ranking similarity. Based on the results, a scoring system has been created for all three methods. Scoring results give different ranges. Thus, ranges in PF-AHP are much narrower, and the differences between the indicators' scores has not been emphasized enough. Compared to that, the IVPF-AHP d method favors significant indicators, and the scoring ranges are much more extensive. Relative to these two methods, the proposed IVPF-AHP p method provides a greater compromise in scoring. Based on the developed three scoring systems, we created the final scoring as the arithmetic mean of the three presented methods. The most significant indicators in the scoring system are bioclimatic design, smart metering, ecological material, and RES. Public-use buildings are used as a case study in the paper. The results of this study can be the basis for future research on buildings that use different fuzzy multi-criteria analysis approaches. The study also highlights the significance of developing a scoring system to evaluate the smartness of architectural buildings. The applied methodology can be used practically in decision-making processes in the urban sector and local self-governments of cities. The determined indicators ranking can be successfully generalized to other purposes for buildings.

Author Contributions: Conceptualization, M.R.M. and D.M.M.; methodology, M.R.M. and D.M.M.; software, D.M.M.; validation, M.R.M. and D.M.S.; formal analysis, M.R.M. and D.M.M.; investigation, M.R.M., D.M.S. and M.K.; resources, M.K. and D.M.S.; data curation, M.R.M., D.M.M. and D.M.S.; writing—original draft preparation, M.R.M. and D.M.M.; writing—review and editing, M.R.M., D.M.M. and D.M.S.; visualization, M.R.M.; supervision, M.R.M., D.M.M. and M.K.; project administration, M.R.M., M.K. and D.M.M. All authors have read and agreed to the published version of the manuscript.

Funding: This research received no external funding.

Institutional Review Board Statement: Not applicable.

Informed Consent Statement: Not applicable.

Data Availability Statement: Not applicable.

Acknowledgments: The authors express gratitude to the Ministry of Education, Science, and Technological Development of Serbia for providing partial support for this paper.

Conflicts of Interest: The authors declare no conflict of interest.

References

1. Lopes, I.M.; Oliveira, P. Can a small city be considered a smart city? *Procedia Comput. Sci.* **2017**, *121*, 617–624. [CrossRef]
2. Desouza, K.C.; Flanery, T.H. Designing, planning, and managing resilient cities: A conceptual framework. *Cities* **2013**, *35*, 89–99. [CrossRef]
3. Global Status Report 2016: Towards Zero-Emission Efficient and Resilient Buildings. Available online: https://www.unep.org/resources/report/global-status-report-2016-towards-zero-emission-efficient-and-resilient-buildings (accessed on 10 January 2023).
4. Li, C.X.; Fong, P.S.W.; Dai, S.; Li, Y. Towards sustainable smart cities: An empirical comparative assessment and development pattern optimization in China. *J. Clean. Prod.* **2019**, *215*, 730–743. [CrossRef]
5. Milošević, M.R.; Milošević, D.M.; Stević, D.M.; Stanojević, A.D. Smart City: Modeling Key Indicators in Serbia Using IT2FS. *Sustainability* **2019**, *11*, 3536. [CrossRef]
6. Milošević, M.; Milošević, D.; Stanojević, A. Making Opportunities for Developing Smart Cities Using Artificial Intelligence. In *Holistic Approach for Decision Making Towards Designing Smart Cities. Future City*; Lazaroiu, G.C., Roscia, M., Dancu, V.S., Eds.; Springer: Cham, Switzerland, 2021; Volume 18, pp. 147–173.
7. Milošević, M.R.; Milošević, D.M.; Stanojević, A.D. Managing Cultural Built Heritage in Smart Cities Using Fuzzy and Interval Multi-criteria Decision Making. In *Intelligent and Fuzzy Techniques: Smart and Innovative Solutions*; INFUS 2020, Advances in Intelligent Systems and Computing; Kahraman, C., Cevik Onar, S., Oztaysi, B., Sari, I., Cebi, S., Tolga, A., Eds.; Springer: Cham, Switzerland, 2021; Volume 1197, pp. 599–607.
8. Milošević, D.; Milošević, M.; Simjanović, D. A Comparative Study of FAHP with Type-1 and Interval Type-2 Fuzzy Sets for ICT Implementation in Smart Cities. In *Intelligent and Fuzzy Techniques for Emerging Conditions and Digital Transformation*; Kahraman, C., Cebi, S., Cevik Onar, S., Oztaysi, B., Tolga, A.C., Sari, I.U., Eds.; INFUS 2021, Lecture Notes in Networks and Systems; Springer: Cham, Switzerland, 2022; Volume 308, pp. 845–852.
9. European-Commission. *Energy Performance of Buildings Directive EPBD, 2018, 844/EU*; European-Commission: Brussels, Belgium, 2018.
10. Love, P.; Bullen, P.A. Toward the sustainable adaptation of existing facilities. *Facilities* **2009**, *27*, 357–367. [CrossRef]
11. Buckman, A.H.; Mayfield, M.; Beck, S.B.M. What is smart building? *J. Smart Sustain. Built Environ.* **2014**, *3*, 92–109. [CrossRef]
12. Arditi, D.; Mangano, G.; De Marco, A. Assessing the smartness of buildings. *Facilities* **2015**, *33*, 553–572. [CrossRef]
13. ICT Solutions for 21 st Century Challenges. Available online: https://smarter2030.gesi.org/ (accessed on 10 January 2023).
14. Tsai, W.H.; Yang, C.H.; Change, J.C.; Lee, H.L. An Activity-Based Costing decision model for life cycle assessment in green building projects. *Eur. J. Oper. Res.* **2014**, *238*, 607–619. [CrossRef]
15. Katz, D.; Skopek, J. The CABA Building Intelligent Quotient program. *Intell. Build. Int.* **2009**, *4*, 277–295. [CrossRef]
16. Wang, Z.L.; Wang, A.; Duonis, I.; Yang, R. Integration of plug-in hybrid electric vehicles into energy and comfort management for smart building. *Energy Build.* **2012**, *47*, 260–266. [CrossRef]
17. Nguyen, T.A.; Aiello, M. Energy intelligent buildings based on users activity: A survey. *Energy Build.* **2013**, *56*, 244–257. [CrossRef]
18. Bayani, R.; Soofi, A.F.; Waseem, M.; Manshadi, S.D. Impact of Transportation Electrification on the Electricity Grid—A Review. *Vehicles* **2022**, *4*, 1042–1079. [CrossRef]
19. Stanojević, A.D.; Milošević, M.; Milošević, D.; Turnšek, B.A.; Jevremović, L.L. Developing multi-criteria model for the protection of built heritage from the aspect of energy retrofitting. *Energy Build.* **2021**, *250*, 111285. [CrossRef]
20. Milošević, M.; Milošević, A.; Milošević, D.; Stanojević, A.; Dimić, V. Multicriteria analysis of contemporary materials for energy-efficient buildings. In Proceedings of the 2nd International Conference "Sfera 2016" Design and Thermal Insulation of Facade Walls—A Traditional and Contemporary Approach, Mostar, Bosnia and Herzegovina, 2 October 2016; pp. 46–51.
21. Kovačević, M.; Ivanišević, N.; Stević, D.; Marković, L.M.; Bulajić, B.; Marković, L.; Gvozdović, N. Decision-Support System for Estimating Resource Consumption in Bridge Construction Based on Machine Learning. *Axioms* **2023**, *12*, 19. [CrossRef]
22. Stanojević, A.; Jevremović, L.j.; Milošević, M.; Turnšek, B.; Milošević, D. Identifying priority indicators for reuse of industrial buildings using AHP method—Case study of Electronic Industry in Nis, Serbia. In Proceedings of the 6th International Academic Conference on Places and Technologies, Pecs, Hungary, 9–10 May 2019; pp. 555–563.
23. Selimi, A.; Milošević, M.; Saračević, M. AHP—TOPSIS Model as a Mathematical Support in the Selection of Project from Aspect of Mobility—Case Study. *J. Appl. Math. Comput. (JAMC)* **2018**, *2*, 257–265.
24. Zadeh, L.A. Fuzzy sets. *Inf. Control* **1965**, *8*, 338–353. [CrossRef]
25. Farooq, D.; Moslem, S. Estimating Driver Behavior Measures Related to Traffic Safety by Investigating 2-Dimensional Uncertain Linguistic Data—A Pythagorean Fuzzy Analytic Hierarchy Process Approach. *Sustainability* **2022**, *14*, 1881. [CrossRef]
26. Zhang, X. Multicriteria Pythagorean fuzzy decision analysis: A hierarchical QUALIFLEX approach with the closeness index-based ranking methods. *Inf. Sci.* **2016**, *330*, 104–124. [CrossRef]
27. Abudayyeh, O.; Zidan, S.J.; Yehia, S.; Randolph, D. Hybrid prequalification-based, innovative contracting model using AHP. *ASCE J. Manag. Eng.* **2007**, *23*, 88–96. [CrossRef]

28. Mahdi, I.M.; Alreshaid, K. Decision support system for selecting the proper project delivery method using analytical hierarchy process (AHP). *Int. J. Proj. Manag.* **2005**, *23*, 564–572. [CrossRef]
29. Cheung, F.K.T.; Kuen, J.L.F.; Skitmore, M. Multi-criteria evaluation model for the selection of architectural consultants. *Constr. Manag. Econ.* **2002**, *20*, 569–580. [CrossRef]
30. Wakchaure, S.S.; Jha, K.N. Determination of bridge health index using analytical hierarchy process. *Constr. Manag. Econ.* **2012**, *30*, 133–149. [CrossRef]
31. Chan, E.H.W.; Suen, H.C.H.; Chan, C.K.L. MAUT-based dispute resolution selection model prototype for international construction projects. *ASCE J. Constr. Eng. Manag.* **2006**, *132*, 444–451. [CrossRef]
32. Taylan, O.; Bafail, A.O.; Abdulaal, R.M.S.; Kabli, M.R. Construction projects selection and risk assessment by fuzzy AHP and fuzzy TOPSIS methodologies. *Appl. Soft Comput.* **2014**, *17*, 105–116. [CrossRef]
33. Antoniou, F.; Aretoulis, G.N. A multi criteria decision making support system for choice of method of compensation for highway construction contractors in Greece. *Int. J. Constr. Manag.* **2018**, *3*, 71. [CrossRef]
34. Antoniou, F.; Konstantinidis, D.; Aretoulis, G. Application of the multi attribute utility theory for the selection of project procurement system for Greek highway projects. *Int. J. Manag. Decis. Mak.* **2016**, *15*, 83–112. [CrossRef]
35. Darko, A.; Chan, A.P.C.; Ameyaw, E.E.; Owusu, E.K.; Pärn, E.; Edwards, D.J. Review of application of analytic hierarchy process (AHP) in construction. *Int. J. Constr. Manag.* **2019**, *19*, 436–452. [CrossRef]
36. Gunatilaka, R.N.; Abdeen, F.N.; Sepasgozar, S.M.E. Developing a Scoring System to Evaluate the Level of Smartness in Commercial Buildings: A Case of Sri Lanka. *Buildings* **2021**, *11*, 644. [CrossRef]
37. Al Dakheel, J.; Del Pero, C.; Aste, N.; Leonforte, F. Smart Buildings Features and Key Performance Indicators: A Review. *Sustain. Cities Soc.* **2020**, *61*, 102328. [CrossRef]
38. Ghansah, F.A.; Owusu-Manu, D.G.; Ayarkwa, J.; Darko, A.; Edwards, D.J. Underlying indicators for measuring smartness of buildings in the construction industry. *Smart Sustain. Built Environ.* **2022**, *11*, 126–142. [CrossRef]
39. Yuliastri, I.R.; Amani, H. Indicators to Measure a Smart Building: An Indonesian Perspective. *Int. J. Comput. Theory Eng.* **2017**, *9*, 406–411.
40. Singh, T.; Solanki, A.; Sharma, S.K. Role of Smart Buildings in Smart City—Components, Technology, Indicators, Challenges, Future Research Opportunities. In *Digital Cities Roadmap: IoT-Based Architecture and Sustainable Buildings*; Solanki, A., Kumar, A., Nayyar, A., Eds.; Wiley-Scrivener: Hoboken, NJ, USA, 2021; Chapter 14.
41. Jain, K. *Development of a Smart Building Evaluation System for Office Buildings*; Technische Universitat Berlin: Berlin, Germany, 2019.
42. Varma, C.R.S.; Palaniappan, S. Comparision of green building rating schemes used in North America, Europe and Asia. *Habitat Int.* **2019**, *89*, 101989. [CrossRef]
43. Omar, O. Intelligent building, definitions, factors and evaluation criteria of selection. *Alex. Eng. J.* **2018**, *57*, 2903–2910. [CrossRef]
44. Benavente-Peces, C. On the energy efficiency in the next generation of smart buildings—Supporting technologies and techniques. *Energies* **2019**, *12*, 4399. [CrossRef]
45. Behzadi, A.; Arabkoohsar, A.; Yang, Y. Optimization and dynamic techno-economic analysis of a novel PVT-based smart building energy system. *Appl. Therm. Eng.* **2020**, *181*, 115926. [CrossRef]
46. Ho, H.C.; Puika, K.S.; Kasih, T.P. Development of IoT-based water reduction system for improving clean water conservation. *Prz. Nauk. Inz. Kształt. Sr.* **2020**, *29*, 54–61. [CrossRef]
47. Amoeda, R. Conservation of Materials Resources by Buildings Reuse and on Site Materials Reuse Strategies. In Proceedings of the Congreso Internacional de Costrucción Sostenible y Soluciones Ecoeficientes, Sevilla, Spain, 25–27 May 2015; pp. 983–994.
48. Dryjanski, M.; Buczkowski, M.; Ould-Cheikh-Mouhamedou, Y.; Kliks, A. Adoption of smart cities with a practical smart building implementation. *IEEE Internet Things Mag.* **2020**, *3*, 58–63. [CrossRef]
49. Fokaides, P.A.; Panteli, C.; Panayidou, A. How Are the Smart Readiness Indicators Expected to Afect the Energy Performance of Buildings: First Evidence and Perspectives. *Sustainability* **2020**, *12*, 9496. [CrossRef]
50. Lawrence, T.M.; Boudreau, M.C.; Helsen, L.; Henze, G.; Mohammadpour, J.; Noonan, D.; Patteeuw, D.; Pless, S.; Watson, R.T. Ten questions concerning integrating smart buildings into the smart grid. *Build. Environ.* **2016**, *108*, 273–283. [CrossRef]
51. Froufe, M.M.; Chinelli, C.K.; Guedes, A.L.A.; Haddad, A.N.; Hammad, A.W.A.; Soares, C.A.P. Smart buildings: Systems and drivers. *Buildings* **2020**, *10*, 153. [CrossRef]
52. Catarinucci, L.; de Donno, D.; Mainetti, L.; Palano, L.; Patrono, L.; Stefanizzi, M.; Tarricone, L. An IoT-aware architecture for smart healthcare systems. *IEEE Internet Things J.* **2015**, *2*, 515–526. [CrossRef]
53. Pozo, A.; Alonso, Á.; Salvachúa, J. Evaluation of an IoT Application-Scoped Access Control Model over a Publish/Subscribe Architecture Based on FIWARE. *Sensors* **2020**, *20*, 4341. [CrossRef] [PubMed]
54. Lin, C.Y.; Chu, E.T.H.; Ku, L.W.; Liu, J.W.S. Active disaster response system for a smart building. *Sensors* **2014**, *14*, 17451–17470. [CrossRef] [PubMed]
55. Yun, J.; Lee, S.S. Human movement detection and identification using pyroelectric infrared sensors. *Sensors* **2014**, *14*, 8057–8081. [CrossRef] [PubMed]
56. Amin, U.; Hossain, M.J.; Lu, J.; Fernandez, E. Performance analysis of an experimental smart building: Expectations and outcomes. *Energy* **2017**, *135*, 740–753. [CrossRef]

57. Sembroiz, D.; Ricciardi, S.; Careglio, D. A novel cloud-based IoT architecture for smart building automation. In *Security and Resilience in Intelligent Data-Centric Systems and Communication Networks*; Elsevier: Amsterdam, The Netherlands, 2018; pp. 215–233.
58. Eini, R.; Linkous, L.; Zohrabi, N.; Abdelwahed, S. Smart building management system: Performance specifications and design requirements. *J. Build. Eng.* **2021**, *39*, 102222. [CrossRef]
59. Atanassov, K. *Intuitionistic Fuzzy Sets*; Springer: Heidelberg, Germany, 1999.
60. Yager, R.R. Pythagorean fuzzy subsets. In Proceedings of the 2013 Joint IFSA World Congress and NAFIPS Annual Meeting (IFSA/NAFIPS), Edmonton, AB, Canada, 24–28 June 2013; pp. 57–61.
61. Peng, X.; Yang, Y. Some results for Pythagorean fuzzy sets. *Int. J. Intell. Syst.* **2015**, *30*, 1133–1160. [CrossRef]
62. Yager, R.R. Properties and applications of Pythagorean fuzzy sets. In *Imprecision and Uncertainty in Information Representation and Processing*; Angelov, P., Sotirov, S., Eds.; Springer: Cham, Switzerland, 2016; pp. 119–136.
63. Zhang, X.; Xu, Z. Extension of TOPSIS to multiple criteria decision making with Pythagorean fuzzy sets. *Int. J. Intell. Syst.* **2014**, *29*, 1061–1078. [CrossRef]
64. Cui, R.; Gallino, S.; Moreno, A.; Zhang, D.J. The Operational Value of Social Media Information. *Prod. Oper. Manag.* **2018**, *27*, 1749–1769. [CrossRef]
65. Oztaysi, B.; Cevik Onar, S.; Seker, S.; Kahraman, C. Water treatment technology selection using hesitant Pythagorean fuzzy hierachical decision making. *J. Intell. Fuzzy Syst.* **2019**, *37*, 867–884. [CrossRef]
66. Garg, H. A novel accuracy function under interval-valued Pythagorean fuzzy environment for solving multicriteria decision making problem. *J. Intell. Fuzzy Syst.* **2016**, *31*, 529–540. [CrossRef]
67. Garg, H. New exponential operational laws and their aggregation operators for interval-valued Pythagorean fuzzy multicriteria decision-making. *Int. J. Intell. Syst.* **2018**, *33*, 653–683. [CrossRef]
68. Bhat, S.A.; Singh, A.; Qudaim, A.A. A New Pythagorean Fuzzy Analytic Hierarchy Process Based on Interval-Valued Pythagorean Fuzzy Numbers. *Fuzzy Optim. Model.* **2021**, *2*, 38–51.
69. Karasan, A.; Ilbahar, E.; Kahraman, C. A novel pythagorean fuzzy AHP and its application to landfill site selection problem. *Soft Comput.* **2019**, *3*, 10953–10968. [CrossRef]
70. Ceballos, B.; Lamata, M.T.; Pelta, D.A. A comparative analysis of multi-criteria decision-making methods. *Prog. Artif. Intell.* **2016**, *5*, 315–322. [CrossRef]
71. Sałabun, W.; Urbaniak, K. A new coefficient of rankings similarity in decision-making problems. In Proceedings of the International Conference on Computational Science, Amsterdam, The Netherlands, 3–5 June 2020; Springer: Cham, Switzerland, 2020.

axioms

MDPI

Article

Prediction of Mechanical Properties of Rubberized Concrete Incorporating Fly Ash and Nano Silica by Artificial Neural Network Technique

Musa Adamu [1,*], Andaç Batur Çolak [2], Yasser E. Ibrahim [1,*], Sadi I. Haruna [3] and Mukhtar Fatihu Hamza [4]

1 Engineering Management Department, College of Engineering, Prince Sultan University, Riyadh 11586, Saudi Arabia
2 Information Technologies Application and Research Center, Istanbul Commerce University, Istanbul 34445, Turkey
3 Department of Civil Engineering, Bayero University Kano, Kano 700223, Nigeria
4 Department of Mechanical Engineering, College of Engineering in Alkharj, Prince Sattam bin Abdulaziz University, Alkharj 11942, Saudi Arabia
* Correspondence: madamu@psu.edu.sa (M.A.); ymansour@psu.edu.sa (Y.E.I.)

Abstract: The use of enormous amounts of material is required for production. Due to the current emphasis on the environment and sustainability of materials, waste products and by-products, including silica fume and fly ash (FA), are incorporated into concrete as a substitute partially for cement. Additionally, concrete fine aggregate has indeed been largely replaced by waste materials like crumb rubber (CR), thus it reduces the mechanical properties but improved some other properties of the concrete. To decrease the detrimental effects of the CR, concrete is therefore enhanced with nanomaterials such nano silica (NS). The concrete mechanical properties are essential for the designing and constRuction of concrete structures. Concrete with several variables can have its mechanical characteristics predicted by an artificial neural network (ANN) technique. Using ANN approaches, this paper predict the mechanical characteristics of concrete constructed with FA as a partial substitute for cement, CR as a partial replacement for fine aggregate, and NS as an addition. Using an artificial neural network (ANN) technique, the mechanical characteristics investigated comprise splitting tensile strength (Fs), compressive strength (Fc), modulus of elasticity (Ec) and flexural strength (Ff). The ANN model was used to train and test the dataset obtained from the experimental program. Fc, Fs, F_f and Ec were predicted from added admixtures such as CR, NS, FA and curing age (P). The modelling result indicated that ANN predicted the strength with high accuracy. The proportional deviation mean (MoD) values calculated for F_c, F_s, F_f and E_c values were −0.28%, 0.14%, 0.87% and 1.17%, respectively, which are closed to zero line. The resulting ANN model's mean square error (MSE) values and coefficient of determination (R^2) are 6.45×10^{-2} and 0.99496, respectively.

Keywords: crumb rubber; fly ash; nano silica; mechanical characteristics; artificial neural network

MSC: 68T07

1. Introduction

Numerous works have been published in the literature to better understand how well concrete performs mechanically, which is one of the most commonly used artificial materials in the construction industry. The conceptualization and construction of civil engineering structures largely depend on the laboratory measurements of the concrete's strength properties, which are subjected to environmental condition such as temperature, humidity, age and concrete compositions etc. [1–3]. In addition, various admixtures modified both fresh and hardeening properties of concrete which include crumb rubber (CR) [4,5] nanomaterials [6–9], polymer materials [10–12], fiber-reinforcement [13–17], and pozzolonic materials [18–20].

Other waste materials/recycing materials were also used for modifications of different types of concrete, for example crushed glass waste was used as partial replacement to aggregates aggregate in concrete and was redported to enhance the flexural strength of the concrete [21]; waste glass powder as partial substitute to cement decreased the slump and mechanical strengths of concrete, but when used as partial replacement to aggregates it improves the concrete's strengths [22,23]; waste lathe scrap were also found to improve the compressive strength and mechanical features of reinforced concrete beams [24]; recycled coal bottom ash as replacement to fine aggregate was found to increase the deflection of reinforced concrete beams [25]; waste marble waste as partial subsitutue to cement was found to reduce the compressive strength and crack behavior of reinforced concrete beams [26]. Therefore, mechanical properties of concrete depends mainly on its constituent material and admixtures [5,27,28]. Presently, artificial intelligent technique have been demonstrating a rubost capacity in training complex dataset of estimating purpose. For instance, Chou, Tsai [29] created an ensemble model using an ANN model, a support vector machine (SVM) for estimating the concrete's strength. The compressive strength of the existing concrete structure has being estimating through different input parameter using ANN model [30]. Chopra, Sharma [31] used genetic programming and an ANN model to analyse the concrete's compressive strength. Rebound hammer and UPV deta sets were applied, as input parameters.The employment of artificial intelligence tools in data forecasting has been widely used recently. Among the artificial intelligence technologies utilised in various technical domains is the ANN, which was inspired by the biological configuration of humans. In certain works of literature, the mechanical characteristics of cement mortars and concrete materials were modelled using ANN. Jang and Xing [32] measured the emissions of ammonia from mortar containing various fly ash types and observed a strongly relationships between the emissions and the fly ash contents, mortar size and age. Then, they used ANN models for predicting the concentration of ammonia under different conditions. The study's results showed that the genetic algorithm ANN models had the least root mean square error (RMSE) when compared to real outputs. Althoey, Akhter [33] compared the performace of different model for Marshall Mix Parameters Using Bio-inspired Genetic Programming and Deep Machine Learning techniques. The comparison analysis result indicates that ANN, ANFIS, MEP and DT-Bagging are all effective and reliable technique for the estimation of Marshall Stability and Marshall Flow. Similarly, Madenci and Özkılıç [34] explore the effect of porosity on free vibration analysis of functionally graded (FG) beams using analytical and numerical approaches. An ANN model and backpropagation technique were used by Felix, Carrazedo [35] to estimate the depth of carbonation in concretes containing fly ash. For networks with two hidden layers, the ANN model that was developed utilizing a collection of 90 data points, can create models with determination coefficient higher than 0.8. The optimized configuration was able to give the smallest RMMSE linked with the highest coefficient of determination. Based on the parametric study, it was found that fly ash and, CO_2 ratio, cement contents and relative humidity were the primary factor which influence the carbonation depth in fly ash-concrete. The suggested models could also be used for simulating the growth of engineering projects focused on durability as well as to anticipate the lifespan of concrete structures. In the study by Pazouki [36], three different models including, group data processing technique, optimization algorithm of ant colony and ANN supported radial based functional neural network are proposed for predicting the compressive strength of the fly ash originated from geopolymer concrete. In this study, 360 samples of fly ash-based geopolymer concrete were used to generate the data set for this investigation. An accuracy and estimation capacity of the models were evaluated with statistical formulas and the models were correlated with an experimental test result. The research revealed that all of the models could predict this mechanical characteristic of fly ash-originated from geopolymer concrete with acceptable accuracy, but that the radial-based function neural network had the best correlation when correlated with the other models. Models to predict the drying shrinkage of alkali-activated fly ash-black furnace mortars were developed by Adesanya, Aladejare [37]. In the experimental study, several factors were taken into account, and the impact of mortars on drying shrinkage was examined. The drying shrinkage of the mortar at 28 days were estimated using multiple linear regression and ANN models. Based on the validations, the experimental results and ANN models were highly correlated. Çelik, Yildiz [38] proposed an ANN model to examine how nano silica combined with a fly ash affects rheological characteristics for cementitious mortars. Experimental research was conducted on the effects of nanosilica as an additive upon the plastic viscosities and values of yield stress for cement-based mortars with varying concentrations of volatile additives as ash mineral additives. In order to use the results of the experiments to evaluate the plastic viscosities and yield stresses of cement originated from mortars incorporating nanosilica, a feedforward backpropagation ANN model has been developed. The proposed models were stated to have very good predictive accuracy.ANN modelling is getting more popularity and has been used to solve several engineering tasks. ANN recorded many successes in civil and structural engineering application. It has been used to predicts concrete durability [39], estimating load-displacement curve of concrete [40], and concrete strength [41]. The fundamental benefit of ANNs is that no particular equation is required. The relationship between variables is automatically managed by ANN, which also is adapted according to the training dataset. Several studies have employed the application of many models, which include ensemble model, hybrid, and boosted model. However, few studies evaluated the concrete mechanical properties using a single model. Due to its extremely robust and effectiveness in solving complicated problems, the study employed ANN model to evaluate mechanical of concrete. Therefore, the aim of this study was to predict the mechanical properties of concrete containing crumb rubber, fly ash, and nano silica. The properties of the concrete predicted includes compressive and flexural strengths, and modulus of elasticity. The predicted models will help to reduce the number of experiments required and save cost and time.

2. Materials and Methods

2.1. Materials

The primary binder material was Grade 42.5R cement (Type I), which meets the standards for cement composition as forth in ASTM C150 [42]. Table 1 provides a summary of the cement's characteristics. A white dispersive powder form of commercially available nanosilica obtained from Zhengzhou Dongshen Petrochemical Technology Co., (Zhengzhou, China) in China was added to the cementitious ingredients by weight. The amorphous structure of the nanosilica made it suitable to be utilized as a pozzolanic material as well as a filler. Table 2 provides a summary of the nanosilica's characteristics. In this investigation, cement was partially substituted in high volume with low-calcium Class F fly ash. The fly ash was obtained from YTL cement Berhad, Kuala Lumpur Malaysia. The fly ash met the ASTM C618 [43] standard criteria. Table 1 provides a summary of the fly ash's characteristics. The fine aggregate utilized was natural sand. The fine aggregate's minimum size is 4.75 mm, it has a 2.65 specific gravity, 1.24% water absorption, and a 2.86 fineness modulus. Figure 1 shows the fine aggregate's particle size gradation. The particle size gradation of the fine aggregate was carried out in accordance with ASTM C136 [44]. For the coarse aggregate, natural gravels were crushed. The maximum particle size for the coarse aggregate is 19 mm, the specific gravity is 2.66, and water absorption is 0.48 percent. The particle size analysis of the coarse aggregate was done in accordance with ASTM C136 [44], and the gradation curve is presented in Figure 1.

Table 1. Characteristics of binder.

Composition of Oxides	Quantity by Mass (%)	
	Cements	Fly Ash
SiO_2 (%)	20.76	57.06
CaO (%)	61.4	9.79
Al_2O_3 (%)	5.54	20.96
Fe_2O_3	3.35	4.15
MgO (%)	2.48	0.033
Na_2O (%)	0.19	2.23
K_2O (%)	0.78	1.53
TiO_2 (%)	-	0.68
SO_3 (%)	1.49	-
Loss of ignition (%)	2.2	1.25
Specific gravity	3.15	2.4
Blaine fineness (m^2/kg)	325	290

Table 2. Characteristics of binder.

Items	Qualities
Average particle size (nm)	10–25
Hydrophobicity	Strong
SiO_2 (dry base) (%)	≥92
SiO_2 (%) (950 °C 2 h)	≥99.8
Specific surface area (m^2/g)	100 ± 25
PH value	6.5–7.5
Surface density (g/mL)	≤0.15
Hear reduction (%) (105 °C 2 h)	≤3
Loss of ignition (%) (950 °C 2 h)	≤6
Dispensability (%) (%) (CCl_4)	≥80
Oil-absorbed value (mL/100 g)	≥250
Hydrophobicity	Strong

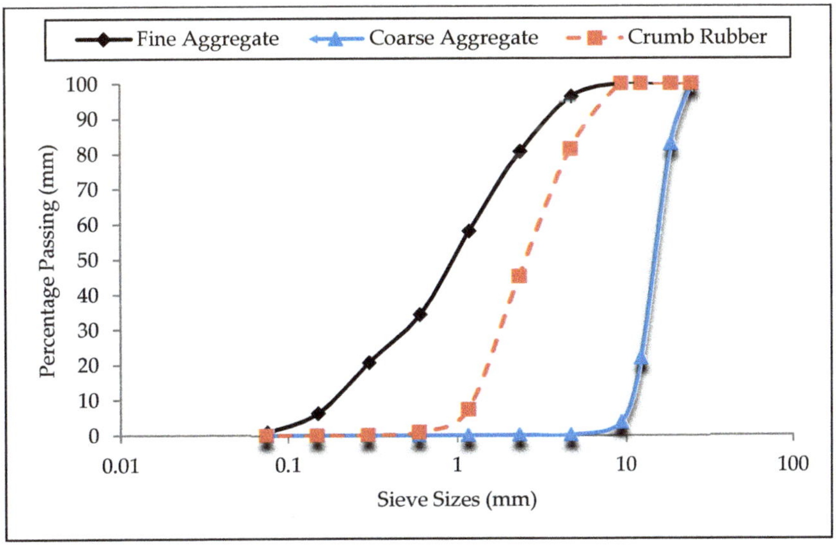

Figure 1. Aggregate's particle size distribution.

CR was used to partially replace fine aggregate. The CR was obtained from scrap tire after it was grinded and reduced to smaller sizes ranging in sizes between 4.75 mm to 75 μm. Before adding to the concrete, the CR was thoroughly washed using clean water to remove all dirts and impurites and then air dried for 48 h to make it completely dry. In order to get the same gradation with the fine aggregate it is replaced, three different sizes of CR were blended together. The sizes ae 3–5 mm sizes, 1–3 mm sizes, and mesh 30 (0.6 mm) sizes, in proportions of 20%, 40% and 40% correspondigly. The particle size gradation of the CR was determined using the standard procedures outlined in ASTM D5644 [45], and the gradation curveis shown in Figure 1 and was found to have similar gradation curve to the fine aggregate it partially replaced. Figure 2 presents the photos of the CR used in this study. The CR had a specific gravity of 0.93 and bulk density of 978 kg/m^3 and water absorpion of 0.6%. The CR was used to replace fine aggregate in different proportions of 0%, 10%, 20% and 30% by volume fraction of the aggregate. The summary of the mass fractions of the chemical components of the CR is summarized in Table 3.

(**a**) Mesh 30 CR (**b**) 1–3 mm CR

(**c**) 3–5 mm CR

Figure 2. Crumb rubber used.

Table 3. Chemical Composition of CR. Reprinted with permission from Ref. [46] Copyright 2023 Elsevier BV.

Chemical	C	O	Si	Zn	S	Mg	Al
Composition by Mass (%)	87.5	9.24	0.2	1.77	1.07	0.14	0.08

2.2. Mix Proportioning

This study's concrete was roller-compacted concrete pavement (RCCP). The mixed design is completed using the geotechnical method of design (soil compaction procedure), depending on a flexural strength target of 4.8 MPa, which is equivalent to C30/37 target compressive strength grade in accordance with the guidelines ACI 211.3R [47] and CRD-C 162 [48]. 13% by weight of the dry aggregates was the cement content used. To achieve the standard gradation and requirements of ACI 211.3R [47] and CRD-C 162 [48] for RCCP, fine sand passing 75 μm sieve was used as mineral filler. The mineral filler added was 5% of the total aggregates. To make the mixtures more consistent, a high-range water reduction additive (superplasticizer) was added. Superplasticizer usage was limited to 1% of the weight of cementitious materials. In all the mixes, the percentage replacement of cement with fly ash was kept to 50%. The CR was added at different proportions of 0%, 10%, 20% and 30% by volume replacement to fine aggregate, and nanosilica was added at 0.0%, 1.0%, 2.0% and 3.0% by weight of binder materials. Table 4 displays the mix proportions and constituent ingredients for each of the mixes used for the ANN modelling.

Table 4. Mix Proportions.

Mixes	Variables (%)			Materials Constituent (kg/m^3)							
	Fly Ash	CR	NS	Cement	Fly ash	NS	Fine Aggregate	CR	Coarse Aggregate	Water	SP
Control	0	0	0	268.69	0	0	1148.05	0	831.88	98.24	2.69
1	50	0	0	134.58	102.54	0	1150.08	0	831.88	96.87	2.37
2	50	0	1	134.58	102.54	2.37	1150.08	0	831.88	96.87	2.39
3	50	0	2	134.58	102.54	4.74	1150.08	0	831.88	96.87	2.42
4	50	0	3	134.58	102.54	7.11	1150.08	0	831.88	96.87	2.44
5	50	10	0	134.58	102.54	0	1035.07	115.08	831.88	96.87	2.37
6	50	10	1	134.58	102.54	2.37	1035.07	115.08	831.88	96.87	2.39
7	50	10	2	134.58	102.54	4.74	1035.07	115.08	831.88	96.87	2.42
8	50	10	3	134.58	102.54	7.11	1035.07	115.08	831.88	96.87	2.44
9	50	20	0	134.58	102.54	0	920.06	230.17	831.88	96.87	2.37
10	50	20	1	134.58	102.54	2.37	920.06	230.17	831.88	96.87	2.39
11	50	20	2	134.58	102.54	4.74	920.06	230.17	831.88	96.87	2.42
12	50	20	3	134.58	102.54	7.11	920.06	230.17	831.88	96.87	2.44
13	50	30	0	134.58	102.54	0	805.05	345.27	831.88	96.87	2.37
14	50	30	1	134.58	102.54	2.37	805.05	345.27	831.88	96.87	2.39
15	50	30	2	134.58	102.54	4.74	805.05	345.27	831.88	96.87	2.42
16	50	30	3	134.58	102.54	7.11	805.05	345.27	831.88	96.87	2.44

2.3. Testing Procedures

The concrete was weighed, batched and mixed in accordance to the procedures outlined in ASTM C192/192M [49] standards using a pan type concrete mixer as shown in Figure 3a. The freshly mixed concrete was cast into the proper moulds after a uniform mix had been achieved in accordancce with the guidelines outlined in ASTM C1435/C1435M [50]. Since RCCP is a dry, rigid mix, adequate compaction cannot be achieved using the usual compaction techniques of a vibration table or tamping rod. Therefore, A 50-Hz vibration hammer is used to compact the mixtures in the molds as shown in Figure 3b. Each layer was then crushed after being poured into the mould until a ring of mortar had formed around the plate's edge that was attached to the hammer. In compliance with the ASTM C1435/C1435M [50], this compaction was carried out. The concrete was left in the laboratory after casting for at least 24 h to settle and solidify. After samples being demolded, then stored in water till the test day.

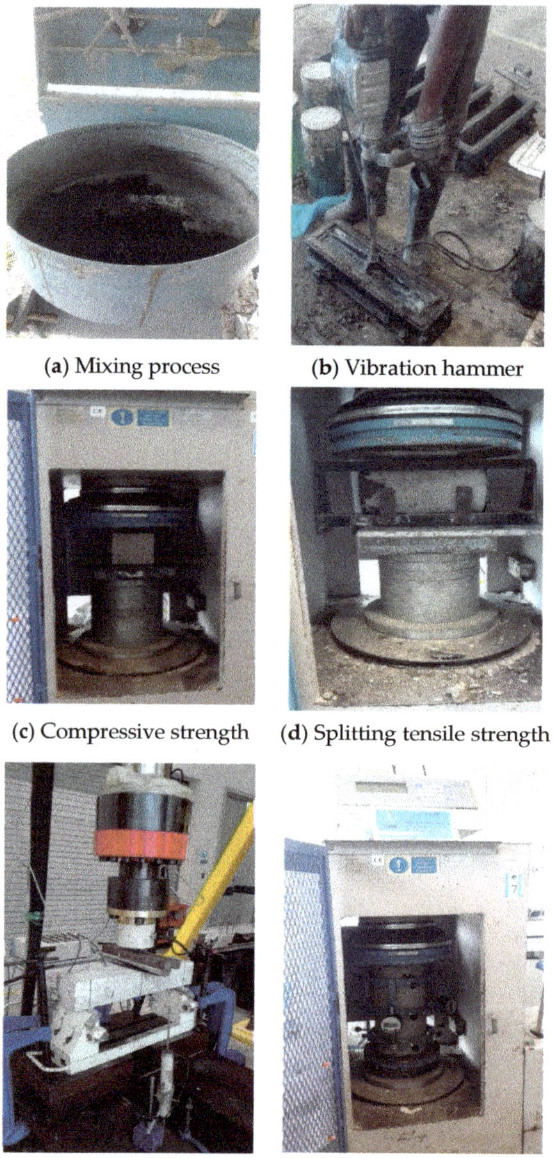

(**a**) Mixing process (**b**) Vibration hammer
(**c**) Compressive strength (**d**) Splitting tensile strength
(**e**) Flexural strength (**f**) Modulus of elasticity

Figure 3. Experimental setup.

According to BS EN 12390-3 [51] requirements, the compressive strength's tests for concrete was conducted using cubic specimen of (100 × 100 × 100) mm at 3, 7 and 28 days using a Universal Testing Machine (UTM) with a 2000 kN capacity as shown in Figure 3c. According to BS EN 12390-6 [52] a cylindrical sample having a diameter and height of 100 mm and 200 mm, respectively was utilized in splitting tensile test as shown in Figure 3d. A 2000 kN capacity UTM was utilized for the splitting tensile strength test. As per ASTM C293/C293M [53] specifications, beam samples measuring (100, 100, 500) mm as shown in Figure 3e were utilized for the flexural strength tests. Beam with center point load method was used for measuring the flexural strength. A self-straining loading frame containing a 500 kN dynamic servo-controlled actuator was used for the testing. The load was applied on the samples at a constant speed of 0.1 mm/s. The modulus of elasticity test was conducted in accordance with ASTM C469/C469M [54] using a 2000 kN UTM [37], utilizing cylinder specimen having diameter and height of 150 mm 300 mm, respectively. Longitudinal and lateral compressormeters of 200 mm effective gauge lengths were mounted centrally at mid-height of each sample to capture the lateral and longitudinal strain during loading as presented in Figure 3f. The longitudinal and lateral strains were used to compute the modulus of elasticity of the samples. For ensure accuracy of each of the tests, three samples were tested for each experiment and the average value was recorded.

2.4. ANN Modelling

For predicting the values of Fc, Fs, Ff and Ec in relation to CR, NS, FA and P parameters, a multilayer perceptron (MLP) ANN model was created. Due to their excellent prediction performance, MLP network models, which possesses a layer design, are one of the most used models of ANN [55,56]. Fc, Fs, F_f and Ec parameters are interpreted as parameters' input in the input's layer of the proposed ANN model, and CR, NS, FA and p values are estimated in the output's layer. Among the problems in creating MLP network is the absent of a rule for estimating neurons' number contained in the hidden layer [57]. To address this issue, performance comparisons of models comprising various neurons' number in the hidden layer led to the MLP model with 15 neurons being favored. Figures 4 and 5 show the architectural configuration and basic composition of the developed MLP network, respectively.

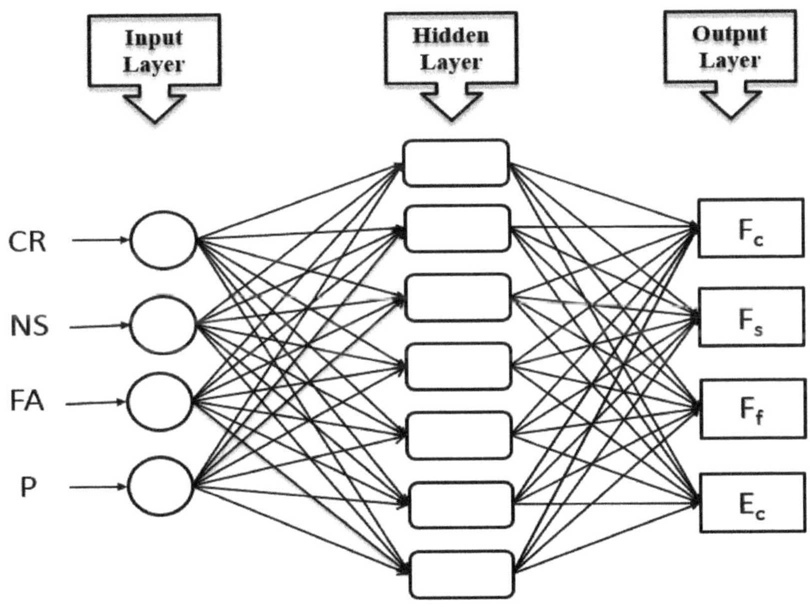

Figure 4. The MLP model's configuration architecture.

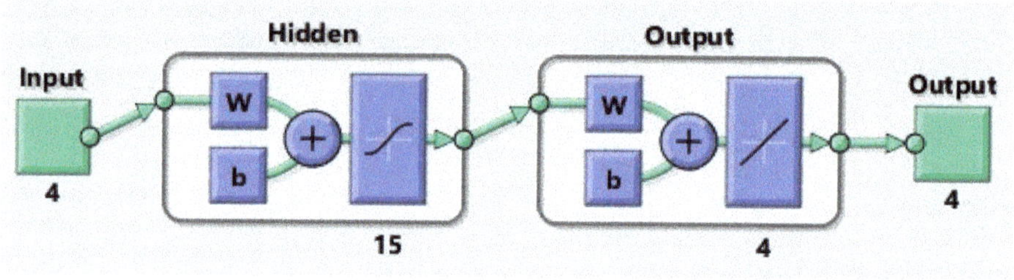

Figure 5. Basic structure of the developed MLP network.

It is crucial to optimise the data collection in the best possible way when creating ANN models [58]. Three major categories that are most frequently utilized in the literature constitute up the data used in the ANN model, which was created employing a total of 448 data sets [59]. 15% of the data were utilized for the model's validation, 15% for the model's testing, and 70 percent of the data were employed for the model's training. The results from the literature studies were used to choose the Levenberg-Marquards training's method that possesses a high capacity for learning, in order to train the MLP network [60]. Below is a list of the Purelin and Tan-Sig functions employed in hidden and output layer [61]:

$$f(x) = \frac{1}{1 + \exp(-x)} \quad (1)$$

$$\text{purelin}(x) = x \quad (2)$$

2.5. Evaluation Matrices

Equations (3)–(5) are the performance metrics employed in this study to assess the learning, training, and predicting capabilities of the developed ANN model. They are frequently used matrices for evaluating how well the proposed model performs. The formulas used to calculate the performance measures known as mean squared error (MSE), determination's coefficient (R), and a margin of deviation (MoD) are provided below [62,63]:

$$\text{MSE} = \frac{1}{N}\sum_{i=1}^{N}\left(X_{\text{targ}(i)} - X_{\text{ANN}(i)}\right)^2 \quad (3)$$

$$R = \sqrt{1 - \frac{\sum_{i=1}^{N}\left(X_{\text{targ}(i)} - X_{\text{ANN}(i)}\right)^2}{\sum_{i=1}^{N}\left(X_{\text{targ}(i)}\right)^2}} \quad (4)$$

$$\text{MoD} = \left[\frac{X_{\text{targ}} - X_{\text{ANN}}}{X_{\text{targ}}}\right] \times 100\ (\%) \quad (5)$$

3. Results and Discussion

3.1. Optimal Choice of Input Parameters

In order to simulate any data-driven model and provide the desired and precise results, the choice of potential input parameters is crucial. Therefore, including inappropriate parameters in artificial intelligent-based modeling reduces the developed model's performance accuracy and increases the computational difficulties [64–66]. However, inadequate input variables can lead to poor prediction accuracy. As a result, in our work, we used sensitivity analysis using Pearson's correlation to choose the critical most input parameter for predicting the fundamental mechanical characteristic for concrete incorporating admixtures. Four output parameters were consider in the modeling, and finding their idividual releationship with input parameters may be unuseful. However, compressive strength being the basic mechanical property was considered and evaluated for its correlation relationship with input parameters as depicted in the Figure 6. It can be seen that, the curing age demonstrate highest correlation value of 0.57 with compressive strength, this indicate curing age is most relevent parameter to mechanical characteristics of concrete incorporating these admixtures. Fly ash, CR and NS, however, show a negative relationship with compressive strength. Table 5 provides a summary of the dataset's statistical description.

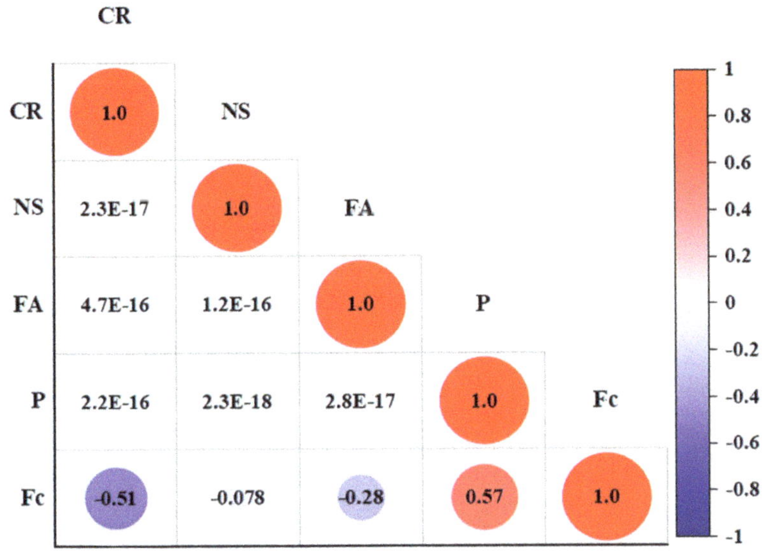

Figure 6. Correlation matrix using person correlation matrix.

Table 5. Descriptive statistic of the experimental dataset.

Direction	Parameter	Symbols	Unit	Min	Max	Mean	SD	Kurtosis	Skewness
Inputs	Crumb rubber	CR	%	0	30	15.00	11.215	−1.365	0.00
	Nano silica	NS	%	0	3	1.50	1.121	−1.365	0.00
	Fly ash	FA	%	0	50	25.00	25.078	−2.025	0.00
	Curing time	P	days	3	365	98.60	137.22	0.017	1.32
Output	Compressive strength	F_c	MPa	11.68	90.86	45.98	17.22	−0.499	0.27
	Splitting tensile	F_s	MPa	1.35	6.41	3.81	1.23	−0.559	0.096
	Flexural strength	F_f	MPa	2.60	8.89	5.32	1.32	0.482	0.707
	Modulus of elasticity	E_c	GPa	5.79	37.78	19.85	7.53	−0.393	0.440

The relative frequency distribution of the experimental dataset employed to predicts Fc, Fs, F_f and Ec is depicted in Figure 7. The distribution plots revealed that some of the variables in the dataset follow the normal or nearly normal distribution, and some datasets do not follow the normal distribution. Most of the dataset for nano silica, crumb rubber, and fly ash have being used. The frequently used value of curing age was between 28 days and 60 days, as shown in Figure 7d. All the independent parameters follows normal distribution with thier mean value of the dataset located at the centre with highes frequency value.

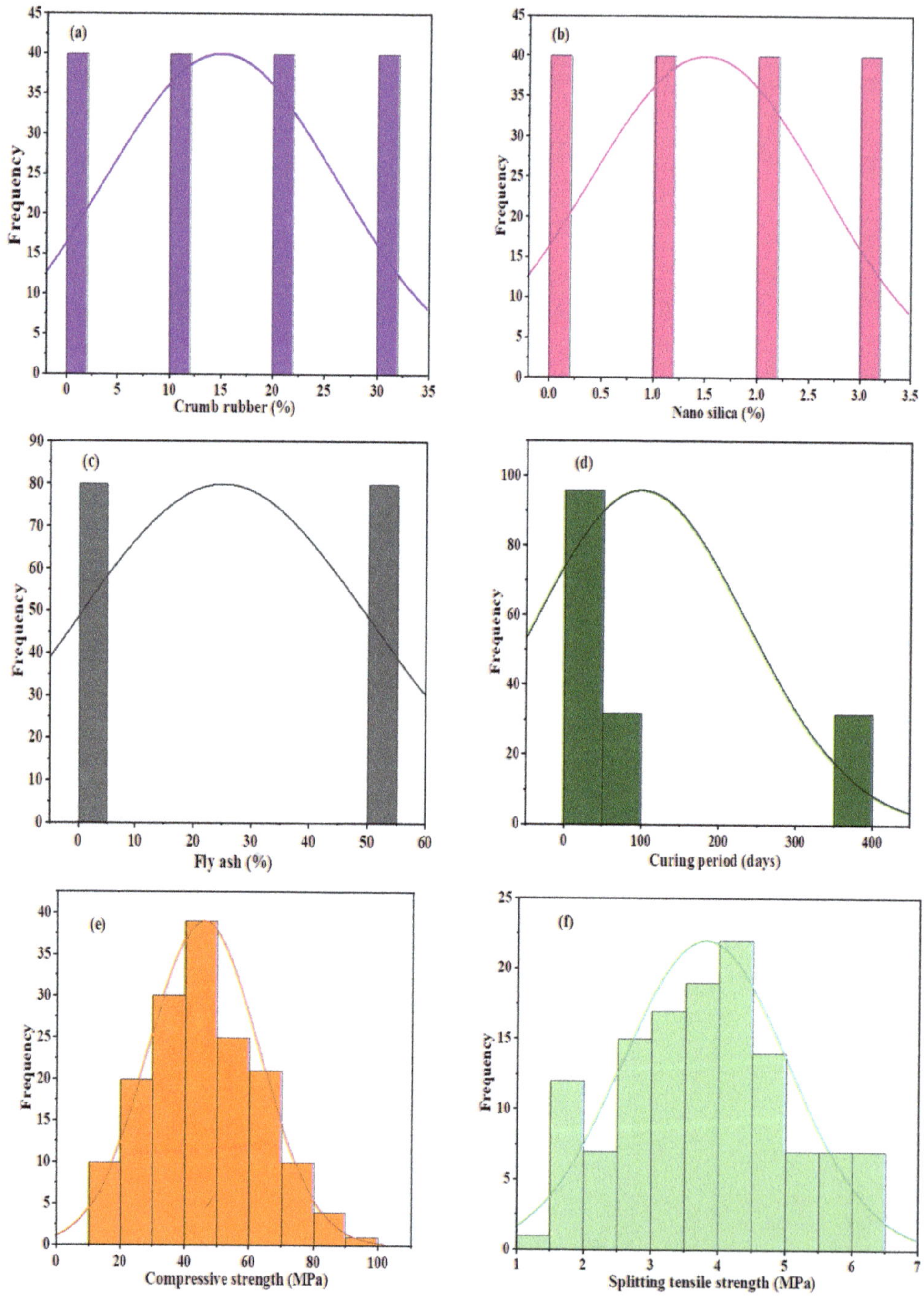

Figure 7. *Cont.*

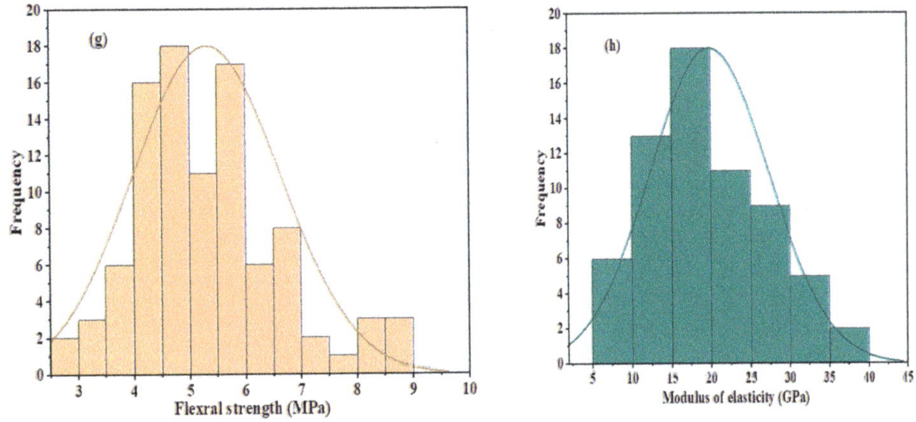

Figure 7. Distribution plot of the experimental dataset.

3.2. Modelling Results

To develop ANN model for the predictiom of mechanical properties of concrete containing admixtures, MATLAB (2021a) toolbox was used in this work. Each model was validated using the 10-fold cross-validation method [66–68]. ANN model was used to train and test the experimental datasets, including CR, fly ash, NS and curing age of the concrete, as the input parameters. On the other hand, the target parameters were calculated including, flexural strength, compressive strength, elastic modulus, and splitting tensile.

Making sure that the learning and training phases of the model are optimally completed is the first step in examining the predictive performance for ANN model. To accomplish this, it was first mandatory to look at the performance graph that the ANN model's training phase had produced. Examining the training performance graph shown in Figure 8, These MSE values are higher at the beginning of the MLP network's training step, can be shown to decrease with each passing epoch. This decline in MSE value is a sign that the deviations between the output layer's Fc, Fs, Ff and Ec values and the actual values are also declining. The 25th epoch, where the best performance was obtained for each of the three phases of the dataset, marked the end for training phase of an ANN model. The results from the performance's graph indicate that the training stage of an ANN model created for estimating the values of Fc, Fs, Ff and Ec has been completed finally.

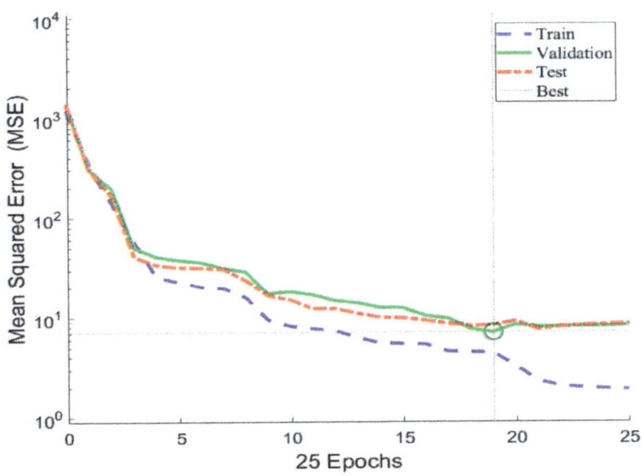

Figure 8. MLP model's training performance status.

The error histogram of the created ANN model is shown in Figure 9. The values of error obtained during the training stage are displayed in the error histogram. Whenever an error histogram is considered, the errors obtained across all three data groups often frequently located near the zero error line. An error histogram reveals that the errors' numerical values are also quite small. An error histogram results demonstrate that the constructed ANN model's training phase was finally completed with very few errors. The accuracy of the predictions acquired via the ANN model should be examined once the training phase has been validated Bulleted lists look like this:

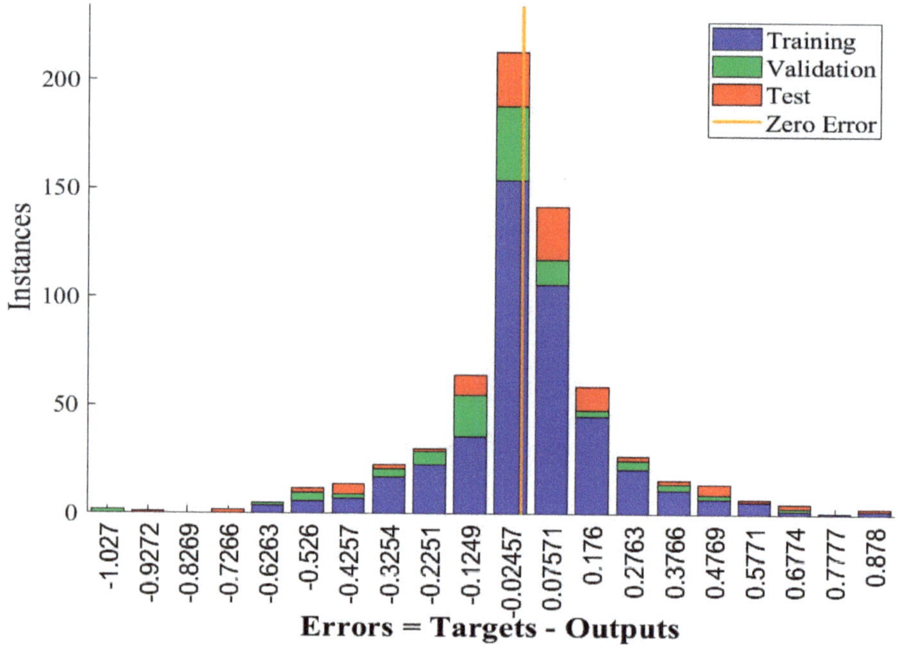

Figure 9. An Error histogram of ANN model.

3.3. *Models Predicted versus Actual Results*

For every one of the Fc, Fs, Ff and Ec parameters, Figure 10 displays an ANN predicted values and target values. The values predicted via the ANN model agree with the goal values perfectly, according to the results obtained in the Figures. The proposed ANN model can predict Fc, Fs, Ff and Ec values with excellent accuracy, as evidenced by the ideal fit between ANN estimations and target values. MoD values were produced for every data points and they are displayed in Figure 11, which expresses the proportional deviations between the values predicted from the proposed ANN model and the goal values. The data points reflecting the MoD values are placed near to the zero line error, when the figures presented for every of the Fc, Fs, Ff and Ec values are examined. The numbers, however, make it very evident that the MoD levels are quite low. The predicted mean MoD values for the Fc, Fs, Ff and Ec values were −0.28%, 0.14%, 0.87% and 1.17%, respectively.

The targeted values of the Fc, Fs, Ff and Ec values differ from the ANN outputs in Figure 12, and a more thorough investigation of the ANN model's predictive ability is planned. The graphs make it abundantly evident that the computed varaition values for every data points are small. The results of the MoD and difference values demonstrate that the constructed ANN model was developed to calculate Fc, Fs, Ff and Ec values with very low errors.

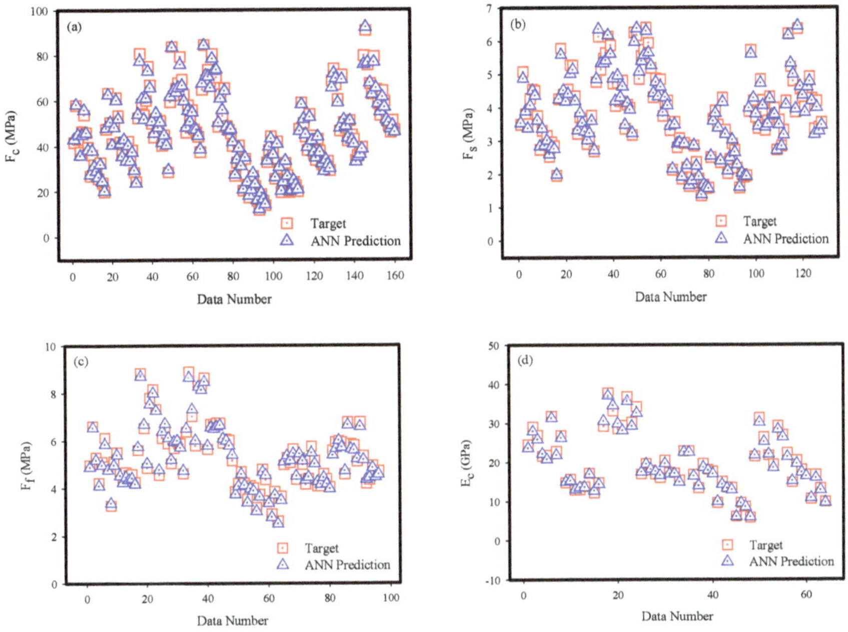

Figure 10. Predictions using ANN and targeting values considering data's number.

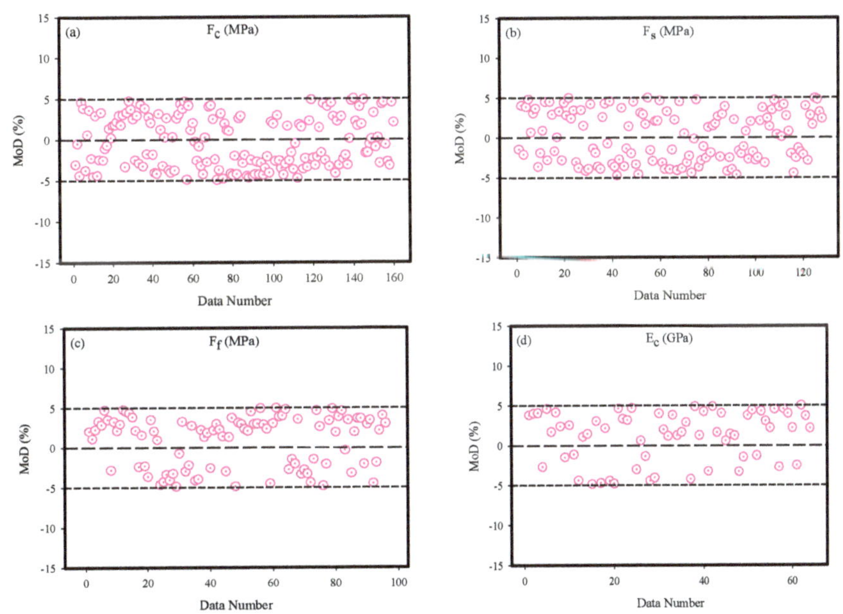

Figure 11. Values of MoD for each output considering data's number.

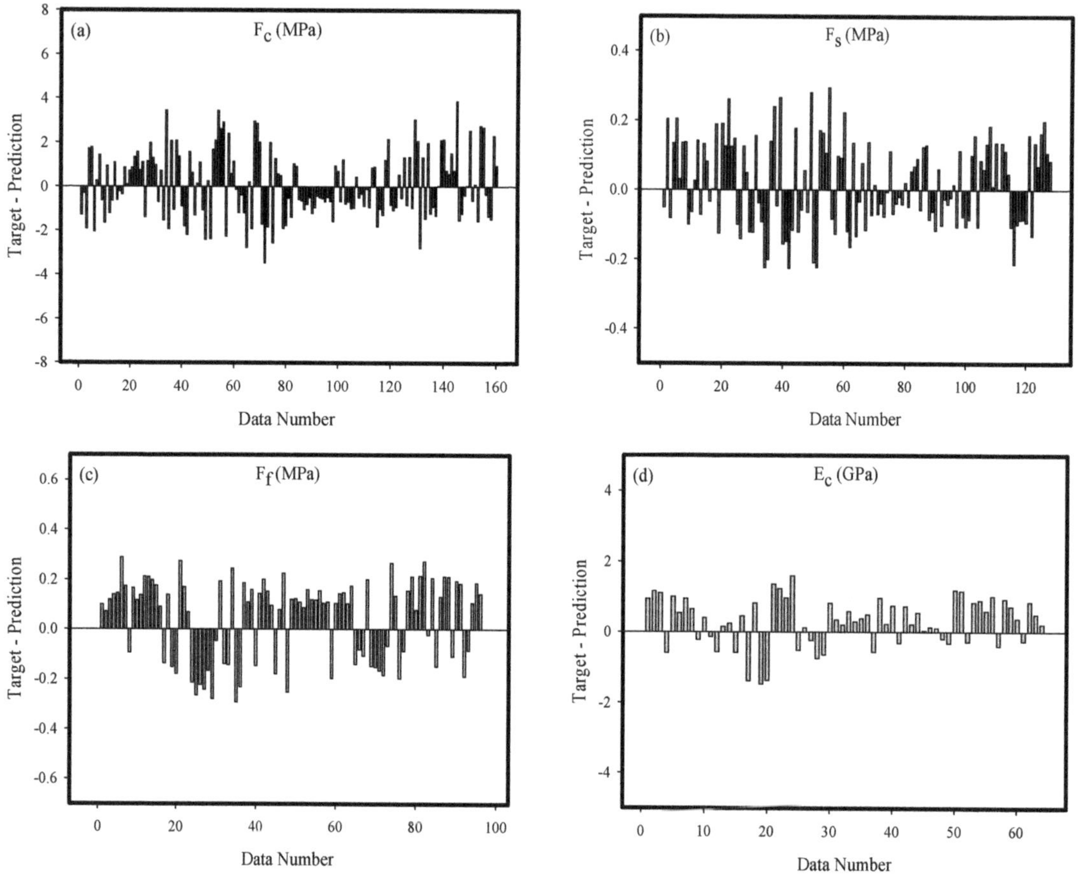

Figure 12. Various values considering data's number.

Figure 13 provides a clearer illustration of the agreement among the targeted values and ANN outputs. Every data point is illustrated to be close to the zero line error when looking at the locations of data points displayed for the Fc, Fs, Ff and Ec values. Additionally, it is noted that the data point fall within the 10 percent error limit. The MSE value for the created ANN model was calculated to be 6.45×10^{-2}, and the R value to be 0.99496. The created ANN model could be utilized in predicting Fc, Fs, Ff and Ec values having high accuracy based on the CR, NS, FA and p values, as can be observed from the perspective of all these results.

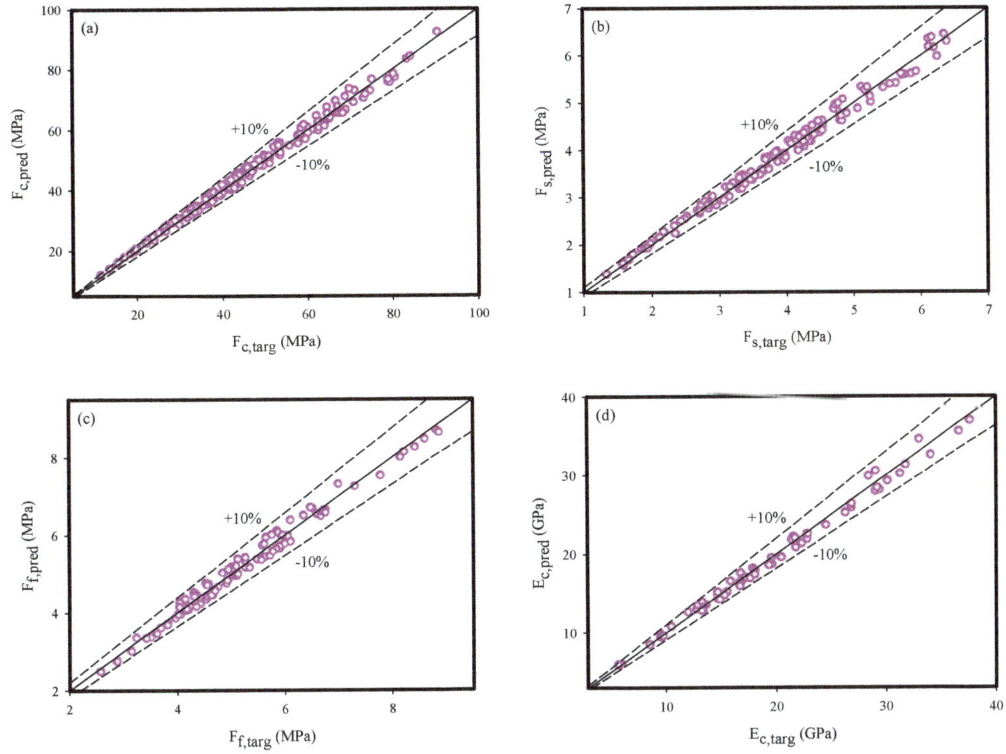

Figure 13. Target and prediction values for each output.

4. Conclusions

The ANN model is utilized to simulate the mechanical characteristics of concrete incorporating crumb rubber, nanosilica, and fly ash, including splitting tensile, compressive strength, elastic modulus, and flexural strength. The dataset for the modeling was obtained from the experimental results. The ANN model demonstrate more robust and accurate prediction skill in estimating the mechanical properties. Sensitivity analysis is utilized to optimize the ANN model's parameters, and compressive strength, a fundamental mechanical characteristic of concrete, is used to determine whether there is a linear or nonlinear relationships among an input parameters and targeted parameters. The outcome suggests that the most important factor in predicting strength is curing age. During the training phase, the proposed ANN model showed relatively low errors. The mean MoD values predicted values for Fc, Fs, Ff and Ec were −0.28%, 0.14%, 0.87% and 1.17%, respectively, which are near to the zero line. Overall, the ANN model predicted the strength with great accuracy. According to the experimental findings, fly ash and crumb rubber both reduced the mechanical strength of the concrete, however, the detrimental impact of the fly ash was only noticeable at young ages. Both the pozzolanic reactivity of fly ash and an impact of crumb rubber on mechanical characteristics of the concrete were partially alleviated by the addition of nanosilica.

Evaluating different properties such as durability generated from the modified concrete through adding admixtures in concrete such as, fibre, nanomaterial, ground glass fibre Therefore, it is recommended to capture and predict the overall concrete behavior considering these materials, and future work should focus on durability-related properties etc.

Author Contributions: Conceptualization, M.A. and Y.E.I.; methodology, M.A. and M.F.H.; software, A.B.Ç. and S.I.H.; validation, A.B.Ç. and S.I.H.; formal analysis, A.B.Ç. and S.I.H.; investigation, M.A. and M.F.H.; resources, Y.E.I.; data curation, M.A.; writing—original draft preparation, M.A., A.B.Ç. and S.I.H.; writing—review and editing, Y.E.I. and M.F.H.; visualization, M.A.; supervision, Y.E.I. All authors have read and agreed to the published version of the manuscript.

Funding: This research has no external funding. The authors acknowledge the support of Prince Sultan University in paying the article processing charges (APC) of this publication.

Data Availability Statement: Not applicable.

Acknowledgments: The authors wish to thank the Structures and Materials Research Laboratory of the College of Engineering Prince Sultan University Saudi Arabia for their viable support. Additionally, the authors would like to thank Prince sattam bin Abdulaziz University for supporting this work under project number PSAU/2023/R/1444.

Conflicts of Interest: The authors declare no conflict of interest.

References

1. Abrams, M.S. Compressive strength of concrete at temperatures to 1600F. *Spec. Publ.* **1971**, *25*, 33–58.
2. Almusallam, A.A. Effect of environmental conditions on the properties of fresh and hardened concrete. *Cem. Concr. Comp.* **2001**, *23*, 353–361. [CrossRef]
3. Kumar, R.; Bhattacharjee, B. Porosity, pore size distribution and in situ strength of concrete. *Cem. Concr. Res.* **2003**, *33*, 155–164. [CrossRef]
4. Mohammed, B.S.; Adamu, M. Mechanical performance of roller compacted concrete pavement containing crumb rubber and nano silica. *Constr. Build. Mater.* **2018**, *159*, 234–251. [CrossRef]
5. Shao, J.; Zhu, H.; Zhao, B.; Haruna, S.I.; Xue, G.; Jiang, W.; Wu, K.; Yang, J. Combined effect of recycled tire rubber and carbon nanotubes on the mechanical properties and microstructure of concrete. *Constr. Build. Mater.* **2022**, *322*, 126493. [CrossRef]
6. Adamu, M.; Haruna, S.; Ibrahim, Y.E.; Alanazi, H. Investigating the properties of roller-compacted rubberized concrete modified with nanosilica using response surface methodology. *Innov. Infrastruct. Solut.* **2022**, *7*, 119. [CrossRef]
7. Sarvandani, M.M.; Mahdikhani, M.; Aghabarati, H.; Fatmehsari, M.H. Effect of functionalized multi-walled carbon nanotubes on mechanical properties and durability of cement mortars. *J. Build. Eng.* **2021**, *41*, 102407. [CrossRef]
8. López-Carrasquillo, V.; Hwang, S. Comparative assessment of pervious concrete mixtures containing fly ash and nanomaterials for compressive strength, physical durability, permeability, water quality performance and production cost. *Constr. Build. Mater.* **2017**, *139*, 148–158. [CrossRef]
9. Murad, Y. Compressive strength prediction for concrete modified with nanomaterials. *Case Stud. Constr. Mater.* **2021**, *15*, e00660. [CrossRef]
10. Ramli, M.; Tabassi, A.A. Effects of polymer modification on the permeability of cement mortars under different curing conditions: A correlational study that includes pore distributions, water absorption and compressive strength. *Constr. Build. Mater.* **2012**, *28*, 561–570. [CrossRef]
11. Haruna, S.I.; Zhu, H.; Ibrahim, Y.E.; Shao, J.; Adamu, M.; Farouk, A.I. Experimental and Statistical Analysis of U-Shaped Polyurethane-Based Polymer Concrete under Static and Impact Loads as a Repair Material. *Buildings* **2022**, *12*, 1986. [CrossRef]
12. Al-kahtani, M.; Zhu, H.; Haruna, S.; Shao, J. Evaluation of mechanical properties of polyurethane-based polymer rubber concrete modified ground glass fiber using response surface methodology. *Arab. J. Sci. Eng.* **2022**, 1–16. [CrossRef]
13. Ong, K.; Basheerkhan, M.; Paramasivam, P. Resistance of fibre concrete slabs to low velocity projectile impact. *Cem. Concr. Comp.* **1999**, *21*, 391–401. [CrossRef]
14. Youn-Čale, B.Y.; Plückelmann, S.; Breitenbücher, R. Round robin test to compare flexural strength test methods for steel fiber-reinforced sprayed concretes. *Struct. Concr.* **2022**, *23*, 255–267. [CrossRef]
15. Malik, M.; Bhattacharyya, S.; Barai, S.V. Thermal and mechanical properties of concrete and its constituents at elevated temperatures: A review. *Constr. Build. Mater.* **2021**, *270*, 121398. [CrossRef]
16. Zeybek, Ö.; Özkılıç, Y.O.; Çelik, A.İ.; Deifalla, A.F.; Ahmad, M.; Sabri, M.M. Performance evaluation of fiber-reinforced concrete produced with steel fibers extracted from waste tire. *Front. Mater.* **2022**, *9*, 1057128. [CrossRef]
17. Aksoylu, C.; Özkılıç, Y.O.; Hadzima-Nyarko, M.; Işık, E.; Arslan, M.H. Investigation on improvement in shear performance of reinforced-concrete beams produced with recycled steel wires from waste tires. *Sustainability* **2022**, *14*, 13360. [CrossRef]
18. Haruna, S.; Malami, S.I.; Adamu, M.; Usman, A.; Farouk, A.; Ali, S.I.A.; Abba, S.I. Compressive strength of self-compacting concrete modified with rice husk ash and calcium carbide waste modeling: A feasibility of emerging emotional intelligent model (EANN) versus traditional FFNN. *Arab. J. Sci. Eng.* **2021**, *46*, 11207–11222. [CrossRef]
19. Jaya, R.; Bakar, B.; Johari, M.; Ibrahim, M. Strength and permeability properties of concrete containing rice husk ash with different grinding time. *Open Eng.* **2011**, *1*, 103–112. [CrossRef]
20. Ramasamy, V.-W. Compressive strength and durability properties of rice husk ash concrete. *KSCE J. Civ. Eng.* **2012**, *16*, 93–102. [CrossRef]

21. Çelik, A.İ.; Özkılıç, Y.O.; Zeybek, Ö.; Karalar, M.; Qaidi, S.; Ahmad, J.; Burduhos-Nergis, D.D.; Bejinariu, C. Mechanical Behavior of Crushed Waste Glass as Replacement of Aggregates. *Materials* **2022**, *15*, 8093. [CrossRef] [PubMed]
22. Zeybek, Ö.; Özkılıç, Y.O.; Karalar, M.; Çelik, A.İ.; Qaidi, S.; Ahmad, J.; Burduhos-Nergis, D.D.; Burduhos-Nergis, D.P. Influence of replacing cement with waste glass on mechanical properties of concrete. *Materials* **2022**, *15*, 7513. [CrossRef] [PubMed]
23. Basaran, B.; Kalkan, I.; Aksoylu, C.; Özkılıç, Y.O.; Sabri, M.M.S. Effects of Waste Powder, Fine and Coarse Marble Aggregates on Concrete Compressive Strength. *Sustainability* **2022**, *14*, 14388. [CrossRef]
24. Karalar, M.; Özkılıç, Y.O.; Deifalla, A.F.; Aksoylu, C.; Arslan, M.H.; Ahmad, M.; Sabri, M.M.S. Improvement in bending performance of reinforced concrete beams produced with waste lathe scraps. *Sustainability* **2022**, *14*, 12660. [CrossRef]
25. Karalar, M.; Bilir, T.; Çavuşlu, M.; Özkiliç, Y.O.; Sabri, M.M. Use of recycled coal bottom ash in reinforced concrete beams as replacement for aggregate. *Front. Mater.* **2022**, *9*, 1064604. [CrossRef]
26. Karalar, M.; Özkılıç, Y.O.; Aksoylu, C.; Sabri, M.M.S.; Alexey, N.; Sergey, A.; Evgenii, M.S. Flexural behavior of reinforced concrete beams using waste marble powder towards application of sustainable concrete. *Front. Mater.* **2022**, *9*, 1068791. [CrossRef]
27. Li, W.-W.; Ji, W.-M.; Wang, Y.-C.; Liu, Y.; Shen, R.-X.; Xing, F. Investigation on the mechanical properties of a cement-based material containing carbon nanotube under drying and freeze-thaw conditions. *Materials* **2015**, *8*, 8780–8792. [CrossRef]
28. Nambiar, E.K.; Ramamurthy, K. Models relating mixture composition to the density and strength of foam concrete using response surface methodology. *Cem. Concr. Comp.* **2006**, *28*, 752–760. [CrossRef]
29. Chou, J.-S.; Tsai, C.-F.; Pham, A.-D.; Lu, Y.-H. Machine learning in concrete strength simulations: Multi nation data analytics. *Constr. Build. Mater.* **2014**, *73*, 771–780. [CrossRef]
30. Asteris, P.G.; Mokos, V.G. Concrete compressive strength using artificial neural networks. *Neural Comput. Appl.* **2020**, *32*, 11807–11826. [CrossRef]
31. Chopra, P.; Sharma, R.K.; Kumar, M. Prediction of compressive strength of concrete using artificial neural network and genetic programming. *Adv. Mater. Sci. Eng.* **2016**, *2016*, 7648467. [CrossRef]
32. Jang, H.-S.; Xing, S. A model to predict ammonia emission using a modified genetic artificial neural network: Analyzing cement mixed with fly ash from a coal-fired power plant. *Constr. Build. Mater.* **2020**, *230*, 117025. [CrossRef]
33. Althoey, F.; Akhter, M.N.; Nagra, Z.S.; Awan, H.H.; Alanazi, F.; Khan, M.A.; Javed, M.F.; Eldin, S.M.; Özkılıç, Y.O. Prediction Models for Marshall Mix Parameters Using Bio-inspired Genetic Programming and Deep Machine Learning Approaches: A Comparative Study. *Case Stud. Constr. Mater.* **2022**, *18*, e01774. [CrossRef]
34. Madenci, E.; Özkılıç, Y.O. Free vibration analysis of open-cell FG porous beams: Analytical, numerical and ANN approaches. *Steel Comp. Struct. Int. J.* **2021**, *40*, 157–173.
35. Felix, E.F.; Carrazedo, R.; Possan, E. Carbonation model for fly ash concrete based on artificial neural network: Development and parametric analysis. *Constr. Build. Mater.* **2021**, *266*, 121050. [CrossRef]
36. Pazouki, G. Fly ash-based geopolymer concrete's compressive strength estimation by applying artificial intelligence methods. *Measurement* **2022**, *203*, 111916. [CrossRef]
37. Adesanya, E.; Aladejare, A.; Adediran, A.; Lawal, A.; Illikainen, M. Predicting shrinkage of alkali-activated blast furnace-fly ash mortars using artificial neural network (ANN). *Cem. Concr. Comp.* **2021**, *124*, 104265. [CrossRef]
38. Çelik, F.; Yildiz, O.; Çolak, A.B.; Bozkir, S.M. Analysing of nano-silica usage with fly ash for grouts with artificial neural network models. *Adv. Cem. Res.* **2022**, 1–16. [CrossRef]
39. Khan, K.; Iqbal, M.; Jalal, F.E.; Amin, M.N.; Alam, M.W.; Bardhan, A. Hybrid ANN models for durability of GFRP rebars in alkaline concrete environment using three swarm-based optimization algorithms. *Constr. Build. Mater.* **2022**, *352*, 128862. [CrossRef]
40. Jula, A.; Sundararajan, E.; Othman, Z. Cloud computing service composition: A systematic literature review. *Expert Syst. Appl.* **2014**, *41*, 3809–3824. [CrossRef]
41. Song, H.; Ahmad, A.; Ostrowski, K.A.; Dudek, M. Analyzing the compressive strength of ceramic waste-based concrete using experiment and artificial neural network (ANN) approach. *Materials* **2021**, *14*, 4518. [CrossRef] [PubMed]
42. *ASTM C150/C150M*; Standard Specification for Portland Cement. ASTM International: West Conshohocken, PA, USA, 2022.
43. *ASTM C618*; Standard Specification for Coal Fly Ash and Raw or Calcined Natural Pozzolan for Use in Concrete. ASTM International: West Conshohocken, PA, USA, 2022.
44. *ASTM C136*; Standard Test Method for Sieve Analysis of Fine and Coarse Aggregates. ASTM International: West Conshohocken, PA, USA, 2006.
45. *ASTM D5644*; Standard Test Methods for Rubber Compounding Materials—Determination of Particle Size Distribution of Recycled Vulcanizate Particulate Rubber. ASTM International: West Conshohocken, PA, USA, 2010.
46. Bisht, K.; Ramana, P. Evaluation of mechanical and durability properties of crumb rubber concrete. *Constr. Build. Mater.* **2017**, *155*, 811–817. [CrossRef]
47. *ACI 211.3R*; Guide for Selecting Proportions for No-Slump Concrete. American Concrete Institute: Farmington Hills, MI, USA, 2009.
48. *CRD-C 162*; Standard Practice for Selecting Proportions for Roller Compacted Concrete (RCC) Pavement Mixtures Using Soil Compaction Concepts. Department of the Army, Corps of Engineers: Washington, DC, USA, 1992.
49. *ASTM C192/192M*; Standard Practice for Making and Curing Concrete Test Specimens in the Laboratory. ASTM International: West Conshohocken, PA, USA, 2015.

50. *ASTM C1435/C1435M*; Standard Practice for Molding Roller-Compacted Concrete in Cylinder Molds Using a Vibrating Hammer. ASTM International: West Conshohocken, PA, USA, 2020.
51. *BS EN 12390-3*; Testing Hardened Concrete Compressive Strength of Test Specimens. British Standard Institute: London, UK, 2019.
52. *BS EN 12390-6*; Testing Hardened Concrete. Tensile Splitting Strength of Test Specimens. British Standard Institute: London, UK, 2009.
53. *ASTM C293/C293M*; Standard Test Method for Flexural Strength of Concrete (Using Simple Beam with Center-Point Loading. ASTM International: West Conshohocken, PA, USA, 2016.
54. *ASTM C469/C469M*; Standard Test Method for Static Modulus of Elasticity and Poisson's Ratio of Concrete in Compression. ASTM International: West Conshohocken, PA, USA, 2022.
55. Güzel, T.; Çolak, A.B. Artificial intelligence approach on predicting current values of polymer interface Schottky diode based on temperature and voltage: An experimental study. *Superlat. Microstruct.* **2021**, *153*, 106864. [CrossRef]
56. Cao, Y.; Kamrani, E.; Mirzaei, S.; Khandakar, A.; Vaferi, B. Electrical efficiency of the photovoltaic/thermal collectors cooled by nanofluids: Machine learning simulation and optimization by evolutionary algorithm. *Energy Rep.* **2022**, *8*, 24–36. [CrossRef]
57. Bonakdari, H.; Zaji, A.H. Open channel junction velocity prediction by using a hybrid self-neuron adjustable artificial neural network. *Flow Meas. Instrum.* **2016**, *49*, 46–51. [CrossRef]
58. Çolak, A.B. An experimental study on the comparative analysis of the effect of the number of data on the error rates of artificial neural networks. *Int. J. Energy Res.* **2021**, *45*, 478–500. [CrossRef]
59. Esmaeilzadeh, F.; Teja, A.S.; Bakhtyari, A. The thermal conductivity, viscosity, and cloud points of bentonite nanofluids with n-pentadecane as the base fluid. *J. Mol. Liq.* **2020**, *300*, 112307. [CrossRef]
60. Ali, A.; Abdulrahman, A.; Garg, S.; Maqsood, K.; Murshid, G. Application of artificial neural networks (ANN) for vapor-liquid-solid equilibrium prediction for CH_4-CO_2 binary mixture. *Greenh. Gases: Sci. Technol.* **2019**, *9*, 67–78. [CrossRef]
61. Akhgar, A.; Toghraie, D.; Sina, N.; Afrand, M. Developing dissimilar artificial neural networks (ANNs) to prediction the thermal conductivity of MWCNT-TiO_2/Water-ethylene glycol hybrid nanofluid. *Powder Technol.* **2019**, *355*, 602–610. [CrossRef]
62. Çolak, A.B.; Yıldız, O.; Bayrak, M.; Tezekici, B.S. Experimental study for predicting the specific heat of water based Cu-Al_2O_3 hybrid nanofluid using artificial neural network and proposing new correlation. *Int. J. Ener. Res.* **2020**, *44*, 7198–7215. [CrossRef]
63. Çolak, A.B.; Karakoyun, Y.; Acikgoz, O.; Yumurtaci, Z.; Dalkilic, A.S. A numerical study aimed at finding optimal artificial neural network model covering experimentally obtained heat transfer characteristics of hydronic underfloor radiant heating systems running various nanofluids. *Heat Transf. Res.* **2022**, *53*, 51–71. [CrossRef]
64. Ahmed, A.A.; Pradhan, B. Vehicular traffic noise prediction and propagation modelling using neural networks and geospatial information system. *Environ. Monitor. Assess.* **2019**, *191*, 190. [CrossRef] [PubMed]
65. Nourani, V.; Abdollahi, Z.; Sharghi, E. Sensitivity analysis and ensemble artificial intelligence-based model for short-term prediction of NO2 concentration. *Int. J. Environ. Sci. Tecnol.* **2021**, *18*, 2703–2722. [CrossRef]
66. Ali, N.M.; Farouk, A.; Haruna, S.; Alanazi, H.; Adamu, M.; Ibrahim, Y.E. Feature selection approach for failure mode detection of reinforced concrete bridge columns. *Case Stud. Constr. Mater.* **2022**, *17*, e01383. [CrossRef]
67. Haruna, S.I.; Zhu, H.; Jiang, W.; Shao, J. Evaluation of impact resistance properties of polyurethane-based polymer concrete for the repair of runway subjected to repeated drop-weight impact test. *Constr. Build. Mater.* **2021**, *309*, 125152. [CrossRef]
68. Farouk, A.I.B.; Jinsong, Z. Prediction of Interface Bond Strength Between Ultra-High-Performance Concrete (UHPC) and Normal Strength Concrete (NSC) Using a Machine Learning Approach. *Arab. J. Sci. Eng.* **2022**, *47*, 5337–5363. [CrossRef]

MDPI AG
Grosspeteranlage 5
4052 Basel
Switzerland
Tel.: +41 61 683 77 34

Axioms Editorial Office
E-mail: axioms@mdpi.com
www.mdpi.com/journal/axioms

www.ingramcontent.com/pod-product-compliance
Lightning Source LLC
Chambersburg PA
CBHW061520210926
51850CB00008B/1984
9783725847457